Mind
— OVER —
Magick

"Destiny dwells in these pages. Any magical practitioner, seeker, or student of life who reads Richard Kaczynski's *Mind over Magick* will discover new personal paths and insights from one of the most erudite, unpredictable, learned, and profound intellects writing today in the magical space. From Richard's chilling, unforgettable opening pages to his finely reasoned psycho-metaphysical insights and breakthroughs—and the practices to accompany them—*Mind over Magick* harbors a fate of its own: an occult classic."

MITCH HOROWITZ, PEN AWARD–WINNING HISTORIAN AND AUTHOR OF *THE MIRACLE CLUB*

"*Mind over Magick* presents a compelling exploration of ritual magick through the lens of psychology and cognitive neuroscience, revealing how structured symbolic practices produce significant shifts in the magician's perceptions, emotions, and behavior. Drawing on peer-reviewed research, Richard Kaczynski offers a clear framework for understanding the psychological foundations of transformative spiritual and magical experience."

DEAN RADIN, MS, PHD, CHIEF SCIENTIST AT THE INSTITUTE OF NOETIC SCIENCE (IONS) AND AUTHOR OF *THE SCIENCE OF MAGIC*

"Richard Kaczynski is a trained social psychologist and statistician who recognizes the presence of 'something' in magick yet also understands the professional practice of science inside and out. Here is a most striking science of magick that is also an implicit theory of popular culture and the ever-present paranormal. We are drawn to things throughout life, it turns out, not because of bad beliefs or misperceptions, but because of who and what we are—magical and material at the same time."

JEFFREY J. KRIPAL, AUTHOR OF
HOW TO THINK IMPOSSIBLY

Mind
— OVER —
Magick

THE PSYCHOLOGY *of* RITUAL MAGICK

Richard Kaczynski

Park Street Press
Rochester, Vermont

Park Street Press
One Park Street
Rochester, Vermont 05767
www.ParkStPress.com

Park Street Press is a division of Inner Traditions International

Copyright © 2025 by Richard Kaczynski

All rights reserved. No part of this book may be reproduced or utilized in any form or by any means, electronic or mechanical, including photocopying, recording, or any information storage and retrieval system, without permission in writing from the publisher. No part of this book may be used or reproduced to train artificial intelligence technologies or systems.

Cataloging-in-Publication Data for this title is available from the Library of Congress

ISBN 978-1-64411-964-8 (print)
ISBN 978-1-64411-965-5 (ebook)

Printed and bound in the United States by Lake Book Manufacturing, LLC

10 9 8 7 6 5 4 3 2 1

Text design by Virginia Scott Bowman and layout by Debbie Glogover
This book was typeset in Garamond Premier Pro with Argent CT, Futura Std, Gill Sans Nova, Gill Sans MT Pro, and Libre Bodoni used as display typefaces

Image credits are provided in the figure captions; images are in the public domain unless otherwise noted. CC BY-SA 3.0: figures 7.7, 11.2, and 11.3; CC BY 4.0: figures 4.5 and 10.4; CC BY 2.0: figure 10.5.

To send correspondence to the author of this book, mail a first-class letter to the author c/o Inner Traditions • Bear & Company, One Park Street, Rochester, VT 05767, and we will forward the communication, or contact the author directly at **https://richard-kaczynski.com**.

Scan the QR code and save 25% at InnerTraditions.com. Browse over 2,000 titles on spirituality, the occult, ancient mysteries, new science, holistic health, and natural medicine.

THIS BOOK IS DEDICATED TO MAEVIUS LYNN, my enthusiastic cheerleader and joy-giver throughout its creation. I couldn't have done it without her light in my life.

I also couldn't have done it without generous help from the following: the legendary Bill Sienkiewicz for use of his artistic example of negative space, and his assistant Sue Karlin for facilitating; Marc Demarest for an image from the Emma Hardinge Britten Archive; William Breeze, Ordo Templi Orientis and the University of London for the Thoth Tarot's Magus artwork; Maevius Lynn for modeling magical gestures; Dean Radin for updating me on the meta-analysis he originally published in *The Conscious Universe*; Mark Stivers for letting me reproduce one of his Saturday Cartoons; Scott Wilde and Keep Silence for the use of scans from Aleister Crowley first editions; Heather Bidzinski, head of Archives and Special Collections at the University of Manitoba, for the scan of Andy Henwood's portrait of Philip, and to Walter Meyer zu Erpen for facilitating and vouching for me; Dr. Lauren Gardner, who read an early version of my manuscript; Jon Graham, Renée Heitman, Jennifer Marx, Manzanita Carpenter Sanz, Mercedes Rojas, and all my other wonderful collaborators at Inner Traditions, who have been an absolute delight to work with; and Ira Firestone, my grad school advisor back in 1993 who supported my dissertation raising weird questions in psychology.

Contents

1 Something — 1

2 Head Like a Whole: The Psychology of Connecting the Dots and Seeing the Big Picture — 17

3 Rigamarole Models: Daily Magical Practices — 40

4 Think Better: The Magick of Yoga and Meditation — 77

5 Greater (and Lesser) Magical Retirements — 100

6 Hold That Thought: Ritual Implements — 108

7 Sacred Head Space: Temples and What We Do in Them — 125

8 Significant Others: Encountering the Divine — 150

9 Full Circle: Group Ritual — 173

10 Initiation: Changing Your Mind — 192

11 The Method of Science and You — 224

12 Last Writes — 250

Notes — 259

Index — 334

1
Something

"YOUR RESUMÉ IS IMPRESSIVE, BUT..."

I was sitting across the desk from the Yale University HR officer. It was my fortieth birthday. I had flown seven hundred miles for this job interview, and here it was: the dreaded *but*. As in, "It never rains but it pours." "It's all over but the crying." "Close but no cigar." Was there a better candidate? Or a problem with the job posting? I took a deep breath and held it. Finally, she continued:

"... what's up with all this stuff about magick?"

Applying for a statistician position, I didn't expect questions about my interests in psychology, let alone my extracurricular writing and speaking on Western esotericism. However, the job *was* in the Department of Psychiatry, so it was a fair question. A question for which I didn't have a prepared response.

I answered from the heart. "The psychology of everyday life isn't very interesting. Most of it happens on autopilot. We get up, eat breakfast, brush our teeth, go to work. Like owning a car, you don't need to know how it works until it breaks down. In the same way, we learn the most about the mind when unusual or unexpected experiences challenge our assumptions. For instance, ecstatic or transformative religious experiences can trigger a sudden change in personality... which we assume to be a stable trait. This breaks the rules. How does that happen?"

She paused to consider my answer, then nodded. "That makes sense."

While my ad-lib answer explained what my interest in magick had to do with psychology, it didn't explain *why* I was so interested. One of my colleagues back at Wayne State University used to quip, "People go into clinical psychology to understand their own mental illness. I went into social psychology because I have no social skills." Well, I pursued a doctorate in psychology because I thought it would explain magick.

How I got there is another story.

Something was in the house.

One night when I was an infant, my half-sister Krys had put me down to sleep in her room. Mom and Dad were at a wedding, and she didn't want to leave me unattended. As she sat there reading by her small nightstand lamp, she heard the familiar sound of footsteps in the house. The hallway light switched on. "Hi Dad," Krys said to the silhouette in the doorway. "Your foreman called to say the worksite was ready for plaster in the morning." He nodded, turned away, and switched off the light.

Not long after, a tapping on the bedroom window alarmed my sister. *What was that?* She moved closer to me, protective. The knocks came again, more insistent. This time she crept out of bed, cautiously drew the curtain, and peered outside.

It was Dad. "I can't find my house keys. Can you let me in?"

That wasn't the last time a mysterious apparition appeared in the house.

On weekends, Dad and his buddies regularly gathered at the house. They drank, smoked, and played pinochle late into the night. Often they would migrate into the basement to Dad's prized possession: the sacred pool table. As a child, I loved watching them play. The sound of racking the balls, the crack of the cue ball striking that triangle of the other fifteen. The adults making bank shots to avoid the other players' balls, doing tricks like putting spin on the cue ball, or shooting with the stick behind their backs. Every time they sank a ball, I enjoyed the sound of the ball falling into the metal tracks inside the table, rolling into the ball return, and stopping with a clink against the neat row of previously sunk balls.

One night when I was four or five, the cue ball bounced off the table. This wasn't unusual, but what happened next certainly was. The ball rolled into the dark half of the basement, coming to rest under the table that served as Dad's wet bar. "I'll get it!" I called out as I ran to retrieve the ball. Once I had it in hand, I paused and glanced at the adjacent storage room where the Christmas tree and decorations sat in boxes during the offseason. Beyond the doorway, in the shadowy darkness of the room, I saw a ghostly apparition. Not the archetypal glowing white figure in a sheet, this specter had a human form with distinct features and clothing. The details were partially obscured by a pale gauzy surface that left deep shadows around the eyes, mouth, and other body parts. It hovered slightly off the floor, rippling in the air. I recall the image vividly to this day.

Naturally, I ran back terrified. The adults took the cue ball from my trembling hands, tousled my hair, and laughed.

"It's just your imagination" was the standard answer whenever I, Krys, or our middle sister, Diahann, reported something inexplicable to Mom. She, like Dad, was a Polish Roman-Catholic immigrant who would brook nothing supernatural beyond the Black Madonna of Częstochowa. Yet these things happened so frequently that we eventually stopped telling Mom, or even each other. Our childhoods were filled with strange sights and sounds. While watching television in the family room, we would hear dishes rattling in the kitchen. When the folks were away at a wedding or other social event, we would hear pool balls knocking together and falling into the gutter; in the morning, we'd go downstairs to find balls on the table (it was strictly forbidden to ever leave balls on the felt after you were done playing). The stories could fill a book . . . but this is not that book.

The incidents begged for an explanation that never came. Was the house haunted? Unlikely, as my father and his construction work buddies built the house. There was no prior owner, so no soul trapped here upon meeting its tragic end. The neighborhood was flat and wooded, so it wasn't like he'd disturbed some ancient burial mound. So what was behind the ongoing creepiness that our family never discussed?

Many years later, as adults enjoying Thanksgiving dinner together, we broke decades of silence with, "Do you remember all the weird stuff that used to happen in the house when we were kids?" We shared stories for a while, including some we'd never told each other. After finally falling silent, we turned to Mom—ever the denier—as she finally confessed, "All that stuff stopped after Dad died."

There was something in the neighborhood.

I was walking home one quiet evening from my godmother's house across the street. I was thirteen or fourteen at the time, and her son was a regular playmate for Dungeons and Dragons and similar distractions. As I traversed the driveway toward my door, the sound of a snapping twig startled me. I looked around and spotted a silhouette beside the neighbor's garage. *Why was the neighbor standing there, alone in the dark, at this hour?* Something was off, however. The silhouette stood as tall as the roof line. And it was walking in my direction.

I didn't wait to ask questions but scooted into the house.

First thing the next morning, I went outside for a reality check. I climbed atop the chain-link fence between us and our neighbors, beside their garage. Teetering between the fence and the garage, I extended Dad's tape measure from the roof to the ground. Eight feet. Hmmm.

I then searched our backyard for any signs of the intruder. At the rear of the yard, in Mom's pristine vegetable garden, I found footprints. Like the silhouette, they were huge. Having seen the cryptid documentary *The Mysterious Monsters* (1976) plus countless episodes of *In Search Of* and *Kolchak: The Night Stalker*,[1] I knew exactly what to do. I grabbed our Instamatic camera, carefully laid Mom's sewing tape measure along one of the footprints, and photographed its seventeen-inch length. (That would've been around a U.S. men's size 26. *My goodness, Grandma, what big feet you have!*)

What could it be? I spent the next days tramping around the woods in the undeveloped areas of the neighborhood, seeking clues while narrating my adventures into a small cassette recorder. In my imagination, the snapped tree I came across could only have been Bigfoot. The dead owl I found must have been a snack—or nuisance—to Sasquatch. My overactive imagination notwithstanding, I found no conclusive evidence.

Fig. 1.1. Something was in Mom's garden last night.
Photo by the author

One evening, Mom pointed to my boots, caked with mud from my woodland adventures. "You're tracking dirt all over the house," she said. "Take your shoes outside and knock off the mud." As bidden, I collected my shoes and carried them to the back door. I opened it to the strangest sight: The storm door, which was on a hydraulic arm, was swinging wildly back and forth like sped-up film footage. In that terrifying instant, I realized I could not see the stars in the sky. Nor the street light. Not the porch, and not the cedar tree just beyond the porch. *Something* was blocking my view of everything beyond the storm door. I slammed the steel door and rinsed my shoes in the basement laundry tub instead.

Eventually, my searches paid off. Wandering a larger area of woods across the main road, I emerged from the thicket into a clearing where a very high chain-link fence demarcated the start of private property. There, on the other side of the fence, in broad daylight, we finally came face-to-face. My quarry looked *exactly* like Bigfoot as portrayed by Andre the Giant in *The Six Million Dollar Man*. Somewhere there's a cassette recording of Detective Rick screaming as he ran all the way home.

Fig. 1.2. Promotional photo of Bigfoot (Andre the Giant) with Steve Austin, the Six Million Dollar Man (Lee Majors). Do our expectations, frame of reference, and popular culture shape our liminal experiences? ABC Photo Archives/© ABC/Getty Images

Of course, Bigfoot wasn't living in suburban Detroit. Neither was a bionic robot or even Andre the Giant. None of that actually happened. But . . . it didn't *not* happen.

Something was occurring in the basement.

That fall found me working my way through the rituals in Israel Regardie's *The Golden Dawn*.[2] I had cobbled together a set of elemental "weapons" using common objects found around the house. For a disk, I had a lopsided circle that I hand cut from a piece of plywood with Dad's coping saw and painted in the requisite four colors of black, olive, citrine, and russet. For a wand, I sawed off the end of a broom that I thought nobody would miss, and painted it red. My chalice was two disposable tapered tumblers from Dad's wet bar, fastened bottom-to-bottom, with the appropriate symbols written in black permanent marker. The dagger was a knife I purchased at the mall: I spray-painted the hilt yellow, and added the Hebrew letters of the Tetragrammaton using purple pinstriping tape. I even made Banners of the East and West using fabric scavenged from Mom's voluminous sewing supplies. The basement became my secret temple.

Several years before, Diahann had done a semester-long independent study in junior high on witchcraft. She interviewed local celebrity Gundella the Green Witch.[3] I remember her returning home from that interview with a bag of goodies: a copy of Gundella's green vinyl record, *The Hour of the Witch*; an Albano-Waite tarot deck; a wooden heart-shaped planchette with a pencil-hole for doing automatic writing; and samples of various kinds of powdered incense. For Diahann, this was a grade: one and done. Sensing my intense curiosity, she eventually gave it all to me. I have the cards and planchette to this day.

Growing up with ghosts, Bigfoot, and witches, I sensed something inexplicable about the world. Did mysterious entities exist on the edge of our perception? Were there astral planes of existence interpenetrating our own, like the radio and television signals all around us? Circumstances ultimately led me to research the occult: Regardie and the Golden Dawn. Blavatsky and Theosophy. Buckland and witchcraft. Crowley and magick. With it came otherworldly experiences of astral projection, altered states of consciousness from pranayama, summoning sphinxlike angels, and so on. The more I studied and practiced, the more my encounters with the unexplained obligingly resembled those of the magicians. My frame of reference seemed to dictate the look of my liminal experiences. Although the shape of my experiences evolved, the underlying question remained: What *was* that?

Something was happening, and it wasn't just me.

After ten solitary years on this journey, I sought like-minded people. I found local groups of unconventional seekers, from Christian mystics to witchcraft gatherings. I found my way to a host of pagan/occult festivals: Covenant of the Goddess, Pagan Spirit Gathering, ConVocation, Pantheacon, Harvest Home Gathering, and Starwood (the latter of which *High Times* touted as an alternative to Woodstock's thirtieth-anniversary concert). I soon became a regular presenter/teacher at these events. Turns out that a lot of people shared my interests and experiences.

This isn't a surprise. Over a million Americans practice some form of witchcraft.[4] Half of all Americans believe in ghosts.[5] Seventy percent have had a paranormal experience.[6] Eighty-one percent believe something spiritual exists beyond the natural world.[7] Ninety percent know their astrological sign.[8] Horror author Whitley Strieber puts these statistics in a remarkable context: After the publication of *Communion*,[9] his autobiographical memoir about being abducted by nonhuman entities, Strieber was inundated by readers sharing similar experiences.

> Between 1987 and 2000, we must have received well in excess of half a million letters, at least a hundred thousand of them detailed accounts. I understand that this seems like a fantastic number, but it is probably accurate. We stopped counting at two hundred thousand, and that was in 1992, and they were still arriving in surprising numbers as late as 1998. We have kept around thirty thousand on file.[10]

That's a lot of people encountering nonhuman entities! Whether it's ghosts, aliens, or some other paranormal experience, even skeptics concede that such unusual experiences are far more common than we tend to think. Historian of religions Jeffrey Kripal leads a collection at Rice University called the Archives of the Impossible, containing about one million documents, many of which record unusual and inexplicable personal experiences. "For all practical or individual research purposes, this material is endless," he remarks.[11] "In historical truth, the phenomenon is *everywhere* and *everywhen*, and its comparative patterns are astonishingly stable and consistent."[12] For these reasons, Christopher Bader and Carson Mencken argue in their *Paranormal America* that the paranormal *is* normal: Those without any kind of paranormal belief are statistically the "oddballs."[13]

Strieber and Kripal's *The Super Natural* calls out skeptics' insistence on a false dichotomy. A phenomenon must be either literally true, or it is dismissed as fake: a hoax, a lie, or a mental illness. Anything that cannot be explained by science must be perpetrated by someone out to fool the gullible and make a buck. More often than not, reports of anomalous phenomena are dismissed on these grounds. If skeptics can reproduce something through trickery, that somehow proves the original phenomenon was also trickery. This argument reminds me of doing a magic trick in my elementary school talent show: I broke eggs, added flour, and mixed milk into my top hat, then, with a stir of my magic wand, transformed the ingredients into fresh cookies. Of course it was trickery. But I guarantee that wasn't how my mother made cookies. Dishonest people will indeed attempt to make a name or turn a profit in any human enterprise—even science.*[14] However, the people I've met in pagan and occult communities are sincere people trying to make sense of the world. Dismissing them as charlatans or mentally ill is gaslighting a huge swath of the population.

Given the ridicule to which believers or practitioners are often subjected, one might wonder why I risk exposing myself to derision with this confessional introduction. Consider the case of Freud's favorite student, Carl Jung. Jung believed in psychic and occult phenomena, but

---

*Fanelli reported that 2 percent of scientists across multiple surveys admitted to fabricating or falsifying or altering data. When reports from 2011 to 2020 are included, that estimate rises to a 2.9 percent rate of falsification, fabrication, or plagiarism, and a 12.5 percent rate of questionable research practices.

the visionary experiments documented in his *Red Book*[15] remained out of the public eye for nearly a century;* this, Jungian analyst Christopher Hauke explains, maintained "the balance between the needs of an information hungry public and the risk of misunderstanding personal psychological material."[16] This misunderstanding was evidenced by scholars, already familiar with the *Red Book*, saying it represented a years-long psychotic episode.[17] Thus, there is good reason to keep these experiences veiled. Similarly, the occult and alchemical interests of Isaac Newton have been downplayed by scholars and biographers to avoid besmirching his reputation,[18] as has been the case with military strategist J. F. C. Fuller.[19] And while some clinical psychologists and psychiatrists have resorted to astrology for clinical assistance, most of them would never admit it.[20] So why am I sticking my neck out?

It comes down to this: Seventy percent of Americans report having had a paranormal experience. The rest of the world is probably in the same ballpark. Yet admitting something so commonplace remains socially and professionally stigmatizing. It's past time to normalize talking about these quotidian human experiences. What they mean may remain elusive, but it's okay to acknowledge that *something* happened. Just as something happens whenever a magician enters their sacred space. It is real. It is memorable. It can be life-changing. And it is worthy of being understood.

Something was going on, but I couldn't explain it. (Or could I?)

I entered university and had to select a major. I chose psychology, hoping it would shed some light on how magick works. I was quickly disappointed. No Grand Unified Theory explained the unexplainable. At that time, the psychological study of religion or spirituality was fringe at best. Anything to do with the paranormal or other anomalous experiences was not psychology at all, but pseudoscience. I shifted my specialization to social psychology and statistics, as these addressed measurable behavior rather than speculating about the mysterious processes of the mind doing the out-of-the-ordinary.

---

*Jung created his Red Book from 1914–1930, drawing from his 1913–1916 notebooks known as the Black Books. *The Red Book* was ultimately published in 2009, and the *Black Books* in 2020.

When I proposed doing my doctoral research on metaphysical beliefs and experiences, my advisor warned me it would be a career killer. Since I already had around forty respectable papers and publications from working as a research assistant—quite a feat for a full-time graduate student—he begrudgingly conceded that I had racked up enough "eccentricity credits" to get away with an embarrassing dissertation.

I struggled to find the requisite three committee members to review and guide my research. Although I proposed to use standard survey and psychometric methods, the faculty I approached said the subject matter was outside their field of expertise. Persistence eventually led me to three cooperative professors.

Diving into the existing literature on anomalous beliefs and experiences was profoundly disheartening. I discovered psychology had a fraught history of approaching the subject with shocking biases and misinformation, leading to demeaning hypotheses to match. Believers and their beliefs were (and still are) regularly described as irrational, unscientific, illogical, pathological, or at risk of psychosis;[21] lumped in with conspiracy theorists; and referred to as "sheep" (as opposed to skeptical "goats").*[22] They were talking about *me*, as well as my friends, mentors, and community. I couldn't think of any other study population that psychologists approached with such fundamental disdain.

The critiques laid out in my dissertation's literature review boiled down to three main points:

First was the disrespectful perception of those who believed, experienced, or were even open to the possibility of anomalous events. Despite these beliefs being persistent and widespread throughout history—including in modern times and popular culture—psychologists conjectured that someone had to be desperately unintelligent, uneducated, or

---

*The terms *sheep* and *goat* for ESP believers and skeptics originated with parapsychology researcher Gertrude Schmeidler, and carried over into the creation of Thalbourne and Delin's Australian Sheep-Goat Scale. Both the nomenclature and scale subsequently crossed into mainstream psychology. Whether a believer or skeptic, being reduced to theriomorphic tropes is dehumanizing; *sheep* and *sheeple* have taken on particularly offensive connotations in recent years. I'm hard-pressed to think of another area of research where human subjects are equated with animals.

illogical to believe these things. Perhaps believers were socially isolated from more reasonable points of view. Or they came from economically, socially, racially, or other disadvantaged backgrounds ... in other words, women, people of color, and the poor. The offensive stereotype proposed by this *marginality hypothesis*[23] didn't describe the people I knew in the pagan or occult communities across the United States. My acquaintances were intelligent, educated, gainfully employed, and voracious readers, of all colors and genders: Just like prominent figures in occult history tended to be well-educated and of financial means (all that secret society equipment, literature, and dues required money!).*

Second were the questions meant to assess belief. They often lumped together a variety of uncommon and not necessarily related beliefs into one big item pool: ESP, UFOs/UAPs, aliens, and Bigfoot sat alongside beliefs in astrology, magick, or the afterlife, with a dash of broken mirrors, walking under ladders, and stepping on a crack to bring bad luck.† Most concerning of all, the individual questions often suffered from the aforementioned biases. Researchers have asked people to rate their agreement with the statement "Witches actually do exist." This is a breathtaking erasure of a widespread and growing spiritual movement.[24] Over the years I've met thousands of people who describe themselves as witches, pagans, and Wiccans. You'd never see a survey that asked whether Muslims, Jews, or Buddhists actually exist.

Other questions seemed to misunderstand the subjects they were asking about. For example, many professional astrologers would disagree with the statement, "The position of planets and stars at birth determines how one turns out." Instead, they may view planetary positions like the hands

---

*Some examples from the Golden Dawn included founding members William Wynn Westcott (a London crown coroner) and William Robert Woodman (a medical doctor); Annie Horniman came from a family of wealthy tea merchants (and founder of the Horniman Museum), and she was educated at the Slade School of Fine Art; and Aleister Crowley similarly came to the Golden Dawn with a large inheritance and a Trinity College Cambridge education.

†While researchers appropriately use factor analysis to identify clusters of items that people tend to answer similarly—forming a conceptual subset of items distinct from other similar clusters—in practice the scale's total, rather than its distinct components, is often examined. This effectively reduces disparate beliefs to a single number.

of a clock. A clock tells the time, but it doesn't cause time. Similarly, the planets themselves don't exert causal force; they merely represent the state of the universe at a given moment.* A better phraseology (which I used in my study) might be, "The positions of planets at one's time of birth tell much about a person." It's a subtle difference, but better reflects the views of people who practice astrology. (Whether or not somebody *agrees* with this view . . . well, that's the point of the questionnaire.)

Some survey questions asked about things that didn't seem unusual or controversial. Take the belief in life on other planets. In 1961, the Drake equation calculated life on other planets in the Milky Way to be a statistical certainty.[25] Some have debated the values that Frank Drake plugged into his equation, but the likelihood of communicative life "out there" has found champions among respected astronomers such as Carl Sagan, and it has animated the Search for Extra-Terrestrial Intelligence (SETI). Similarly, belief in the afterlife is a tenet shared by the world's major religions, yet it is considered marginal when believed by Spiritualists.†

Taken together, these concerns about questionnaire wording and subject matter raised doubts about whether they accurately represent the breadth of beliefs, or whether they are a funhouse mirror of what laypeople *think* these beliefs look like.

---

*This interpretation is nothing new. Back in 1902, Alvidas wrote, "The planets are like the hands of a clock pointing out what is happening in those other invisible worlds without themselves being the causes of the influence." See Alvidas, *Science and the Key of Life: Planetary Influences*, vol. 2 (Detroit, Astro Publishing Company, 1902), 471.

†Few researchers include religion in their belief scales, but one notable exception is Tobacyk and Milford's popular Paranormal Belief Scale, whose "traditional religious beliefs" component reflects only "the traditional Christian religious belief system." See Jerome Tobacyk and Gary Milford, "Belief in Paranormal Phenomena: Assessment Instrument Development and Implications for Personality Functioning," *Journal of Personality and Social Psychology* 44, no. 5 (1983): 1029–37 (p. 1029). Nearly forty years later, researchers lament that most research in the psychology of religion focuses on the idea of a person-like God, when faiths commonly include other types of beings, forces, or more abstract conceptions of the divine. See Kathryn A. Johnson, "God . . . Karma, Jinn, Spirits, and Other Metaphysical Forces," *Current Opinion in Psychology* 40 (2021): 10–14 and Julie J. Exline and Joshua A. Wilt, "Supernatural Attributions: Seeing God, the Devil, Demons, Spirits, Fate, and Karma as Causes of Events," *Annual Review of Clinical Psychology* 19 (2023): 461–87.

My third and final critique dealt with the research subjects themselves. The tried-and-true recruitment method in psychology is to offer course credit to Psych 101 undergraduates who volunteer for university research studies. I questioned whether Psych 101 undergraduates—except for odd ducks like myself—were invested in their opinions on paranormal beliefs, or whether they had engaged in a meaningful way with liminal experiences, spiritual questions of life and the nature of the universe, the existence of the soul, or practices of occultism. One thing was certain: Studies of college freshmen did not represent the practitioners I knew. Such samples likely don't produce the full range and diversity of beliefs, and instead represent only a narrow range of opinions. When I encountered research on *behaviorally committed* subjects,[26] the light bulb lit up. Everyone has an opinion, but few are so invested in their opinions that it shapes their behavior. It's the difference between believing in witchcraft versus belonging to a coven.

Consider the 2016 study of skeptics versus believers in psychic ability conducted by University of East London researcher Anna Stone. In an apparent confirmation of prior studies, Stone found that believers in psychic abilities were more likely to engage in intuitive (as opposed to rational) thinking. They also viewed their lives as being more influenced by external factors rather than being self-directed (a concept psychologists call *locus of control*). Importantly, when Stone narrowed the group of believers to individuals who had written articles on the subject, were teaching it, had taken advanced training, or had given at least one hundred psychic readings (in other words, were behaviorally committed to their beliefs), this group was just as rational as skeptics, and they had the highest internal locus of control scores. Stone concluded that "practitioners may have rationalized their beliefs and constructed a coherent model of psychic phenomena that satisfies a propensity for rational thinking within a community of belief," and stressed to fellow researchers (emphasis mine): "This highlights the importance of *considering level of involvement* with psychic practice in understanding the thinking styles of believers."[27] In a similar vein, there is a fundamental difference between the armchair magician and one who does the work. Alas, only a few researchers had made this point when I offered the same argument in my 1993 dissertation, drawing my sample from actual members of the pagan community: those whose behavior indicated they were engaged with their beliefs by participating in pagan circles, frequenting occult bulletin board systems (pre-Internet online computers reached using dial-up modems), or attending magical conferences and festivals.

Thus, I cashed in my eccentricity credits on a dissertation topic that I was passionate about. My study of behaviorally committed participants in the occult did not support the marginality hypothesis. It also showed that the best predictor of having had a transformative religious or spiritual experience was whether one's belief system involved actively learning and seeking new experiential insights (as opposed to believing all the answers could be found in whatever doctrine they espoused).[28]

From there, I continued on my prior professional course, acting as a scientist, professor, researcher, and statistician in areas including sociology, psychology, public health, psychiatry, medicine, pharmacy, orthodontics, and dentistry. However, my interest in the history and enduring power of magick continued, and I pursued it as an independent scholar. In that world, I've written critically well-received books such as *Perdurabo: The Life of Aleister Crowley* and *Friendship in Doubt*,*[29] presented at academic conferences such as the Association for the Study of Esotericism, and given a keynote address at the first Trans-States conference at the University of Manchester.

Looking back after more than thirty years into this split personality of a career—the skeptical scientist on the one hand, the freethinking practitioner on the other†—the questions about magick that originally

---

*Being a bit of an expert on Crowley—one of the most influential occultists of modern times—I reference him frequently in this book. As they say, write what you know.

†Psychologist Gerhard Mayer, director of the Society for Anomalistics, once remarked that "in Germany it would be barely conceivable that an academic author such as Richard Kaczynski, who has also published numerous articles in well-respected medical journals, could give lectures to occult groups and writes papers for occult magazines under his real name." See page 182 in Gerhard Mayer, "Magicians of the Twenty-First Century: An Attempt at Dimensioning the Magician's Personality," *Magic, Ritual and Witchcraft* 4, no. 2 (2009): 176–206.

motivated me to become a psychologist now appear in a different light. Religion and spirituality are accepted areas of study. Ritual, broadly speaking, has been the subject of accepted research. The transformative experiences of magick *do* involve psychological processes that are well understood from other contexts. The answers to my questions were always there. Like a five-hundred-piece puzzle, all it took was opening the box and putting the pieces together.

This is that book.

WHAT THIS BOOK IS AND ISN'T

In these pages, we will explore the transformative practices of magick as reflected in psychology research. This means scientific experiments and empirical data from peer-reviewed journals in favor of untestable theories or "fringe" topics. (Curious readers can, and should, pursue these other topics to supplement what's covered here.) Before wrapping up the book with chapter 12, chapter 11 will review the basics of the scientific method for readers who may have limited experience with it, and illustrate how you can use it to critically evaluate your magical work.

I am *not* saying that everything about magick is psychological. There are also social, cultural, anthropological, and religious aspects as well as nonscientific matters of faith or experience. Likewise, if I cite an occult author for ideas that parallel psychology research, I am not suggesting that *everything* they say is scientific. The same author may also espouse beliefs that lie beyond scientific inquiry.

This evidence-based survey will show that psychology has plenty to tell us about the mind of the magician and how psychological principles contribute to the powerful experiences underlying magick.

2

Head Like a Whole

The Psychology of Connecting the Dots and Seeing the Big Picture

1976: The NASA Viking 1 orbiter photo of the Cydonia mesa reveals what quickly becomes world famous as the "Face on Mars."

1977: Over six thousand people flock to the New Mexico home of Maria Rubio to see the face of Jesus that miraculously appeared on a griddled tortilla.[1]

2004: Online casino Golden Palace pays $28,000 for a ten-year-old grilled cheese sandwich with a likeness of the Virgin Mary.[2]

2011: Social media is flooded with photos of coat hooks with the caption "Drunk octopus wants to fight you."

Incidents like these reflect the human propensity to see patterns in the world. And so do you whenever you look in the sky and see the Big Dipper, the Man in the Moon, or a cloud in the shape of a familiar object. Why do we have this tendency to see things that may not be there?

Evolutionary biologists say we are pattern-seeking animals. The ability to quickly assess an environment for danger, even when the situation is unclear—a predator rustling in the bushes!—gave early humans a selective advantage. The same is true for recognizing patterns over

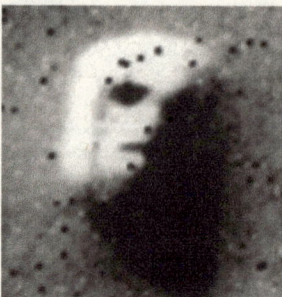

Fig. 2.1. Viking face on Mars.
The Planetary Society

time, such as "Every time one of us eats those berries, they get sick and die." These characteristics allowed our species to survive when human beings were the new kids on the savanna. They remain hardwired into our biology today. Although the world is very different, we continue to make sense of it by looking for patterns. Even the suggestion of a pattern will do. This evolutionary wiring for patternicity has profound implications for human psychology and the psychology of magick, as shown by the perceptual laws of Gestalt psychology.

Gestalt psychology emerged in Austria and Germany during the early twentieth century as a reaction to the structuralist approach prevalent in psychology at the time. Structuralists argued that understanding human perception required reducing things to their individual, elemental components. The Gestalt school argued (as did Aristotle) that the whole is greater than the sum of its parts. We cannot understand water by looking at its component gases, hydrogen and oxygen, separately. The same is true of human psychology. The Gestalt school's holistic approach was a precursor to what would become known—in a broader, cross-disciplinary sense—as systems theory: the study of how the components of a system interact with each other.

The *phi phenomenon* is a classic example of how separate perceptions interact to create an impression that is more than its separate components. In a darkened room, two points of light shown one at a time in quick succession will be perceived as a single light moving. This same phenomenon adds the "motion" to motion pictures: Rather than appearing as a series of static photographs, we see a continuous flow of action.

DEMONSTRATION 1: PERCEPTUAL GROUPING

Gestalt psychology lays out several principles that govern perceptual grouping:

Similarity: We see like objects as going together.
Proximity: Objects that are near each other belong together.
Common region: Objects occupying the same space flock together.
Continuity: We see shapes in the simplest, most continuous way.
Completeness: Our minds fill in the blanks when information is missing.

Figures 2.2 to 2.11 on the following pages 20–24 demonstrate each of these.

Fig. 2.2

Fig. 2.3

Figs. 2.2 and 2.3. The *similarity* of shapes determines whether we see these images in rows (*above, fig. 2.2*) or columns (*below, fig. 2.3*).

Fig. 2.4. The *proximity* of objects to one another can override perceptual grouping based on similarity.

Fig. 2.5

Fig. 2.6

Figs. 2.5 and 2.6. While the similarity in the above image compels us to visually group the Mars symbols on the left separately from the Venus symbols on the right (*above, fig. 2.5*), adding a *common region* causes us to group them differently (*below, fig. 2.6*).

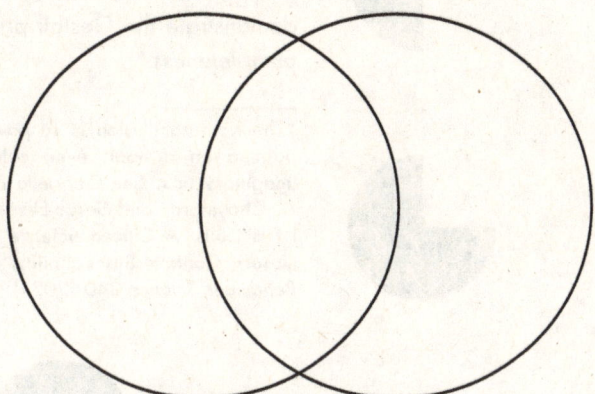

Fig. 2.7. The vesica piscis.

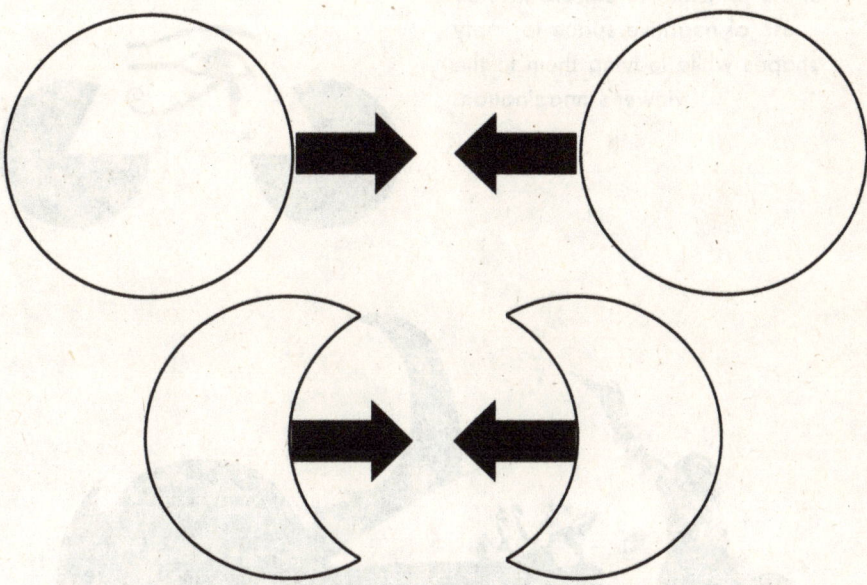

Fig. 2.8. The Gestalt principle of *continuity* means we tend to see the vesica piscis as two overlapping circles (*top*) rather than two crescents touching (*bottom*).

Fig. 2.9. Kanizsa-style square and triangle illusions, in which we perceive shapes that aren't really there, demonstrate the Gestalt principle of *completeness.**

_____
*The Kanisza illusion is so powerful that, when painted on a floor, even cats will sit in the imaginary box. See Gabriella E. Smith, Philippe A. Chouinard, and Sarah-Elizabeth Byosiere, "If I Fits I Sits: A Citizen Science Investigation into Illusory Contour Susceptibility," *Applied Animal Behaviour Science* 240 (2021): 105338.

Fig. 2.10. Artists take advantage of the principle of closure in their use of negative space to imply shapes while leaving them to the viewer's imagination.

Fig. 2.11. One of my favorite examples of the principle of closure is "Gal art Bend negative space" by Bill Sienkiewicz.

DEMONSTRATION 2: CONTEXT, CULTURE, AND PERCEPTUAL EXPECTANCY

In addition to the Gestalt principles of grouping, we gather contextual clues from our surroundings to shape our expectations. *Perceptual expectancy*, in turn, can affect how we perceive things and "fill in the blanks." Take the following four words:

MIDNIGHT; NOON; DAWN; D*SK

Based on the first three words, most people would read the fourth word as "dusk." Change those first three words, however, and how we read the last one changes:

DAGGER; WAND; CUP; D*SK

For anyone familiar with magick ritual implements or "elemental weapons," the last word would logically be "disk."

Various internet and social media fads rely on our ability to use contextual clues to determine meaning in situations that are ambiguous or violate our expectations. This includes leet speak (or 1337 5p34k), in which letters are swapped with similarly shaped numbers; lolspeak, the spelling-challenged pronouncements of lol cats, such as when a kitteh says "I can haz cheezburgr?"; and textspeak, such as "I am ded." The same principle was at work with Jim Beam's 2021 "6ourbon 7ime" ad campaign, seeking to reclaim 6–7 pm as happy hour.

Just as context plays a role in how we fill in missing or ambiguous information, language and culture play a role in how we group objects. In one study, subjects were given a "One of these things is not like the other" challenge with word lists such as the following:

PANDA; MONKEY; BANANA
SEAGULL; SQUIRREL; TREE
CARROT; RABBIT; EGGPLANT
TEACHER; DOCTOR; HOMEWORK

Those who kept together panda and monkey, seagull and squirrel, carrot and eggplant, or teacher and doctor, tended to be American, applying analytic or taxonomic categories. Those who kept together monkey and banana, squirrel and tree, carrot and rabbit, or teacher and homework, tended to be Chinese, reflecting a thematic or holistic view of which things appear together in nature.[3]

PAREIDOLIA AND APOPHENIA

The examples at the beginning of this chapter—from Jesus on a tortilla to the Man in the Moon—illustrate famous instances of *pareidolia*: the tendency to interpret ambiguous environmental cues as familiar things. It is a side effect of our brains looking for patterns. This can be linked to visual ambiguity or uncertainty activating areas of the brain associated with curiosity.[4] Pareidolia isn't limited to vision, however. Some of the most striking examples are based on how we (mis)hear things. A most notorious example happened in the early 1980s when televangelists claimed that Led Zeppelin's classic song "Stairway to Heaven," when played backward, contained secret messages such as "Here's to my sweet Satan" and "He'll give you 666." The hunt for Satanic messages in rock-and-roll music became a national obsession. The State of California Assembly's "Consumer Protection and Toxic Materials Committee" even considered a bill requiring warning labels for records with purported backward messages.[5]

Demonstrations of so-called backward masking would set up the nonsense sounds of reversed music by saying something like, "You're going to hear the phrase 'The Lord turns me off.'" Such instructions prime the listener with a perceptual expectancy that is, unsurprisingly, confirmed.[6] And once someone "perceives" something (or is suggested to perceive something), it is hard for them to un-see, or un-hear, it.[7] Scientist and skeptic Michael Shermer potently demonstrated this phenomenon with the Led Zeppelin track:

> I played a portion of Led Zeppelin's "Stairway to Heaven," first forward with the words on the screen.... Then I played this portion of

the song backward with no words on the screen, and almost everyone heard "Satan," with some also hearing "sex" or "666." Finally, I played it again after priming their brains with the alleged lyrics on the screen.... Everyone could now clearly hear: *Oh, here's to my sweet Satan / The one whose little path will make me sad / whose power is Satan/ He'll give you / Give you 666 / There was a little tool shed where he made us suffer, sad Satan*. The effect is stunning to audiences, who, with their unprimed ears, can hear one or maybe two words, but when primed can make out the entire lyrical score.[8]

This moral panic ultimately fizzled out, as there is no evidence that any band intentionally created lyrics that sounded one way forward and another backward; and, even if they did, the human brain cannot detect, let alone be influenced by, backward audio.[9] A similar situation is arguably implicated in *electronic voice phenomenon* (EVP): intelligible-sounding messages heard in the static of recording devices in haunted houses. While listening back to static recorded in their investigations, investigators will sometimes hear voices whose words pertain to the haunting being investigated. When broadcast as reality television, shows will tell audiences in advance what to listen for, or subtitle the recording, much like televangelists a generation before told audiences what satanic message they were about to hear played back. As expected, audiences hear it.

Pareidolia is a special case of the brain's tendency to see patterns or causal connections where none exist. This broader phenomenon is called *apophenia*. The term was originally coined by Klaus Conrad to describe an early symptom of schizophrenia: perceiving abnormal meaningfulness between unrelated things.[10] It has also been implicated in people's tendency to embrace conspiracy theories.[11] However, while some studies support a link between apophenia and schizotypy, others do not.[12] Still others find intermediary associations between apophenia and factors such as enhanced attention,[13] vivid imagination,[14] and hallucination-proneness.[15] Indeed, the experience of apophenia in general is extremely common in clinically healthy individuals.[16]

A 2018 study by van Prooijen and colleagues underscores how

common this patternicity phenomenon is. To test individuals' propensity to find patterns in randomness, they took a randomly generated string of coin tosses—fifty heads and fifty tails—and subdivided it into ten sets of ten coin tosses. Some of those segments—such as the symmetrical HTHHHHHHTH—did indeed appear systematic even though, in the context of the full string, it was not. As the authors noted, "Truly random sequences typically display less variation—and hence form more clusters—than people intuitively expect, creating the feeling of meaningful patterns that in fact occurred at random."[17] Because of this tendency to see patterns where none exist, programmers of music devices have had to develop complex algorithms to make "shuffle" play seem more random than an actual random order; we'll dig deeper into this topic in chapter 11.

FROM SEEING THINGS TO *NOT* SEEING THINGS

Our expectations can fool us in other ways. What we focus on can also cause us to *not* see other things. This includes not seeing the unexpected. "Looked but failed to see" automobile accidents are collisions in which a driver is attentive but fails to see a hazard. These incidents may account for roughly 10 percent of traffic accidents.[18] Perceptual blindness is best illustrated through a pair of famous studies by Daniel Simons and colleagues.

In the first study, Simons and Daniel Levin staged a scenario on the Cornell campus in which one experimenter with a campus map stopped a pedestrian to ask for directions to a nearby building. As they spoke, two people carrying a door passed between them. During this brief visual interruption, the experimenter was replaced by a second experimenter in different clothing and with a different voice. The majority of people, their attention divided by the direction-giving task, did not notice the switch. The "door study," as it has come to be known, is an example of *change blindness*.[19]

In another study, Simons and Christopher Chabris played a brief video of two teams—three people in white, three in black—walking around and passing a basketball between their teammates. Participants in the study were asked to count how many times one of the teams passed the ball to each other. A little over halfway through the video, someone dressed in a gorilla suit walks into the middle of the frame, thumps their chest, and walks off. Of roughly two hundred participants, half did not notice the gorilla. The "invisible gorilla" study illustrates *inattentional blindness*.[20]

Stage magicians routinely exploit these phenomena through misdirection and similar strategies, allowing their trick to pass undetected.

SOMETHING OUT OF NOTHING AT ALL

So far, our survey has examined how we see, think we see, or fail to see things in our environment, thanks to our biological wiring for patternicity. But what happens when we are in a situation where there is no meaningful sensory input? Our eyes, ears, and brains want to impose structure so badly that they will find patterns even when nothing is there.

Zalmoxis was an ancient Thracian who has been described variously as a slave, a student of Pythagoras, a shaman, or a religious reformer. He retired to a cave in the classic Greek trope of *katabasis*: an initiatory death or underworld journey. Presumed dead by his peers, he emerged three years later promoting the life-changing revelations he had experienced underground. He preached the immortality of the soul, demanded that his followers be vegetarians (as did Pythagoras before him), and became regarded by the Thracian Getae as a god, god-king, or man-daimon.[21] What was revealed to Zalmoxis in that cave that so transformed him?

The cave is a frequent motif in Greek lore. It can be a place of obfuscation (as in the allegory of Plato's cave) or a place of revelation (in the initiations of Pythagoras and his followers). It is a place of monsters. It is a place of oracles. Yulia Ustinova suggests that the initiatory cave ordeals of Zalmoxis and others parallel the experiences of miners during a tunnel collapse (even more dramatic forms of this experience will be explored in chapter 8). Trapped in total darkness for an extended period, they start to see shapes, colors, and images emerge from the blackness: a sign of a brain struggling to impose structure or order on the absence of visual input. Similar experiences have been described by Arctic and Antarctic explorers after seeing nothing but a visual field of snow for days at a stretch. Prisoners in solitary confinement report similar experiences with such regularity that the phenomenon is known as the *prisoner's cinema*. These visions in the darkness, Ustinova argues, are what the ancient Greeks interpreted as divine revelations.[22]

The Pythagorean cave or prisoner's cinema experience finds echoes in the writing of the Book of Mormon. Joseph Smith used a "seer stone" to facilitate visions of the golden tablets, which he translated and dictated. According to David Whitmer's account (italics mine):

> Joseph Smith put the seer stone into a hat, and put his face in the hat, drawing it closely around his face to exclude the light; and *in the darkness the spiritual light would shine*. A piece of something resembling parchment would appear, and on that appeared the writing. One character at a time would appear, and under it was the interpretation in English.[23]

The uniform, snowy white visual field of mountains has likewise been associated with unusual visions, mystical experiences, and even mysterious beings.[24] We will explore these spectacular manifestations in chapter 8.

Magicians and seers through the ages have harnessed the visionary possibilities of gazing into a featureless surface. Lecanomancy—divination using a dish of water—goes back at least as far as Babylon,[25] occurs across Africa,[26] and continues to be practiced by modern-day pagans.[27] Aztecs, meanwhile, believed the black reflective surface of obsidian protected against evil spirits. A magick mirror or "shew-stone" of this Mexican volcanic glass somehow made its way to Europe and into the possession of Queen Elizabeth I's court astrologer, John Dee (1527–1608).[28] For ten years, Dee worked with his scryer, Edward Kelly (1555–1597), who gazed into its stygian surface to receive communications from angels, often in their native tongue of Enochian.[29]

Head Like a Whole ☆ 31

Fig. 2.12. Edward Kelly served as the seer for John Dee's angelic experiments with Enochian magick, reporting visions seen in an obsidian scrying mirror.
From Meric Casaubon, *A True and Faithful Relation of What Passed for Many Yeers between Dr. John Dee and Some Spirits* (London: 1659).

A similar ancient practice "in almost every known culture"[30] is crystallomancy, or divination with crystals. In the nineteenth century, Francis Barrett's *The Magus* (1801) included a translation of Renaissance occultist Johannes Trithemius' *The Art of Drawing Spirits into Crystals*:

Procure of a lapidary good clear pellucid crystal, of the bigness of a small orange, *i.e.* about one inch and a half in diameter; let it be globular or round each way alike; then, when you have got this crystal, fair and clear, without any clouds or specks, get a small plate of pure gold to encompass the crystal round one half; let this be fitted on an ivory or ebony pedestal as you may see more fully described in the drawing. . . . On the other side of the plate let there

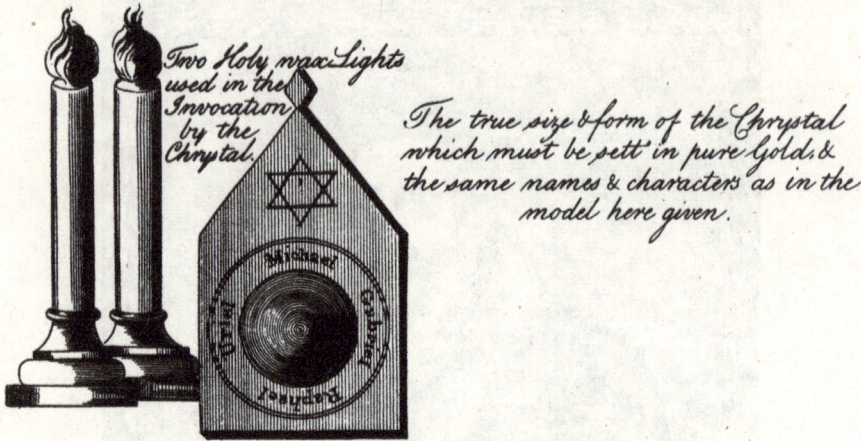

Fig. 2.13. The Crystal (and Holy Lights) as described in Francis Barrett's *The Magus, or Celestial Intelligencer* (London, 1801).

be engraven "*Michael, Gabriel, Uriel, Raphael;*" which are the four principal angels ruling over the *Sun, Moon, Venus* and *Mercury*.*

The Magus was a hugely influential text in the magical practices—including divination—of a new generation of occultists. This included purported Barrett protegee Frederick Hockley (1809–1885),[31] whom Godwin called "the most persistent crystallomancer of the century,"[32] and his friend, the Rosicrucian Freemason Kenneth R. H. Mackenzie (1833–1886).[33] American Spiritualist Emma Hardinge Britten (1823–1899) recounted how, as a child, she served as a seer for a group of magicians she called the Orphic Society or Orphic Circle.[34] As she recalled in her memoir *Ghost Land*,

> During our residence in London we were constant attendants and welcome visitors at a circle which for distinction I shall name the

---

*Francis Barrett, *The Magus, or Celestial Intelligencer; Being a Complete System of Occult Philosophy* (London: Lackington, Allen & Co., 1801; rpt. Secaucus, NJ: Citadel Press, 1967), IV: 135. The "valuable Latin manuscript" from which this material was translated does not appear to exist prior to its appearance in *The Magus*, suggesting that the material is a pseudepigraphical fabrication.

Orphic Circle. Its president and "Grand Master" was a noble gentleman whom I shall call Lord Vivian. . . . The seers, of whom Lord Vivian's society numbered several, conducted their experiments through the mirror and crystal, and the young ladies especially who attended these interesting seances, were particularly happy in attracting pure and noble planetary spirits in response to their call. . . . I recall a special séance wherein I was myself the clairvoyant. Professor von Marx had as usual magnetized me by a single wave of his hand, and enjoined me to describe to those present various visionary scenes in which they were interested.[35]

The birth of Spiritualism in the mid-nineteenth century brought crystallomancy to a wider audience, becoming a stereotype for mediums and fortune tellers. Robert Fryar (1844–1909), a boutique occult book publisher from Bath, not only wrote on crystal-gazing but was also a British importer of Bhattah mirrors from India for divination purposes.[36] According to one description, Bhattah mirrors were a "crystal, with a coating of paranaphthalin saturated, by a special ceremony, with the magnetism of boys and girls who have not yet reached the age of puberty."[37] Fryar's visionary experiences with scrying included:

> landscapes, emblematical groups, events transpiring by land and sea, whether in the snowy fastnesses of the far north or on the burning sands of southern climes. The forms of deceased friends flit across them in visions of the past, present, or future. Figures of men and animals are seen in motion, also carriages, the waving of foliage, ships and steamboats arriving or departing.[38]

American Spiritualist, Rosicrucian, and sex magician Paschal Beverly Randolph (1825–1875) wrote extensively about scrying,[39] and he advertised a superior method of magnetizing mirrors:

> merely two plates of French glass, with strips of wood around their edges to keep them half an inch apart, and so that a fluid poured between them shall not escape. Nothing depends for success upon

Fig. 2.14. A scrying crystal and box, ca. 1900, from
Emma Hardinge Britten's *Two Worlds*.
Image courtesy of the Emma Hardinge Britten Archive

either the box, the curtain, or the glasses, but all depends upon the peculiar fluid between them, which is . . . of a dark brown color, but at a distance, quite inky to the eye.⁴⁰

Given its widespread popularity, crystallomancy was even practiced by authors Charles Dickens and Lord Edward Bulwer-Lytton.* In the United States, Emma Hardinge Britten's *Two Worlds* newspaper cashed in on the craze by selling its own crystal-gazing kits.

Into the twentieth century, when Aleister Crowley and his student Victor Neuburg recorded their encounters with the thirty Enochian Æhyrs as *The Vision and The Voice*, Crowley carried on the tradition of

---

*The crystal ball used by Charles Dickens is in the Wisbech and Fenland Museum, while Bulwer-Lytton's is on display at Knebworth, the manor home of the Lytton family.

a bygone era by gazing into a topaz shewstone, dictating his visions while Neuburg transcribed them.* For example, in the 28th Æthyr, we read:

> There cometh an Angel into the stone with opalescent shining garments like a wheel of fire on every side of him, and in his hand is a long flail of scarlet lightning; his face is black, and his eyes white without any pupil or iris. The face is very terrible indeed to look upon. Now in front of him is a wheel, with many spokes, and many tyres; it is like a fence in front of him.
>
> And he cries: O man, who art thou that wouldst penetrate the Mystery? for it is hidden unto the End of Time.[41]

Crystallomancy was also advocated in the twentieth century by New Thought pioneer William Walker Atkinson (1862–1932),[42] Crowley's heir apparent Frater Achad (1866–1950),[43] and American psychic and syndicated astrologer Jeane Dixon (1904–1997).[44]

Unsurprisingly, crystal gazing also attracted scientific attention. As early as 1898, Morton Prince, one of the founders of psychology, began studying hallucinations produced when subjects gazed into a glass bulb.[45] He concluded that "the content of visualizations thus produced shows that they are identical in structure and action with many of the hallucinations of the insane as well as with the spontaneous hallucinations of the sane (Joan of Arc, Fra Angelico, Catherine of Siena, Margaret Mary of the Sacred Heart, Arch-duke Charles of Austria, *et alii*)."[46] His observational and qualitative study of crystal-gazing in healthy individuals sought to understand the mechanisms underlying hallucinations among those considered "insane" (a pejorative term no longer used in psychology). Most telling is that Prince's examples of "spontaneous hallucinations of the sane" quoted above are all people who experienced ecstatic religious visions.

---

*"I had with me a great golden topaz (set in a Calvary cross of six squares, made of wood, painted vermillion) engraved with a Greek cross of five squares charged with the Rose of forty-nine petals." Aleister Crowley, Victor B. Neuburg, and Mary Desti, *The Vision and the Voice with Commentary and Other Papers*, The Equinox Volume IV Number II (York Beach, ME: Samuel Weiser, 1998), 15.

In 1930, German Gestalt psychologist Wolfgang Metzger coined the term *Ganzfeld* ("whole field") to describe the undifferentiated visual conditions responsible for the "prisoner's cinema" and an accompanying altered state of consciousness.[47] The Ganzfeld effect was tricky to induce in the laboratory. Researchers have had subjects stare at a large sheet of paper or smooth wall, often with blinders to control for eye movements or changing posture. Then, in 1951, Julian Hochberg and colleagues introduced the ingeniously simple method of placing halves of a ping-pong ball over the subject's eyes.[48] This quickly became a standard method of creating a blank visual field, and it is used in Ganzfeld studies to this day. Subjects in Schmidt and Prein's study of the visual Ganzfeld reported various images, including dots; mandala-like geometric patterns; and faces, eyes, or other facial features.[49] In addition, participants in Wackermann and colleagues' study reported percepts such as a horse, a forest, or a cave. Some reported extraordinary details, such as "a hand holding a piece of chalk and writing on a black-board something like a mathematical formula" and a figure that was "all in black, had a long narrow head, fairly broad shoulders, very long arms and a relatively small trunk. . . . He approached me, stretching out his hands, very long, very big, like a bowl."[50]

The cryptographic complexity of Enochian magick, the apocalyptic detail of *The Vision and the Voice*, and the sacred text of the Book of Mormon are far more significant than mere optical illusions or light patterns. The elaborate examples of Ganzfeld imagery described above may indicate that the phenomenon is a key that opens the door to more profound revelations.

IMPLICATIONS FOR MAGICK

The natural proclivity of the human brain to impose structure on its environment plays a large role in the magical practices covered in this book. Magical work generally involves altering one's consciousness, inhabiting liminal spaces, and seeking inspiration. It is often said that once somebody sets foot on a magical path, they will start to notice curious events around them. Paul Foster Case, American occultist and founder of Builders of the Adytum, said that this is, in fact, a *goal* of magical work: "The Universe is rational. It is composed according to a pattern intelligible to the mind of Man. That pattern may be seen, provided we train ourselves to look for it. Its characters are written on the mechanism of Nature, and we may read them."[51] Granted, magicians seeing patterns and coincidences in the world could be the result of priming one's perceptual expectancies—belief in the supernatural is associated with apophenia, after all[52]—but could there be more to it than simply seeing patterns or connections where none exist?

Whereas some clinicians link patternicity with mental illness, Carl Jung normalized it with his concept of *synchronicity*. This term has been variously defined as perceiving an "acausal connection through meaning,"[53] or "a meaningful coincidence of an outer event with an individual's inner state in which there is no apparent causal relationship."[54] Atmanspacher and Fach elaborate, "The way they are connected is not due to some causal interaction—nor is it due to chance. Rather, it is based on their joint meaning, which is constituted by their relationship with one another."[55] In short, synchronicity refers to the subjective experience of a meaningful coincidence between seemingly unrelated internal and external events. These coincidences reveal meaning about the world or, at the very least, about the mind of the person perceiving a connection. Among Jungian psychologists, synchronicity is not an unusual phenomenon associated with mental illness, but a normal phenomenon or universal human experience.[56]

The Jungian concept of "meaningful coincidence" muddies the waters over what is a real or meaningful connection. As Dietrich and Fields point out, who decides what is and isn't random can be a tautological argument:

> We must appeal to a division of perceptible patterns into the "real" and "meaningful" on the one hand and the "not real" or "meaningless" on the other. Common sense or, more recently, science is the arbiter of this division. Both common sense and science are, however, themselves both pattern recognizers that operate on an assumption that some patterns are meaningful while others are not.[57]

While such epistemological questions are beyond the scope of this book, the bottom line is that, in analytical psychology, those muddied waters of synchronicity open the door to asking the question "Why?"

The experience of meaningful coincidences can reveal things not only to a patient but also to a magician. Synchronicity is often associated with religious, mystical, and paranormal events.[58] Indeed, the very concept of synchronicity emerged from Jung's study of the Chinese method of divination by yarrow stalks, I Ching:

> A few years after my first experiments with the reeds, the *I Ching* was published with Wilhelm's commentary. I instantly obtained the book, and found to my gratification that Wilhelm took much the same view of the meaningful connections as I had. But he knew the entire literature and could therefore fill in the gaps which had been outside my competence.*[59]

Just as a student taking their first steps on a magical path will often begin to notice interesting coincidences in their lives, this likewise happens in the Jungian therapeutic setting. As Connolly wrote, "There is an increasing consensus that there is something in the nature of the analytical relationship that increases the probability of the occurrence of synchronistic events."[60] Similarly, Aleister Crowley's system of magick calls on those who aspire to the elevated degree of Master of the Temple to vow "that I will interpret every phenomenon as a particular dealing of God with my soul."[61] It is a literal exhortation to recognize a deeper meaning in all things.

In interviews with forty-five adults "who have undergone one or more experiences of unpredictable instances of coincidence or synchronicity," Russo-Netzer and Icekson's phenomenological analysis revealed that the experience of synchronicity is predicated on receptiveness to these experiences.[62] My own study of metaphysical beliefs and

---

*Richard Wilhelm's translation of the *I Ching* appeared in 1923; Jung would provide an introduction to the text for the 1950 Bollingen Series XIX (New York: Pantheon Books).

experiences similarly found that the best predictor of whether someone has had a transformative spiritual experience is whether they are *questing* (actively being open to new information and experiences to inform their spiritual understanding).[63] According to Russo-Netzer and Icekson, a chief determinant of synchronistic experiences is *intention*. Intention is, likewise, a fundamental concept for magical practitioners. Magick involves trying to make something happen. In Aleister Crowley's definition of magick as "the Science and Art of causing Change to occur in conformity with Will,"[64] any intentional act is a magical act. Similarly, as Christopher Penczak's *The Inner Temple of Witchcraft* describes the requirements for a practitioner, "First, you must have strength of will."[65] And Thorn Mooney's *The Witch's Path* says, "Intention triumphs above all else."[66] Intention may well prime the practitioner to spot synchronicities.

CLOSURE

In this chapter we have seen how the human brain structures perceptions and seeks order in the world. This process is governed not only by Gestalt principles of organization but also by culture, context, perceptual expectations . . . and sometimes even coincidence and pareidolia. The predilection for finding meaningful connections between seemingly unrelated things or events can run the gamut from mental illness to mysticism. As Joseph Campbell is often quoted as saying in his lectures, "The psychotic drowns in the same waters in which the mystic swims with delight."[67] Between these extremes, patternicity is a common human experience. These Gestalt concepts of the whole being larger than the sum of its parts—and the brain's innate desire to perceive that whole whenever possible—is a powerful idea that will resurface throughout the following chapters.

3
Rigamarole Models
Daily Magical Practices

IF YOU ARE A MAGICIAN, odds are pretty good that you have spiritual practices that you do daily, or as often as you can. And if you know any people from other traditions, odds are that they have a daily practice, too. A daily (or regular) practice is fundamental for many magicians. In *Everyday Witchcraft*, Deborah Blake discusses integrating spiritual practices into even the busiest life in just a few minutes every day.[1] Jenn Stevens' *The Mindful Witch* encourages daily meditation.[2] Organizations like A∴A∴, Temple of the Silver Star, and the Typhonian Order expect new students to begin some kind of daily ritual. A Golden Dawn–based group may recommend the Lesser Ritual of the Pentagram. Students of Israel Regardie may practice the Middle Pillar exercise.[3] Other regular practices may include prayers, affirmations, offerings, or devotionals; lighting a candle or burning incense; or some sort of divination, such as drawing a daily tarot card. This chapter will explore common daily practices and the psychological principles behind them. (We'll save meditation and yoga—a huge topic!—for the next chapter.)

WHAT IS A RITUAL, ANYWAY?

Psychologists and other social scientists have written extensively about ritual. Their definitions, however, are broad and include things that are not part of magical practice. For example, Graybiel's 2008 overview for the *Annual Review of Neuroscience* includes habits and other daily routines, which are defined as "sequential, repetitive, motor, or cognitive behaviors . . . that, once released, can go to completion without constant conscious oversight." In other words, "habits are performed almost automatically, virtually nonconsciously."[4] For a magician, if your rituals are done almost automatically or virtually nonconsciously, then your heart isn't in it, and your rituals probably aren't very effective. That's because magick rituals require being mentally present.

Imber-Black and Roberts' definition of daily rituals includes eating, sleeping, saying hello, and saying goodbye; other nondaily rituals can include family traditions, holidays, and weekend rituals.[5] Examples appearing in *Ritual: How Seemingly Senseless Acts Make Life Worth Living*, by University of Connecticut anthropologist Dimitris Xygalatas, include courtroom procedures, state functions, and attendance of concerts or sporting events (it's a great book, especially if you're interested in the social functions of rituals).[6] Liénard and Boyer, from Washington University in St. Louis, seemingly throw in the towel, declaring, "There is no clear criterion by which cultural anthropologists or other scholars of religion or classics determine that a particular type of behavior is or is not an instance of a ritual."[7]

Other researchers are more sensitive to magical practitioners with their definitions. Parker and Horton, for instance, specify that:

> in the Western magical tradition, which is based in alchemical, Cabalistic, and Hermetic models of self-transformation, there are three main types of rituals: (a) banishing rituals, which aim at removing harmful forces; (b) evocation or invocation rituals, which enlist the aid of helpful forces; and (c) consecration rituals, which involve a sacred celebration or aim at the magical transmutation of oneself or a sacred object.[8]

They classify rituals as serving one of three functions: liberation, transformation, or celebration/commemoration. Whitehouse, on the other hand, identifies two distinct types of religious rituals: *doctrinal* (routines meant to instill religious knowledge) and *imagistic* (infrequent and stimulating rituals that instill vivid memories).[9] Finally, Legare and Souza's study of Brazilian *simpatias* noted that the perceived efficacy of these folk magick rituals revolved around repetition, number of steps, and "transcendental influence" (such as the presence or use of religious icons).[10]

Most researchers have settled around a working definition of ritual that involves three characteristics: (1) A *predefined sequence of words and actions*, marked by formality, rigidity, and repetition. (2) It draws on a larger *system of symbolism*. (3) The ritual actions are *causally opaque*, which is to say actions in the ritual are not connected to the goal in an obvious cause-effect way.[11] A magician's daily practices generally tick most of these boxes.

BENEFITS OF A REGULAR MAGICAL ROUTINE

During the COVID-19 pandemic, much of the population discovered the importance of having a daily routine. Perhaps this realization occurred when closures or shifting to work-from-home disrupted a familiar work schedule. Or when health professionals encouraged continuing routines, such as getting dressed for work in the morning, to combat feeling lost or rudderless. Or when old routines gave way to new ones. For instance, I started taking walks every day for exercise. Regardless, the pandemic laid bare the importance of routines for structuring time, getting through the day, increasing resiliency, and combatting depression.[12] These benefits also apply to a magician's daily practice.

When discussing the Augoedies ritual for Knowledge and Conversation of the Holy Guardian Angel, Aleister Crowley stressed the importance of persisting every day regardless of what obstacles life presented, including the death of his infant daughter. Maintaining daily rituals can help life seem normal—especially in times of stress[13]—by maintaining the natural rhythm our minds have come to expect. While Crowley frames it as an act of defiance against adversity or a test of one's dedication to the Great Work, persistence likely helped him cope with the loss of a child by preserving something familiar in his day.

Adverse life events such as those described above are persistent stressors. Over time, they are detrimental to health and well-being. In contrast, any boost we get from *positive* events tapers off quickly. This phenomenon is called *hedonic decline*. Alas, major positive life events are all too uncommon. Here's where a daily practice comes into play: According to research by Mochon and colleagues, "certain seemingly minor events—such as attending religious services or exercising," presumably including the benefits of a daily magical practice, may provide "small but frequent boosts; if people engage in such behaviors with sufficient frequency, they may cumulatively experience enough boosts to attain higher well-being."[14] This is a case of slow and steady wins the race.

For those just starting, the idea of beginning a magical routine may sound daunting. It's a commitment, true. But it's a commitment to yourself (as opposed to the many commitments we make to others). As Francis King and Stephen Skinner wrote in *Techniques of High Magic*, a book on which I cut my teeth as a young magician, "It is most important to commence by establishing a rhythm of work, a regular practice which one performs every day no matter what circumstances arise. This makes the student continually aware that magic is a part of his life, not a 'once in a blue moon' experiment."[15] David Conway, another of my early influences, concurred, writing, "It is far better to keep up five minutes a day than have much longer, but irregular, sessions."[16]

Aleister Crowley recommended a simple but effective ritual often referred to as "Saying Will," to be done in conjunction with the main meal of the day. It may resemble the religious practice of saying grace over one's food, but this dialogue is meant to remind the magician of the Great Work:

"Do what thou wilt shall be the whole of the Law."
"What is thy will?"
"It is my will to eat and to drink."

"To what end?"
"That my body may be fortified thereby."
"To what end?"
"That I may accomplish the Great Work."
"Love is the law, love under will."

This dialogue can also be adapted to solitary use, for example: "It is my will to eat and to drink, that my body may be fortified thereby, that I may accomplish the Great Work." One could similarly adapt language from whatever tradition you follow. One example might draw from the Wiccan cakes and ale consecration, "O Queen most secret, bless this food into our bodies; bestowing health, wealth, strength, joy, and peace, and that fulfillment of love which is perfect happiness."[17] As magician-educator Maevius Lynn remarks, observations like these are "meant to inject intention and mindfulness into mealtime. It turns the mundane act of eating into a magical one: you are converting food into spiritual substance."[18]

One function of Saying Will is to stop whatever we're doing and remind ourselves of our magical goals. Rodney Orpheus—magician and lead singer for The Cassandra Complex—tells the aspiring practitioner about Saying Will at mealtime, "At first it will seem a bit of a chore, but after a while it becomes a habit, until you begin to do it naturally every time you sit down to eat."[19] Saying Will, however, isn't the only way to remind us of our magical goals. Magicians can apply practices like these more broadly. Thelemite and psychologist David Shoemaker writes, "This sort of mindfulness is hardly limited to mealtime—you can extend this concept to *any* task. Anything that you are doing during the day can and should be recognized as a contribution to the execution of your Great Work."[20]

The ideal for a magician is not to be mindful occasionally, but constantly. As Rodney Orpheus tells us, "To be a good magician, you must be a magician all the time."[21] This succinctly echoes the words of Éliphas Lévi a century and a half earlier: "Magic is exercised at all hours and at all moments.... All the faculties and all the senses must take part in the work, and no part of the priest of Hermes can remain idle."[22]

Everything a magician does should be mindful and intentional. Occultist Lon Milo DuQuette spells this out in no uncertain terms: "Any *un*willed action is an *un*magical act: reaching for a cigarette; ordering that fourth Martini; or any *habitual or reactive behavior that overrides the momentum of one's life focus*."[23] Like Orpheus above, DuQuette echoes Lévi's writings from over a century before:

> All intentions which are not manifested by acts are vain intentions, and the words which express them are idle words. It is action which provides life, and it is also action which provides and certifies the will. It is also said in the symbolic and sacred books that men shall be judged, not by their thoughts and ideas, but by their works. To be, one must do.[24]

The goal of ever-mindfulness may seem lofty and elusive, but it begins with the small step of adopting a regular magical practice. This habit forms a solid foundation on which to build.

The hardest part of a routine is getting it established. Lally and colleagues determined that people take, on average, sixty-six days (just under ten weeks) to establish new health habits. Individuals took anywhere from eighteen to 254 days for the behavior to become automatic. The health habits studied included simple practices like eating a piece of fruit while watching TV, drinking a glass of water after breakfast, or running for fifteen minutes before dinner. More complex routines like banishing or grounding rituals might take longer to establish. If you miss a day, don't get discouraged: Study data suggest that missing a day does not impact the habit-formation timeline, so long as the routine continues to be followed.[25] We are creatures of habit, so pick yourself up, dust yourself off, and keep going!

For our discussion of specific daily rituals, we will group the practices as intellectual, active, or receptive. *Intellectual* practices are those brainy things that can feel like homework: journaling, studying, and memorizing things like correspondences, rituals, or other texts. *Active* practices involve doing something with an intended effect, such as banishing, solar or lunar adorations, prayers, and blessing food or other things. *Receptive* practices refer to entering an introspective state of mind to take in information from the external world. Examples of these practices are astral projection, pathworking, and divination. This three-category scheme may not be perfect—is memorizing a ritual active?—but it's a useful framework for exploring relevant psychological research.

INTELLECTUAL PRACTICES: MEMORY AND MAGICK

One of the magician's best tools is the journal, diary, or magical record. Keeping a record of your practices is recommended by many groups, schools, and authors. In the Hermetic Order of the Golden Dawn tradition, Chic and Sandra Cicero write, "We encourage students to keep a magical journal of all esoteric practice: meditations, exercises, rituals, and readings. . . . Always include the date, time, and circumstances of the working, along with any results or feelings that occur afterward."[26] Writing from a witchcraft perspective, Arin Murphy-Hiscock suggests, "Keeping records of your work allows you to consult notes regarding herbal or incense blends, timing, success and failures, origins of ideas, references, and experiments with energies of various supplies and components."[27] Similarly, in *How to Study Magic*, Sarah Lyons writes, "To keep track of these things in the early stages of your study, it's a good idea to keep a magical journal. . . . Whether you use it for keeping track of divination that you do, logging what comes up during meditation, or taking notes on what worked and what didn't work in a spell, a magical journal can be a great way to figure out what works best for your magical practice."[28] James Wasserman has devoted an entire volume to the importance of the magical record.[29]

Think of a journal as your lab notes. It's data you can revisit to reflect on your work at a later time, whether to evaluate your successes (as we'll discuss in chapter 11), to note your progress, or simply to recall events of your past. A Thelemite may gain insight into understanding their True Will. Others may see evidence of karmic patterns or the path of destiny laid out (as they say, hindsight is 20/20).

Looking back on events from years ago and seeing forgotten details can be sobering. It really shouldn't surprise us, because we know our recollections can be inaccurate. Anyone who has experienced the Mandela effect knows the unsettling feeling of their memories being at odds with the facts. Some would rather believe they have passed into an alternate universe than accept that their recollections—like everyone else's—are imperfect. Memory is the ultimate unreliable narrator.

Rather than being a faithful record of reality—like a film of our life events—memories reflect our *experience* of reality. This, in turn, is influenced by the meaning we assign to the event, and whatever knowledge base or frame of reference we bring to the experience. We don't relive memories so much as bring them into the present. This means the circumstances that call a memory to mind also influence how we interpret those impressions in the present. Finally, we store only fragments of any given experience: enough to recall the gist of it, but not photographic recall of every detail. Whenever we recall an event, we reconstruct it from the pieces we remember. We also reconstruct memories in a way that brings coherence to the self-story of our lives. As University of Oxford anthropologist Valerie van Mulukom writes, "Rather than veridical accounts of past experiences, memories may be fictions that are continuously revised and shaped in the service of ongoing ideas and attitudes."[30]

This is especially true with magick ritual, which can be quite emotionally charged. One prevailing theory promoted by anthropologist Harvey Whitehouse suggests that highly arousing religious rituals create "flashbulb memories" that are stored and recalled in vivid detail.[31] In the mundane world, these infrequent but significant moments are the answers to questions like "Do you remember what you were doing when January 6 happened?" or "Where were you when the Challenger space shuttle blew up?" However, Xygalatas found that recollections of participants in a Spanish fire-walking ritual had poor factual recall of the details. This supports the counter-hypothesis that highly arousing religious rituals overwhelm or exhaust our cognitive capabilities and impair episodic memory formation.[32] Mulukom offers an alternative interpretation, which is that fire-walking is a significant ritual for participants, whose memories may focus more on the *meaning* of the ritual instead of factual details.³³ In any case, two months after fire-walking, participants were more confident of the details they remembered . . . but these recollections were also more inaccurate. As Xygalatas and colleagues concluded, this increase in fire walkers' memory errors "suggests that they continued to construct memories of the event in the weeks following the ritual. . . . [T]hese were based on cognitive elaboration rather than on retrieval of perceptual memories."³⁴ The bottom line here is that recollection of magical rituals, like other memories, becomes more inaccurate over time.

This is where journaling comes to the rescue. Write down important impressions and details of your rituals *as soon as possible*. Do it while your memory is fresh. Don't wait until the next day. Seriously. Vivid details fade surprisingly quickly. Journaling also involves rehearsing the memory of a fresh event, which aids memory formation. Writing also helps people process their experiences.³⁵

While autobiographical memory is prone to inaccuracy, we have a great capacity for accurate memorization of facts, correspondences, rituals, and texts. Such things may seem daunting to a new magician, but the typical person already has a great deal of information stored in their brain, whether it be song lyrics, lines from a favorite movie, or trivia about a chosen fandom. Occultism has an age-old tradition of memorization, or *ars memoriae*, about which Frances Yates wrote the seminal work *The Art of Memory*.³⁶ The ancient Art of Memory involves the following two main steps:

1. Encode bits of information into memorable tableaus. Suppose I'm trying to memorize the phrase "health and wealth and strength and joy and peace" from the Gnostic Mass. In that case, I might visualize a doctor, with a white lab coat and stethoscope, arm-in-arm with a billionaire in a top hat and monocle on one side, and a circus strong-man in a leopard-skin off-the-shoulder singlet on the other. They are skipping giddily down the road. The billionaire and strong man are flashing the peace sign with their free arms.
2. The Method of Loci, or memory palace, associates these tableaus with rooms in an imaginary cathedral, mansion, or other location.

Moving through this imaginary space can help recall, and string together, longer pieces of information.

Over the Renaissance and Baroque periods, practitioners developed iconography to communicate their abstract ideas to others. The often-bizarre images of alchemy have been called "flashcards for the insane."[37] Kabbalah has a tradition of iconography around the Tree of Life.[38] In Freemasonry, diagrams called *tracing boards* serve as teaching aids or reminders of one's initiatic lessons. Likewise, tarot cards are potent repositories of symbolism, whose images may be more memorable than books made up of imposing rows and columns of correspondences. Interestingly, University of Manchester professor emeritus Susan Llewellyn sees parallels between the bizarre images associated with the Art of Memory and REM sleep, during which episodic memories are encoded as dreams; if this proves true, then both phenomena may reflect similar neurobiological processes.[39]

Fig. 3.1. The bizarre ars memoriae for alchemical processes—such as this illustration from Michael Maier's *Tripus Aureus* (1618)—earned them the sobriquet "flashcards for the insane."

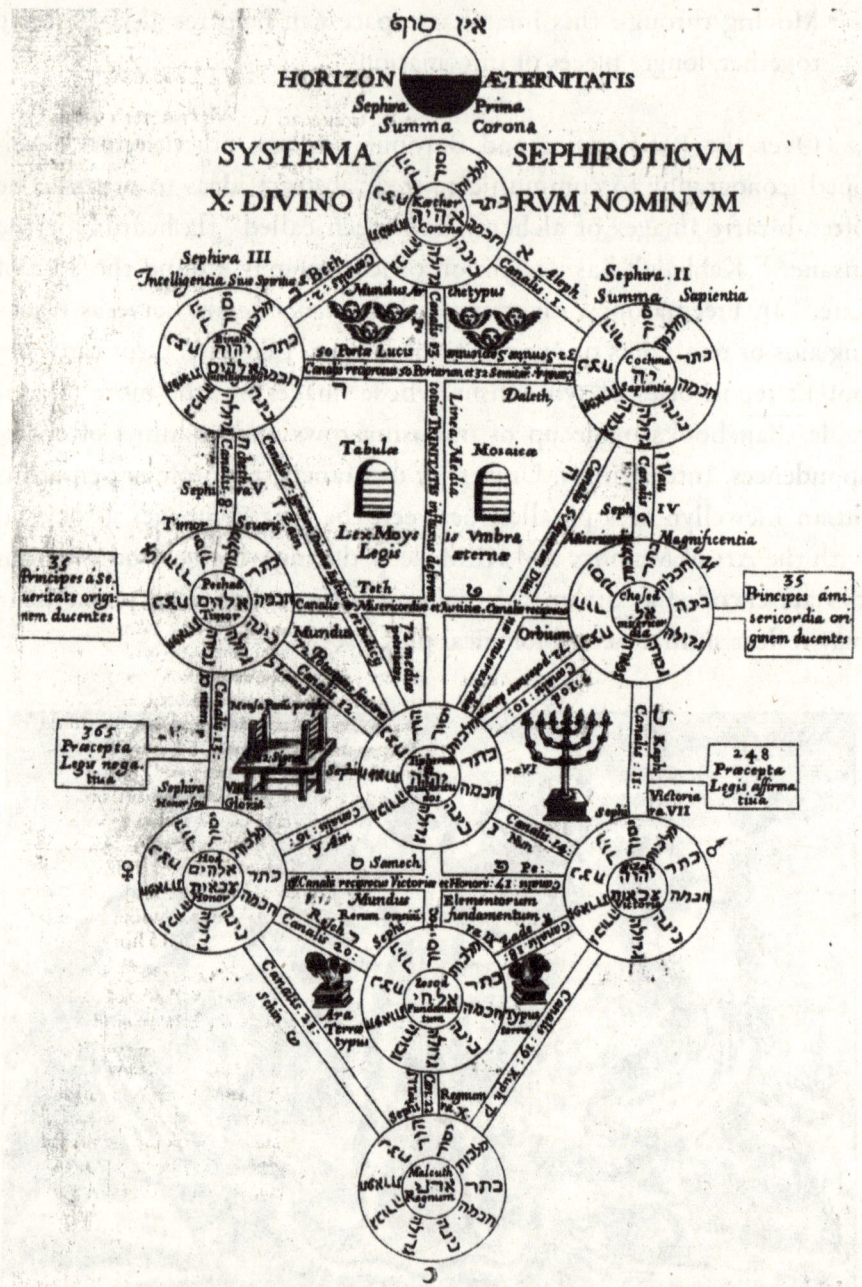

Fig. 3.2. Athanasius Kircher's *Œdipus Ægyptiacus* (1652) demonstrated how the Kabbalistic Tree of Life could serve as a memory palace, inspiring the systems of correspondence popularized in ceremonial magick traditions of nineteenth-century France and England.

Rigamarole Models ☆ 51

Fig. 3.3. This lithograph, published by Currier & Ives circa 1876, illustrates the variety of symbols that appear in Masonic tracing boards as memory prompts.
Image courtesy of the Library of Congress

Fig. 3.4. The Thoth Tarot of Aleister Crowley and Frieda Lady Harris (1944) was the first to incorporate Golden Dawn colors and other correspondences into the cards' designs, making them memorable tableaus for magicians to learn from.
"Atu I, The Magus," courtesy Ordo Templi Orientis and the University of London

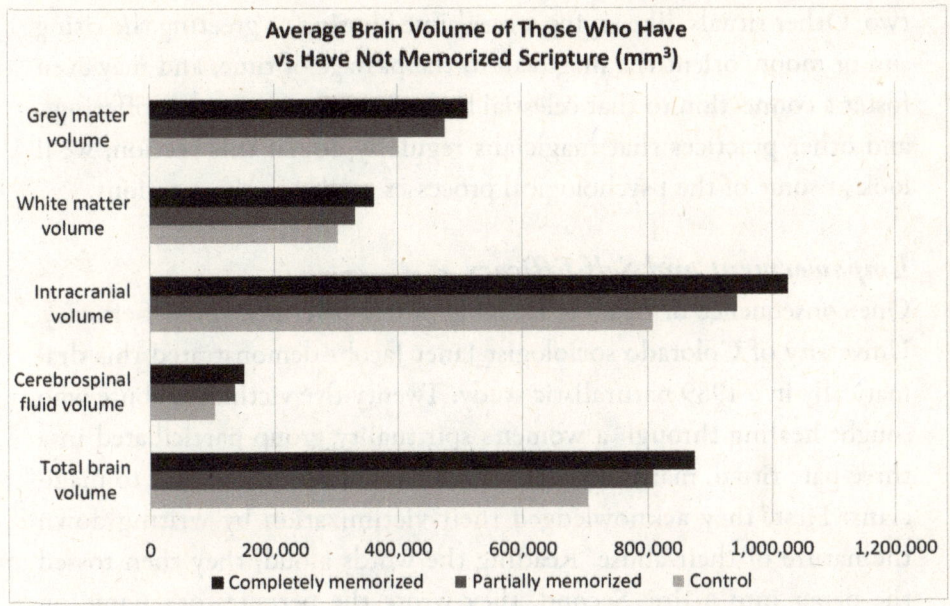

Fig. 3.5. Summary of memorization study findings from Rahman et al.
Image by the author using data from Rahman et al., "Association between Scripture Memorization and Brain Atrophy Using Magnetic Resonance Imaging."

Memorization of rituals and other texts internalizes the words and ideas at a much more profound level than one gets from simple familiarity. Being able to do a ritual without holding notecards or a script is but one benefit of memorization. One study found that subjects who had memorized scripture (in this case, the Qur'an) had significantly larger volumes of gray and white matter, cerebrospinal fluid, intracranial volume, and total brain volume than those who had not. These findings suggest that memorization may boost brain health by fostering a cognitive reserve, fending off natural cognitive decline.[40]

ACTIVE PRACTICES: DOING THE MAGICK

Many daily practices involve rituals to accomplish something. A banishing ritual or calling the quarters purifies a space. Centering or grounding rituals such as the Middle Pillar connect the magician either with themselves, the world around them, or the relationship between the two. Other rituals, like saying a mealtime blessing or greeting the rising sun or moon, orient the magician to the passage of time, and may even foster a connection to that celestial body. So too with prayers, offerings, and other practices that magicians regularly do. In this section, we'll look at some of the psychological processes at play in these actions.

Empowerment and Self-Efficacy

One consequence of ritual is a feeling of empowerment or self-efficacy. University of Colorado sociologist Janet Jacobs demonstrated this dramatically in a 1989 naturalistic study: Twenty-five victims of abuse who sought healing through a women's spirituality group participated in a three-part ritual, many elements of which will sound familiar to magicians. First, they acknowledged their victimization by writing down the nature of their abuse. Reading the words aloud, they then tossed the paper into a fire. Second, they wrote the perpetrator's name on an egg, which they smashed on the floor while shouting their abuser's name. Finally, they did a guided meditation in which they envisioned themselves as whatever goddess was personally meaningful to them, confronting their abuser to internalize the strength and power of that divine form. Participants reported that the ritual was effective in reducing fear (40 percent), releasing anger (60 percent), reducing emotional pain (60 percent), increasing one's sense of power (73 percent), and improving their overall mental health (76 percent). While the feeling of empowerment was temporary, over half of the participants (52 percent) reported that the feeling lasted a month or more.[41]

Empowerment translates into greater discipline, willpower and control.[42] According to Albert Bandura's self-efficacy theory, "People's perceptions of their capabilities affect how they behave."[43] These perceptions determine "how much effort will be expended, and how long it will be sustained in the face of obstacles and aversive experiences."[44] Self-efficacy is associated with better academic performance,[45] as well as pain tolerance, diet, weight loss, following medical regimens, and recovery from myocardial infarction and substance abuse.[46]

Skeptics may scoff and say that the empowerment and behavior changes that come from rituals are the result of self-delusion and wish-

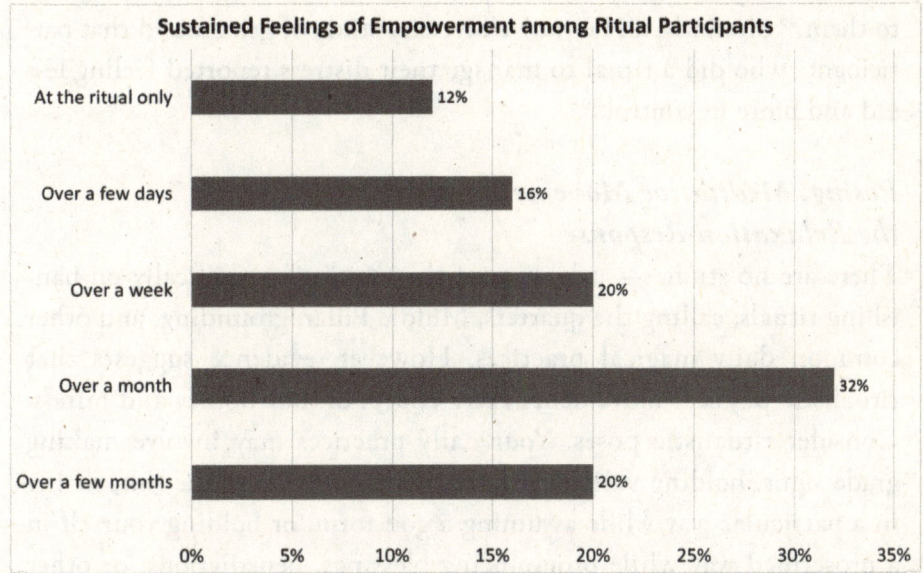

Fig. 3.6. Long-term effect of a healing ritual to promote feelings of empowerment among victims of abuse.
Image by the author using data from Jacobs, "The effects of ritual healing on female victims of abuse."

ful thinking. However, research demonstrates that rituals *do* make a difference. Athletes' rituals—which can include things as varied as eating a special meal, wearing a certain pair of underwear, calling on the dead, being first/last to walk onto the court, or spinning a ball or bouncing it before shooting—indeed improve performance.[47] Some question whether self-efficacy is the operative factor. For example, in a study of anxiety-inducing situations like singing karaoke or doing a math test, Alison Wood Brooks and colleagues determined that rituals reduce anxiety, which in turn leads to better performance. Or, as they put it, "Simple, novel rituals reduce anxiety, lower elevated heart rates, and improve performance—provided they are imbued with symbolic meaning."[48] Regardless of whether the key is self-efficacy or reduced anxiety, the result is that ritual makes people feel like they have control over a situation. Thus, for example, top-ranking Dutch athletes with an internal locus of control "exhibited greater levels of ritual commitment" than those who felt that success was more influenced by factors external to them.[49] Similarly, a Harvard University study of grief found that participants who did a ritual to manage their distress reported feeling less sad and more in control.[50]

Posing, Meditative Movement, and the Relaxation Response

There are no studies—at least as of this writing—specifically on banishing rituals, calling the quarters, Middle Pillar, grounding, and other common daily magical practices. However, evidence suggests that ritualistic physical movements exert effects on our bodies and minds. Consider ritualistic poses. Your daily practices may involve making grade signs, holding various gestures while addressing the sun, sitting in a particular way while assuming a god form, or holding yourself in a proscribed way while pronouncing blessings, benedictions, or other intentions. Magician and author Donald Tyson has even proposed a system of "kinesic magic" based entirely on hand gestures and bodily poses.[51] In whatever way these signs are part of your work, it turns out that bodily postures induce emotional and cognitive responses. These are called *bottom-up* responses because impulses flow from the nervous system up to the brain to influence mood and other mental states. (By contrast, a *top-down* approach is one where the mind exerts an influence on lower-level functions of the body.)

Back in 1974, James Laird famously reported that subjects reported feeling happier while smiling, and angrier while frowning. Cartoons were also rated as funnier when participants were smiling rather than frowning.[52] This finding has been widely replicated, including a recent multicenter study involving 3,878 culturally diverse participants from nineteen countries.[53] The conclusion is that peripheral feedback from the face influences one's emotional experience in a bottom-up fashion: Smiling literally makes you feel happier.

But what about the rest of the body? Another classic study, this time by Riskind and Gotay (1982), looked at the effect of physical posture on motivation and emotion. In their study, subjects who were temporarily placed in a slumped or hunched posture subsequently (i.e., after they were no longer in that position) showed lower persistence on a challenging task and reported greater feelings of stress, compared to subjects who had been in a relaxed position. This led to the bottom-up conclusion that "physical postures are not just diagnostic of internal states, but can influence the *susceptibility* of a person to such states."[54] Similarly, Price and colleagues demonstrated that different postures influence basic reflexive and electrocortical reactions: When presented with erotic (vs. neutral) images, emotive responses like eyeblink and EEG (event-related potential) were greater when subjects had "heightened approach motivation embodied via leaning forward" than those placed in a reclined (satiated) posture.[55] Recently, Wieneck and colleagues found that "power postures"—leaning forward, tilting the head up, arms akimbo, or an open bodily position—increased subjective feelings of power. These gains were lost by the one-week follow-up, leading the authors to conclude that "longer periods of sustained practice are required to achieve lasting change."[56]

In the context of Christian devotional practices, Cappellen and colleagues determined that expansive and upward-oriented postures were associated with praise, worship, adoration, and thanksgiving; these in turn resulted in positive affect and better engagement in worship services. Meanwhile, downward and constrictive poses, such as kneeling, were indicative of confession or prayer and associated with negative affect.[57] Perhaps French polymath Blaise Pascal (1623–1662) wasn't too far off when he said, "Kneel and you will believe."

Taken together, these studies demonstrate that bodily postures play a bottom-up role in eliciting feelings of happiness, anger, depression, helplessness, power, adoration, or contrition. It doesn't seem much of a stretch to assume feelings of empowerment—or other experiences—could result from adopting ritual postures, whether they be the Golden Dawn LVX signs, Crowley's NOX signs, the degree signs from some magical order, and so on. Indeed, anthropologist Felicitas Goodman's cross-cultural study of shamanic trance postures made a startling discovery:

> If we consider in how many different ways we are able to hold our bodies and heads and can place our hands, arms, feet, and legs, it

is truly astounding that these roughly thirty specific combinations should appear over and over again worldwide.... The greatest mystery of all, however, is the agreement in visionary content. Where we do have evidence in local traditions, it is clear that cross-culturally the postures elicit almost identical experiences.[58]

Bodily postures, it seems, are capable of not only eliciting specific moods or feelings, but of unlocking cross-culturally consistent mystical experiences.

If this is true about static poses, what does research tell us about dynamic gestures and other types of actions? In an ethnographic study of Spiritist practices among Puerto Rican *brujos* ("witch healers"), anthropologist Raquel Romberg recognized "the religious significance of gestures, the emotions they elicit, the religious subjectification process they constitute and the spiritual healing they can promote," arguing that ritual gestures are "affective and practical technologies for constituting the religious subject within Spiritism."[59] In other words, Romberg's focus is less on what gestures *mean*, so much as on what they *do*: "I claim that it is through these gestures that followers may become and feel like Spiritists and thus be healed as Spiritists."[60]

Within psychology, a large body of literature focuses on *meditative movement*, or practices characterized by mindful bodily movements, regulated breathing, meditative mindset, and deep relaxation.[61] Examples in the literature include practices both Eastern (t'ai chi, qigong, chi kung, aikido, Sufi dance, yoga) and Western (Somatics, Alexander Technique, Feldenkrais). These characteristics also describe the magician doing the Lesser Banishing Ritual of the Pentagram, Middle Pillar, and similar

Figs. 3.7–3.12. (opposite page) A selection of magical gestures: A receptive pose, common in paganism and other traditions (fig. 3.7); conferring blessing, also called the Ornate Gesture in Ordo Aurum Solis (fig 3.8); prayer or adoration, called the Flame Pose in the Gnostic Mass, also found in yoga (fig 3.9); the Hailing Sign of a Magician (fig 3.10); sign of a Practicus 3 = 8 in the Golden Dawn (fig 3.11); and Mulier, one of the NOX signs in Aleister Crowley's A∴A∴, also the Goddess Posture in Wicca (3.12).

Photos courtesy of Maevius Lynn

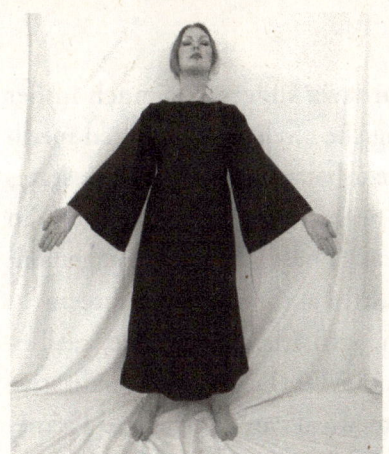

Fig. 3.7

Fig. 3.8

Fig. 3.9

Fig. 3.10

Fig. 3.11

Fig. 3.12

exercises. Neopagan and ecofeminist Starhawk suggests as much in her seminal book *The Spiral Dance*: "Casting the circle is an enacted meditation."[62] In addition to promoting relaxed, balanced, or attentive states of mind, meditative movement has also been shown to be beneficial in an array of health and mental health areas. These include management of mood, stress, anxiety, depression, cognitive ability, and self-esteem, as well as inflammation, immune function, arthritis, cancer care, cardiovascular risk factors, diabetes, obesity, and ADHD.[63] While meditative movement is no replacement for proper medical care, Payne and Crane-Godreau found that practitioners of meditative movement fared better managing mental health conditions like stress, anxiety, and depression, with results being generally as effective as other therapeutic interventions.[64] The main caveat in trying to extend these benefits to the meditative movements of daily magical practices is that a session of t'ai chi or qigong may last considerably longer than a banishing ritual; thus, any benefits may be less pronounced depending on the duration of one's daily practices.

One powerful mechanism by which postures and meditative movement may impact well-being is through the *relaxation response*. Coined in the mid-1970s by Harvard University physician Herbert Benson and colleagues,[65] the relaxation response is the body's ability to de-stress. Characterized by a state of deep rest on both the physical and emotional levels, it is the flip side of the fight-or-flight response (which we discuss in chapter 10). According to Benson, eliciting the relaxation response is very straightforward:

> Once or twice a day for 10 to 20 minutes, sit in a relaxed position, eyes closed, and repeat a word or sound as you breathe. Some people use such words as "love" or "peace." Others say traditional prayers. If your thoughts stray—which is normal and expected—just refocus on the word repetition. . . . Anything that breaks the train of everyday thought will evoke this physiological state.[66]

The list of age-old practices from around the world that elicit the relaxation response looks a lot like the who's who of meditative movement listed in the previous paragraph: t'ai chi, qigong, meditation, yoga, breathing exercises, progressive muscle relaxation, biofeedback, and repetitive prayer. Many daily magical practices share features with, or incorporate, these practices.

Hundreds of peer-reviewed studies have demonstrated the efficacy of the relaxation response in treating a range of medical conditions caused or exacerbated by stress, including cardiovascular, autoimmune, and other inflammatory conditions, as well as psychological conditions such as anxiety, panic disorder, and mild-to-moderate depression. It can improve the lives of those with chronic conditions and boost the immune system.[67] One year out, participants in long-term training on the relaxation response and resiliency saw their healthcare utilization drop by 43 percent.[68]

The key to maximizing the benefits of the relaxation response is sustained regular practice. While some changes in gene expression have been noticed in the short term, some beneficial changes only happen after prolonged practice. Furthermore, changes seen in the short term become more pronounced in long-term practitioners. These findings have led Manoj Bhasin and colleagues to say, "Regular daily practice of techniques that can be used to elicit the R[elaxation]R[esponse] are often recommended for sustaining its beneficial effects."[69] And so it goes for regular magical practices.

Savoring

Another powerful yet simple psychological technique to incorporate into daily magical practice is *savoring*: pausing to enjoy a positive experience. As Fred Bryant and Joseph Veroff, who wrote the book on the subject, put it, savoring is "a search for the delectable, delicious, almost gustatory delights of the moment."[70] While it resembles mindfulness—being aware of a moment—savoring is different in that it actively "upregulates" positive emotions.[71] By consciously acknowledging your pleasure, expressing it by smiling or other nonverbal expressions, and engaging all your senses, savoring enhances and prolongs one's enjoyment.

If enhanced joy doesn't convince you to incorporate savoring into your daily practice, consider the following: Much like the benefits of meditative movement and the relaxation response, savoring has been linked to optimism, well-being, life satisfaction, and resilience against depression.[72] It can reduce chronic pain and opioid misuse.[73] In older adults, savoring is associated with better general health, energy, and social functioning.[74] Garland and Fredrickson even propose that savoring fosters self-transcendence by "inducing absorptive experiences of oneness between subject and object, amplifying the salience of the object while imbuing the sensory-perceptual field with affective meaning."[75]

Some people are predisposed to savoring and the benefits thereof, but anyone can cultivate this skill.[76] To start, Hurley and Kwon suggest recalling three moments that you could have savored. Once you have practiced recognizing opportunities to savor, it's time to start a savoring log (or magical journal, if you prefer). To actually engage in savoring, Bryant and Veroff offer three directions:

1. To the extent possible, disconnect from or de-emphasize whatever stresses, worries, or other conditions may interfere with savoring.
2. Focus on the present.
3. Focus on the positive experience.[77]

They also suggest creating "contexts for savoring" by regularly setting aside time for this practice: "A basic strategy that enhances opportunities to savor is to purposely take 'time outs' from ordinary ongoing life."[78] This is precisely what daily magical practices do: They pause the routine of mundane life to remind us of our spiritual work, and the goals we attach thereto.

Thus, if you are saluting the sun, go outdoors for a literal encounter with that fiery orb. Pause to feel its warmth on your face, or the breeze against your skin. Smell the air. Appreciate the quality of light, whether it be dawn breaking on the horizon or the warm glow of sunset's golden hour. Enjoy the sound of birdsong around you. Tune out whatever distracts you from these pleasures. Then, when you have immersed yourself in the rich splendor of that experience, speak your words of adoration with true conviction.

Likewise, if you are accustomed to Saying Will or a blessing with your meal, don't end the exercise when you pick up your knife and fork. Extend your practice to the meal itself. Take a moment to appreciate the smell of your coffee brewing, or the sound of the coffee maker burbling away. Appreciate the warmth of cupping a mug of tea in your hands. Peer into your glass to notice the color and legs of your chosen wine. Roll that aged whiskey, kombucha, or whatever around on your tongue, and take the time to detect its different flavor notes.

By incorporating savoring of meals into one's daily practice, the magician has an advantage over other savorers: Rituals enhance enjoyment. Vohs and colleagues tested the theory that ritualistic behavior potentiates and enhances ensuing consumption. In other words, ritualistic behavior (vs. random gestures) increases the perceived flavorfulness and value of everything from chocolate to lemonade to carrots.[79] Similar findings were reported by Kapitány and Nielsen, in a study where participants rated ritualistically poured wine as more special and desirable than the same wine poured without the ritual.[80] However, as Vohs and colleagues point out, this effect is greatest for those who performed, rather than observed, the ritual, "because of the greater involvement in the experience."[81] So get out there and do some rituals!

RECEPTIVE PRACTICES: LETTING THE MAGICK FLOW THROUGH YOU

In the previous section, we saw how active ritual practices can potentially boost feelings of self-efficacy, confidence, relaxation, and enjoyment . . . all of which have physical and mental health benefits. What of common daily practices—such as pathworking, astral projection, vision questing, and divination—in which the magician enters a receptive state of being in communion (or communication) with their divinatory tools, the universe, or the divine? The contents of an astral journey or pathworking are less directed by the magician than they are a stream of consciousness, an observation of a novel landscape and its inhabitants. As Israel Regardie wrote, when exercises like divination are "practiced sincerely and intelligently and assiduously by the real students, consciousness gradually opens itself to a deeper level of awareness."[82]

Rather than directing, these practices are about listening and free association. One might experience a reduced sense of personal agency, as these practices involve being receptive to whatever presents itself to the practitioner. Marc Andersen and colleagues found exactly this in their study of American Ouija board users recruited at a paranormal conference: Participants who agreed that "the Ouija board can be used to contact entities such as spirits, ghosts, demons, angels, etc." reported a lower sense of personal agency and felt that the planchette moved on its own (i.e., by contacting a supernatural agent).[83] This begs the question: What leads us to perceive agency—supernatural or otherwise—in events around us?

Agenticity and the Hyperactive Agency-Detection Device

In 2000, Justin L. Barrett coined the term "hyperactive agency-detection device" (HADD) to describe the human "bias towards detecting human-like agency in their environment . . . when data is ambiguous or sketchy."[84] Sometimes simply called *agenticity*, the tendency to see an actor behind environmental stimuli is the sibling of patternicity. Agenticity would have been evolutionarily adaptive, as *not* detecting a nearby predator, hostile other, or similar danger could have proved fatal. In the modern world, this self-preserving instinct may have unintended consequences. As van Elk suggests, "The perceived presence of other agents in ambiguous situations . . . may reinforce people's belief in the continuous presence of external agents, such as ghosts, spirits or gods."[85]

To test this theory, van Elk created a video of a dozen points of light arranged and animated to look like a human walking. From this footage, he created a series of two-second snippets. Half the snippets consisted of a scrambled set of frames so that the sequence was discontinuous. The other half of the snippets were left as-is (i.e., a normal, continuous piece of video). Subjects rated whether each video did or did not depict a walking human figure. They also completed a survey measuring their paranormal belief. Consistent with Barrett's theory, believers and skeptics agreed on the videos where the answer was obvious—that is, there clearly was (or was not) a walking figure. However, for videos where the answer was ambiguous, believers were more likely than skeptics to say the video represented someone walking. Interestingly, the tendency to see agency in these ambiguous videos was unrelated to belief in either traditional religion or witchcraft. The HADD kicked in for believers in ESP, spiritualism, and superstition.

Studies of paranormal belief often treat skeptics as the "gold standard" against which believers are compared unfavorably. However, with HADD, the sword cuts both ways. Paranormal believers may be more likely to suspect agency in ambiguous situations where none exists. However, skeptics may be more likely to overlook agency in ambiguous situations where it *does* exist. (Similarly, in chapter 11 we will see that skeptics are less able to distinguish real faces from those with scrambled features.)

Mental Imagery

Pathworking and astral projection provide practitioners with imaginal (some would argue extrasensory) experiences of either an interior world or a world inaccessible through our conventional five senses. Regardless of how one thinks these experiences work, they rely upon mental imagery. As with other psychological phenomena discussed in this chapter—memory palaces, meditative movement, and the relaxation response—mental imagery has a long history of therapeutic use in practically every culture around the world: from ancient Greeks, Native Americans, and Indigenous people, to Hindus, Judeo-Christians, and Chinese medicine practitioners.[86] In the early twentieth century, guided imagery became an effective tool in psychotherapy, having "been shown to help clients make meaning of their inner worlds, improve performance, increase empathy and resiliency, and manage distressing symptoms of mental and physical health disorders."[87] Consequently, guided imagery found its way into scientific studies and clinical practice as a complementary therapy.

What do we mean by *imagery*? It is using the imagination to create mental images involving all of one's senses.[88] Mental imagination can be done alone; with a facilitator, guide, or therapist; in group settings; or through technology such as prerecorded scripts, telemedicine, telehealth, and the like. Consider the following example of guided imagery from a psychologist:

> Imagine you are walking through a beautiful meadow. The sun is shining in the midmorning day. Through your hair, you feel a gentle breeze blowing that is not too cold and not too hot; it just feels pleasant. Butterflies are flying about the many wildflowers. You stop for a moment to enjoy the beauty of the world around you and count your favorite colors and shapes within the flowers. The fragrance of wildflowers is mild but ever present. As you continue walking, you can hear the swish of the tall grass. The grasses feel soft and are not scratchy or itchy; they remind you of the velvet curtains that hung in your grandmother's living room. As you are moving through the tall velvety grasses, you come to a small door hidden in the field. You recognize this as the door to a magical place your heart has been dreaming of. You reach for the golden handle, twist the knob, and walk inside. What is around you? What do you see? Who is with you in this magical place, or are you alone? What does it feel like to be here? Spend some time enjoying this space, and when you are ready, open your eyes.[89]

Compare that to a common practice in witchcraft called *grounding*, *rooting*, or *centering*. In this exercise, the practitioner visualizes themself as a tree: Close your eyes and take several deep, calming breaths. Imagine tree roots growing out of your legs, penetrating deep into the Earth, encountering moisture, nutrients, cool soil, and all the life teeming therein, until you feel a deep connection to Mother Earth. Draw that energy up through the roots and into yourself, circulating that energy up your trunk and pushing into the branches and leaves that are growing out of the top of your body. These branches and leaves are also reaching upward toward the sun. Feel the breeze blowing through your branches. Notice the birds and other living creatures singing or resting there. Feel the warmth of the sun beating down upon your canopy of leaves, where that light is photosynthesized into nutrients and energy. Circulate that down your body, through your trunk and down to your roots. Feel the vitality of the Earth and sky circulating up and down through the tree that is you.[90]

The effectiveness of guided meditations relies upon vivid imagery. Visualization exercises are therefore fundamental. Some of Aleister Crowley's magical diaries contain accounts of him visualizing various objects during his early concentration exercises:

OBJECT MEDITATED UPON	REMARKS
Winged-Globe.	The entire meditation was bad.
Winged-Globe and Flaming Sword.	Meditation on both of these was only fair.
Pendulum.	Good as regards plane kept by the pendulum; but thoughts wandered.
Winged-Globe.	The result was pretty good.
Ankh (green).	Not bad.
Pentagram.	Rather good.*

*This is a selection of the examples appearing in Crowley's diaries, as quoted in J. F. C. Fuller, "The Temple of Solomon the King," *The Equinox* I. no. 4 (September 1910): 41–196 (p. 107–108).

In this example, recording both bad and good outcomes is important, as it allows the magician to track their progress. So important is visualization that David Conway devotes an entire chapter to it in *Magic: An Occult Primer*. He recommends five to fifteen minutes of practice daily. "In view of its importance in magic, colour must be visualized with special ease, and this too requires practice."[91] The goal is for the mental image to be "'projected' into the real world," that is, "to 'see' the mental picture just as if it were a part of your normal physical surroundings."[92] Morwyn makes similar recommendations in *Secrets of a Witch's Coven*: "Once you are able to hold the image of a three-dimensional object in your mind with your eyes open, try to imagine the object from various angles.... These exercises strengthen your powers of observation, recollection, visualization, and projection, all of which are employed by the Witch at work."[93] Similar exercises are found in David Shoemaker's *Living Thelema*.[94] The emphasis on these exercises illustrates how important visualization is to pathworking, astral projection, and other "clairvoyant" practices.

Sports psychologists also recommend visualization exercises. Daniel Gould and colleagues' program for coaching athletes in visualization training is remarkably similar to a magician's regimen:

> Mental skills are like physical skills. Becoming proficient in the use of imagery requires a commitment throughout the training season. It is unrealistic to think that either a physical or mental skill will be effective in a competitive situation when it is never practiced at any other time. Ideally imagery training should become an integral part of daily practice.[95]

Just as magicians keep a journal, athletes may keep logs to help them "in monitoring imagery practice and progress."[96] The athletes' proposed curriculum begins with vividness training, which can be a difficult task for some. Their advice is as sound in magick as it is for sports:

> If athletes have very poor imagery skills, the sport psychology professional or coach might recommend that they start with a simple exercise, such as imagining the details of their bedroom or a piece of equipment associated with their sport (e.g., a football, running shoes). As their imagery skills develop, they can begin to imagine more complex skills associated with their sport performance.[97]

From there, athletes practice controlling and manipulating mental images regularly, then evaluate "whether the program is meeting its objectives"[98] (this evaluation will be the topic of chapter 11).

By this point, you may be able to predict the psychological and physiological benefits of visualization and guided imagery, as they are similar to those of the other practices described in this chapter. One main benefit is reduced stress,[99] which in turn counteracts stress-impacted conditions like immune system functioning[100] and pain management.[101] In one study, fibromyalgia patients reported decreased pain and anxiety, plus improved sleep, at four and eight weeks after a guided visualization intervention.[102]

These benefits come with some caveats: First and foremost, magical exercises are not a replacement for proper medical care. If you have a serious physical or mental health condition, seek treatment from a medical professional. For instance, the stress-reducing effect of guided imagery was most pronounced among people reporting relatively low levels of stress.[103] These practices may improve the well-being of average healthy individuals, and give them resilience against more serious conditions, but they cannot counteract pathology (though they may be used as complementary tools in the medical treatment or management of a serious illness). Second, using guided imagery in cancer pain management produced mixed results, and suggests that success hinges on the patient's ability to generate and be absorbed in their mental images. While the term *imagery* implies vision, the practice is flexible and can accommodate individuals with aphantasia or other sensory deficits. This underscores the importance of engaging *all* the senses in these exercises, not just sight.[104]

Projective Techniques in Psychology

In chapter 2, we touched briefly on how the "filling in the holes" processes in Gestalt psychology and related phenomena like patternicity may play a role in divination by helping diviners see the connection between, say, different tarot cards in a spread, or how one I Ching hexagram changes toward another. Let's take a closer look at some related work in psychology. "Filling in the holes" also describes the underlying process in psychology's use of projective techniques.

The American Psychological Association's *Encyclopedia of Psychology* defines projective techniques as "a fixed series of relatively ambiguous stimuli designed to elicit unique, sometimes highly idiosyncratic, responses."[105] Early in the development of psychology, various clinical tools emerged around this concept. These include sentence completion and word association tests from Francis Galton or Carl Jung (1910); the famous Rorschach inkblots (1921); and the Thematic Apperception Test (1935), with pictures used as storytelling prompts. Their use became controversial over the ensuing century,[106] with fewer graduate schools today offering training in these techniques.[107] Much of the controversy revolved around the underlying theory of what projective tests reveal and how they are interpreted. Both answers have evolved significantly. How a person responds to the ambiguity of a projective technique can provide insights into "how an individual constructs meaning in well-specified but relatively ambiguous conditions."[108] Proponents argue that this methodology—so different from standardized tests with validated numerical scores and clinical cutoffs—can play a complementary role in therapeutic settings. As Blatt notes, "The skill of the clinician plays a central role in the use of projective techniques."[109] These interpretive skills vary widely from clinician to clinician.

In this way, interpreting projective techniques in psychology can be as much art as it is science . . . recalling Crowley's definition of magick as the Science and Art of causing Change to occur in conformity with Will. The similarities to divination or projection in magick are strikingly similar. Consider this observation from Choca and Rossini (2018) about the sometimes-subtle art of interpreting projective techniques:

> At times, there is a Rorschach marker, a response, a TAT story, a self-report test profile, or something else, that offers a portrait of the individual with uncanny clarity, sort of like the painting of a face that almost shows what the person is thinking.
>
> On many other occasions, however, you have to work at it. In those cases, it may be useful to commit to memory as much of the data as possible and let it sit. Go for a walk, go swimming, take a long shower, have a seat in your thinking armchair, and do whatever you do when your brain is likely to produce one of your great insights.[110]

As another example, let us return to the APA description of projective techniques eliciting "unique, sometimes highly idiosyncratic devices."

Our response to prompts from an oracle deck, shells, bones, or other medium can produce similarly idiosyncratic responses. Divination allows us to access deeper rational, creative, or intuitive ways of understanding situations. By seeing things from a different angle, we may find solutions or avenues we hadn't considered. An acquaintance of mine was fond of pointing out that pathworking or astral projection experiences where you see what you expect (e.g., consistent with the correspondences you are familiar with) don't reveal much and may merely reflect your subconscious expectations. When your visions produce something completely unexpected, yet appropriate, *that* is when things get interesting.

Skeptics, however, may dismiss psychology's projective techniques outright, saying "these techniques lack reliability and validity and ... are no better than reading tea leaves."[111] But, to misquote Joseph Campbell, the mystic drinks the tea upon which the skeptic frowns.

A Word about Psi

You may be wondering about divination practices that predict the future. Aren't patternicity and projective techniques only part of the story? Don't diviners utilize some form of precognition (seeing things before they happen), clairvoyance/remote viewing (seeing things in the present without any explainable way of accessing that information), or similar psychic ability?

In talking about research in psychology, I leave open the question of what else may be going on beyond that. The reader can explore and decide for themselves the utility of additional explanations. Parapsychology is one such area that you may (or may not) incorporate into your worldview. It might seem like a subfield of psychology: *psychology* is right there in the word, and research is done by trained scientists affiliated with respected universities. However, the vast majority of psychologists regard parapsychology as pseudoscience. This is a good place to briefly address the twin elephants in the room: What have studies of parapsychology found, and why is psychology so hostile to it?

Psi has an enormous body of research. Although groups like the

Society for Psychical Research date back to 1882, J. B. Rhine established the field of parapsychology within psychology in 1930, founding a parapsychology laboratory at Duke University that operated for thirty-five years. Since then, many studies and meta-analyses around the world have lent support to the existence of a small but significant psi effect.[112] For example, the perceptual Ganzfeld (discussed in the previous chapter) is popular in psi research to induce a relaxed, altered state of consciousness for "receiving" information from a remote sender. Research using this technique supports anomalous—which is to say "inexplicable"—information transfer.[113] Honorton and Ferrari's 1989 meta-analysis of 309 forced-choice precognition experiments published from 1935 to 1977, involving sixty-two different investigators and over fifty thousand subjects, described a small but significant hit rate (Rosenthal effect size $z/\sqrt{n} = 0.02$, $z = 6.02$, $p = 1.1 \times 10^{-9}$, which is to say chances are less than nine hundred million to one that the finding is spurious).[114] This is in line with the results of Radin's meta-analyses, and its 2024 update by Tressoldi and Storm, which concluded that this effect does not guarantee success every time, but may represent a slight tipping of the odds in one's favor.[115] Radin offers the metaphor of the baseball player who is considered extraordinary and paid millions of dollars if they can hit a ball one-third of the time.

The dashed horizontal line represents the chance rate of a correct hit. Dots represent the hit rate reported in each study. Vertical lines represent the 95 percent confidence interval around the observed hit rate; results where the confidence interval does not intersect the chance rate are statistically significant. The rightmost vertical line represents the results of meta-analysis, which combines all the studies into a single result. Numbers in parentheses indicate how many subjects were in each study (larger studies have narrower confidence intervals, which is to say more observations ensure more certainty).

The discussion of psi in psychology took off in 2011 when respected Cornell University professor Daryl Bem—the originator of self-perception theory and the Bem Sex Role Inventory—published the results of nine experiments in precognition . . . or what he described as "the anomalous retroactive influence of some future event on an

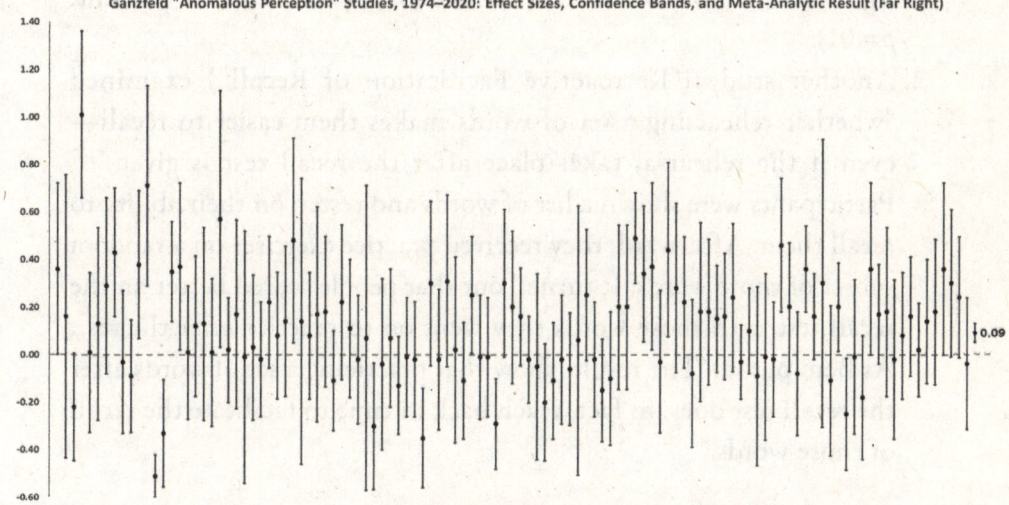

Fig. 3.13. Results of all Ganzfeld telepathy experiments 1974–2020.
Image by the author using data reported from Tressoldi and Storm,
Stage 2 Registered Report: Anomalous Perception in a Ganzfeld Condition:
A Meta-analysis of More than 40 Years Investigation."

individual's current responses, whether those responses are conscious or nonconscious." This wasn't Bem's first foray into parapsychology. He had been a defender of the Ganzfeld methodology for two decades. But what raised eyebrows was that his paper—involving nearly a thousand participants—passed peer review to appear in the preeminent *Journal of Personality and Social Psychology*.[116] Describing all nine studies in his paper is impractical, but here are a couple of examples:

1. In one study ("Precognitive Detection of Erotic Stimuli"), subjects were asked to guess which of two curtains shown on a computer screen had a random photograph behind it (the other had a blank image). Unknown to the subjects, the computer did not randomly place the picture until *after* the subject made their guess. Compared to neutral images, those trials involving erotic images (thus having higher valence/reward value) were correctly guessed

significantly more often than chance (53.1 percent vs. 50 percent, $p=.01$).

2. Another study ("Retroactive Facilitation of Recall") examined "whether rehearsing a set of words makes them easier to recall—even if the rehearsal takes place after the recall test is given."[117] Participants were shown a list of words and tested on their ability to recall them. Afterward, they received practice exercises on a random subset of those words. It turned out that people scored better on the recall test with those words they went on to practice *after* the test. As Bem put it, "The results show that practicing a set of words after the recall test does, in fact, reach back in time to facilitate the recall of those words."

These findings generated intense controversy. Bem and colleagues subsequently published a meta-analysis of ninety replications of his research, taking place in thirty-three laboratories in fourteen countries, resulting in the calculation of a small but significant effect size of 0.09. In statistics, effect sizes are often classed as small (0.30), medium (0.50), and large (0.70). Thus, the effect of psi is quite small, but statistically significant: $p = 1.2 \times 10^{-10}$ (in other words, the odds of the results from so many studies falling this far from zero due to chance alone is one in 8 billion).[118] On the other hand, a group of researchers self-identifying as the Transparent Psi Project attempted to replicate Bem's study and found a 49.89 percent correct guess rate (statistically indistinguishable from the chance rate of 50 percent).[119]

This controversy underscores how toxic the subject of parapsychology is to many psychologists. In a 1979 survey of 1,188 college professors, psychologists were more likely to reject the existence of psi than their colleagues in other disciplines (34 percent vs. 16 percent).[120] Similarly, in a 2020 study, one hundred subjects who either had a psychology degree or were psychology majors (either undergraduate or graduate) evaluated one of two nearly identical article abstracts. Both described peer reviews of eighteen meta-analyses representing 1,461 studies that noted that, despite some methodological flaws in the studies, most of the results were statistically significant, with small effect sizes in line with findings for other phenomena in psychology. The only difference was that one abstract was about psi phenomena, while the other was about memory storage in the hippocampus. Despite the information in the abstracts being identical, participants rated the psi version as less valid and reliable than the neuroscience version.[121] This finding points to a bias against parapsychology.

One objection to psi is that findings are presented with no acceptable scientific explanation or mechanism for how it occurs. Bem, however, argues (echoing the sentiments of other colleagues) that no amount of evidence is enough to convince some staunch skeptics; and even when a successful study is done to their specifications, the goalposts are moved to demand even more changes in response to having their skepticism challenged.[122] One argument says parapsychology research creates a paradox that logically leads to two equally untenable (and absurd) conclusions:

1. If we assert that psi simply cannot exist because there is no plausible scientific explanation—and yet hundreds of studies using the rigorous tools of accepted science (research design and methodology, laboratory protocols, statistical analysis, etc.) support the existence of psi—then these findings mean there must be something fundamentally flawed with the scientific method. *Therefore, this calls all research findings in every scientific field into question.*
2. If psi does exist, then it is possible that the effects obtained are not due to the subjects, but due to the researcher psychically influencing the outcome of the study. "Even if a significant effect is found at each step, there is no way to conclude anything . . . is it from the participants? From the experimenter? Is it from each experimenter separately? Or is a stronger influence from the first one who analyze [sic] the data?"[123] This applies not only to parapsychology studies, but to *all* research. *Thus, all of science is once again called into question!* "It means that a direct relationship between an intention and reality is possible"[124] . . . which is pretty much the definition of magick.

76 ☆ Rigamarole Models

Given that there is plenty of other psychological research free of intense controversy or bias, readers can explore this subject on their own. If you want to link your magical practice with psi, Mat Auryn's books *Psychic Witch*, *Mastering Magick*, and *The Psychic Art of Tarot* are a great and popular place to start.[125]

4

Think Better

The Magick of Yoga and Meditation

YOGA EXISTS IN A DIZZYING VARIETY THESE DAYS: Vinyasa. Kundalini. Ashtanga. Bikram. Yin. Aerial. Acro. Partner. Restorative. Prenatal. Baby. Hot. Cold. Nude. Goat. Do you want to do yoga with your bros? Try broga. Do you want some alcohol with your lotus position? Sign up for Zin(fandel) yoga or gin yoga. If you want it, odds are there's a type of yoga out there for you.

Whatever your preference, some practices are common across forms. These include *asana* (poses or positions), *pranayama* (focus on breath), *mantra* (repetition of a word or phrase), possibly visualization, and usually some form of meditation. The latter can range from calm free association to specific practices such as *mahasatipatthana*, *dharana*, or *dhyana*. The previous chapter on daily practice addressed related concepts such as meditative movement, magical gestures, and visualization. But yoga is such a huge topic—both in variety and research—that it gets a chapter all to itself.

Yoga is so prevalent in our culture today—turning up everywhere from community centers to grade schools—that it's easy to forget that this ancient Indian cultural practice was new to the West 150 years ago. One of its most prominent Western expressions—though by no means the first—came through the Theosophical Society, which was founded in New York City in 1875. For all its talk, however, members were frustrated that the society avoided practical instruction. Other groups like the Hermetic Society and Golden Dawn subsequently stepped in to fill the gap. Thus, in its earliest days in the West, yoga was embraced by occultists. Swami Vivekananda attended the World Parliament of Religions in 1894, and his subsequent book *Rāja Yoga* (1896) marked the moment that yoga came to wider popular attention in the West.[1]

As a sign of how ahead of the curve magicians were, consider that Austrian inventor and industrialist Carl Kellner—widely considered the "spiritual father" of Ordo Templi Orientis—wrote a booklet about yoga for the International Psychological Association meetings in the same year as Vivekananda's book. Kellner's chargé d'affaires and prime organizer of O.T.O., Theodor Reuss, taught about yoga and the chakras, perplexing students and scandalizing outsiders.

Y.O.G.A. IN THE U.S.A.: THE EARLY YEARS

A similar checkered history of yoga-related hyperbole and scandal played out repeatedly in the United States in the first quarter of the twentieth century.

In 1900, a self-proclaimed professor offered New Yorkers a two-week training in the career of mental healing, covering a mishmash of popular trends including "magnetic healing, personal magnetism, hypnotism and vital magnetism; vibrations of color and 'hatha yoga,' which includes concentration, and 'yoga breathing.'"[2]

In 1902, Ida Craddock killed herself rather than report to federal prison for mailing marital pamphlets deemed obscene by notorious censor Anthony Comstock; newspapers nationwide recalled her not as a sex educator but as the "High Priestess of Yoga" for her short-lived Church of Yoga in Chicago two years earlier (and which involved little actual yoga).[3]

In 1906, the *St. Louis Post Dispatch* promoted hatha yoga to its women readers as the secret to beauty and long life.[4]

In 1908, the wife of Purdue University President Winthrop Ellsworth Stone deserted her husband and two sons after nineteen years

Fig. 4.1. Purdue University President Winthrop E. Stone attempted to resign in disgrace after his wife abandoned him and his family to study yoga.
Image from *Chicago Defender*, July 29, 1911.

of marriage to become a yogi. This was such a widely reported scandal that Stone attempted to resign his position.[5] Her behavior was blamed on a "fad" course in yoga philosophy that was attended by "many women and some men" in the college town of Lafayette, Indiana. In 1911, Stone was ultimately granted a divorce on grounds of abandonment.[6]

Sri Agaymya Guru Paramahamsa—colloquially known as the Tiger Mahatma—was for a time teacher to European occultists like Carl Kellner, J. F. C. Fuller, and Aleister Crowley. When he came to the United States in 1907, his New York followers set up the Parliament of Infinite Wisdom to house him and host his lectures. After he returned to Europe, however, disgruntled donors sued the founders of the Parliament for the return of their money;[7] Paramahamsa himself, meanwhile, was jailed in London for sexually assaulting applicants to the secretary position he had advertised.

In 1911, a New York lawsuit sought to set aside the will of Sarah Chapman Bull—who left her vast fortune to Vivekananda's Vedanta Society rather than her daughter—by arguing that she had gone insane through the practice of raja yoga, which was dangerous for those with "little brains and weak intellects," including, they argued, ninety-nine out of one hundred women.[8]

In 1915, the custody case between Rudolph and Dorothy Gerber ended with neither parent being awarded custody of their daughter, after it was discovered that Mrs. Geber engaged in nudism and improper extramarital conduct with Ralph M. De Bit, leader of the Beaux Arts yoga village's Christian Yoga group.[9]

Meanwhile in 1915, Aleister Crowley—who had come to the United States a year before—promoted yoga as an integral piece of his scientifically based system of magick.[10] In the context of the prevailing uninformed attitudes of the times, Crowley was radical in integrating yoga practices throughout his Golden Dawn offshoot, A∴A∴, and writing about it in *Book 4*, part 1 (1912). Consequently, yoga has been a central focus of magical practitioners, turning up in books like J. F. C. Fuller's *Yoga* (1925), Crowley's own *Eight Lectures on Yoga* (1939), and Nancy Wasserman's *Weiser Concise Guide to Yoga for Magick* (2007).[11] As occultist and psychologist David Shoemaker informs students of magick, "You need to have the basics of yoga in your practice; specifically, *asana* (posture) and *dharana* (concentration). These practices will aid in focusing the mind."[12] Morwyn gives similar advice to new witches: "In order to 'get things done' the Witch must train, discipline, and perfect the most important tool of the trade—the mind."[13]

In 1919, when Pierre Arnold Bernard moved his yoga studio to a lavish estate in Nyack funded by wealthy New York City socialites such as the Vanderbilts, the "Omnipotent Oom" and "Loving Guru" (as the press dubbed him) was dogged by old rumors of "abduction and criminal assault growing out of orgies attending the initiation of members."[14] Men and women mixing socially in loose-fitting clothing was too scandalous for the times. Although he was one of the first to introduce and promote yoga in the United States, he remains an obscure figure in the history of yoga. More celebrity is lavished a generation later, as yoga became better understood and normalized in the public's mind, on his nephew Theos Casimir Bernard (1908–1947), who promoted hatha yoga and Tibetan Buddhism in his books.[15]

Fig. 4.2. On the day after Christmas, 1915, Aleister Crowley expounded magick, yoga, and science in the *Washington Post*.

Fig. 4.3. C. W. Kahales' April 15, 1917, syndicated comic strip shows detective Hairbreadth Harry exposing the Omnipotent Oom to be his archnemesis, Rudolph Rassendale. It illustrates public misgivings about yogis, swamis, mysticism, and the use of hypnotic powers to dupe the innocent. (Hypnosis will be discussed further in chapter 10.)
Image courtesy of the Library of Congress

YOGA BECOMES A GLOBAL PHENOMENON

The 1960s saw the emergence of modern postural yoga, such as that popularized by B. K. S. Iyengar. Coincidentally, an important behind-the-scenes figure in this movement is Gerald Yorke, Aleister Crowley's former student and sometimes benefactor.* Yorke served as a reader for British publishers Rider & Co. and Allen & Unwin, helping them source books on Hinduism and Buddhism. These included British editions of two books on yoga by Theos Bernard: *Heaven Lies Within Us* (1941) and *Hatha Yoga* (1950). In addition, Yorke championed early drafts of Iyengar's *Light on Yoga* (1966), helping to fine-tune the author's English so much that Iyengar declared Yorke his "literary guru."[16]

Modern postural yoga turns out to have more to do with already-familiar Western bodybuilding, calisthenics, gymnastics, and female physical culture.[17] As historian Anya P. Foxen notes, "There is a Western history of practice here that was overwritten by the imported language of yoga... Modern transnational yoga is ultimately a deeply syncretized and amalgamated entity resulting from the interaction of Indian yogic traditions with this Western body of thought and practice, among others."[18] This wildly popular amalgamation quickly became the predominant form of yoga throughout the Western world. Much as has happened with tantra[19] and chakras,[20] yoga's Westernization has fed back into and reshaped Eastern ideas and practices.

YOGA IN PSYCHOLOGY

Due to its long history, immense popularity, and claimed benefits, yoga has received so much intense medical and psychological scrutiny that an entire book could be devoted to it. Such books have indeed been written. These include Shapiro and Walsh's *Meditation: Classical and Contemporary Perspectives* (1984), Monro and colleagues' *Yoga Research Bibliography* (1989) with over 1,350 entries, Ospina's *Meditation*

---

*Yorke spent his energies preserving Crowley's literary legacy in a massive archive housed at the Warburg Institute.

Practices for Health: State of the Research (2007), Rao's *Foundations of Yoga Psychology* (2017), and Srinivasan's *Meditation* (2019).[21] We obviously can't cover in one chapter every claim and counterclaim about yoga. However, this large body of research allows us to focus on literature reviews and meta-analyses to highlight where there is consensus.

Rao writes in *Foundations of Yoga Psychology*,

> Meditation is the central focus of yoga practice. Yoga is equated, however, in the public mind with a physical culture involving bodily and breathing exercises, which are included in Patañjali yoga among the preliminary steps leading to meditation. . . . [T]here has been an explicit recognition that bodily processes influence mental states. Consequently, a study of the effects of these exercises on human psyche and soma is of interest on its own, independent of the goals of yoga. However, it should be recognized that these exercises are essentially aids to meditation and may not be confused with meditation per se.[22]

In this spirit, we will start by examining these preliminary practices or aids to meditation—relaxation, asana, pranayama, and mantra—before tackling the central subject of meditation.

PROGRESSIVE MUSCLE RELAXATION

A calm, relaxed state of body and mind is a good first step before beginning spiritual work, whether it be yoga or some other practice. Of the Golden Dawn system of magick, Torrens stresses, "Before starting any breathing exercises it is essential to attain complete muscular relaxation as far as possible. Be seated or lie down comfortably. Start relaxing the muscles of the feet and legs, then relax those of the arms starting with the fingers, next the abdomen, chest, neck and head. When a degree of calm has been achieved start breathing deeply."[23] Relaxing your body to ease into yoga shares many features with grounding rituals and similar exercises (discussed in the previous chapter), which are often preparatory for astral projection and the like. Just as those findings apply here, so do the findings below apply there.

Progressive muscle relaxation (PMR) facilitates "a deep state of relaxation via repeated tensing and relaxing of muscle groups combined with breathing exercises," marked by gradually decreasing activity in certain areas of the brain: the superior frontal gyrus, inferior frontal gyrus, and posterior cingulate cortex.[24] These areas of the brain govern self-awareness, language processing, and the "default mode network" (the parts of your brain that are active when you are at rest and not focusing on anything). Reduced activity in these areas is consistent with many forms of meditation, thus making the case that manipulation of semivoluntary body functions such as breath can affect consciousness. This effect is not just for experienced practitioners: As Kobayashi and Koitabashi note in their fMRI study, "Even novices may be able to induce such a focused mental state."[25] This makes PMR an ideal exercise to prepare or "ground" oneself for yoga.

Research among cancer patients demonstrates that PMR produces a significant increase in self-efficacy[26]... another theme discussed in the last chapter on daily practices. Among an unemployed sample in Greece, a PMR intervention reduced depression, anxiety, and stress, and increased coherence, health-related quality of life, and general well-being.[27] Other benefits of PMR include "decreased blood pressure, better balance of heart rate, decreased headaches, better management of cardiac rehabilitation, better quality of life after bypass surgery, improved quality of life of people with multiple sclerosis, and better emotional balance."[28]

A technique related to PMR is *autogenic training*. This is a form of self-suggestion or autohypnosis that promotes feelings of warmth and heaviness in the arms, legs, and abdomen, along with steady respiration and heartbeat. A meta-analysis of the research literature on this technique found consistent improvement in headaches and migraines, hypertension, heart disease, asthma, pain, anxiety, sleep disorders, and mild-to-moderate depression. The effect was most pronounced with psychological disorders, producing medium to large changes comparable to those found in standard psychological treatments. For psychosomatic disorders—that is to say, physical problems caused or exacerbated by psychological distress—the impact of autogenic training was more modest, in the small-to-medium range. Autogenic training was most effective when part of an ongoing practice, rather than as a brief or temporary intervention.[29] This underscores the point made in the previous chapter about the value of a regular daily practice.

ASANA (YOGA POSTURES)

Asana, or yoga postures, are one of the ashtanga, or eight limbs of yoga. Unlike modern yoga, which often focuses on doing a series of postures during a session, in the classic sense it involves settling into a posture to facilitate a meditative state. In a study of established yoga practitioners, sixty minutes of asana produced a statistically significant 27 percent increase in GABA levels, which counters the effects of depression and anxiety. Subjects in the control group showed no change after sixty minutes of reading.[30] This impact on depression and anxiety parallels the findings described above with PMR.

Another study, by the National Institutes of Health and McGill University, found that years of yoga experience and hours of weekly practice correlated with more gray matter. This study teased apart the unique contribution of postures, breathing, and meditation, and found that yoga posture was the most significant predictor of gray matter volume. This suggests that yoga offers a neuroprotective effect against typical decreases in gray matter volume that result from normal aging. (Change in gray matter is a common metric of brain age.) In other words, yoga with asana may prevent or delay age-related decline of gray matter.[31] These findings about brain volume will repeat in studies of other yoga practices.

For related ideas, see the discussion of the psychological effects of magical postures, poses, and gestures in the previous chapter.

PRANAYAMA AND OTHER BREATHING EXERCISES

Breathing is the only automatic process over which we can exert conscious control. This suggests that breath control may have a top-down effect on the body: By intentionally changing our respiration, we in turn alter other autonomic functions. Yogic breathing exercises run with this idea in many varieties. The most basic form is simply mindful breathing (focusing on one's respiration). From there, it encompasses a variety of practices. Among these are *chandra bhedana* or moon breath (inhaling through the left nostril and exhaling through the right); *nadi shodhana* or alternate nostril breathing (inhaling through one nostril, exhaling through the other, then switching); along with varieties such as *shitali* (cooling breath), *kapalabhati* (breath of fire), *ujjayi* (ocean breath), and so on. Modern fast-breathing techniques for inducing therapeutic or altered states outside of yoga have also emerged, such as holotropic breathwork,[32] holorenic breathwork, rebirthing breathwork, and conscious connected breathing.[33]

Given Western esotericism's embrace of yoga, breathing exercises naturally find their way into magick. Ráma Prasád's *Nature's Finer Forces* was a highly influential text, introducing both breathwork and elemental *tattwa* imagery into the Theosophical Society and the Golden Dawn.[34] Across the ocean, American spiritualist prophet Thomas Lake Harris's *The Breath of God with Man* promoted the life-extending properties of "divine breath" from a Christian perspective.[35] Golden Dawn member Edward Berridge, under the pen name Respiro, published digests of Harris's works and promoted them within the London Order. It is no surprise, then, that Golden Dawn Neophytes received instruction in a technique called the Fourfold Breath, which consisted of breathing in for four seconds, holding the breath four seconds, exhaling four seconds, and holding for another four seconds.[36] This simple exercise of observing the space between breaths is commonly used today by clinical psychologists as an exercise to relax and center clients in the present.

While this "square breathing" involves segments of equal length, other variations are possible. In *The Equinox*, J. F. C. Fuller offered the practice of inhaling for four seconds, holding the breath for sixteen, and exhaling for eight.[37] Aleister Crowley's "Liber RV," meanwhile, instructed, "Let the Zelator ... endeavour to master a cycle of 10. 20. 40 or even 16. 32. 64. But let this be done gradually and with due caution."[38]

One popular form of slow breathwork is *coherent breathing*. Its target of roughly 5.5 breath cycles per minute evenly divided between inhaling and exhaling supposedly synchronizes with cardiovascular rhythms to promote physical and mental well-being. However, a 2023 randomized control trial with four hundred subjects found that coherent breathing and a "placebo" group with breathwork at twelve breath cycles per minute (the low range of normal respiration) both produced similar decreases in stress, anxiety, depression, and improved well-being.[39] The message seems not to refute coherent breathing so much as affirm that breathwork of all types can be beneficial.

Indeed, despite its various styles, yogic breathing exercises—including practices that are not strictly pranayama—are generally effective and produce similar physiological results.[40] These benefits appear shortly after beginning one's practice, which is great news for novice practitioners and old hands alike. The exact physiological mechanism is unclear, but yogic breathing benefits patients struggling with hypertension, cardiac arrhythmia, bronchial asthma, tuberculosis, cancer symptoms, and smoking cessation. The low cost makes breathing exercises an appealing complementary therapy.

Despite some reviews suggesting that all breathing exercises have similar outcomes, others suggest that pranayama involving manipulation of the nostrils is better. Jeniffer Brandani and colleagues' survey of thirteen clinical trials tentatively suggests that slow breathing through the left nostril is more effective in reducing blood pressure.[41] Singh and colleagues, meanwhile, did a study concluding that single nostril breathing, depending on the nostril, produces greater oxygenation and blood volume in different parts of the brain: The right nostril is associated with the left prefrontal cortex, while the left nostril affects the right prefrontal cortex.[42] This may provide the neurological background for practices like chandra bhedana and nadi shodhana.

One interesting physiological finding is the *meditation paradox*: While pranayama purports to calm the mind and relax the body, it may actually produce physiological arousal. In examining heart rate dynamics in different types of breathing exercises, Peng and colleagues observed that breathing exercises accompanied high amplitude oscillations among those practicing the relaxation response, segmented breathing, Chinese chi and kundalini yoga. Breath of fire increased heart rates. This led to the conclusion that "these results support the concept of a 'meditation paradox,' since a variety of relaxation and meditative techniques may produce active rather than quiescent cardiac dynamics."[43]

This meditation paradox extends beyond cardiac dynamics and pranayama. Our autonomic nervous system has complementary modes that, normally, either arouse (sympathetic) or calm (parasympathetic) our involuntary functions. However, Andrew Newberg—the leading researcher in the emerging field of neurotheology—notes of certain meditation practices, "Although typically only one side of the autonomic nervous system turns on at a time, there is growing evidence that they sometimes can turn on together, particularly when one side is turned on to a very high degree."[44] Corroborating evidence comes from researchers at the University of Wollongong, who reported that electroencephalography and skin conductance level measured during mindfulness meditations reveals a state of relaxed alertness.[45] Similar arousal and release phenomena emerge from self-reported spiritual experiences ranging from Buddhist jhāna yoga to Christian speaking in tongues.[46] Finally, evidence from a study of tantric meditation suggests that this paradoxical autonomic activation occurs chiefly in experienced meditators, while inexperienced meditators show autonomic relaxation.[47] This observation mirrors the finding that mindfulness-based emotion regulation is a top-down phenomenon in short-term practitioners but bottom-up in long-term practitioners.[48]

Yogic breathing also produces subjective psychological responses. In a study of eighty-six college undergraduates, a twelve-week course in breath-focused yoga was more effective than meditation alone for improved energy, focus, awareness, and stress reduction.[49] Similarly, after six weeks of daily practice of a form of pranayama called *shambhavi mahamudra kriya*, 142 participants reported less stress and better general well-being than they reported beforehand.[50]

In an evaluation of the primary school program Breathing Break Intervention, von Salisch and Voltmer found that short daily breath-based mindfulness practices among third- and fourth-grade girls resulted in increased prosocial behaviors and perception of a supportive classroom environment.[51] These findings confirm other research showing that school-based mindfulness increases prosocial behavior.[52] The COVID-19 pandemic prompted a switch to distance learning shortly after the planned follow-up test, and teachers led Breathing Break sessions less frequently: instead of daily, sessions occurred several times a week (12 percent), once a week (12 percent), once a month (50 percent), or not at all (25 percent). At the five-month follow-up, most prosocial gains had disappeared.[53] This may be due to the disruption of the normal classroom setting, or it may indicate that mindfulness exercises are most effective when done more frequently.[54] The Breathing Break study and the supporting literature that Salisch and Voltmer cite are specific to school children, but the lesson applies to the daily practices of magicians: These exercises are beneficial, but for the benefits to continue, the magician needs to keep up their regular practice.

By enhancing resilience and reducing stress (a major cause of illness), meditative pranayama may increase longevity. As Brown and Gerbarg wrote in the *Annals of the New York Academy of Science*, "Our hypothesis is that yoga breathing provides a neurophysiological 'work-out' that leads to greater flexibility and plasticity in the nervous system."[55] In this sense, Thomas Lake Harris may have been at least slightly right about the life-extending powers of "divine breath" (despite yoga practitioners not reaching the amazing ages of the biblical patriarchs).

MANTRA, CHANTING, AND PRAYER

A mantra is a special word or phrase that is repeated either aloud or silently as part of meditation to achieve "union of the practitioner's consciousness with . . . the pure consciousness of the divinity manifested in the mantra."[56] According to some traditions, a mantra is specially selected by the guru for their disciple and kept secret from all others lest it lose its efficacy. However, the research presented here involves mantras chosen by a researcher for all participants. Thus, the mantra is not tailored to the needs of the individual, nor is it secret. Nevertheless, studies report significant effects of mantra. Literature reviews suggest that the "magic" lies in the act itself and is not limited to the special meaning of a particular word or sound: Intoning a mock mantra such as "one" is equally effective as intoning "om."[57] As Delmonte writes, "There is thus little evidence to support the notion that uniquely tailored mantras suited to individual needs are critical to the outcome of meditation."[58] That said, in chapter 7 we will explore the psychological value of treating words, objects, and ideas as secret, consecrated, or special.

Setting aside secrecy, sacred syllables, and bespoke mantras, the line between mantras and other repetitive vocal or subvocal meditative exercises blurs to include chanting and repetitive prayer, such as saying the rosary. As Perry, Polito, and Thompson note, "Rhythmic, repetitive singing or speaking of sounds and phrases either vocally or mentally" is a global practice, including yogis, Sufis, monks of various traditions, and Indigenous Australians. Their survey of 464 regular chanters across thirty-three countries showed that over half (60 percent) had experienced a mystical state while chanting. Adherents of some spiritual traditions, however, were more likely to report mystical states than others, as summarized in figure 4.4. Those who experienced mystical states also scored higher in focus, altruism, and religiosity; ecstasy, peace, and tranquility; and feelings of ineffability ("a sense that profound experiences cannot be described in words"). These findings held whether the practice was vocal or silent; solitary or in a group setting.[59] In another study, those who prayed the rosary reported similar enhanced feelings about "orientation in life, peace, security and a contemplative connection with the Divine."[60]

Gao and colleagues examined whether the effects of religious chanting differed from those of meditation. They studied twenty-two Mahayana Buddhist practitioners who followed the traditional daily practice of chanting the name of Amitābha Buddha for at least one year. EEG, fMRI, ECG, and respiratory data were collected in three conditions: (1) religious chanting (silently chanting "Amitābha Buddha"), (2) control (resting with eyes closed without chanting), and (3) nonreligious chanting (silently chanting "Santa Claus").*

---

*In Chinese (the language of the research subjects), the names "Amitābha Buddha" and "Santa Claus" are similar linguistically in that they consist of four characters of comparable complexity, and both figures have similarly positive connotations.

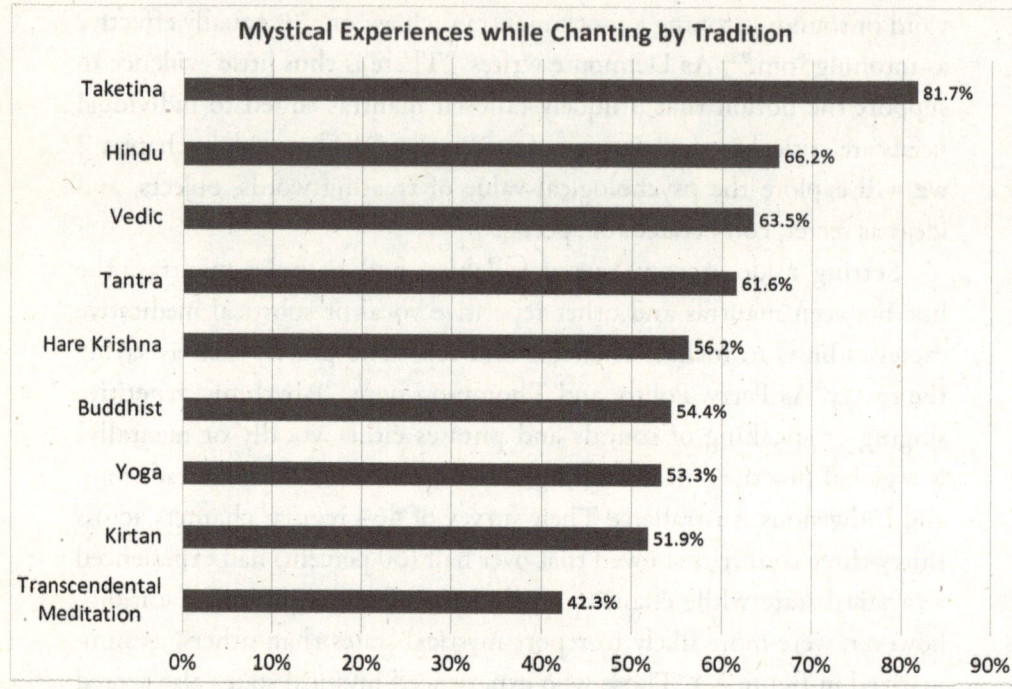

Fig. 4.4. Reports of mystical experiences while chanting differed by spiritual tradition.
Image by the author based on data from Perry et al., "Rhythmic Chanting and Mystical States across Traditions"

Compared to the other two conditions, religious chanting produced strong delta brain waves similar to those found in meditation, and which are thought to represent internally focused concentration. According to this study, "Mental states dominated by delta-band activity are considered as evolutionarily ancient states, in which compensatory and restorative mechanisms replenish biological resources in the brain and peripheral organs, resulting in beneficial effects encompassing biological and cognitive domains."[61] Religious chanting was also associated with increased stability in cardiac function. These and other differences led Gao and colleagues to conclude that "the neurophysiological correlates of religious chanting are somewhat different from those of mindfulness meditation and those of other types of religious prayer."[62]

Khalsa and colleagues, meanwhile, scanned the brains of eleven practitioners of kirtan kriya, which involves chanting in succession one the primal sounds—Sa, Ta, Na, and Ma—while touching the thumb to each finger of the hand. Compared to when they were not meditating, scans taken while chanting showed increased activity in some parts of the brain (right temporal lobe and posterior cingulate gyrus) and decreased activity in others (left parietotemporal and occipital gyri). That chanting increases or decreases activity in different parts of the brain presents the possibility that future research could establish different chanting or meditative techniques targeting specific areas of the brain: "Different modes of meditation might ultimately be prescribed when clinical evidence suggests that certain functional brain regions are hypoactive or hyperactive."[63]

MEDITATION

Like the other forms of yoga practice discussed so far, meditation takes on myriad forms both within and across cultures. This poses a challenge for an evidence-based assessment: Should all studies of meditation be pooled together, lumped into a few broad categories, or assessed separately based on the style of meditation? Cramer and colleagues' review of 306 randomized control trials falls into the first category, concluding that "different yoga styles do not differ in their odds of reaching positive conclusions . . . [T]he choice of an individual yoga style can be based on personal preferences and availability."[64] Fox and colleagues' review of seventy-eight neuropsychology studies falls into the latter category: "While several regions [of the brain] may be equally involved in many forms of contemplative practice, differences in neural activity greatly outnumber similarities. *Commonality across meditation categories is the exception rather than the rule.*"[65] A 2024 study of monks and *geshes* at a Tibetan monastery in India likewise demonstrated differences in neural activity based on which of two types of Tibetan Buddhist meditation they were doing: concentrative versus analytical. Compared to analytical meditation, concentrative meditation produced substantial increases in EEG power in the theta, alpha, and beta ranges, suggesting "a non-ordinary state of consciousness different from wakefulness and sleep."*[66]

If one strikes a middle ground and combines the many types of meditation into categories, this approach poses questions: Should these categories be based on similarity in geography, practices, or resulting brain wave patterns? As Travis concluded, "Grouping meditations by their described procedures yields defining neural imaging patterns within each category, and clear differences between categories."[67] As shown in the illustration from Travis's study (fig. 4.5), different types of meditation impact different areas of the brain. While these areas are known to govern or represent different mental and autonomic functions, what is less clear is how this activity connects to the meditative experience, or how this activation affects the brain.

One finding emerging from the literature is that long-term meditation alters the brain. Not just momentarily, while meditating, but changing its physical structure over time. Neuroimaging shows that long-term meditation practitioners of various types have greater structural connectivity between regions of the brain than do nonmeditators,[68] along with changes in gray and white matter.[69] Raja yoga practitioners have higher gray matter volume in reward-processing centers of the brain, with greater volume correlating with self-reported happiness.[70] Practitioners of sahaja yoga have higher gray matter volume across the whole brain, particularly in areas associated with attention, self-control, compassion, and interoceptive perception.[71] Overall, Fox and colleagues' review and meta-analysis of twenty-one neuroimaging studies with approximately three hundred meditation practitioners "found eight brain regions consistently altered in meditators, including areas key to meta-awareness . . . , exteroceptive and interoceptive body awareness . . . , memory consolidation and reconsolidation . . . , self and emotion regulation . . . , and intra- and interhemispheric communication."[72] Consistent with the other studies

---

*Similar differences in EEG power for mindfulness meditators versus controls were reported by Brittany McQueen, Oscar W. Murphy, Paul B. Fitzgerald, and Neil W. Bailey, "The Mindful Brain at Rest: Neural Oscillations and Aperiodic Activity in Experienced Meditators," *Mindfulness*, 15 (2024): 2484–2502.

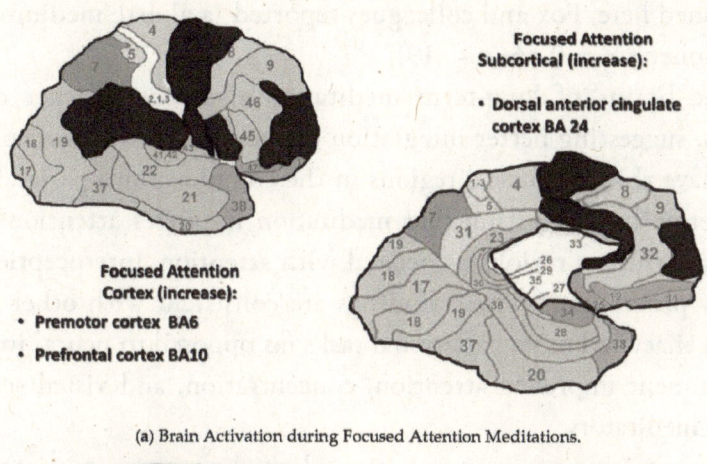

(a) Brain Activation during Focused Attention Meditations.

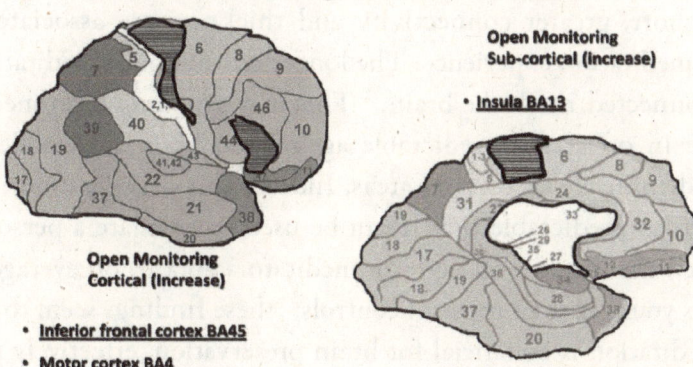

(b) Brain Activation during Open Monitoring Meditations.

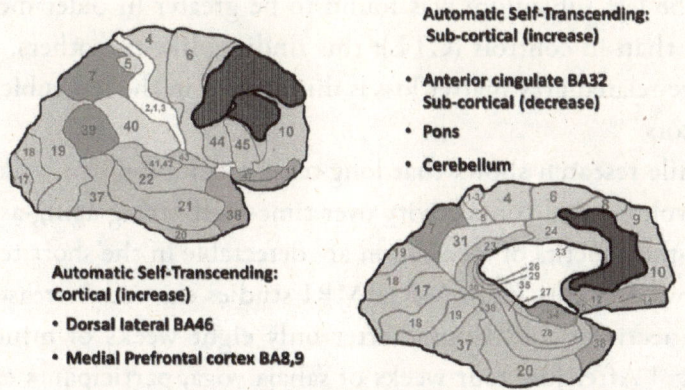

(c) Brain Activation during Automatic Self-Transcending Meditations.

Fig. 4.5. Different types of meditation activate different areas of the brain (Travis, 2020).

mentioned here, Fox and colleagues reported "a global 'medium' effect size (Cohen's $d = 0.46$; $r = .19$)."[73]

The brains of long-term meditators also have thicker callosal regions, suggesting better integration of the brain's two hemispheres.[74] They have thicker cortical regions in the cingulo-fronto-parietal attention networks, suggesting that meditation improves attention.[75] And they have thicker regions associated with attention, interoception, and sensory processing.[76] These findings are consistent with other studies of yoga that used more traditional tasks (as opposed to neural imaging) to document improved attention, concentration, and visual scanning among meditators.[77]

In short, greater connectivity and thickness are associated with greater meditation experience: The longer one has been meditating, the more connected/thick the brain.[78] This may give long-term meditators an edge in offsetting predictable age-related brain matter degeneration and thinning of cortical areas. Indeed, this degeneration in brain matter is so predictable that it can be used to estimate a person's age. However, the brains of long-term meditators appear, on average, to be 7.5 years younger than those of controls; "these findings seem to suggest that meditation is beneficial for brain preservation, effectively protecting against age-related atrophy with a consistently slower rate of brain aging throughout life."[79] In another study, the amount of gray matter in the left subiculum was found to be greater in older meditators (MED) than in controls (CTL); this finding, like the others, suggests that "age-related gray matter loss is diminished in the left subiculum in meditators."[80]

While research shows that long-term meditation can bulk up our brain's volume and connectivity over time—offsetting aging-associated losses—the benefits of meditation are detectable in the short term, too. A review of twenty-eight MRI/fMRI studies showed increased activity, connectivity, and volume after only eight weeks of mindfulness training.[81] After just four weeks of sahaja yoga, participants exhibited increased gray matter density and brain activity coherence in regions associated with attention, self-control, and self-awareness.[82] Short-term meditation training also improved brain energy metabolism,[83] network plasticity,[84] and reaction times;[85] and reduced anxiety, depression and even irritable bowel syndrome.[86] On an interpersonal level, nine months of loving-kindness meditation training in older adults resulted in significant increases in feelings of awareness, connection, and insight.[87]

A ten-week lockdown during the highly stressful initial stages of COVID-19 in Spain provided the perfect opportunity for a naturalistic experiment. Sixty-one subjects participated in several guided meditation sessions over Zoom. Compared to sixty-five controls, the meditation group reported increased self-compassion and reductions in anxiety, stress, and depression. However, these improvements dissipated by the two-month follow-up, suggesting that the practice of meditation needs to be ongoing to perpetuate its benefits.[88] Granted, the existential threat of the pandemic may have erased the benefits of meditation by the two-month follow-up, something that might not have occurred in typical circumstances. Indeed, a recent meta-analysis on mindfulness and mental health indicated that the benefits can be observed one to six months postintervention,[89] while Galante and colleagues found that the University of Cambridge's Mindfulness Skills for Students program produced spiritual feelings that persisted up to a year later.[90] An ongoing practice, however, maximizes these benefits. A study at the University of Bristol found that students who kept up the "happiness hacks" taught in their Science of Happiness course had significantly better well-being, and lower loneliness and anxiety, one to two years later compared to students who did not continue the practices.[91]

CONNECTIONS

Interesting parallels appear in the system of Contrology advocated by Joseph Pilates. In the 1920s, he introduced his system of mind-body exercise that—like yoga—emphasized breathing, concentration, and mental control over the body. Pilates' original exercises called for nothing more than a mat, but in the decades since, studios have introduced apparatuses such as the Reformer, Cadillac, Magic Circle, and specially designed chairs, barrels, straps, rollers, balls, and so forth. The purpose of these tools is to accelerate the timeline with the method's mind-body exercises.[92]

Similarly, a magician could use yoga alone to achieve certain goals, particularly those seeking knowledge and development of the self. However, adding various apparatuses to one's practice can facilitate the journey. The subject of magical implements will be explored in chapter 6.

CAUTIONS

Overall, research suggests the benefits of both short- and long-term practice of yoga range from reduced stress to increased brain matter and connectivity, which ultimately fosters greater health, wellness, and even resilience against the effects of aging. In the magical quest to unite with the divine, experience oneness with the universe, become more spiritually present or aware, obliterate one's ego in the ordeal of the Abyss, or whatever you may call it, there is a downside: The quest

Fig. 4.6. The danger of the quest for self-enlightenment: egotism. Comic by Mark Stivers, *Saturday Cartoons*, March 30, 2008.
© 2008 Mark Stivers

for self-enhancement can have the opposite effect, leading to feelings of superiority, spiritual narcissism, egotism, and supernatural overconfidence.[93] This echoes what Crowley described as the Black Brothers: those failed Aspirants who cling to their egos and elevate themselves to the godhead. Strive to become the best version of yourself, but remember that it doesn't make you better than others.

5
Greater (and Lesser) Magical Retirements

WHEN A MAGICIAN NEEDS TO DO A RITUAL for a substantial goal beyond the scope of their daily practices, they will commonly prepare for such a working by undertaking a magical retirement. This traditionally involves a retreat from one's daily routine, devoting oneself to preparations that could include contemplation, prayer, fasting, or abstinence. Think of it how an athlete trains for a marathon or the Olympics, except the magician is working out spiritually (and psychologically).

A magical retirement can be long or short, depending on the preparation required, either by the ritual itself or the practitioner's desires. A protracted retreat is sometimes called a Great Magical Retirement (GMR), which implies the existence of a shorter Lesser Magical Retirement. A classic example of a GMR is the Abramelin Working. The name is taken from an eponymous seventeenth-century grimoire that uses a system of alphabetic magick squares with specified purposes such as "to make people into animals (and animals into people)" or "to obtain lost books, hidden manuscripts, and such." In this tradition, the magician undertakes an intense devotional period of contemplation and prayer ranging from six to eighteen months (depending on the version of the manuscript)[1] to purify themself sufficiently to be worthy of wielding such powerful magick. The ultimate goal of this purification is attaining the so-called Knowledge and Conversation of the Holy Guardian Angel. What exactly the Holy Guardian Angel (or HGA) is has been a matter of some debate. As occult maestro Lon Milo DuQuette puts it, one approach is "to consider the magician as being a spiritually incomplete *human* unit until united with the Holy Guardian Angel—and to consider the Holy Guardian Angel as being a spiritually incomplete *angelic* unit until it has become one with the magician."[2]

The English translation of an Abramelin manuscript at the Bibliothèque de l'Arsenal appeared in 1898 courtesy of Samuel Liddell MacGregor Mathers, then head of the Golden Dawn. The book became popular among its members and later offshoots. The notion of Knowledge and Conversation of the Holy Guardian Angel became the central attainment of the A∴A∴ system, with "Liber Samekh" given as an alternative route to this goal.[3] We'll say more about the HGA and similar entities in chapter 8.

In practice, most people can't easily step away from their work or family responsibilities for an extended period of magical devotion, and

Fig. 5.1. Title page of S. L. MacGregor Mathers's *The Book of the Sacred Magic* (1898), art by Mina Mathers.

they instead find a way to balance retirement time with these other demands. Aleister Crowley's "John St. John" diary, published in the first number of *The Equinox*, demonstrated that a magician could indeed thread this needle, living in the world while also going on a spiritual retreat... lasting, in this case, a dozen days.[4]

ISOLATION AND RETIREMENT

When the last plane of the upcoming winter season leaves the Amundsen-Scott South Pole research station, the remaining skeleton crew of fifty scientists and staff are isolated for nine months in the coldest and most inhospitable place on Earth. Temperatures can dip below -100 degrees Fahrenheit. For six months, the sun will never rise. And the air is so dry, it's technically the planet's largest desert. Frequent gale-force winds buffet the station.

Located on a two-mile thick ice sheet, the station sits at an elevation of 9,300 feet... nearly twice that of the famous Mile High City of Denver, Colorado. This adds the ongoing challenges of dehydration, exhaustion, and altitude sickness. The eight-hundred-mile flight from the Antarctic coast, over the Transatlantic Mountains, to the station is only possible during a brief three-month window during the summer, weather permitting. For the rest of the year, darkness, wind, and cold render the journey impossible: Planes' AN-8 fuel turns to gel at -76 degrees Fahrenheit, and extreme cold makes the planes too stiff and fragile to fly safely. For nine months, the fifty over-winter inhabitants are cut off from the rest of the world, except for a daily two-to-four-hour window when communication satellites pass overhead, allowing brief internet access.

Work days are long, given the rare opportunity to do research here. Off-hour amenities include a galley, library, greenhouse, lounge, game room, music room, craft room, gym, and sauna. Rituals and traditions have emerged for observing birthdays, holidays, midwinter, and other events. When the last plane for nine months leaves, one ritual is a group screening of John Carpenter's classic Antarctic horror film, *The Thing* (1982); and, at midwinter, they watch Stanley Kubrick's adaptation of

Stephen King's snowed-in story of ghosts and madness, *The Shining* (1980). Another ritual involves initiation into the "300 Club": when temperatures outside dip to -100 degrees Fahrenheit, participants warm up in the 200-degree sauna and then walk outside naked (except for boots) to circle the South Pole marker, thus experiencing a 300-degree temperature change within minutes. Aspiring initiates must carefully walk at a brisk enough pace to avoid frostbite, but slow enough so as not to inhale too much and freeze their airway. According to 300 Club Initiate and senior scientist Denis Barkats, "The sensation is amazing. Your brain tells you, 'You should be freezing,' because you know it's negative-100 degrees outside, and yet your body has accumulated enough heat that you actually feel quite comfortable for three to five minutes. I did it during my winter and it was so incredible, I repeated it immediately afterwards."[5]

A pilot study of nine scientists wintering over at the Amundsen-Scott South Pole Station 1976–1977 found that the winter-overs, at the end of the season, displayed a higher degree of hypnotizability or suggestibility. Without giving away the subject matter of the study, the experimenter measured hypnotizability at the beginning and end of winter using a paper-and-pencil scale, electroencephalogram (EEG), and a clever intervention: Subjects were presented with six items to smell, and asked to describe them; however, only four had an odor. According to Barabasz, "Increases in hypnotizability bring increases in individuals' capacity and probability of experiencing . . . positive or negative hallucinations, changes in perception of odors, increases or decreases in vigilance performance, dissociate, or fugue, states, and increases in deep imaginative involvement and absorption."[6]

A separate study of seven summer-overs—in which scientists experienced similar conditions but with no nighttime—followed subjects three months after they returned to normal life. At this extended time point, no signs of suggestibility remained, suggesting that the psychological effects of isolation were more immediate and of a short duration.

Life at an Antarctic research station is indeed harsh, but such extreme conditions are not necessary to produce psychological changes. According to psychologist Andrew Neher, the absence of information or stimulation from one's environment—including among "religious ascetics in isolated quarters"—can produce altered states of consciousness including "hallucinations and delusions of various kinds."[7] For example, fifty-seven psychology students participated in a floatation tank study. The flotation-restricted environmental stimulation technique (or flotation-REST) typically lasts forty-five minutes, and it is known to reduce stress, improve sleep quality, lower blood pressure, and sometimes even produce altered states of consciousness such as feeling weightless, altered experience of time, and mental imagery. After the session, participants completed several self-report questionnaires measuring their sensitivity to people and events in their surroundings; their experience of altered states of consciousness during flotation-REST; and prior mystical experiences. Students who were highly sensitive to their surroundings were more likely to experience an altered state of consciousness during the study ($p < .05$), and to have had prior mystical experiences ($p < .01,$).[8]

The solitude of a magical retirement offers more than altered states of consciousness and mystical experiences (as interesting as those things are!). A review of the literature reveals several other benefits relevant to magicians. Christopher Long and James Averill with the University of Massachusetts Department of Psychology define solitude (which is distinct from loneliness) as a state of relative social disengagement from the immediate demands of other people.[9] Its benefits include enhanced feelings of freedom, creativity, and spirituality. Solitary backpackers, for instance, cite being able to act and think freely as one of the most important benefits.[10] These freedoms of thought and action can promote creativity, including the opportunity for self-transformation . . . and that's ultimately the goal of magick. According to Long and Averill, "By separating us from our usual social and physical environments, solitude can remove those people and objects that define and confirm our identities . . . [B]y extracting us from our customary social and physical contexts . . . solitude facilitates self-examination, reconceptualization of the self, and coming to terms with change."[11] Transformative experiences are often associated with experiences of the divine or numinous; indeed, the founders of major religions such as Moses, Jesus, Mohammed, and the Buddha experienced divine encounters during periods of solitude, as have countless prophets, mystics, and ascetics around the world and through the ages. Thus, a magical retirement has the potential to be a profound time of refocusing, reevaluation, and spiritual transformation.

NOT SO FAST! THE PSYCHOLOGY OF FASTING AND ASCETICISM

Temporarily giving up something pleasurable is a tradition in many religions. Christians may give up sweets for the forty days of Lent or abstain from meat on Fridays. Muslims may give up food, water, and other sensual activities between sunup and sundown during the month of Ramadan. Jews may fast for twenty-five hours on Yom Kippur. Other devotees may adopt more extreme forms of renunciation, such as early Buddhist monks who possessed only three robes and a begging bowl.

In a magical retirement, ascetic choices are expressions of intention, dedication, willpower, and discipline. They also represent an effort to purify or detox both the body and mind. Through these practices, changes in consciousness become possible. As Bradford wrote in his psychological review of asceticism, "Corporeal asceticism addresses the body, and through the body, it changes the mind."[12] Nineteenth-century French occultist Éliphas Lévi echoed this sentiment when he advised, "The purification of the Magus consists in the renunciation of coarse enjoyments, in a temperate and vegetarian diet, in abstinence from intoxicating drink, and in regulating the hours of sleep."[13] Crowley, on the other hand, was not a fan of sexual abstinence, finding the practice more distracting than the act of indulgence. Recalling his college years, he wrote in his *Confessions*, "I certainly found even forty-eight hours of abstinence sufficient to dull the fine edge of my mind."[14] For Crowley, it came down to a state of chastity . . . which he equated not with abstinence, but with devoting one's actions to the Great Work. He spelled this out in *Little Essays Toward Truth*: "Chastity may thus be defined as the strict observance of the Magical Oath; that is, in the Light of the Law of Thelema, absolute and perfect devotion to the Holy Guardian Angel and exclusive pursuit of the Way of the True Will."[15]

One benefit of temporary renunciation in a magical retirement is its effect on *hedonic adaptation*. According to the *Wiley Encyclopedia of Personality and Individual Differences*, hedonic adaptation is "the process by which an individual's emotional response to both positive and negative experiences diminishes over time."[16] In other words, the more often we experience something, good or bad, the less our reaction to it. Returning to baseline levels and slowing hedonic adaptation are both useful strategies for enhancing pleasure and happiness. In one of the few empirical tests of this theory, fifty-five undergraduates were given a piece of chocolate in exchange for completing some questionnaires, then asked to return in a week. These students were assigned to one of three groups: The restricted access group was told not to eat any chocolate during the ensuing week. The abundant access group was given two pounds of chocolate and told to eat as much as they comfortably could. Finally, the control condition received no instructions at all. Returning to the lab a week later, they were given another piece of chocolate. Those who gave up chocolate for a week savored the chocolate more and had more positive emotions than either of the other two groups.[17]

Of the various forms of renunciation available to magicians, one of the most common is fasting. This includes *intermittent fasting*, a recurring cycle during which few, if any, calories are consumed for an extended time (typically twelve to forty-eight hours). *Periodic fasting* is similar, except it extends to longer periods, up to twenty-one days. Both practices can optimize physiological functioning, which results in enhanced performance and slowed processes of aging and disease.[18] Specific health benefits in the aging and disease domain include ameliorating the effects of diabetes, cancer, heart disease, stroke, and Alzheimer's and Parkinson's.[19] Evidence also suggests that intermittent metabolic switching—alternating cycles of fasting/exercise and eating/rest/sleep—may also promote neuroplasticity.[20]

Finally, a 2025 study from Tübingen, Germany, found that fasting affects what types of information our brains consolidate into memory. Food deprivation resulted in prioritizing facts at the cost of context. In other words, fasting causes us to emphasize the "what" over the "where" and "when."[21] Physiologically, this indicates a shift away from short-term memory processing in the hippocampus, favoring language, cognition and consciousness functions in the cortex. Fasting thus creates a change in our consciousness . . . a change which may influence how we recall our magical experiences. This underscores the importance of updating your magical record promptly, while the details are fresh in your memory.

LESSER MAGICAL RECAP

Disconnecting from the routines and commitments of mundane existence is a popular way to prepare for a substantial magical working. Devotional practices like bhakti yoga can bring the mindfulness and tranquility discussed in the previous chapter. Fasting or variations on intermittent fasting can have beneficial physical and psychological effects. Abstaining from things we enjoy can increase our enjoyment of those things when the retirement concludes. But most importantly, the increased freedom, creativity, and spirituality of a magical retirement—not to mention a potentially altered state of consciousness—creates conditions for personal change and transformative experience. The ritual toward which the retirement is building provides just that impetus.

6

Hold That Thought

Ritual Implements

PICTURE AN ICONIC MAGICIAN OR WIZARD, and what do you see? Perhaps they're fictional, such as the Harry Potter clan with their wands. Mickey Mouse as the sorcerer's apprentice with his hat and robe. Gandalf with his staff. Doctor Strange with his cloak of levitation and the Eye of Agamotto. Or perhaps you imagine a real-life practitioner: A Wiccan priestess clad with the triple moon, or a priest wearing the crown of the Horned One. The all-white clothing of a Santería initiate. Someone with a pendant, ring, or other jewelry representing their tradition. Odds are, your mental picture includes the accessories of an occultist. In this chapter, we'll examine the role played by these physical trappings, from implements to robes (or the lack thereof).

Most magicians use some kind of altar or table, upon which rest their various implements. The specifics vary from tradition to tradition: A ceremonial magician may orient their altar to face east, the direction of the rising sun. A Wiccan might place their altar in the north, which is associated with Mother Earth. There may be a cup, disk, wand, and dagger. The dagger may be called an athame. The cup may be referred to as a chalice. In any case, these implements are typically associated with the four cardinal points and the four elements corresponding to those points. The implements therefore represent qualities of the magician that correspond to those elements. For instance, the yellow dagger represents the element of Air, the sharpness of one's intellect. The red wand represents Fire, the force of will. And so on. As such, these implements are external projections of the magician's internal qualities. When a magician holds their wand, they are literally holding their intention.

For this reason, implements are customarily designed and crafted by the magician themself, who also consecrates them (which is to say they dedicate their tools to purely magical use).

In addition to the standard elemental "weapons," other items on the altar or elsewhere in the magician's space may include incense, oils, or other perfumes; candles and altar cloths of various colors; musical instruments; some kind of consumable sacrament, such as cakes and wine; or other items specific to one's tradition.

Fig. 6.1. Archetypal image of a magician, from the tarot deck designed by writer Arthur Edward Waite and artist Pamela Colman Smith (1909).

These tools of the trade are central to the magician's practice, and are special indeed. Psychology provides several perspectives to help account for what makes ritual implements so magical.

WE ARE WHAT WE HAVE

Unlikely as it seems, consumer psychology has a lot to tell us about a magician's paraphernalia. In a 1988 issue of the *Journal of Consumer Research*, Russell Belk's concept of the *extended self* proposed that our possessions are extensions of our identity, "comprising not only that which is seen as 'me' (the self), but also that which is seen as 'mine.'"[1] Our possessions not only reflect ourselves, but they also preserve our past, indicate where we are at present, and point to where we are going. "Self-extension," Belk writes, "occurs through control and mastery of an object, through creation of an object, through knowledge of an object, and through contamination via proximity and habituation to an object."[2] Nowhere is that truer than with a magician's tools, which are literal representations of parts of the self. As Crowley writes in *Book Four*, "As the Magick Wand is the Will, the Wisdom, the Word of the Magician, so is the Magick Cup his Understanding.... The Magick Sword is the analytical faculty.... [T]he Pantacle [Pentacle] shall be his body, the Temple of the Holy Ghost."[3]

Our possessions can also undergo a process of sacralization when associated with a fandom or celebrity. Debraix and Decrop found that many fans of football (or soccer, as it's known in the States) have team memorabilia that assumes especially symbolic and even sacred significance. This sacralization is particularly the case with fan-made mementos of one's favorite team. "It seems that a home-made scarf is embedded with more meaning than a replica bought in a fan shop."[4] Even noted skeptic Michael Shermer recalls visiting Mellow Johnny's—the bicycle shop of seven-time tour de France winner and Livestrong cancer foundation namesake Lance Armstrong—and how wearing his newly acquired Livestrong T-shirt and black-and-yellow socks under his suit made him feel more confident at that evening's debate.[5] If this happens with a favorite athlete, imagine the impact of one's handcrafted magical tools.

WE ARE WHAT WE MAKE

When sales of time-saving instant cake mixes began to flatten in the 1950s, Ernest Dichter—psychologist, marketing consultant, and the person who coined the term *focus group*—interviewed homemakers and determined that mixes were perceived as being too easy: They minimized the labor of baking. They didn't count as real cooking. Using them felt guilty. In response, advertisers began to emphasize decorating the finished product to give it that personal touch. This shifted the emphasis from baking to what the cook did after the cake emerged from the oven. Thus, cake mixes took off again as a pantry staple.[6] The resistance and guilt expressed by consumers revealed something about human nature: "Infusing the task with labor appeared to be a crucial ingredient."[7] This observation was confirmed in a study in which sixty participants tasted a milkshake that either they or somebody else made. Not only did participants prefer the self-prepared milkshake, but they also drank more of it.[8]

In 2012, Norton and colleagues coined the term *IKEA effect* to describe how consumers value things that they make or assemble themselves more than identical objects put together by others. In short, the more effort that goes into making something, the more they value it. The IKEA effect has been documented with origami, Legos, a science kit, and an actual IKEA cube.[9] Prevailing explanations posit that the effort of completing an assembly project enhances one's feelings of competence and ownership.[10] As March, Kanngiesser, and Hood write, "Perhaps when a product is created, a special link between this item and the creators' self-identity is forged. This link results in the object becoming an extension of the creators' self-identity, which is valued over-and-above an identical item created by someone else."[11]

Consider, for example, the tradition that the wood for a wand be cut from a living tree with a single stroke of a blade, harvested on the day of Mercury at sunrise, and taken from a species with special significance to that path.[12] The tools of the trade require commitment! A magician would heartily agree that the effort of making one's implements creates a special "link" with that object.

WE ARE WHAT WE TREAT

One crucial aspect of preparing ritual implements is that, upon completion, they are consecrated—which is to say a ceremony purifies the object and dedicates it exclusively to magical work. After that, these tools may be wrapped in silk, stored in an altar, or never touched by anyone other than the magician who consecrated it. It turns out that there is a psychological basis for these acts of sanctification and treating ceremonial objects as special.

Vohs and colleagues did three experiments to see how rituals around food affected consumption. In one study, participants received a candy bar with the following "ritual": "Without unwrapping the chocolate bar, break it in half. Unwrap half of the bar and eat it. Then, unwrap the other half and eat it." In the second study, subjects ate carrots while following instructions to knock on the desk, breathe deeply, and briefly close their eyes at specified moments. In the final study, subjects prepared lemonade from a mix by first preparing half the mix in a glass, waiting thirty seconds, adding the rest of the power, topping off with water, stirring, then waiting another thirty seconds before drinking it. Compared to people who did not do these simple rituals, participants enjoyed the experience more, found the food more flavorful, savored eating for a longer time, and valued what they ate more. In short, performing the food ritual caused subjects to enjoy consumption more than they would otherwise.[13]

Similarly, in a study of ritual and consumption by Kapitány and Nielsen, participants watched videos of wine being poured into glasses. The ritual condition involved waving a napkin, gesturing, and humming along with the explanation that "the actions in this video can be seen in [ceremony name] of [location]," with a fictitious name and location inserted. The control group watched wine poured with random, nonritualized behavior. Despite the videos using the same wine, which was not altered by either intervention, participants perceived the wine in the ritual condition as somehow "special," and preferred that wine to the identical control wine.[14] Interestingly, the researchers also manipulated "valence" by associating the ritual in some conditions with Satanism, Voodoo, or Wicca, expecting that the wine would be *less* desirable due to negative misrepresentations in the media and pop culture, but subjects preferred the ritual wine regardless of the ritual's supposed origins. This study led the authors to conclude that "we eat the cake, not in spite of its strange preparation, but because of it."[15]

Treating something as special *makes* it special. The examples above demonstrate this with simple rituals. Imagine the power of a more elaborate ritual!

Then again, "specialness" can also be imparted to objects without a ritual. In a study at the California Institute of Technology, participants rated two wines, one a ninety-dollar-a-bottle variety and the other costing ten dollars a bottle. The more expensive wine scored higher not only on subjective reports, but its consumption also accompanied increased activity in the medial orbitofrontal cortex (a part of the brain connected to pleasant experiences). Unbeknownst to the study participants, both wines were exactly the same, but believing they were drinking a more "special" bottle of wine produced both subjective and neurological differences in perception.[16] Even this finding, however, has a parallel in magical practice: When it comes to acquiring the necessaries of a ritual, one is advised not to cut corners or cheap out, but to "buy a perfectly black hen, without haggling."[17]

It is not necessary to make everything from scratch or to spend beyond one's means. An item may be special if commissioned from an admired artisan, or found while traveling or in another special location. The idea is that the more special the implements are to the magician, the more psychological impact they will have when used in ritual.

CORRESPONDENCES AND COLORS

One of the most striking features of the Golden Dawn's ritual implements is the high level of detail and specificity in their designs. Every feature, every inscription, every sigil, and every color, has a very specific meaning with which the initiate would be familiar.[18] Other traditions vary from being highly particular to totally freeform (as may be the case with, say, Chaos Magicians). The Golden Dawn offshoot

A∴A∴ specifies numerous details—the implements must be fashioned by the magician, with a diameter, height, or length of eight inches—but particulars of the design are left to the "understanding and ingenium" of the initiate.[19] Regardless of the tradition, the Golden Dawn represents an archetype that looms large in the ritual magick world. So where do all those highly specific details come from?

It comes down to correspondences. This idea runs through much of magick, dictating details of ritual such as color, incense, and timing. It is premised on recognizing an agreed system by which like things go together. Take, for instance, the four cardinal points: East, the direction of the rising sun, is associated with the element of Air and the color yellow. South, the noonday sun, is attributed to Fire and the color red. West, the setting sun, corresponds to Water and the color blue. And north, the cool night, goes with Earth and earthy colors like black, olive, citrine, or russet. Thus, the wand is painted red and placed in the south on the altar, while the cup is blue and goes in the west, and so on.

William Butler Yeats's Golden Dawn pentacle (fig. 6.2) is representative of what members would make themselves. We find the following: *Demon Est Deus Inversus* (Latin, "the Devil is God Inverted") is Yeats's magical motto. The Hebrew words around the perimeter include names like Adonai ha-Aretz ("Lord of the Earth," the name of God corresponding to the element of Earth) and Uriel ("Light of God," the archangel of Earth). Also included are sigils made by tracing the letters of these words over the Rose Cross lamen. The center is divided into four quadrants colored in the Earth tones of black, olive, citrine, and russet. Other implements are likewise painted in the corresponding color, with inscriptions made in the complementary color (what the Golden Dawn referred to as "flashing colors").

Correspondences provide a common vocabulary of associations by which magicians can communicate their thoughts and experiences using an agreed-upon symbol set. Learning basic associations is thus an important early step in a magician's education. Crowley expressed disappointment that, upon initiating, the Golden Dawn tasked him with the "secret" of memorizing the Hebrew alphabet; yet, as he would discover, this was the key to their elaborate system of correspondences (which he

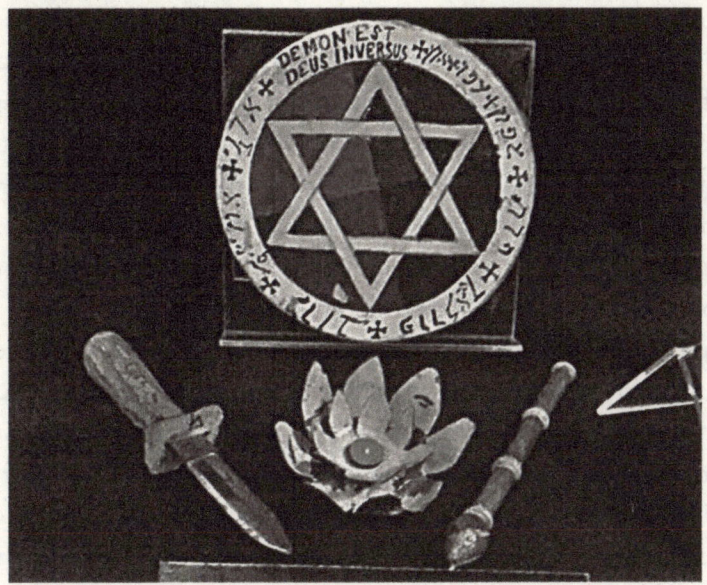

Fig. 6.2. Some of William Butler Yeats's Golden Dawn implements, as shown in the National Library of Ireland.
Photo by the author

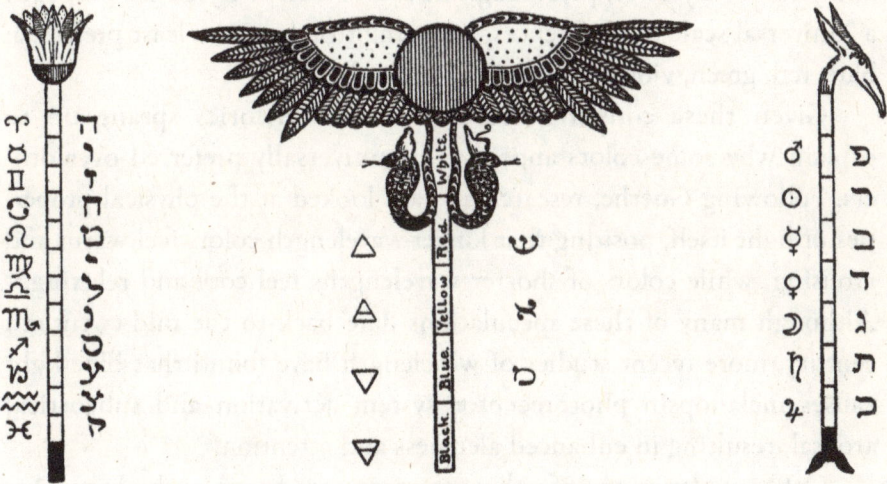

Fig. 6.3. Golden Dawn wands used in the Adeptus Minor degree, painted in bands corresponding to (*left* to *right*): the twelve signs of the zodiac, the four elements, and the seven planets of classical astrology (from Aleister Crowley's *The Equinox* 1910, I, no. 3).
Scan courtesy of Keep Silence

later collated, expanded, and published anonymously as *777*). As British occultist Dion Fortune emphasized, "A system of Correspondences consists of a set of symbols which the concrete mind can apprehend and knowledge of the association chains which connect them with each other; this knowledge is absolutely essential for occult development."[20]

Since correspondences play such a large role in the magician's toolkit, we naturally wonder: Is there anything to it? For those all-important color correspondences, psychology has plenty to say.

That people have color preferences, and some colors are more popular than others, has been pondered well before the question was taken up by research psychologists. Goethe's 1810 work on the *Theory of Color* categorized colors as either plus (action, light, force, warmth) or minus (negation, shadow, weakness, attraction). He placed yellow, orange, and reddish shades of yellow in the plus category, and blue and reddish shades of blue in the minus.[21] Jastrow's survey of color preferences of 4,556 visitors to the 1893 Chicago World's Fair ranked twelve colors in popularity. Half the people liked blue, red, light blue, and blue-violet, while the least-liked colors were orange and its combinations with red and yellow.[22] By 1941, psychological studies such as Eysenck's proposed a "universal scale of preferences," running from most to least preferred: blue, red, green, violet, and orange/yellow.[23]

Given these consistent results, various theories sprang up to explain why some colors appear to be universally preferred over others. Following Goethe, researchers have looked at the physical properties of light itself, positing that longer-wavelength colors feel warm and arousing, while colors of shorter wavelengths feel cool and relaxing.[24] Although many of these speculations date back to the mid-twentieth century, more recent studies of wavelength have found that blue light causes melanopsin photoreceptor system activation and subcortical arousal, resulting in enhanced alertness and attention.[25]

Other explanations of color preference are based on biology. One such theory involves the contrast between foreground and background colors for S-cones (short wavelength) versus M- and L-cones (medium and long wavelength), with universal, evolutionary sex differences occurring due to differential use of color vision, such as food gathering focusing on red fruit and green leaves.[26] In related publications, Changizi argued that trichromatic vision evolved to allow our primitive ancestors to assess the emotional state of others based on changes in blood flow beneath the skin.[27] *Ecological Valence Theory* (EVT), meanwhile, proposes that color preferences are ecologically adaptive for survival, based on colors associated with liked or disliked objects. Thus, we evolved a preference for blue because it is associated with clear skies and clean water, and we dislike brown because it's the color of feces and rotten food.[28] *Color-in-Context Theory*, meanwhile, offers a nuanced take on biological versus learned color associations, saying that color preferences may depend on the context in which they are encountered. For instance, a blue ribbon may have positive associations, while a blue piece of meat is revolting.[29]

Problematically, these studies of "universal" color preferences tend to focus on industrialized cultures, in which color preferences may share a common influence other than biology or evolution, such as global media or consumer culture. A survey of the Himba—an Indigenous, nonindustrialized society in rural Nambia—found none of the so-called universal color preferences or sex differences described in surveys of industrialized cultures.[30] A cross-cultural study at the University of Wollongong also questioned the idea of universal color preferences, finding that the use of color in marketing varies dramatically by culture: White represents purity and happiness in the West, while in the East it represents death and mourning. Red can reflect masculinity, aggressiveness, love, lust, or anger in the West, but symbolize love, happiness, and luck in China. Black is a color of mourning in the West, while in the East it represents power.[31]

Rather than go with an all-or-nothing approach, Taylor and colleagues propose that color preference may reflect a diverse combination of all of the above: evolution, the biology of color vision, and learned social/cultural associations.[32]

While these theories seek to explain why some colors are more popular than others, the more relevant question for magicians is whether there's any basis for thinking that different colors have different psychological effects. University of Wales researcher W. R. Crozier sees color preferences being based on philosophical-religious attitudes.[33] Meanwhile, Elliot and Maier could almost be speaking about magicians' learning and using of color correspondences when they write, "Color effects are thought to be rooted in the repeated pairing of color and particular concepts, messages, and experiences; over time, these pairings create strong and often implicit color associations such that the mere perception of the color evokes meaning-consistent affect, cognition, and behavior."[34]

Color does more than merely signal learned correspondences. Numerous studies demonstrate that it shapes behavior. Looking at sports statistics, football and hockey teams with black uniforms are more aggressive, ranking near the top for the most penalties. Laboratory studies suggest that this is due to a combination of self-perception prompting more aggressive behavior, and referees' biased perceptions of black-clad athletes.[35]

When two sports teams are about evenly matched, the team that wears red has a higher chance of winning.[36] This may be related to a separate study that found people who prefer the color tend to be more hostile.[37] This effect of the color red isn't universal, however. A study in China found that red produced lower IQ scores among college students, but enhanced IQ scores among stockbrokers; this suggests that "colour effects may manifest through culturally learnt associations that are specific to country, geographical region or even cultural group."[38]

The *Dental Research Journal* recently ran an article looking at 132 pediatric dental patients aged six to nine who were receiving local anesthetic. Researchers manipulated the color of the dentist's attire and operatory curtains. Findings indicated that the lowest levels of anxiety and stress—as measured by self-report, heart rate, and pulse rate oximeter—occurred with blue and pink, and the highest levels with red and black.[39] This finding is consistent with prior research showing an association between colors and pediatric dental patient perceptions, in which red and black connected to negative perceptions while blue and pink yielded positive perceptions.[40]

In a study by researchers at the University of Leeds, the background color of computer-based tests influenced arousal, impulsiveness, logical ability, and spatial imagination in various ways:

> **Purple:** Lowest arousal
> **Green:** Highest arousal
> **Yellow:** Least impulsive
> **Blue:** More errors

This finding led researchers to conclude that colors do indeed influence our cognitive abilities.[41]

If color preferences are learned rather than universal, then where did that so-influential color scheme of the Golden Dawn come from? Typical of their penchant for synthesizing different systems into a harmonious whole, the Golden Dawn color scales have multiple influences, from Goethe to Blavatsky, from occultism to science.[42] Thus the planets are assigned colors based partly on traditional associations in grimoires and partly on primary and secondary colors. The circular band of the zodiac divides the color wheel into twelve segments. Also typical of the Golden Dawn, they arrived at a highly complex system. They didn't settle for one set of color correspondences attributed to the Kabbalistic Tree of Life. No, they had four (!) different systems. With ten sefirot and twenty-two paths on the Tree of Life, the Golden Dawn's four color scales involve a whopping total of 128 color correspondences.

Describing in words so many subtle variations in color is challenging and subjective, so—in an apparent attempt at standardization—some of these scales used terminology from the widely popular Winsor & Newton watercolor palette.[43] Nevertheless, various temples and offshoots altered the color scales over the years.[44] This includes Crowley's tables of correspondences in *777* and Regardie's monumental *The Golden Dawn*.[45] In practice, most occultists stick to a simpler single system that combines parts of the "King" and "Queen" scales.[46] But even this system isn't universal outside of Golden Dawn–based groups.

Take the planet Venus, for instance. It isn't assigned the traditional Valentine's Day color red (that color is reasonably assigned to the red planet Mars) but with green for the goddess's association with cultivated fields and gardens. Wicca and other earth-based traditions, however, associate green with Mother Earth or the Green Man. Meanwhile, French occultists like Éliphas Lévi and Gérard Encausse associate Venus with the color blue.[47] Neither of these match the associations in Jewish Kabbalistic texts, which describe Netzach (attributed to Venus in Western esotericism) as red shading to white[48] and Binah (the sefira of Saturn) being green.[49] Clearly, color correspondences in magick are not universal but fall into the category of connections that are made within particular cultures or traditions through repeated association in ritual, study, and practice.

THE CLOTHES MAKE THE MAGUS

In the 1956 Merrie Melodies short "Bugs' Bonnets," a pothole and a poorly latched delivery truck sends an array of hats floating into the woods, where they randomly fall on the heads of Bugs Bunny and his bungling but persistent nemesis, Elmer Fudd. With each hat that lands on their heads, Bugs and Elmer automatically assume the personality associated with that headgear. Hilarity ensues. Introduced as a mock educational film on psychology, it was truly prescient, as research decades later would support the idea that our clothes indeed influence how we perceive ourselves and even how we behave. What is true for hats or other clothes extends to what the magician wears (or doesn't wear) in ritual. Let's examine the evidence.

Back in 1890, pioneering Harvard psychologist William James placed clothing second only to the body in defining *Self*... even ahead of one's own family:

> The body is the innermost part of *the material Self* in each of us; and certain parts of the body seem more intimately ours than the rest. The clothes come next. The old saying that the human person is composed of three parts—soul, body and clothes—is more than a joke. We so appropriate our clothes and identify ourselves with them that there are few of us who, if asked to choose between having a beautiful body clad in raiment perpetually shabby and unclean, and

having an ugly and blemished form always spotlessly attired, would not hesitate a moment before making a decisive reply. Next, our immediate family is a part of ourselves.[50]

More recently, *self-perception theory*[51] proposed that we evaluate ourselves on the same factors that we use to form impressions of others, including appearance. In other words, how we dress influences how we see ourselves. In line with this prediction, a study by Kellerman and Laird at Clark University found that subjects who were given glasses to wear perceived themselves as more stable, scholarly, and competent, and believed that they performed better on hidden figure and intelligence tests than those who were not asked to wear glasses in the study.[52] Likewise, Peluchette and Karl's human resources study asked white-collar employees to recall how they felt at work when wearing formal versus business casual or casual attire. Respondents reported feeling authoritative, trustworthy, and competent when dressed formally, and feeling friendlier while wearing business casual or casual clothing.[53]

Further research suggests that clothes affect not only how we see ourselves, or how we feel, but they also influence our *behavior*. In Stanford University psychologist Philip Zimbardo's classic study on deindividuation, participants whose identities were obscured by lab coats and hoods were more prone to socially undesirable behaviors such as swearing and administering electrical shocks.[54] A follow-up study by Johnson and Dowling looked at administering electrical shocks purportedly as part of a study in learning. The person receiving the shock was really an actor who behaved as either "nice" or "obnoxious." When the person administering the shock wore a nurse's uniform, they pressed the shock button for a shorter duration for the nice actor than the obnoxious one. But when the person administering the shock wore an identity-obscuring coat and hood reminiscent of the Ku Klux Klan, not only did they administer longer shocks, but they administered them more-or-less indiscriminately to both nice and obnoxious partners.[55] Findings like these beg the question of whether wearing the clothes was necessary for these behaviors, or were the behaviors simply reactions to prosocial/antisocial cues that the clothes represented, regardless of whether those clothes were worn or not?

In 2012, Hajo Adam and Adam Galinsky at Northwestern University introduced the concept of *enclothed cognition* to describe how clothes can cause changes in intrapersonal processing and even in our *abilities*. In their supporting study, subjects who wore a doctor's white lab coat displayed increased selective attention. This change in attentional ability did not happen when the lab coat was in the room but the subject did not wear it, nor when the coat was described as being a painter's smock.[56] This established two necessary conditions of enclothed cognition: (a) the physical act of wearing a piece of clothing, and (b) knowing the symbolic meaning of said clothes. The startling finding that enclothed cognition can alter our innate abilities was picked up by the *New York Times*, to whom Galinsky remarked, "Clothes invade the body and brain, putting the wearer into a different psychological state."[57]

Subsequent research has found evidence that the altered psychological state of consciousness associated with clothing can improve or diminish abilities other than attention. In one study, the enhanced attention associated with wearing a white lab coat hindered abstract/insight problem-solving in participants with lower working memory capacity.[58] In another study, wearing a business suit in a negotiation task elicited dominance behavior, while donning sweatpants and a T-shirt lowered participants' testosterone levels (researchers misdirected participants away from guessing the purpose of the study by claiming they were testing sensors that were sewn into the clothing they were asked to wear).[59] When Slepian and colleagues reported that participants wearing formal work clothing experienced enhanced abstract processing ability,[60] headlines declared that casual Fridays kill creativity.[61] Other abilities enhanced by clothing include better attention and information processing while wearing reading glasses (vs. wearing a baseball cap sideways)—but only for those who do not regularly wear glasses[62]—and greater empathy when wearing nursing scrubs (as opposed to simply being in the room with the scrubs, or when the scrubs were identified as those of a cleaner).[63]

More provocatively—and coming full circle to our Bugs Bunny metaphor—Civille and Obhi at McMaster University found that students wearing a police uniform give more attention to apparently low-SES targets, such as individuals wearing hoodies, and concluded that "uniforms might exert their effects on cognition by virtue of the power and cultural associations they evoke in the wearer."[64] Similarly, Mendoza and Parks-Stamm found that participants wearing police uniforms were more likely, in a simulation, to shoot unarmed targets.[65] Findings like these prompted Galinsky—one of the co-authors of enclothed cognition—to warn that militarization of the police encourages brutality.[66]

Given the amount of supporting laboratory research, Adam and Galinsky have called for more naturalistic experiments on enclothed cognition. In other words, we need more studies done in the real world rather than under artificial conditions. "Potential effects such as the boost of self-confidence when wearing an individually tailored suit or dress for a job interview, the feeling of pride when wearing a decorated uniform displaying one's military achievements, or the sense of relaxation when dressing down for Casual Fridays may be difficult to capture in a laboratory setting."[67] The same can be said of a magician wearing consecrated jewelry, robes, or other ritual attire.

While some attempts to replicate Adam and Galinsky's original enclothed cognition study have been unsuccessful,[68] the possible reasons why pose more questions than answers. The effects of enclothed cognition "depend on both the significance attached to the clothing and that participants actually wear it,"[69] but a failed replication set in the classroom rather than a laboratory led the researcher to propose that "enclosed cognition may only be effective when the symbolic meaning associated with the surrounding environment matches that of the article of clothing that is being used to potentially alter an individual's cognition."[70]

COLLECTING OUR THOUGHTS

Enclothed cognition tells us that wearing a piece of clothing with symbolic associations—a lab coat, hood, hat, even a watch—can alter our consciousness and affect how we see, experience, and interact with ourselves and the world around us. How much more powerful might this effect be with the trappings of the magician? These are not the uniform of some generic third person in a laboratory study, but the very possessions of the magician. As King and Skinner advised would-be magicians,

> Strictly speaking there is no reason why you should not wear your everyday clothes, be they a dark suit with collar and tie, or jeans and sweatshirt. In practice, however, it makes the work of the imagination and the building up of a secondary *magical* personality much easier if you have a garment, or garments, worn only when you are engaged in occult work. . . . [Y]ou will find that having some particular garment associated exclusively with the magical aspect of your daily activities helps your creative imagination to transform an ordinary room into a Temple of the gods.[71]

Clothing and implements are part of our extended self (which everyone from William James to consumer psychology would agree with). Furthermore, these extensions of our identity are imbued with extra salience through learned correspondences, the IKEA effect of being hand-made, and being consecrated for magick. The strength of this altered psychological state of enclothed cognition may depend on the appropriate setting, such as the magician's temple or other sacred space (as opposed to, say, a fancy dress ball).* And that brings us to the topic of our next chapter.

---

*Former Golden Dawn member Elaine Simpson reportedly wore her robes to a fancy dress ball in Shanghai and took first place. See Aleister Crowley, *The Confessions of Aleister Crowley*, ed. John Symonds and Kenneth Grant (London: Jonathan Cape, 1969), 230.

7
Sacred Head Space
Temples and What We Do in Them

The temple represents the external Universe.
ALEISTER CROWLEY, *BOOK 4*, PART 2, CHAPTER 1

IF THE TOOLS OF A MAGICIAN are extensions of the self—made particularly salient by the specialness accorded to them—then the sacred space in which a magician works is similarly special: a space set aside, or converted temporarily, for ritual, filled with consecrated tools and other necessaries of the ritual. The act of banishing, calling the quarters, casting a circle, or in other ways demarcating and preparing a sacred space for magick sanctifies it even more. According to occultist William Gray, "To construct a Magic Circle is to create Inner Cosmos according to Intention."[1] The maxim abbreviated as *quod superius, quod inferius* ("as above, so below") indicates the belief that both the magician and their temple are a microcosm, and what happens there is reflected in the macrocosm.

A temple need not be an architectural space. Many rituals are done outdoors: in a clearing, in the woods, at a crossroads, in a desert, or in some other designed space according to one's tradition. Contact with nature promotes authenticity, which is the feeling of that one is acting in alignment with their true self (or, arguably, one's "True Will").[2]

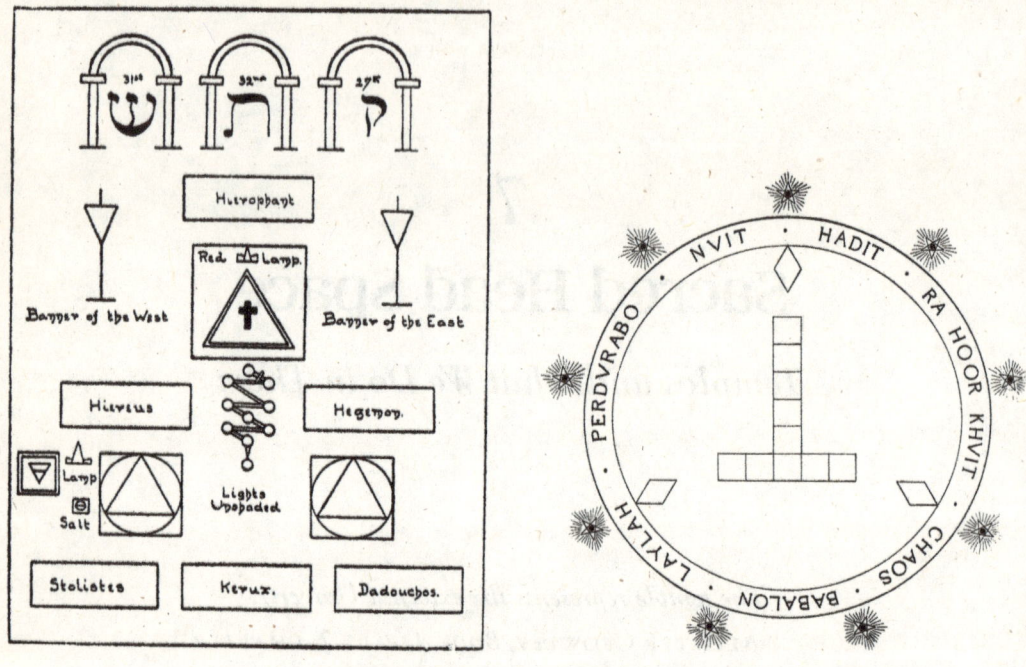

Fig. 7.1. *Left:* The arrangement of a Golden Dawn temple for the Zelator degree (from Aleister Crowley's *The Equinox* 1910, I, no. 2).

Fig. 7.2. *Right:* The magical circle from Aleister Crowley's *Book 4*, part 2 (1913).

Images courtesy of Keep Silence

Nature also brings with it a plethora of mental health benefits, including reduced stress, better sleep, greater happiness, attenuated aggression, and improvement in ADHD symptoms[3] and increased prosocial behavior such as donation willingness, cooperation, and helping behaviors.[4] Visitors to coastal areas, woods, or mountains report feeling restored.[5] As little as fifteen minutes walking in a forest is enough to decrease anxiety and improve mood.[6] Additional mental and physical health benefits come from longer exposure to nature: According to a study of nearly twenty thousand people, that magic number is 120 minutes a week, whether all at once or broken up over multiple days.[7] Imagine combining that time with intense spiritual work.

For a magician, being in a sacred space is a small part of the picture, however. More important is what the magician *does* in their sacred space: ritual. Overall, ritual draws on and impacts human psychology. Many routine features of ritual also have documented psychological effects. Let's start wide and then dig into specifics.

Rituals play an important role in society by marking rites of passage; transmitting and enforcing social norms; and reinforcing group cohesion.[8] They also have a powerful impact on the solo or solitary practitioner. As a mundane example, the ritual of going to a doctor has beneficial effects regardless of whether the patient receives treatment, a placebo, or no treatment at all. This has prompted Harvard Medical School researcher Ted Kaptchuk to redefine the placebo effect as "the positive health benefits people receive in the context of a clinical interaction that's due to the rituals, symbols, and behaviors that surround the pill. When a person's sick and goes to a healer, the drama of medicine by itself is a potent form of healing."[9] As Brian Resnick elaborates on this quote in his article for *Vox*, "Medicine is a type of theater. A pill is a prop in the story of medicine. A doctor wearing a lab coat and being, like, really attentive to you is a character in the story of medicine."[10] The journey from pills and lab coats to ritual implements and robes is very short.

Whether we attribute it to placebo, suggestion, or belief, medical research demonstrates the power of this phenomenon. *How* it works remains mystifying. Psychotherapist Gary Greenberg summed it up best in the *New York Times*:

> Tell someone a normal milkshake is a diet beverage, and his gut will respond as if the drink were low fat. Take athletes to the top of the Alps, put them on exercise machines and hook them to an oxygen tank, and they will perform better than when they are breathing room air—even if room air is all that's in the tank. Wake a patient from surgery and tell him you've done an arthroscopic repair, and his knee gets better even if all you did was knock him out and put a couple of incisions in his skin. Give a drug a fancy name, and it works better than if you didn't.[11]

Deception isn't even necessary for the placebo effect to work. *Open-label placebos* involve telling a patient upfront that they are being prescribed sugar pills, and explaining that this has been found to be effective in treating their condition. A meta-analysis on open-label placebos—involving eleven clinical trials with 654 participants—revealed a statistically "significant, medium-sized effect" on conditions including back pain, allergies, depression, irritable bowel syndrome, attention deficit hyperactivity disorder, menopausal hot flashes, and cancer-related fatigue.*[12] Mind over body is real and can potentially play a role in ritual, whether that ritual involves a patient going to the doctor or a magician stepping into their sacred space.

The benefit a patient experiences from the ritual of going to the doctor is just one piece of the full picture of medical care. So, too, is it with ritual. One commonly documented outcome is the anxiolytic (anxiety-reducing) effect of ritual, which becomes more prevalent in times of uncertainty. Purportedly, ritual provides a sense of structure and order, boosting its practitioners' feelings of control over external events.[13]

Neurotheologist Andrew Newberg contends that the repetitive or rhythmic movements of ritual—such as music, chanting, and dance—drive brain activity from the bottom up. That is to say, these rhythmic elements engage lower areas of the nervous system, which in turn cause changes in higher levels of functioning. The "speed" or the intent of the ritual determines whether the result is highly exciting (sympathetic nervous system), as in a Sufi dance, or blissfully calm (parasympathetic nervous system), like a Gregorian chant. In some cases, one state can break through the other, such as extreme arousal that blooms into a sudden mystical experience of serenity.[14] Hobson and colleagues, meanwhile, offer a literature review and framework in which ritual has both bottom-up and top-down processes that can regulate emotions, performance, and interpersonal connection.[15]

Ritual, thus, can impact practitioners' bodies and minds through a potent combination of belief (or placebo, if you prefer), stress-reduction,

---

*While the authors appropriately describe this as a "medium-sized" effect, it's worth noting that the effect size, or observed standard mean difference (SMD = 0.72), approaches the conventional "large" end of the scale (0.80). The 95 percent confidence interval puts the "true" effect size at somewhere in the range of 0.39 – 1.05.

empowerment, and neurological responses both bottom-up and top-down. Let's now dig deeper into specific facets common to ritual, and explore their relationship to psychology.

SMELLS AND BELLS

One of the legendary acts of ritual magick is the time French magician Éliphas Lévi conjured the shade of Apollonius of Tyana to visible appearance. As recounted in his *Doctrine and Ritual of High Magic*:

> I lit the two braziers with the required and prepared substances, and I began reciting, in a low voice at first, then raising my voice by degrees, the invocations from the Ritual. The smoke expanded, the flames made all the objects which they illuminated shimmer, and then they went out. The white smoke slowly rose above the marble altar. I seemed to feel the earth tremble; my ears were ringing and my heart beat strongly. I put several branches and perfumes in the braziers, and as the flames rose again, I distinctly saw, in front of the altar, the larger-than-life figure of a man, which then dissipated and faded away. I renewed my evocations, and I had just placed myself within the circle I had drawn beforehand between the altar and the tripod: it was then that I saw appear within the mirror in front of me, behind the altar, a white form, getting larger and appearing to draw nearer. I closed my eyes and called out to Apollonius three times, and when I opened them again, a man stood before me, entirely covered in some kind of shroud, who seemed to me to be more gray than white: his form was thin, sad, and beardless, which was not exactly the image I had of Apollonius beforehand. I felt an extraordinarily cold sensation, and when I opened my mouth to question the ghost, I was unable to utter a sound.[16]

From Catholic priests swinging censers of frankincense to santeros blowing tobacco to greet the Orishas, perfume and incense have been standard components in rituals since ancient times. Smell is the most potent sense, capable of triggering powerful memories unlike any other.[17] Conventional wisdom tells us that smells can also improve our mood, concentration, and relaxation. The complementary practice of aromatherapy is rooted in this idea. But is there anything to it?

The psychological effect of scent is anything but straightforward. While some studies conclude that ambient odors influence well-being, others do not. As Oxford University researcher Charles Spence notes cautiously:

> It is by no means guaranteed to occur. Furthermore, as yet, there isn't a clear sense of what the key factors determining whether an effect of ambient scent will be demonstrated or not . . . People's belief about the efficacy of ambient scent, and its likely effect(s), also seems to play a role . . . Conditioned associations resulting from prior exposure also represent an important factor determining the effect of specific odorants.[18]

In their paper, Smeets (Utrecht University) and Dijksterhuis (University of Copenhagen) elaborate, "Repetition priming refers to the phenomenon that a stimulus can act as its own prime. When presented again, an odor is processed faster because its representation in memory was activated just before, and there is still a memory trace available."[19]

Further complicating matters: While studies may report soothing effects of, say, lavender scent, they are often unclear about which of the forty-five species or 450 varieties are being used, or whether that might even make a difference in the outcome.[20] This conundrum is clear in Sowndhararajan and Kim's sprawling literature review: Their paper contains a multipage table listing all the different fragrances tested—lavender, rosemary, peppermint, green tea, and so on for five pages—and their documented effects. Broadly speaking, the research literature supports the idea that olfactory stimulation interacts with the nervous system to change physiological measures like blood pressure, muscle tension, pupil dilation, skin temperature, pulse rate, and brain activity. However, among the vast array of fragrances summarized in this paper, few studies have been replicated, limiting what conclusions can be drawn about the psychophysiological effect of any particular scent.[21]

Mutsumi Ijima and colleagues at Tokyo Women's Medical University reported that olfactory stimulation by incense enhances alpha wave activity as measured by EEG. This indicates increased vigilance while also having a relaxing effect on brain activity. Their finding is consistent with previous studies, which found that essential oils such as lavender, sandalwood, and chamomile have a similar effect on alpha waves and relaxation.[22] Sowndhararajan and Kim's aforementioned literature review supports this finding: Lavender is the most commonly studied plant, and the body of available research demonstrates its anxiolytic, mood stabilizer, sedative, and analgesic properties.[23]

As with color preference, there may or may not be sex differences in preferences for ambient fragrance. Other variables include the concentration or intensity of the scent. Since the stress-reducing effect of fragrance tends to be small, it may not manifest in subjects who are not already stressed.[24] (This is consistent with studies cited in previous chapters, e.g., that reductions in anxiety or depression most benefit those with severe symptoms.) Furthermore, it remains unclear how scent interacts with other perceptions in a multisensory setting . . . as is the case in ritual, when all the senses are engaged. As Ba and King report, in urban environments "there is a masking effect between audition and olfaction that is reflected in the finding that when one stimulus is stronger, the other has weaker perceptual intensity."[25]

Another popular ritual device is the use of sound. The shofar—traditionally made from a ram's horn—has appeared in Jewish religious ceremonies since biblical times and continues to be used in synagogues to the present day (e.g., on Rosh Hashanah). The iynx or strophalos—a disc spun on a cord to produce the birdlike sounds after which it is named—figures into the Chaldean Oracles, Greek Magical Papyri, and other magick traditions. Ceremonial magick and masonic-influenced rituals commonly incorporate numerically significant knocks, claps, and other kinds of rapping (or patterns thereof). But far and away the most prevalent ritual sound is the bell. Bells appear in religious rituals throughout the Far East. They sound in many a Mass to accompany blessing the host, and also in the Catholic rite of excommunication.

They are also a tool on many a witch's altar. According to the Wiccan author Lisa Chamberlain:

> In ritual, the bell may be used to invoke the Goddess, and/or the Elements. Some will ring it after casting the circle to seal the energy within, while others will ring it after releasing the circle to disperse any remaining energy. It can also be used to mark different sections of a longer ritual, such as the end of invocations and the beginning of the main body of the ritual. Bells also makes [sic] a lovely way to seal different kinds of spellwork.[26]

In the 1970s, singing bowls (also known as standing bells) became a popular New Age trend, leading to their widespread adoption everywhere from yoga to paganism. They can be rung for a bell-like tone; or rubbed with a wooden striker to create a sustained, swelling tone at the bell's resonant frequency through the same stick-slip motion used in singing glasses. Their immense popularity accounts for them being the most-studied ritual tool for producing sound.

Note that a couple of these studies describe singing bowls as part of ancient tradition, but their present-day use is entirely Western and modern. In the last few years, people have become more aware of this fact, and suggest that calling singing bowls "Tibetan" or "Himalayan" not only echoes misleading marketing jargon but perpetuates harmful racial stereotypes related to the West's long history of orientalism and fetishizing of the East.[27] I will stick with the term *singing bowl* here.

In one study of fifty-one adults, exposure to singing bowls versus silence both produced drops in blood pressure, heart rate, and affect state, but the amount of change in the singing bowl condition was greater. This led to the conclusion that "responses were enhanced by . . . singing bowl exposure, suggesting this may be a useful adjunct to directed relaxation."[28] Other studies link exposure to singing bowls to decreased anxiety and better adjustment to stress in metastatic cancer patients;[29] reduced sleepiness in women after relaxation;[30] and reduced tension, anger, fatigue, and depressed mood, especially in those experiencing singing bowl sound meditation for the first time.[31] Stanhope and Weinstein's systematic review of the research literature, however, pumps the brakes on any hasty recommendations: "Given there were few studies and the potential risk of methodological bias, we cannot recommend singing bowl therapies at this stage. As the evidence suggests positive health effects, we recommend that future studies consider the effect of singing bowl therapies using more robust study methods, allowing for evidence-based recommendations to be made to reduce the disease burden."[32]

MAGICK CIRCLE OR MOOD RING?

The effect of illumination on our emotions is so ingrained that there's even a term for it: mood lighting. Just as magicians can use smell or sound to set the stage for a ritual, so too can lighting. This can take the form of lights whose colors have symbolic correspondences, or lighting to conjure the feel of a particular time of day. It can signal a change from one part of a ritual to another. It can be extreme—like a flash, strobe lighting, or sudden darkness for disorientation. Or it can be subtle—just a hint of something to set a mood.

Like color, which we discussed in chapter 6, lighting is a complex topic. Light exists on a spectrum, and it can vary in terms of color, warmth, softness, brightness, distance, direction, and movement. Most studies do not account for all these factors, which renders their findings incomplete at best. Furthermore, as we move away from traditional incandescent bulbs toward LED lighting with a drastically different spectrum, the impact of these new light sources is only gradually being understood. Vision itself is also complex. In addition to the familiar rod and cone photoreceptors in our eyes whose signals the brain turns into vision, our eyes also have nonimage forming photoreceptors that can affect circadian rhythm, alertness, sleep, melatonin, pupillary restriction, mood, and cognitive functioning. This secondary system was discovered around the turn of the twenty-first century, and it interacts with the visual pathway, leaving much yet to be discovered.[33] That said, a few experimental findings bear repeating.

Deguchi and Sato, for example, ran a pilot study where a higher color temperature light (7500 degrees Kelvin) had more impact than a 3000 degree Kelvin light on the reticular activating system, which is related to expectancy, motivation, intent, and attention.[34] An fMRI study by Campbell and colleagues demonstrated in real time how illuminance during a concentration-intensive task altered activity in areas of the hypothalamus related to alertness and cognition.[35] Mu and colleagues' meta-analysis of twenty-nine studies likewise concluded that light exposure is associated with alertness in both daytime and nighttime conditions.[36] This effect extends to backlit LED screens, where the light they emit suppresses both natural melatonin and feelings of sleepiness.[37] Findings like these have prompted advice to avoid screen time before bed, especially for people having difficulty sleeping at night. Magicians can take advantage of these findings to manipulate attention and alertness during ritual.

In a study by Igor Knez, mood, memory, and problem-solving varied according to the quality of light (dim vs. bright, and warm vs. cool); the optimal condition was not the same for all participants, however, including differences by sex.[38] Similarly, McCloughan and colleagues found that long-term (i.e., more than thirty minutes) effects of lighting on mood involved a complex interaction between brightness, color temperature, and sex. The initial or short-term effects of lighting were more clear-cut: Dimmer light was associated with compensatory sensation-seeking.[39] This latter finding is supported by subsequent studies, which found that the lack of sensory information in dark conditions results in increased cooperation to reduce social distance,[40] and feelings of liberation that promote creativity and risky behavior.[41] Thus, rituals in low light can promote creativity in solitary settings, or promote affiliation or cohesion in groups.

Many people associate darkness with fear, but this is more a function of circadian rhythms and time of day rather than being in a dark room during daytime.[42] The idea that time of day plays a role has practical implications for magicians. For instance, a ritual under a full moon will always be at night. Similarly, when magicians schedule their rituals based on planetary hours, rising sign, or astronomical positions, the time of day may also be a factor in the magician's state of mind.

DO SOUNDS HAVE SHAPE? BARBAROUS NAMES AND SIGILS

The Papyri Graecae Magicae (PGM, or Greek Magical Papyri) are among the most celebrated ancient magical texts, and they are more popular with magicians today than ever before.[43] Their conjurations are notable for their use of barbarous names, so-called because they are unfamiliar words borrowed from other cultures or groups, and outsiders are historically perceived as barbaric, heathen, or uncivilized. In addition to sacred names borrowed from other cultures (sometimes altered or garbled in the process), the Greek Magical Papyri also feature incoherent yet heady strings of sounds. Here is a typical example, from PGM XIII.585–590:

> I call on you, lord, as do those gods who appeared through you that they may have power, ACHEBYKRŌM, whose name is glory, AAA ĒĒĒ ŌŌŌ III AAA ŌŌŌ SABAOTH ARBATHIAO ZAGOURE, THE GOD ARATH ADŌNAI BASYMM IAŌ.
>
> I call on you lord, in birdglyphic, ARAI; hieroglyphic, LAILAM; Hebraic, ANAG, BIATHIARBAR BERBI SCHILATOUR BOURPHOUNTŌRM; Egyptian ALDABAEIM; baboonic, ABRASAX; falconic, CHI CHI CHI CHI CHI CHI CHI ti ti ti ti ti ti ti; hieratic, MENEPHŌIPHŌTH CHA CHA CHA CHA CHA CHA CHA.[44]

Some of these barbarous names are recognizable Hebrew names of God such as צבאות (Tzevaot or Sabaoth, "hosts"), אדני (Adonai, "Lord"), and יהוה (the Tetragrammaton, sometimes transliterated into Greek as Ἰαω). Others represent fantastical languages such as birdglyphic and falconic, which appear to be onomatopoeic; yet others involve sonorous intonations of various vowels that I liken to a human didgeridoo.

Another example, from Wicca, is the chant that Gerald Gardner published in *High Magic's Aid*,[45] and which has been adopted in other pagan traditions:

> *Eko, eko, azarak. Eko, eko, zomelak.*
> *Bagabi lacha bachabe, Lamac cahi achababe.*

> *Karrellyos.*
> *Lamac lamac bachalyas.*
> *Cabahagy sabalyos. Baryolos.*
> *Lagoz atha cabyolas. Smnahac atha famolas.*
> *Hurrahya.*

While some have argued that the chant is in the Basque language (or a garbled form thereof), the words are assembled from spells appearing in J. F. C. Fuller's article on "The Black Arts" and Rutebeuf's *Le Miracle de Théophile*.[46] Whether they have meaning or not, the ambiguity around these words, plus their provenance from Gerald Gardner himself, make these barbarous words a popular choice, chanted around many a festival bonfire.

Conventional wisdom has it that the power of barbarous words resides in their sound, not their meaning: They are intentionally nonsensical, made up, or borrowed from other languages specifically to be unrecognizable. Instead, by their sound alone, they draw the magician into an altered state of consciousness. As Hereward Carrington wrote on this topic, "They devised a whole series of mechanisms to overcome the impenetrability of the supposed barrier between the two levels of the psyche by resorting to chanting, long prayers, barbarous words of evocation."[47] Kenneth Grant, meanwhile, indicated that "the barbarous names of evocation and invocation . . . are peculiarly adapted to the unsealing of subconsciousness. Their potency lies chiefly in the fact that they are unintelligible to the conscious mind."[48] And, as Crowley specified, "The long strings of formidable words which roar and moan through so many conjurations have a real effect in exalting the consciousness of the magician."[49] Occultist and Reichian psychotherapist Israel Regardie offered a lovely summation of the thinking behind barbarous names:

> [The use of barbarous names] is not unique, nor does it confine itself exclusively to ceremonial or Theurgical work. One very frequently reads of poets becoming entranced, as it were, by the repetition of rhythmic verse and names . . . One hears too of preco-

cious children being singularly affected by those readings from the Bible in which occur long lists of weird Hebrew names and places. Thomas Burke, the eminent novelist, once informed the writer that when a young man the names of cities and countries in the South American continent were to him as magical spells almost of enchantment, occult in their power. Names such as Antofagasta, Tierra del Fuego, Antananarivo, and Venezuela are indeed barbarous names to conjure with. I remember too reading at one time a poem by William J. Turner, the music critic, in which he recounts that as a boy, Mexican words and names exerted a fascinating charm: Popocatépetl, Quexapetl, and Chimborazo, and the like. The names themselves convey nothing to a fertile and developed imagination; the exaltation of consciousness is due almost entirely to rhythm and its music, the witchery of the names entering into the realm of the imagination, where it is seized upon to arouse a peculiar frenzy or excitation.[50]

The use of unfamiliar words and sounds, as seen in the quotes above, is believed to "exalt" the consciousness of the magician. The power lies in their rhythm and unfamiliarity. We see this idea in magick—both real and fictional—where spells and magick words are often in Latin, or spoken in rhyming couplets.

Names, both barbarous and sacred, often assume graphical form as sigils or seals. While seals of angels and demons are as old as the history of magick, the Golden Dawn introduced a new way of creating them based on the spelling of the entity's name. This method employed their Rose Cross lamen, at whose center was a twenty-two-petaled rose, each of which contained one of the twenty-two Hebrew letters. A sigil would be created by tracing a divine name in connect-the-dots fashion. Adonai, for instance, would be sigilized as in figures 7.3–7.5 on page 138.

Occult artist Austin Osman Spare (1886–1956) took a more intuitive approach to magical sigils. His images contained mixtures of elaborate sigils and simpler glyphs. These latter he referred to as the Alphabet of Desire. Rather than being based on purely mechanical rules like those of the Golden Dawn, his sigils drew from his subjective feelings

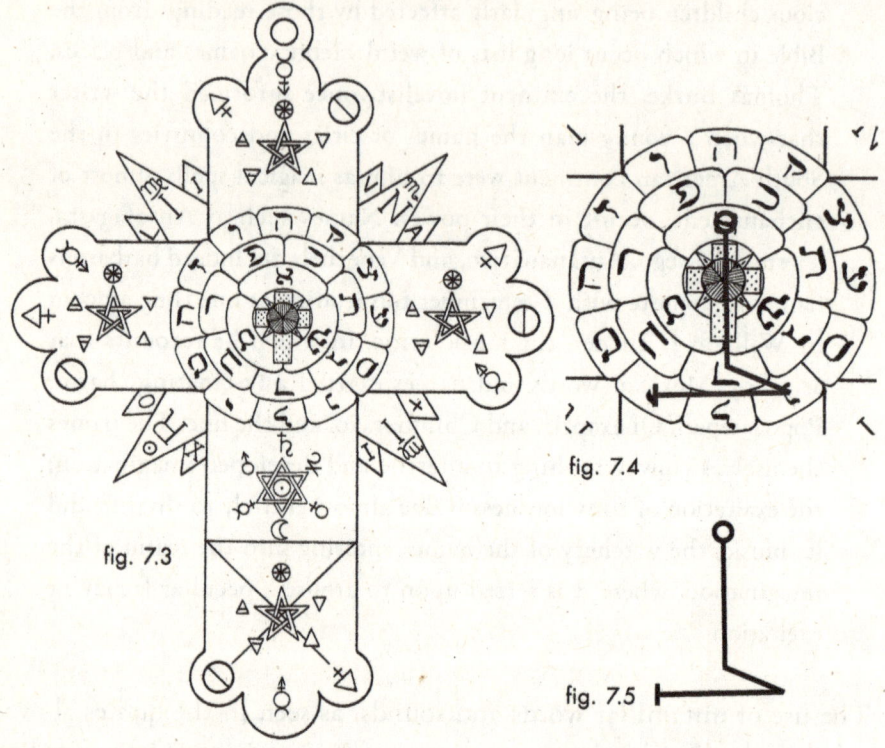

Figs. 7.3, 7.4, and 7.5. Examples of a Golden Dawn sigil: (7.3) the Rose Cross lamen, (7.4) detail of alphabetic rose with Adonai (אדני) traced, and (7.5) the resulting sigil.

of shape as expressions of his underlying intentions. He claimed that his system expressed the subconscious, rather than the rational, mind. Grant explains Spare's method: "His graphic symbology represents a definite language designed to facilitate communication with the psychic and subliminal world. It was Spare's opinion that for this language to be truly effective, each individual should evolve his own, creating his sigils from the material nearest to hand—his own subconscious."[51] Chaos magick extended one of Spare's other approaches to making sigils, popularizing a hybrid approach to sigil creation: The magician writes out a simple statement of their intent. Next, strike out all vowels and any duplicate letters. Arrange the remaining letters into a glyph, to be consecrated and/or visualized. Although the resulting glyph's meaning is

Fig. 7.6. An example of Austin Osman Spare's sigils and Alphabet of Desire, from the chapter "Sigils: The Psychology of Believing" in *The Book of Pleasure: The Psychology of Ecstasy* (1913).

unintelligible to the rational mind, practitioners of this method propose that the sigil works its magick subliminally.*

These are some pretty ambitious claims about the psychological power of sigils and barbarous names. Yet some sounds and shapes are indeed connected in our minds. Gestalt psychologist Wolfgang Köhler first noted the phenomenon in 1929: Presented with one smooth and one jagged abstract shape, and asked which of two nonsense words goes with which, most people without hesitation associate "baluma" with the smooth shape and "takete" with the jagged shape.[52] One study reported an extraordinary 95 percent agreement rate.[53] Over years of study and replication, the nonsense words have been adjusted. For example, at one point "maluma" replaced "baluma" when some suggested that the latter sounded too much like "balloon." A consensus settled around two words—which gave their name to the *bouba-kiki effect*. Related terms in psychology for sound-shape associations include crossmodal correspondences (the association of different sensory modalities with each other) and synaesthesia (when stimulation of one sense produces an impression in another sense, such as sounds having color).[54]

Fig. 7.7. The bouba-kiki effect: Which shape is "bouba" and which one is "kiki"? Most people match "bouba" with the image on the *right* and "kiki" with the image on the *left*.

---

*This is but one of the ways sigils may be created in chaos magick. For a general overview of sigils in all their various forms, see Frater U∴D∴, *Practical Sigil Magic: Creating Personal Symbols for Success* (St. Paul, MN: Llewellyn, 1990).

The bouba-kiki effect demonstrates a consensual link between sound and shape, even when the sounds and shapes have no concrete meaning. These nonarbitrary preferences are consistent across different languages and cultures.[55] The effect has also been shown in infants as young as three years of age.[56] According to a study published in the *Philosophical Transactions of the Royal Society*, the mapping of sounds to shapes happens *automatically and unconsciously* (i.e., when the sound is first heard and *before* the shape is even seen); "congruent" pairings (e.g. when "kiki" is followed by the spiky image) are processed faster than noncongruent pairings, such as when "kiki" is followed by the smooth shape.[57] Findings like these indicate to some researchers that the effect is universal.[58]

Admittedly, there is a chasm between the bouba-kiki effect and the sigils and barbarous words of magicians. Between bouba-kiki and, say, the PGM's BOURPHOUNTŌRM or SCHILATOUR. Or between Köhler's abstract shapes and Spare's Alphabet of Desire. At best, we have a path to potentially connect the two. The closest science has come to testing sigil magick was Newberg's study of 125 symbols: a mix of religious, nonreligious, and neutral symbols. Religious symbols tended to involve circles, stars, and crosses but, interestingly, no squares. Furthermore, fMRI showed that the visual area of the occipital lobe responded more to religious symbols.[59] Is it possible that we are hardwired to respond to certain shapes? Future research may provide more insight into this question.

TABOO AND TRANSGRESSION

Ask a magician what is the key to a successful ritual, and odds are they'll say something like "raising energy." Anything that punctuates a ritual's climax can work. Wiccans may point to the cone of power or spiral dance. Other examples include chanting, singing, and drumming. One powerful tool is transgression, or the breaking of taboos. For instance, Tantra refers to the transgressive *panchamaka* or *panchatattva* (Sanskrit, "five elements"), sometimes referred to as the "Five M's." These traditionally forbidden substances are *madya* (alcohol), *māṃsa* (meat), *matsya* (fish), *mudrā* (dry grain), and *maithuna* (sexual intercourse or sexual discharge).

Breaking taboos can be magically powerful, but it becomes less effective over time. After all, is something truly taboo if you do it repeatedly? This matches the psychological phenomenon of *hedonic decline* (previously mentioned in chapters 3 and 5): The more we experience a stimulus, the less we enjoy it. Many factors play a role, including satiation, adaptation, and habituation, as well as changes in how we perceive ourselves or the stimulus itself.[60]

The opposite—called *hedonic escalation*—is also possible, in which case one's enjoyment increases. This can happen, for instance, with foods that offer a complex mix of flavors and textures, and one's attention is drawn to different flavors with each bite. Similarly, with a fine wine, one may attend to the aroma, legs, taste, and finish—or how it pairs with chocolate or other foods. In these cases, each taste can get better and better.[61] The key here, as discussed in previous chapters, is mindfulness.

TO WHAT END?

As we have seen, daily practices develop proficiency in magical techniques, with all their psychological impact; a magical retirement builds up expectation and anticipation; and ritual provides the release. This much is clear. We now naturally ask: To what end?

One potential function of extensive magical preparation is to facilitate accessing a state of consciousness that makes ritual efficacious. Just as a pump is primed by adding some water to it, so, too, can behaviors be primed. The phenomenon in psychology is even called *priming*. It can be described as the process whereby an external stimulus increases sensitivity to related constructs, thereby affecting behavior. Primes can be conscious or subconscious, and they can involve sound, sight, smell, or any of the other senses.[62] In the case of magick, all the senses may be engaged.

As an example, in *The Science of Magic*, Gustav Kuhn describes a magic trick in which a person is led into a toy store and asked to choose one from among the thousands of toys on display. To their amazement, the magician had predicted that the toy would be a giraffe. The subject, however, hadn't noticed that along the way they had passed prepositioned pictures of giraffes, giraffe patterns, giraffe toys, and signs containing the word "giraffe." At one point while walking, the magician even softly whispered the word "giraffe" in her ear![63]

As another example, are you able to fill in the blanks below to form a word?

P E _ _ _ _ _ A M

If you were, you may have been subconsciously primed by the image on the previous page.[64]

Priming is a controversial topic. Consumer psychology has long since debunked claims about subliminal advertising. Remarkable findings in priming studies—such as aging-related words causing subjects to move more slowly—have failed to be replicated.[65] Nevertheless, the phenomenon of priming is widely demonstrated and debated. While the possibilities here are fascinating, let's not put our eggs in one basket. There are other more intriguing possibilities to explore.

It's a familiar story: The soloist walks onto the stage, and from the moment they sit at the piano, they and their instrument are one. Musical notes fly effortlessly. Difficult passages are fluid. The musician is in a rhapsodic trance, unaware of time, space, or self. They are in control of the moment, achieving their personal best and enjoying every blissful moment.

This state is an example of *peak performance*, being *in the zone*, *in the groove*, or simply *flow*. It can be defined as "a state of optimal performance denoted by smooth and accurate performance with an acute absorption in the task to the point of time dissociation and dissociative tendencies."[66] A ten-year longitudinal study found that people are an astonishing 500 percent more productive when in a flow state.[67] Yet its inner workings remain opaque and mysterious to researchers. Flow happens spontaneously and unconsciously. It cannot be forced. Stopping to think about it will interrupt the experience.[68] As a pianist, I've experienced this myself many times: My playing is clean and effortless . . . until I start to think about how well I'm playing, removing myself from the experience. And my performance invariably falls apart. It's like breaks in meditation; except with flow, you can't just jump back into it.

So how does one remain in a state of flow without the mind interrupting it? I'm reminded of the story of the aspiring student of yoga who goes to their guru and asks, "Oh, master, how may I achieve enlightenment?" To which the master replies, "You must wade into the Ganges up to your waist. But whatever you do, don't think of your belly button." The overconfident student rushes off to his certain date with illumination, only to return dejected: "Master, I did as you instructed, but all I could think about was my belly button." Nodding wisely, the guru replies, "When you can *not* think of your belly button, then you will be enlightened."

This is among the concentration skills that a magician practices.

Another benefit of the magician's work is that it prepares them for a smooth and effortless execution. Mihaly Csikszentmihályi, the "father of flow," enumerated nine characteristics of the flow experience: challenge-skill balance; merging of action and awareness; clarity about one's goals; immediate, unambiguous feedback; concentration; the paradox of control; transformation of time; loss of self-consciousness; and autotelic experience.[69]

Challenge-skill balance is the best understood of these factors, and the most studied. Dating back to 1908, the Yerkes-Dodson law plotted the relationship between arousal and performance of a challenging task as an inverted U.[70] In essence, too little stimulus results in boredom; too much stress is overwhelming. But there is a Goldilocks spot where the level of stress is just right to eke out optimal performance. (For simple tasks, arousal has little impact.) Calling this relationship a "law" is an overstatement, and modern research describes it simply as "the inverted U-shaped dose-response curve." Researchers of flow have found that the relationship between flow and cortisol (a marker of stress) follows this same curve, in which an optimum level of cortisol facilitates flow.[71] A related study of the video games *Pong* and *Tetris* determined that the difficulty level best suited for a given individual player—neither too hard nor too easy—promoted flow (as indicated by self-report, attention, autonomic activity, and higher oxygenation of the frontoparietal regions).[72] This is consistent with an earlier video game–based experiment that similarly reported activation of the prefrontal cortex of the frontoparietal regions.[73]

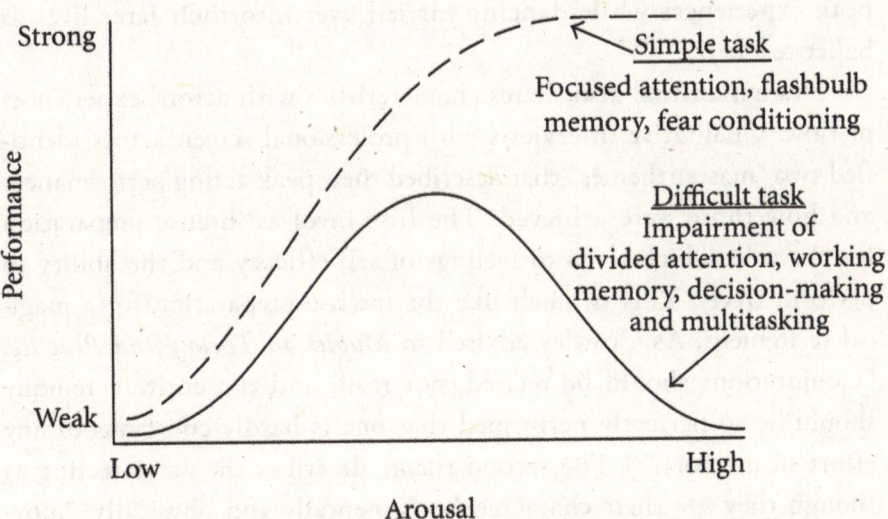

Fig. 7.8. This graph of Yerkes-Dodson law illustrates the inverted-U relationship between stress/arousal and performance of a difficult task, with optimal performance associated with moderate levels of arousal.

While flow does not occur at will, one can take steps to help it happen. Athletes—for whom the performance boost associated with flow is most desirable—may engage in a series of exercises to set the appropriate arousal level. This includes visualization or relaxation to either boost or cut arousal; going through a fixed routine (i.e., ritual) before each game; and focusing attention on and savoring events as they happen.[74] Flow thus overlaps somewhat with mindfulness, but flow also involves muscle memory: the automatic execution of a thoroughly rehearsed response. Furthermore, whereas mindfulness tends to be inward-focused, flow is outward-focused on performance.[75]

Flow experiences are highly consistent with experiences of meditation, mindfulness, hatha yoga, and qi (the flow of energy in Chinese philosophy). Yoga practitioners report higher flow experiences doing yoga than with other types of physical activities.[76] Indeed, flow states share features with recorded transcendent spiritual experiences dating back centuries.[77] Like other religious experiences, flow experiences that are perceived as spiritual can also be transformative. Ballet dancers report that spiritually significant peak experiences while dancing carried over into their later lives as ballet teachers.[78]

Dramatic ritual also shares characteristics with actors' experiences of flow. Qualitative interviews with professional screen actors identified two "master themes" that described their peak acting performances and how those were achieved. The first involves intense preparation for the role, which leads to feelings of self-efficacy and the ability to perform freely. This is much like the intense preparation for a magical retirement. As Crowley advised in *Magick in Theory and Practice*, "Conjurations should be recited, not read: and the entire ceremony should be so perfectly performed that one is hardly conscious of any effort of memory."[79] The second theme describes the actor feeling as though they *are* their character, both mentally and physically, "moving beyond cognitive processes and into active experiencing."[80] These feelings are familiar to a magician who, donning their robes, entering a temple or other sacred space, and casting the circle, sets aside mundane concerns and shifts into a spiritually focused frame of mind. Occultist W. E. Butler, for instance, discussed how a magician in training should cultivate a different persona or character—that of the magician—that they assume whenever they don a particular ring or other piece of ritual gear.[81] This connects to our prior discussion of the extended self in chapter 6.

Arne Dietrich's explanation of flow from a neurocognitive perspective has some interesting applications to magick. It is based on differences between the explicit and implicit systems of human memory. The explicit system involves conscious and intentional recollection, while the implicit system works subconsciously and procedurally. A great example of the latter is how someone can drive to work or another familiar place without consciously having to think about each turn along the way, or stopping and going at each traffic signal. Dietrich suggests that a complex task—such as writing or free jazz improvisation—involves a wide range of thoroughly practiced microtasks, rules, and decisions that combine into a unique performance. The possible combinations and permutations are enormous: an explosion of possibilities beyond the capability of the conscious, explicit system. While the overall goal may be steered consciously, the many steps and decisions making up its execution occur at the subconscious, reflexive level of the implicit system.[82] As Dietrich writes:

> It is the central proposal of this paper that optimal performance involving a real-time sensory-motor integration task is associated with maximal implicitness of the task's execution. Given that the explicit system is subserved by prefrontal regions, it follows from this proposal that a flow experience must occur during a state of transient hypofrontality that can bring about the inhibition of the explicit system.[83]

In this model, entering a flow state requires *inhibiting* the explicit system. This can be done volitionally, and Dietrich offers two methods. First, "flexing the muscle of attention" to focus narrowly on the task at hand buffers the explicit system and maximizes the implicitness of the execution. A magician's exercises in yogic concentration provide these tools. The second method suggests that tasks involving bodily motion create competition for metabolic resources. "Because sensory-motor integration tasks require massive and sustained activation of sensory, motor, and autonomic systems, an individual may need to inhibit neural activity in regions performing functions that the individual can afford to disengage. These regions are, first and foremost, the higher cognitive centers of the prefrontal cortex, and thus the explicit system."[84] In other words, a complex sequence of physical behaviors—such as those involved in performing a ritual—may tax the explicit system to the point that the subconscious, implicit system takes over.

I submit that one feature of ritual magick is that it employs a host of rehearsed behaviors, along with a host of learned associations (correspondences): colors and tarot cards on the altar, incense and implements with symbolic meaning, sonorous intonations and other tones, and so on. These, as in Dietrich's model, tax the conscious, explicit system's bandwidth, allowing the subconscious system to come to the fore. As Neher writes, in cases of extreme bombardment with sensory stimuli, "We sometimes respond to this condition of 'sensory overload' by going into an altered state of consciousness."[85] To quote Crowley again:

> The mind must be exalted until it loses consciousness of self. The Magician must be carried forward blindly by a force which, though in him and of him, is by no means that which he in his normal state of consciousness calls I. Just as the poet, the lover, the artist, is carried out of himself in a creative frenzy, so must it be for the Magician.[86]

This, in turn, can lead the magician to experience remarkable results in ritual. As Regardie writes, bringing in concepts from his training as a psychotherapist:

> Magical ritual is a mnemonic process so arranged as to result in the deliberate exhilaration of the Will and the exaltation of

the Imagination, the end being the purification of the personality and the attainment of a spiritual state of consciousness, in which the ego enters into a union with either its own Higher Self or a God.[87]

We will explore these encounters in the next chapter.

8

Significant Others

Encountering the Divine

> *Who is the third who walks always beside you?*
> *When I count, there are only you and I together*
> *But when I look ahead up the white road*
> *There is always another one walking beside you*
> *Gliding wrapt in a brown mantle, hooded*
> *I do not know whether a man or a woman*
> *—But who is that on the other side of you?*
> T. S. ELIOT, THE WASTE LAND (1922), LINES 360–66

IN AUGUST 1914, Ernest Shackleton and his crew sailed the *Endurance* on the Imperial Trans-Antarctic Expedition, the first land-crossing of Antarctica. Their boat's name was prescient, as circumstances transformed their voyage into a years-long ordeal of endurance and survival. The Weddell Sea's ice pack trapped the *Endurance*, drifting it slowly northward over the long Antarctic winter. After nearly ten agonizing months, the ice finally crushed and sank the boat, stranding the crew of twenty-eight on the ice with three lifeboats and whatever supplies they managed to salvage from the *Endurance*. The crew sailed these lifeboats to Elephant Island, a frozen and uninhabited land off the Antarctic Peninsula, and set up camp. From there, Shackleton and five others took their sturdiest boat on a seventeen-day voyage nearly eight hundred miles northeast. Over treacherous ocean waters, their destination was the nearest outpost of civilization: a whaling station on the far side of South Georgia. A hurricane forced them to land on the opposite side of the island, leaving them no choice but to traverse the mountainous terrain on foot: a journey of twenty-four miles. Half of this skeleton crew stayed with the boat, while the rest—Shackleton, Frank Worsley, and Tom Crean—trekked toward the station under harsh conditions, without proper tools or supplies. They ultimately reached their destination, and rescue teams set out to both the other side of Georgia and Elephant Island. Not a single crew member was lost.

During their trek across South Georgia, the three bedraggled explorers shared a most unusual experience. As Shackleton recalled,

> I know that during that long and racking march of thirty-six hours over the unnamed mountains and glaciers of South Georgia it seemed to me often that we were four, not three. I said nothing to my companions on the point, but afterwards Worsley said to me, "Boss, I had a curious feeling on the march that there was another person with us." Crean confessed to the same idea.[1]

Poet T. S. Eliot immortalized the experience of Shackelton and his companions in *The Waste Land*.[2] The poem gave a name to the mysterious extra party member, now widely known as the Third Man (even though for Shackleton and company it was a fourth man). This Third Man experience can be considered a form of the prisoner's cinema, as discussed in chapter 2.

A mysterious figure appearing during a hopeless situation in a remote setting is not an isolated incident. Here are a few other examples:

- The Shepperton Mine disaster in August 1963 trapped two workers in a nine-by-fourteen-foot space three hundred feet below the surface. Following their rescue fourteen days later, both miners reported seeing Pope John XXIII (among other things) during these blackout conditions, looking at him incredulously "about 5,000 times."[3]
- Frank Smythe tried to summit Mt. Everest in 1933, writing of the

solo portion of his climb, "All the time that I was climbing alone I had a strong feeling that I was accompanied by a second person. . . . It even seemed that I was tied to my 'companion' by a rope, and that if I slipped 'he' would hold me. I remember constantly glancing back over my shoulder, and once, when after reaching my highest point, I stopped to try and eat some mint cake. I carefully divided it and turned round with one half in my hand. It was almost a shock to find no one to whom to give it."[4]

- In the twenty-second hour of the first grueling trans-Atlantic flight (1927), Charles Lindbergh sensed "ghostly presences—vaguely outlined forms, transparent, moving, riding weightless with me in the plane. . . . Without turning my head, I see them as clearly as though in my normal field of vision. . . . These phantoms speak with human voices—friendly, vapor-like shapes, without substance."[5]

- Eric Shipton, climbing Mount Kenya with H. W. Tilman in 1930, "experienced that curious feeling, not uncommon in such circumstances, that there was an additional member of the party—three of us instead of two."[6]

- Adrift for weeks on a raft in the Straits of Malacca, one of the two passengers recalled that, before his companion was attacked and devoured by sharks, "For the whole voyage I'd had the strange feeling that someone else was with me, watching over me, and keeping me safe from harm. . . . It was as if there were sometimes three people on the raft, not two."[7]

- Setting out in 1895 to circumnavigate the globe solo on a thirty-seven-foot oyster boat, Joshua Slocum at one point took seriously ill and passed out during a dangerous storm. "When I came to . . . I saw a tall man at the helm. His right hand, grasping the spokes of the wheel, held them as in a vise. One may imagine my astonishment. His rig was that of a foreign sailor, and the large red cap he wore was cockbilled over his left ear, and all was set off with shaggy black whiskers. . . . 'Señor,' said he, doffing his cap, 'I have come to do you no harm.' . . . 'Lie quiet, señor captain,' he added, 'and I will guide your ship to-night.'"[8] This strange sailor reappeared to Slocum at other points in his journey.

Fig. 8.1. "The apparition at the wheel" by Thomas Fogarty (from Slocum, *Sailing Alone Around the World* (1900), 40).

Slocum's account stands out as not just a vague feeling of someone else being present, but of a vivid and visible person capable of interaction. Similar experiences have occurred into the present day.

Six-year-old Haley Zega got lost in Arkansas's Upper Buffalo Wilderness Area on April 29, 2001. Her grandparents had taken her on a nature trip to the Ozark National Forest, a ninety-minute drive from her home in Fayetteville. It was her first time in the woods. From their rented cabin, they hiked to the Hawksbill Crag sandstone outcropping, renowned for its spectacular overlook of the ravine where the Buffalo River flowed two hundred feet below. According to a contemporary description, "The area is rugged country with deep hollows and high cliffs. The Buffalo River cuts a 1,200-foot-deep valley across the county, but dozens of tributaries slice into the hillsides as well."[9] The hike is rated moderately difficult; visitors are cautioned to stay away from edges of the bluff and to keep an eye on children and teenagers. The unwary have been known to fall to their deaths.

As Haley and her grandparents made their way back to the cabin for lunch, they passed the top of a waterfall. Haley insisted on seeing the bottom, a treacherous descent even for skilled climbers. To coax the recalcitrant child away from her fixation, her grandparents walked ahead, frequently turning and keeping an eye on her. Haley lagged petulantly behind.

In a moment, she disappeared.

Haley recalled twenty years later that the trail was overgrown and poorly marked. When she lost sight of her grandparents, she followed a line of trees intending to intercept them. Instead, she became hopelessly lost. Calling and searching by her frantic grandparents failed to locate her. The largest search-and-rescue mission in Arkansas history ensued, with hundreds of law enforcement officers, park rangers, and volunteers searching the area by ground, by helicopter, and with tracking dogs. A child her age, with no survival training, was at risk of dehydration, starvation, falling to her death, or being killed by mountain lions. As nightfall settled in, prospects looked grim.

A second day of searching proved equally fruitless.

Finally, after fifty-one hours, Haley was found two miles away, dangling her feet in the Buffalo River. Her thought was to follow the river to a bridge, from which she could find a road, a gas station, and a telephone to call home. But how did a child manage to descend those deadly cliffs and survive for three days?

According to Haley, an "imaginary friend" guided her. Her name was Alecia (and that, she insisted, was the correct spelling). She was four years old with straight black hair in pigtails. She dressed in bell-bottoms and a red sweatshirt with purple sleeves. With a flashlight in hand, she led Haley to the river. Alecia kept Haley company "from the moment I was lost until the moment I was found."[10] They sang songs and told jokes. Even as Haley grew weak—suffering from exhaustion, hunger, and exposure—Alecia's presence comforted her. As Haley recalled the incident many years later, "I was fully aware that this was a non-corporeal being that was with me. And she was a little girl, and we had conversations, we told stories, we played patty-cake, and she was just a very comforting presence.... I one hundred percent did not think there was another child with me. I knew, physically, I was alone."[11]

Remarkably, Haley had never had an imaginary friend, either before or since. She was not raised with religious beliefs, and thus wouldn't have interpreted this figure as a guardian angel. Indeed, at age six, she would not have had many cultural norms or expectations to shape this encounter with another. Even today, Haley resists trying to define what "Alecia" was. However, her experience at such a young age suggests that this phenomenon is an innate part of human psychology.

FROM THIRD MEN TO GUARDIAN ANGELS

Experiences of a Third Man—or a "sensed presence," as the phenomenon is called in psychology—are so numerous that entire books have collected Third Man accounts triggered by extreme situations.[12] Furthermore, sensed presence phenomena aren't confined to extreme conditions. Indeed, Suedfeld and Mocellin contend that—contrary to thinking that these experiences are hallucinations or other manifestations of serious psychiatric symptoms—they are, in fact, common and possibly even adaptive.[13] Bader and colleagues report that four out of five Americans say a guardian angel has saved them from harm.[14]

In *The Angel Effect*, explorer and author John Geiger collects sensed presence accounts of people in which the encounter is interpreted as a guardian angel, including the extremely common experience of sensing the spirit of a deceased loved one "looking over" them (around half of U.S. adults "say they've ever been visited by a dead family member in a dream or some other form," according to the Pew Research Center).[15]

These guardian angels aren't necessarily momentary encounters, but in some cases can become "an ongoing part" of one's life.[16] According to British neurologist Macdonald Critchley, "The notion of an *angelo custode* is a common teaching and is depicted in religious art,"[17] and "it is not surprising therefore to find that a supernatural or theistic interpretation is adduced by the religious as the obvious explanation of the idea of a presence... The 'Guardian Angel' motif is inescapable to those with strong beliefs."[18] And thus we cross into the realm of encounters typical of magicians who practice *evocation*.

PSYCHOLOGY OF SENSED PRESENCE

Psychologists have been aware of the sensed presence since its early days. William James—the first person to teach a psychology course in the United States—wrote in his pioneering *Varieties of Religious Experiences*,

> It is as if there were in the human consciousness a *sense of reality, a feeling of objective presence, a perception* of what we may call "something there," more deep and more general than any of the special and particular "senses" by which the current psychology supposes existent realities to be originally revealed.... It often happens that an hallucination is imperfectly developed: the person affected will feel a "presence" in the room, definitely localized, facing in one particular way, real in the most emphatic sense of the word, often coming suddenly, and as suddenly gone; and yet neither seen, heard, touched or cognized in any of the usual "sensible" ways.[19]

A century later, despite various theories proposed to explain the phenomenon, there is no consensus. In 2010, a group of researchers in

Montreal outlined three fundamental properties of sensed presences: They are (1) always *apparent*, i.e., recognizable, (2) *localized* in space, and (3) *intentional*.[20]

The sensed presence shares qualities with various other conditions well-understood in psychology and medicine. These include psychosis, epilepsy, and dementia. Yet the vast majority of people experiencing a sensed presence do not have these conditions. There may, however, be some common underlying mechanism that sheds light on the phenomenon common in nonclinical individuals. Take, for example, a sensed presence being localized in a particular point in space, often just behind the person having the experience. Patients suffering from Parkinson's disease, or dementia with Lewy bodies, often report a sensed presence. Alderson-Day collected several such patient reports. One stated that "someone was sitting on his left side when he was driving or at his desk." Another reported, "The image is behind me." And in one study of Parkinson's with fifty-two patients who reported a sensed presence, it was "often placed specifically behind or to the side of the person experiencing them."[21]

In a 1997 study, nine out of fifteen volunteers exposed to weak magnetic fields also experienced a sensed presence. As with the examples cited above, the presence moved either behind or to the opposite side of the study participant when they tried to focus on its location.[22] This localization behind the experiment is similar to reports of mediums, those reporting sensory experiences of the dead, or those encountering a guardian angel.[23] Indeed, Cook and Persinger asserted in their 1997 study that the sensed presence "may be the common phenomenological base from which experiences of gods, spirits, angels, and other entities are derived."[24]

EVOCATION

Geiger coins the term *angel switch* for the mix of circumstances that trigger a sensed presence. Given that it manifests in varied situations, these conditions can be as hard to pin down as an explanation for the sensed presence itself. Geiger posits that the key comes down to "beliefs and expectations coupled with stress and emotional arousal."[25] This echoes Stanford University anthropologist Tanya Luhrmann's observation that "more recent research suggests that expectation may actually generate the nonpathological unusual sensory phenomena."[26] In addition, we can look to locations other than mountains, shipwrecks, or glaciers. As Solomonova and colleagues point out, "Some environments seem to be more conductive and more linked to felt presence experiences than others. Sacred spaces, or places where the divine are thought to dwell, are endowed with this capability, in both theological, culturally dependent and in tacit, almost imperceptible ways."[27]

All of this begs the question asked by Geiger: "Can this capacity be evoked intentionally? Can angels be summoned?"[28] The answer is, of course, yes. Neher, for instance, provides the following example of "the process involved in creating visions, together with considerable prior preparation."[29] Psychologist and hypnotist George Estabrooks whiled away his time recuperating in hospital by hypnotizing himself to be able to conjure up a pet polar bear simply by counting to five. As he reported:

> This animal would parade around the hospital ward in most convincing fashion, over and under the beds, kiss the nurses and bite the doctors. It was very curious to note how obedient he was to 'mental' commands, even jumping out of a three story window on demand.
>   But autosuggestion has a certain menace which this phantom bear illustrated. He became so very familiar that he refused to go away. He would turn up in the most unexpected places and without being sent for . . . He also had a nasty habit of turning up in dark corners at night, all very well when one realized he was just made of ghost-stuff but rather hard on one's nerves for all that. So he was banished and told never to return.[30]

In an interview with Alderson-Day, Luhrmann proposed that intentionally evoking a sensed presence comes down to talent, practice, and an open mind.[31] Elsewhere, Luhrmann adds, "It is also true that spiritual training may make sensory overrides more likely."[32] Alderson-Day himself asserts, "This capacity can be evoked intentionally."[33] Through the expectations created by daily practice, magical retirement, and performing rituals with consecrated tools in a specially prepared space, magicians take advantage of this human capacity for the sensed presence to open the doors to evocation, and to the aspiration of Knowledge and Conversation with the Holy Guardian Angel.

Consider how similar the accounts of sensed presence are to Aleister Crowley's description of encountering his Holy Guardian Angel, Aiwass, during the Three Days of the Writing of *The Book of the Law*:

> The Voice of Aiwass came apparently from over my left shoulder, from the furthest corner of the room. It seemed to echo itself in my physical heart in a very strange manner, hard to describe. . . . The voice was passionately poured, as if Aiwass were alert about the time-limit . . .
>
> The voice was of deep timbre, musical and expressive, its tones solemn, voluptuous, tender, fierce or aught else as suited the moods of the message. Not bass—perhaps a rich tenor or baritone.
>
> The English was free of either native or foreign accent, perfectly pure of local or caste mannerisms, thus startling and even uncanny at first hearing.
>
> I had a strong impression that the speaker was actually in the corner where he seemed to be, in a body of "fine matter," transparent as a veil of gauze, or a cloud of incense-smoke. He seemed to be a tall, dark man in his thirties, well-knit, active and strong, with the face of a savage king, and eyes veiled lest their gaze should destroy what they saw. The dress was not Arab; it suggested Assyria or Persia, but very vaguely. I took little note of it, for to me at that time Aiwass was an "angel" such as I had often seen in visions, a being purely astral.[34]

Similar interactions are central to great works by Carl Jung and William Butler Yeats. Jung's gnostic *Black Books, Red Book,* and *Seven Sermons to the Dead* resulted from exploring visionary states of consciousness with his spirit guide, Philemon. He recounts one early episode in his memoirs (circa January 1916):

Around five o'clock in the afternoon on Sunday the front doorbell began ringing frantically... but there was no one in sight. I was sitting near the doorbell, and not only heard it but saw it moving. We all simply stared at one another. The atmosphere was thick, believe me! Then I knew that something had to happen. The whole house was filled as if there were a crowd present, crammed full of spirits. They were packed deep right up to the door, and the air was so thick it was scarcely possible to breathe. As for myself, I was all a-quiver with the question: "For God's sake, what in the world is this?" Then they cried out in chorus, "We have come back from Jerusalem where we found not what we sought." That is the beginning of the *Septem Sermones* [Seven Sermons].[35]

Fig. 8.2. Elizabethan magicians John Dee and Edward Kelly summoning the spirit of a deceased person, from Ebenezer Sibly, *Astrology, A New and Complete Illustration of the Occult Sciences* (London, 1806).

Similarly, Yeats collaborated with his wife George in a three-year exploration of automatic writing that started in 1917. William was the questioner and George the scribe. The resulting fragmentary and esoteric writings would form the basis of W. B. Yeats' book, *A Vision* (1925). He spent the better part of a dozen years heavily revising—some might say redacting—the text, whose definitive edition appeared in 1937.[36]

None of this is meant to dismiss these experiences as mere hallucinations. Geiger, having experienced the angel effect himself, suggests that "the sensed presence represents a real encounter with some actual entity or being,"[37] with this rhetorical question: "So is the brain triggering a sensed presence? Yes, perhaps so. Or it may simply be revealing a presence that is already there. The angel switch in the brain may be more like one of English writer Aldous Huxley's 'doors of perception.'"[38]

INVOCATION

Evocation—calling forth an angel, spirit, daimon, or other entity—is one side of the coin of divine encounters a magician may have during ritual work. The other is invocation, which involves inviting some aspect of the divine to enter the magician: By identifying with a chosen deity, the idea is that those qualities may "rub off on" the magician. Mars for courage. Thoth for learning. Aphrodite for love. And so on. In other words, whereas evocation summons a presence outside of the magician, invocation temporarily invites an influence to dwell within the magician.

Psychology has some adjacent acquaintance with this idea through research on actors and cosplayers. Ella Embry's bachelor's thesis on student actors cast in a production of *You Can't Take It With You* studied "how getting into a specific costume affects an actors' perception of themselves in relation to and independent of their character for a certain show."[39] Actors' pronoun usage shifted when discussing their character; namely, while in costume, they tended to refer to the character in the first person ("I") rather than third person ("he/she"). In other words, while in costume, actors identified more with their characters. This led Embry to posit that "a relationship exists between a theatrical costume and a noticeable change in an actor's sense of self."[40]

In her memoir *Some of Me*, actor Isabella Rossellini recalled filming David Lynch's controversial 1986 film, *Blue Velvet*. Even in rehearsals, when actors were not in costume, Rossellini needed to put on red nail polish to embody her character:

> When I played Dorothy Vallens in *Blue Velvet*, I needed my red nails even when we rehearsed on Sundays. Obviously I can't see my own face, so I didn't make myself up for rehearsal, but if my un-made-up hand, gesticulating, had flown past my eyes while I was working on one of the sadomasochistic scenes, it could have taken me right out of character. My red nails gave me enough "distance," "fantasy," "play-pretend," "be-someone-else" to help me feel it wasn't me.[41]

This calls to mind method actors who so immerse themselves in their role that they refuse to break character between takes. These examples recall the concept of enclothed cognition introduced in chapter 6: What we wear can change out state of consciousness (and that concept extends to ritual garments).

Similar clothing-based identification occurs among cosplayers: Those who dress up as fictional characters for conventions or other events tend to choose characters they identify with, either for some psychological characteristic or as an idealized self-persona. This, in turn, contributes positively to their well-being and self-concept.[42] Rahman and colleagues state that "cosplay is a form of identity-transformation from an 'ordinary person' to a 'super hero' . . . that transforms an individual's identity through the reproduction of an idealized character."[43]

Aleister Crowley's poem "Hymn to Pan" is a great example of this shift of perspective. It begins with the speaker/magician calling on the Greek god Pan:

> *THRILL with lissome lust of the light,*
> *O man! My man!*
> *Come careering out of the night*
> *Of Pan! Io Pan!*
> *Io Pan! Io Pan! Come over the sea*

> *From Sicily and from Arcady!*
> *Roaming as Bacchus, with fawns and pards*
> *And nymphs and satyrs for thy guards,*
> *On a milk-white ass, come over the sea*
> *To me, to me.*[44]

Yet toward the end, the words shift to an identification with Pan himself:

> *I am Pan! Io Pan! Io Pan Pan! Pan!*
> *I am thy mate, I am thy man,*
> *Goat of thy flock, I am gold, I am god,*
> *Flesh to thy bone, flower to thy rod.*
> *With hoofs of steel I race on the rocks*
> *Through solstice stubborn to equinox.*[45]

Much like actors in- versus out-of-costume in Embry's study, this poem is potent as an invocation of the deity being hymned.

In practice, the experience of invocation can vary widely depending on the expectations and cultural norms of the practitioner. For example, some traditions may seek identification with a particular quality of an entity. Others may find an opportunity to interrogate an entity for information about a particular question, about itself, or for some kind of prediction. Still others may enter a kind of mediumistic trance, taking on the persona of the entity to speak or act within the confines of the ritual. An extreme form of this occurs in certain Afro-Caribbean traditions such as Voudoun, in which ritualists are "ridden" by the gods like "horses."[46]

It is useful to distinguish invocation from possession, at least the sensational image culturally imprinted by films like *The Exorcist* (1973). Anthropologist Erika Bourguignon's 1968 study of spiritual practices of seven hundred cultural groups noted that "trance" and "possession" are found worldwide, in normal (i.e., nonpathological) individuals. However, these states—and combinations of them, such as "possession trance" and "non-possession trance"—have very different beliefs associated with them.[47] In 1980, Colleen Ward made similar distinctions in terms of mental health: *ritual possession* refers to a temporary, socially sanctioned event occurring within a ritual context, while *peripheral possession* refers to long-term, involuntary possession by intruding spirits and is often associated with psychological pathology.[48]

DISTINGUISHING FACTORS BETWEEN RITUAL AND PERIPHERAL POSSESSION

RITUAL POSSESSION	PERIPHERAL POSSESSION
1. Generally voluntary, reversible, and short-term	1. Involuntary, long-term
2. Supported and encouraged by cultural beliefs	2. Evaluated negatively by culture
3. Induced in ritual ceremonies	3. Induced by individuals' stress
4. Functions as a defense mechanism	4. Constitutes a pathological reaction
5. Irrelevant to cultural concepts of illness	5. Connected with physical and mental illness
6. No curatives sought	6. Curatives sought

Source: Ward, "Spirit Possession and Mental Health," 158.

Invocation—whether it be a low-key identification with some facet of a god or full-on possession by a spirit—falls into the category of voluntary and short-term ceremonial experiences.

WORDS, WRITTEN AND SPOKEN

Encounters with a spirit or other divine power in ritual can take on myriad forms. In this section, we'll look at two common expressions for which some psychological research exists: (1) inspired, dictated, or automatic writing, and (2) glossolalia.

As mentioned above, texts like *The Book of the Law*, *Seven Sermons to the Dead*, and *A Vision* represent written material originating from an encounter with some sort of entity. Such works can be the product of transcribing what the magician hears, or of having their actual hand controlled while the medium is unaware of what is being written (automatic writing). It can also be something in between. Crowley has described himself as simply being the "stenographer" of *The Book of the Law*, yet the text itself suggests that the speaker, Aiwass, was also in control of the writing itself. Crowley is told early on, "Change not as much as the style of a letter; for behold! thou, o prophet, shalt not behold all these mysteries hidden therein."[49] Toward the end, the importance of the handwritten manuscript is emphasized again, because "in the chance shape of the letters and their position to one another: in these are mysteries that no Beast shall divine."[50] Meanwhile, in the middle of it all, Aiwass proclaims, "I see thee hate the hand & the pen; but I am stronger."[51]

The experience of an external force compelling a hand to write can be a symptom of hypergraphia: a condition related to some forms of mood disorder or epilepsy characterized by a compulsion to write, draw, or paint.[52] However, the experience has been noted in nonclinical cases as well. As early as 1890, psychologist William James said of automatic writing, "We must admit that organized systems of paths can be thrown out of gear with others, so that the process in one system give rise to one consciousness, and those of another system to another *simultaneously* existing consciousness. Thus only can we understand the facts of automatic writing."[53] In other words, certain mental processes can fall out of sync and produce a "doubling of the self" in which both consciousnesses seem to act independently.

More recently, a study of twenty highly hypnotizable volunteers were given simple sentence stems, such as "The dog _____." They were then either (a) asked to think of a short suitable ending for the sentence (*control condition*), (b) given the suggestion that "you will have the experience that an engineer is inserting a sentence ending into your mind" (*thought insertion*), or (c) given the suggestion that "you will have the experience that an engineer is controlling your hand movements as you write" (*alien control of movement*). Regardless of the condition, the subjects then wrote out the sentence ending. The last two conditions—administered under hypnosis—replicated aspects of automatic writing, mediumship, spirit possession, shamanism, and similar practices widely reported across cultures and throughout history. The authors found that "targeted suggestions produced a double dissociation between the thought and movement components of writing."[54] They also concluded that:

> the beliefs, expectancies, and attributions through which suggestive processes exercise their effects on cognition, brain function, and experience are therefore likely to be accessible in different ways ... The experience of automatic writing may conform to expectancies derived from largely implicit cultural learning and social modeling.[55]

Unexpectedly, some subjects even reported impressions of the hypnotically suggested engineer, both visual (e.g., "blonde hair in a ponytail") and nonvisual (e.g., a sensed presence that was felt rather than seen) ... which brings us full circle to the beginning of this chapter: The sensed presence sought by magicians may be facilitated by a dissociative or self-hypnotic state of consciousness.

Altered states of consciousness can also result in glossolalia, or speaking in tongues. The phenomenon is particularly associated with Pentecostal and charismatic Christian worship, but it can manifest in other settings. Despite sharing some characteristics with schizophrenia, glossalists generally show no signs of psychopathology.[56] They do, however, outperform controls in linguistic skills, such as extracting statistical regularities from verbal information (for grammar and phoneme sequence), learning the rules of artificial grammar, and retaining this information for twenty-four hours.[57] This suggests that glossalists possess an innate understanding of language, and they have an ability to produce (or transmit) strings of sounds that convincingly resemble some kind of natural language.

Turning (again) to Crowley, his *Vision and the Voice* is the result of obtaining visions corresponding to thirty "calls" in the artificial language of Enochian. While heavily influenced in tone and language by his fundamentalist upbringing and the King James Bible, the records of these visions also contain examples of different languages: Bathyllic,

Lunar, and even one communicated by placing various tastes on his tongue. Here is an example of Bathyllic, from the 2nd Æthyr:

> Ōmărĭ tēssălă mărāx,
> tēssălă dōdĭ phōrnĕpāx.
> āmrĭ rādără pōlĭāx
> ármănă pīliŭ,
> āmrĭ rādără pīliŭ sōn';
> mārĭ nārýă bārbĭtōn
> mādără ānăphăx sārpĕdōn
> āndălă hrīlĭu.[58]

Given Crowley was a poet—and familiar with a smattering of languages including Latin, Greek, Hebrew, Arabic, French, German, Russian, Spanish, Egyptian, Pali, and Sanskrit—it is perhaps unsurprising that he, too, would have an innate sense of linguistic structures... whether he is drawing inspiration from within, or preserving communications from an external source.

WRAPPING IT ALL IN AWE

An encounter with the divine or numinous in ritual is an experience rich with awe and wonder. This is true whether invoked or evoked, in an altered state of consciousness, or any other circumstance. The psychological study of awe is a relatively new field—pioneered in 2003 by Dacher Keltner and Jonathan Hadit[59]—and is informed by diverse fields from art and aesthetics to religion and spirituality. Awe is defined as "the feeling of being in the presence of something vast that transcends your current understanding of the world."[60] But this doesn't quite capture experiences that blow your mind, are "big and baffling," make you go "Woah," and can prompt either dread or joy.[61] Piercarlo Valdesolo emphasizes awe's epistemic aspect, saying, "Your normal way of understanding the events that you experience in your life isn't allowing you to comprehend what is in front of you,"[62] while Jennifer Stellar stresses "the self-transcendent quality of awe."[63] My favorite definition of awe comes from Zhao and colleagues: "Awe is an intense emotional response to perceptually vast stimuli that dramatically transcend one's ordinary reference frame and provoke a need to adjust the current mental structures."[64]

In developing a psychometric scale to assess awe, Yaden and colleagues identified six reliable dimensions making up this construct: (1) altered time perception, (2) self-diminishment, (3) connectedness, (4) perceived vastness, (5) physical sensations, and (6) need to accommodate this new information/experience. These elements were identified in a survey of 501 participants and then confirmed with a second sample of 636.[65] All six do not necessarily occur in every awe experience, but they are the principal components that, to a greater or lesser degree, typify the tremendously varied forms of awe. Notably, these six dimensions are very similar to psychologists' descriptions of the religious experience. For instance, Saver and Rabin write:

> The core qualities of religious and mystical experience, assented to by a wide variety of psychologists of religion, are the noetic and the ineffable—the sense of having touched the ultimate ground of reality and the sense of the unutterability or incommunicability of the experience. Frequent additional features are an experience of unity, an experience of timelessness and spacelessness, and a feeling of positive affect, of peace and joy.[66]

Fingelkurts and Fingelkurts, meanwhile, define religious experience as:

> the very moment of experiencing of ultimate divine reality or ultimate divine truth, a transcendence of events or universe, timelessness, spacelessness, and divine being and/or union with it in any combination with an accompanied memorable feeling of reality, emotions and thoughts with a religious context.[67]

This, then, anchors our discussion of awe within the context of the mystical experience, and of the magician encountering some aspect of the divine as a result of their ritual work.

In short, awe is the feeling of juxtaposing oneself against something mind-boggling in vastness, beauty, or sublimity. It can be transformative, causing you to reevaluate what you know about the world and your place in it. Typical examples include seeing the Grand Canyon; hearing a stirring concert performance; or encountering nature's fierce face in the form of earthquakes, hurricanes, or tsunamis. Those lucky enough to observe the Earth from space have their own term to describe this transcendent experience of awe: the *overview effect*.[68] A high-profile account of the overview effect came from actor William Shatner—famous for playing Captain James T. Kirk in *Star Trek*—when he, at age ninety, had the opportunity to actually go into space on October 13, 2021, aboard the *Blue Origin* space shuttle. For Shatner, the contrast between seeing the Earth in one direction and the expanse of space in the other was overwhelming:

> I saw a cold, dark, black emptiness. It was unlike any blackness you can see or feel on Earth. It was deep, enveloping, all-encompassing. I turned back toward the light of home. I could see the curvature of Earth, the beige of the desert, the white of the clouds and the blue of the sky. It was life. Nurturing, sustaining, life. Mother Earth. *Gaia*. And I was leaving her. . . .
>
> I had thought that going into space would be the ultimate catharsis of that connection I had been looking for between all living things—that being *up there* would be the next beautiful step to understanding the harmony of the universe. . . . I discovered that the beauty isn't out there, it's down here, with all of us. Leaving that behind made my connection to our tiny planet even more profound. . . .
>
> I was so thoroughly unprepared for this experience. It was among the strongest feelings of grief I have ever encountered. The contrast between the vicious coldness of space and the warm nurturing of Earth below filled me with overwhelming sadness. Every day, we are confronted with the knowledge of further destruction of Earth at our hands: the extinction of animal species, of flora and fauna . . . things that took five billion years to evolve, and suddenly we will never see them again because of the interference of mankind. It filled

me with dread. My trip to space was supposed to be a celebration; instead, it felt like a funeral.[69]

While most of us will never have the experience of seeing the Earth from orbit, immersive virtual-reality presentations of spacious natural settings can also produce feelings of selflessness, positive affect, and loosened boundaries between one's body and one's environment.[70]

While the vastness of nature or space is indeed powerful, it is also possible to cultivate awe for things we may take for granted every day: walking in nature, viewing architecture, or appreciating friends and loved ones.

Encounters with the divine also fall into the category of awe. For instance, the terrifying and awe-ful appearance of angels has become the stuff of "Be Not Afraid" memes. When the biblical Daniel encountered an angel, he was so terrified that he fell on his face.[71] The prophet Ezekiel, meanwhile, described cherubs as having four faces (human, eagle, ox, and lion), four wings, and bull's hooves for feet.[72] A far cry from the chubby children with wings often depicted in art!* Whatever form an angel or other entity takes, the experience of awe upon encountering the divine is as true for magicians as it is for religious prophets and ascetics.

Most importantly, the experience of awe can be transformative. In a study of 563 Chinese adults, Zhao and colleagues found that the tendency to experience awe (*dispositional awe*) correlated with well-being. In other words, the more open someone is to experiencing awe, the

---

*Divine beings are often anthropomorphized in ceremonial magick, too. Donald Michael Kraig describes the archangel Raphael as "dressed in yellow robes which have some purplish highlights. The figure carries a caduceus ... and the figure's robes wave in the wind" (*Modern Magick* [St. Paul, MN: Llewellyn, 1988], 41), while William Gray describes Raphael as "a young being with brown hair and grey eyes, lively voice and engaging disposition. His colours are associated with Springtime and the dawn, pale blues, delicate greens, etc. His robes are of these tints ... and his girdle is deep blue" (*Inner Traditions of Magic* [New York: Weiser, 1978], 129). Gray also released a portfolio of ten lithographs representing anthropomorphic representations of the *sefirot* of the Tree of Life. See William G. Gray and Bruce G. Griffin, *Magical Images* (Dallas: Sangreal Foundation, 1972).

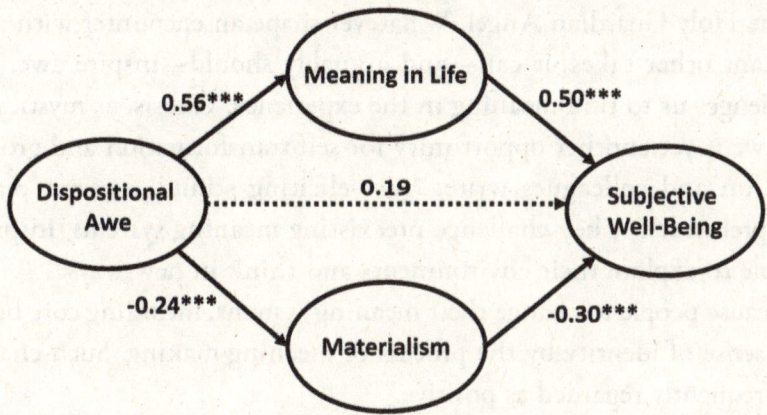

Fig. 8.3. The influence of awe on well-being, through its effects on materialism (-) and meaning in life (+). Asterisks (***) indicate statistically significant pathways; the direct path between awe and well-being is not significant.
Image by the author based on data from Zhao et al., "Why Are People High in Dispositional Awe Happier?"

more satisfied they are with their lives. This increased well-being occurs because dispositional awe influences two other traits: In the positive direction, awe bolsters meaning in life, which in turn promotes well-being. In the negative direction, awe suppresses materialistic tendencies (and materialism's contribution to lower life satisfaction).[73]

Awe also fosters spiritual sentiments. In a series of five studies, Claremont McKenna College psychologists Piercarlo Valdescolo and Jesse Graham linked awe to *agency detection*—the tendency to interpret events as being caused by a purpose-driven agent—in both supernatural and mundane contexts. According to the authors, "in the moment of awe, some of the fear and trembling can be mitigated by perceiving an author's hand in the experience."[74]

IN OTHER WORDS

A magician may encounter the divine in many contexts: Confronting a spirit conjured to visible appearance. An astral journey. A *unio mystica* or sense of identification with a patron deity. A revelation of previously unknown information. A channeled text. Knowledge and Conversation of the Holy Guardian Angel. Whatever shape an encounter with a significant other takes, it can—and arguably should—inspire awe. Awe challenges us to find meaning in the experience. Gnosis, as mystics call it. Awe is yet another opportunity for self-transformation and growth. As Ihm and colleagues write, "Awe-eliciting stimuli are not readily comprehended. They challenge preexisting meaning systems, inspiring people to explore their environments and think in new ways. . . . This can cause people to change their meaning systems, including core beliefs and sense of identity by the process of meaning-making. Such changes are frequently regarded as positive."[75]

9

Full Circle
Group Ritual

IN SEPTEMBER 1972, eight members of the Toronto Society for Psychical Research got together to create a ghost.

Their reasoning? They suspected that the textbook results of séances—raps, table-turning, and other physical manifestations—originated not from the spirit world, but unconsciously from the sitters' latent psychic abilities. If so, these results could be reproduced without resorting to either a medium or the deceased. Furthermore, it didn't require any of the sitters to have demonstrated psychic ability (which none of these eight researchers had). The setting of the séance itself would coax psychic effects from them.

Thus, the Toronto Eight collectively invented the character of Philip, a seventeenth-century English aristocrat in the time of Oliver Cromwell. His skeletal, if tropey, backstory ran as follows: He lived at Diddington Hall in Warwickshire* in a loveless marriage to his wife Dorothea. While riding one day, he came upon a Romani caravan and fell instantly in love with Margo, whom he moved into the gatehouse as his secret lover. When Dorothea eventually discovered this love nest, she accused Margo of using witchcraft to steal her husband. Philip—

---

*Coincidentally, about four miles from Aleister Crowley's birthplace in Leamington Spa, Warwickshire.

afraid of losing his reputation, not to mention his property—failed to defend Margo, who was consequently burned at the stake. Philip began remorsefully pacing the ramparts of Diddington Hall, mourning his lost love. Then one day, his body was discovered on the rocks below, an apparent suicide. Legend has it that his ghost still walks those ramparts to this day.

If a séance with fictitious Philip yielded raps or other manifestations, it would prove they were not caused by summoning the spirit of the deceased. Instead—as two of the participants, Iris Owen and Margaret Sparrow, wrote—"it would prove, to the group's satisfaction at any rate, that it arose from their collective minds."[1] What they did next sounds remarkably like the long period of preparation typifying a magical retirement.

The group met weekly, sitting in a circle around a table and meditating on Philip, initially for ten minutes but later expanding to thirty. They then discussed their impressions from the meditation, followed by further meditation. They immersed themselves in studying the era in which Philip lived, collecting books, documents, and other memorabilia related to Philip's time and place, and arranging them around the Toronto SPR room that had been dedicated to this experiment. They continued to flesh out his backstory. One of them even produced a "police sketch" based on their collective physical descriptions of Philip, which they placed in the center of the table to aid in visualizing him and coaxing him into visible form. After a year of these weekly meetings, however, Philip failed to appear.

Undaunted, they tried another approach described by British psychic researchers:[2] recreating the social mood typical of Victorian salons. Instead of being somber researchers sitting in silent meditation, be jolly. Tell jokes. Sing songs. Chide the table and invite it to join them. Much to their surprise, after only two attempts, they began to hear raps from the table. Faint at first, the raps became louder and more distinct. As Owen and Sparrow put it, "The year's building up of rapport now paid off."[3] Philip was communicating with them. He would rap once for yes, twice for no. A soft, delayed rap indicated uncertainty. A series of rolling knocks was his "laughter." He even had favorite songs from the

Fig. 9.1. A group consensus sketch of the imaginary ghost Philip, created in 1972 by Diana Andrienne "Andy" Henwood (1933–2012).
University of Manitoba Archives & Special Collections,
Lorne and Andy Henwood fonds, MSS 457 (A15-07), Image 1

era in which he "lived," to which the table would knock along. At the beginning of each session, each sitter would say "Hallo, Philip," and would receive a welcoming rap underneath their hands. They said goodbye in a similar manner at the end of each session.

As the sitters sat in a circle, their fingers resting on the table top, the table shook, moved, and tilted, either to one side or up on a single leg. Philip—for Philip and the table were essentially one—became playful, chasing different members or visitors around the room while the eight did their best to keep their hands in contact with the recalcitrant table. On one occasion it flipped over entirely. On another, the table levitated an inch off the ground, gliding in the air for four or five feet.[4]

Despite his often-playful nature, Philip also displayed manners and empathy. One of the Toronto group disliked cigarette smoke. Whenever she was present, Philip would answer the question "Is it okay if we smoke?" with a single rap (no). The table would tip and the ashtray would slide right off. But if this person was not present, Philip would answer with a yes, and no matter how much the table tilted, the ashtray would stay put.

These sessions continued for several years. Over time, the group became so adept that they could quickly summon Philip at will. Curious visitors flocked to the sittings as their reputation spread. And not just in the dedicated room at the Toronto SPR. Philip could now be summoned at other locations, whether it was a Halloween party or a television studio. The journal *New Horizons* began to publish their results. In January 1974, a documentary filmed the sittings to prove they weren't the result of mass hallucination or trickery. In December 1974, four of the team gave a Christmastime demonstration for psychologists and physicists at Kent State University in Ohio.[5] Two of the team would write a book about the sessions, *Conjuring Up Philip*, which came out in 1976.[6] And in November 1976, they did a demo on television for the Larry Solway Show.[7]

Others followed suit by creating their own fictitious ghosts with an equally colorful cast of characters: Lilith. The Artful Dodger. Santa Claus. Even a talking dolphin named Silk! The challenge in reproducing the Toronto group's results was maintaining weekly meetings of a tight-knight group over such a long period. Many of those seeking to replicate Philip-like manifestations were unable to sustain the necessary commitment, and achieved only partial results.

From these experiences and others, the group concluded, "It is clear that in some way that we cannot yet understand a group of people can create a thought-directed force which can be expressed in a physical way."[8]

The Philip experiment shares obvious parallels with Theosophical, Spiritualist, and occult concepts such as the thought-form, collective entity, collective consciousness, group mind, egregore, tulpa, servitor, or astral bot. Indeed, the Toronto group drew inspiration from the entry on "Artificial Entities" in *Zolar's Encyclopedia of Ancient and Forbidden Knowledge*.[9] In this section, Zolar writes:

> These artificial entities . . . are the creations of the minds of men, and are really a highly concentrated class of thought forms. They are not entities, in the strict sense of the term, having no life or vitality except that which they borrow, or have been given by their creators. . . . [M]any magicians have learned the art of creating them consciously, in an elementary form of magic, white or black. . . . Another and quite a large class of these artificial Astral entities, consists of thought-forms of supernatural beings, sent out by the strong mental pictures of the persons creating them.[10]

The experiment itself strongly resembles a ritual: The group met regularly to follow the procedure, in a room dedicated exclusively to the working (i.e., a temple), decorated with items related to Philip, including a visual image on the table around which they gathered (i.e., an altar) where they visualized Philip with the initial goal of evoking him to visible appearance.

Skeptics have questioned or dismissed the Philip working. Richard Reichbart, a New Jersey psychoanalyst and parapsychologist (whom one might expect to be sympathetic) criticized the reports for their lack of clear evidence: The published accounts do not provide dates, nor how many meetings were held. The available narrative overlaps events from different sittings, making it impossible to determine how things progressed. Also, the way the group spoke of Philip strayed from scientific objectivity well into subjective anthropomorphism. "What I saw in the Philip experiment and in the book," he observed, "is an unintentional case study of the formation of a religious group."[11]

Other skeptics attributed the results of the Philip experiment to ideomotor action,[12] a phenomenon first explored in the mid-nineteenth century by the likes of physician William Benjamin Carpenter, surgeon James Braid, scientist Michael Faraday, and psychologist William James. Ideomotor action refers to the body having minuscule and often unconscious or reflexive muscular reactions to thoughts or images. It has been invoked to explain an array of then-mysterious phenomena such as hypnotism, table-turning, spirit or Ouija boards, dowsing, and automatic writing.

While ideomotor action has been used to dismiss the phenomena of séances and Spiritualism, a study by Gauchou and colleagues at the University of British Columbia offers a fascinating wrinkle: Twenty-one university students completed a test of general knowledge (e.g., "Is Buenos Aires the capital of Brazil?" or "Were the 2000 Olympics held in Sydney?"). For each question, they answered either yes or no, and also indicated whether they were guessing or knew the answer (volitional condition). These same students also answered the knowledge questions using a Ouija board (ideomotor condition). The surprising result was that, when guessing the answer to a question, the Ouija board was more accurate than the volitional condition (italics mine):

> In essence, when participants believed that they guessed, accuracy for volitional report was at chance (50%). But for ideomotor responses to the same questions, accuracy was 15% points higher (65%), well above chance. *These results suggest that nonconscious knowledge can indeed be expressed through ideomotor actions, even when it cannot be accessed consciously.*[13]

In short, ideomotor action can access sources of knowledge that are inaccessible to the conscious mind. Gauchou and colleagues propose that this information resides in "implicit long-term semantic memory." For the mystical-minded, the collective unconscious and other liminal doors of perception suddenly become candidates for what ideomotor action taps into.

Sympathetic voices have countered that while the ideomotor phenomenon shares similar features to the Philip experiment, it does not account for all the data. For instance, Owen and Sparrow noted of their Toronto sittings that "the floor was thickly carpeted, and in ordinary circumstances it was very difficult to move the table by pushing on this floor."[14] At the Kent State demonstration,

> The table used there was an antique, heavy wooden chess table with wheels on castors—one of which was broken; the other three needed oiling, and squeaked when the table was pushed. Nevertheless the

table glided around the carpeted floor, without the wheels squeaking, and without making track markings on the carpet. One two occasions, one of the men present sat on the table and was thrown off, once quite violently.[15]

Also at this demonstration, "A strain gauge was used to measure the upward thrust of the table. On several occasions when the sitters' hands were all on top of the table the gauge registered a force of more than 20 pounds, thus showing that the table was indeed pushing upwards."[16]

Peter Lamont of the University of Edinburgh noted that, in the Victorian era, the skeptic's reaction to séances was to explain away what evidence they could, either as trickery or based on known scientific principles (such as the ideomotor action); what they couldn't explain they would deny could possibly have happened.[17] More recently, historian Carlos Eire's *They Flew: A History of the Impossible* explores how impossible or miraculous events in the early modern era coexisted in tension with the ascendance of skepticism, atheism, and science.[18] As fellow historian Francis Young writes in his book review, "Although Eire acknowledges that certainty about such events is ultimately impossible to attain, entertaining the possibility that they really happened leads us to a startling conclusion: It would mean that the material reality we perceive is subject to the intervention of a much more powerful being, one not subject to the laws of physics."[19]

Whatever the explanation may be, the Philip working stands as an example of how a group working together—ritualistically, I would argue—can produce astonishing results. Let's take a look at what else may be going on when magicians get together to do ritual.

SPELLCASTING A WIDE NET

Up to this point, we have focused on how magick affects the individual. Group ritual, however, has an enormous literature that overlaps psychology, sociology, and anthropology. The prevailing idea is that ritual serves as a sort of social glue, bonding members of society together and transmitting/reinforcing cultural norms.[20] The phenomenon is universal, occurring across cultures and throughout human history. As an example, Sohi, Singh, and Boopanna showed that participation in the Sikh ritual practice of *seva* correlated significantly with social well-being, sense of community, reinforcement of needs, membership, influence, and shared emotional connection.[21]

Nor is this effect limited to religious rituals. Charles and colleagues compared traditional churchgoers to participants in the Sunday Assembly, a secular movement in London, England, "doing church without god."[22] Its meetings are structured like an evangelical Christian church service, except in place of hymns the congregation sings uplifting popular songs, such as U2's "It's a Beautiful Day"; and instead of a sermon, attendees hear a TED-style talk. As Charles and colleagues note, "Were one to see a video of a Sunday Assembly taking place without sound, it would be largely indistinguishable from many evangelical churches."[23] Researchers found that Sunday Assembly attendees showed the same increase in positive affect and social bonding as those who attended a traditional Christian church service: "This work is the first to demonstrate that secular rituals, much like religious rituals, promote feelings of social bonding."[24]

Similar effects are found with communal meals, which are often a feature of rituals. In a series of studies involving 1,476 participants, Woolley and Fishbach found that people who ate from a shared plate (e.g., family style) behaved more cooperatively during negotiations. As the study notes, "The effect of sharing a plate on cooperation occurred among strangers, which suggests that sharing plates can bring together more than just allies."[25] Cao and colleagues replicated these findings with the added wrinkle that this effect was manipulated to create the opposite result: "If a ritual highlights a sense of separateness, such as separate eating, it may decrease cooperation."[26] Granted, one expects that typical group rituals would strive to promote social harmony.

Ritual's powerful effect of bonding a community around tradition is also responsible for another phenomenon: resistance to change. Moral outrage often confronts changes to established rituals. Stein and colleagues conducted several experiments on group activities with a range of ritualization, such as fraternity initiations, circumcision, the Pledge of Allegiance, and the Jewish Passover ritual. They concluded that "because group rituals symbolize sacred group values, even minor alterations to them provoke moral outrage and punishment."[27] While I was completing this book, the National Collegiate Athletics Association revised women's volleyball rules to allow double-touching the ball in certain circumstances (provided the ball is not played over the net). The change provoked the same kind of controversy among players and fans alike.[28]

Changes in rituals within the magical community are often met with remarks of, "That's not how we did it back in my day!" Indeed, Stein and colleagues similarly noted that "moral outrage was particularly pronounced among individuals who were more strongly committed to the group in which the ritual originated and among those who more strongly believed that the ritual symbolizes group values."[29] In my experience, changes in occult traditions—even minor—may be met with either resistance or adulation. Within Freemasonry, for example, the historical expansion from the so-called 25-degree Rite of Perfection (also called the Order of the Royal Secret) into the 33-degree system that became the Scottish Rite went pretty smoothly. Yet, when the more esoteric Rite of Memphis reduced its system of 96 degrees to a more manageable 33, members like Calvin C. Burt (1819–1902) rejected this reorganization and formed the Egyptian Masonic Rite of Memphis, retaining the original and expansive degree system. Within an international organization like Ordo Templi Orientis, some "local customs"—unique regional practices that add to or deviate from the ritual text—can be difficult to reign in, particularly when people believe their unauthorized change is an improvement. The addition of gender-inclusive or gender-neutral language has generally been applauded; however, some initiates from the old days insist they were initiated as a Man and a Brother, not as a Woman and a Sister, and they plan to keep it that way. Consistent with the research described above, such holdouts are anecdotally those who ascribe deep meaning to the ritual as they went through it.

Xygalatas extensively explores the concept of ritual as the glue that holds society together, particularly in his book chapter titled "Glue."[30]

While interesting and valuable, my goal here is to focus on the individual magician and how group ritual affects them.

Participants in the extreme BDSM "Dance of Souls" generally report psychological changes in consciousness, affect, stress, intimacy, and sexual arousal; however, physiologically speaking, those dancing—while temporarily pierced with weights attached—had increased cortisol levels compared to preritual levels, while other participants (piercers, piercing assistants, observers, drummers, and event leaders) experienced a decrease in cortisol. According to Lee and colleagues, "Overall, the ritual appeared to induce different physiological effects but similar psychological effects in focal ritual participants (i.e., pierced dancers) and in participants adopting other roles."[31]

Similarly, Fischer and colleagues reported that participants in a Mauritanian Hindu fire-walking ritual experienced increased heart rate and postritual happiness, while non-fire-walkers and spectators experienced greater fatigue . . . suggesting a sort of empathy response.[32] In another study, the arousal experienced by fire-walkers extended to observers who were their friends or relatives, but not other bystanders.[33] In a more secular vein, Baranowski-Pinto and colleagues revealed that in-person attendance of a basketball game was more physiologically arousing and socially bonding than watching the same game on television with a small group. "Our findings suggest that the social effects of sports depend substantially on the inter-personal dynamics unfolding among fans, rather than being prompted simply by watching the game itself."[34] In short, being *in* a ritual is a very different experience than being an observer.

That ritual participation differs from simply watching it is not new to occultists. Among magicians, one may encounter the idea that gnosis—experiencing something—is different from simply knowing it. Anyone who has read a ritual in a book and subsequently attended its performance knows how much more powerful the latter is. In the age of YouTube and other types of streaming, it is easy to see that rituals come across very differently on a phone or computer screen than in person. Something vital is lost in translation. A team of Yale University researchers recently reported that neural activity differs for in-person versus online face-to-face interactions, with in-person interactions producing "increases in neural activity within the dorsal visual stream, increases in neural coupling as measured by cross-brain coherence, changes in visual sensing, increases in arousal as indicated by variations in pupil diameter, and increases in electrocortical responses in the theta band."[35] Extending this finding to the occult community, where magicians have successfully been doing rituals online from the very beginning,[36] the physiological and psychological effects are nevertheless more powerful in person.

SYNCHRONY

One key psychological factor in the power of group ritual is *synchrony*: spontaneous interpersonal coordination of rhythmic behavior. As Jasmin and colleagues note, "Synchronized behavior (chanting, singing, praying, dancing) is found in all human cultures and is central to religious, military, and political activities, which require people to act collaboratively and cohesively."[37] In experiments outside of the magical or spiritual setting, synchrony has been found to influence both affiliation and cooperation. For example, in one study participants tapped their fingers in time with a metronome. The experimenter, in turn, did one of three things: (1) did not tap at all (control), (2) tapped to a different, out-of-sync metronome (asynchronous), or (3) tapped along with the subject (synchronous). Participants in the synchronous condition liked the experimenter significantly more than in the other two settings ($p =.017$, which means that the probability of this occurring by chance alone—roughly 1 in 59—is highly unlikely; $p < .05$, or 1 in 20, is commonly the threshold for statistical significance).[38]

Rauchbauer and colleagues' fMRI study found evidence that subjects' mimicry of happy facial expressions "is driven by distinct affiliative goals" and "seems to denote reciprocation of an affiliative signal."[39] Similarly, Cacioppo's neuroimaging study found that affiliation works the other way around too; when the other person appears to be synchronizing with the study subject, the subject expressed greater perceived affiliation with a synchronous partner. These feelings involved brain

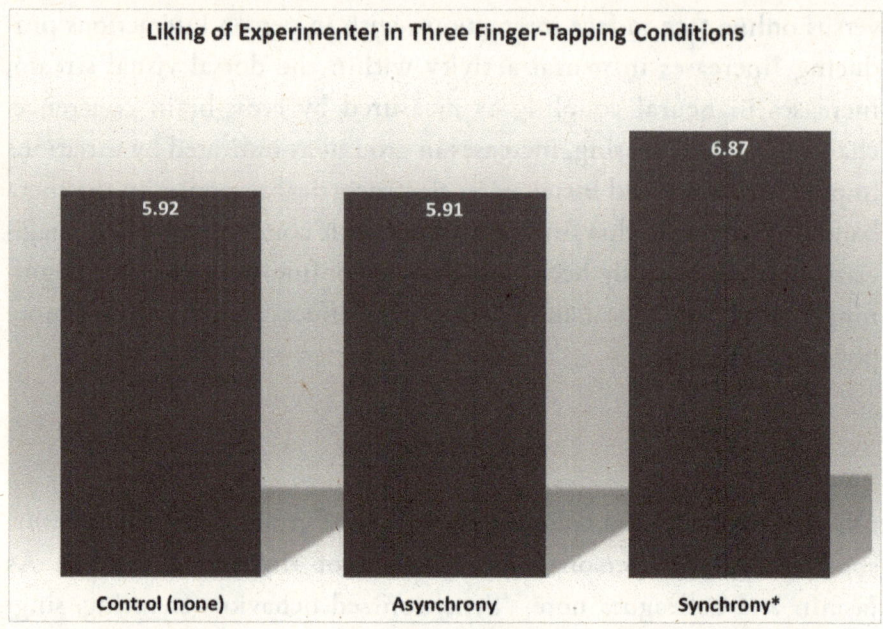

Fig. 9.2. This figure shows the average degree of liking an experimenter in three finger-tapping conditions (Hove and Risen, 2009).

areas associated with social cognition, enclothed cognition, self-other expansion, and action observation.[40] In short, synchrony promotes positive feelings and indicates, or is interpreted as, a desire for affiliation.

Synchrony has a similar effect in enhancing cooperation. Wiltermuth and Heath did several experiments on this phenomenon. In one study, they organized campus walks in which half the groups walked casually, while the other half walked in step. They found that synchrony led to greater social attachment and cooperation. In their other studies, this relationship held even when personal sacrifice was required. The social benefit was tremendous:

> Our results suggest that cultural practices involving synchrony (e.g., music, dance, and marching) may enable groups to mitigate the free-rider problem and more successfully coordinate in taking potentially costly social action. Synchrony rituals may have therefore endowed some cultural groups with an advantage in societal evolution.[41]

Reddish, Fischer, and Bulbulia, meanwhile, found that synchrony, when combined with a shared intention, resulted in the greatest levels of cooperation.[42] Intention, of course, is fundamental to any ritual. Imagine the interconnectedness prompted by collective intentional actions like making the Sign of the Cross, exchanging Masonic handshakes, or giving the Hailing Sign of a Magician.

Moving into research on ritual, a study of varying levels of ritual synchrony looked at nine different activities, classified as exact synchrony (e.g., yoga, Buddhist chanting, kirtan), complementary synchrony (capoeira, drumming, choir, church service), and no synchrony (cross-country running, social poker). Participants were measured before and after the activity. The largest increase in prosocial attitudes occurred in (a) the exact synchrony situations, and (b) activities judged to be sacred. Data analysis concluded that "ritual synchrony increases perceptions of oneness with others, which increases sacred values to intensify prosocial behaviors."[43]

Synchrony is powerful, and rituals often involve various ways for attendees to participate together, including singing, chanting, drumming, and dancing.

SYNCHRONOUS RITUAL ACTIONS

Numerous studies report that group drumming reduces stress, anxiety, depression, and anger. It also leads to improved mood, self-esteem, motivation, and empowerment. After a group session, drummers feel themselves more wakeful, relaxed, cheerful, and friendly.[44] Fancourt and colleagues found that ten weeks of group drumming not only improved depression, anxiety, resilience, and well-being in comparison to a control group, but these improvements held up three months later.[45] In short, group drumming promotes positive shifts in well-being.

Kokal and colleagues conducted a clever study that involved fMRI brain scans of eighteen women (nonmusicians) drumming alongside an experimenter, who played either synchronously or out of sync. After the fMRI scan was done, the experimenter "accidentally" dropped eight pencils. The number of pencils that the study participant helped to pick up was recorded as an indicator of prosocial behavior. Patients in the synchronous condition showed greater activity in the caudate, part of the brain's basal ganglia associated with physical movement. The greater the caudate activity, the more pencils the participant picked up. Thus, the authors "provide preliminary neural evidence for how experiencing synchrony in joint drumming could be linked to increased prosocial behavior."[46]

Singing and chanting represent other opportunities for synchrony effects in group ritual. Congregants associate singing during Roman Catholic Mass with feelings of community and spiritual experience.[47] Similar positive effects occur in the Muslim practices of *salat* (prayer) and *dhikr* (chanting).[48] This supports our earlier observation that group ritual promotes social cohesion. But what about synchronous vocalization's effect on the individual?

A literature review of eighteen studies found that group singing had a range of benefits for the individual. These included boosts in confidence, mood, and social support.[49] While group chanting is associated with a heightened positive mood, this isn't necessarily always the case. Bensimon and Bodner found that audience chanting during football (soccer) games leads to aggression, hostility, and destructive impulses, compared to those who did not chant.[50] Such emotions, properly channeled, can lead to outcomes other than unfortunate postgame fistfights and riots. Eleusyve Productions' rock opera adaptation of Aleister Crowley's *Rite of Mars* incorporated ensemble singing and chanting in the cast, along with martial moves inspired by the traditional Māori haka, to ritualistically generate the energy of the god of war.[51] This demonstrates that synchrony can generate a range of responses, depending on the *intention* driving the ritual.

Changes also happen at the neurological level. Regular choir singing is associated with greater white matter structural connectivity, suggesting this activity could support brain health across the entire lifespan.[52] In Buddhism, chanting of Amitābha Buddha incorporates the practices of *samatha* (concentration) and *vipassana* (mindfulness) on Buddha Amitābha as the object of meditation. Gao and colleagues found neurophysiological changes that are (a) due to something other than cardiac, respiratory, or language processing activity, and (b) different from the activity seen in simple meditation or prayer. These neurological changes did not occur in a nonreligious control condition, in which the name of Santa Claus was chanted. Untangling the meaning of these results awaits further research.[53]

Even more intriguing, when two people recite the same sentence in unison—the type of thing that happens, in the real world, when people recite the Pledge of Allegiance, or when a congregation recites its creed, profession of faith, the Lord's Prayer, or similar passages—the auditory cortex processes one's own speech as if it were other- rather than self-produced. Jasmin and colleagues conclude from their study, "This may contribute to our understanding of synchronized behavior as a group-bonding tool."[54] One wonders if this also contributes to altered states of consciousness in ritual settings.

Synchrony effects do not require actively singing, chanting, or drumming. Merely *listening* to such activities is enough to trigger synchrony. Across eleven different classical music concerts in Berlin, nearly seven hundred attendees' heart rate, heart rate variability, and skin-conductance response synchronized. The greatest physiological synchrony happened among those who welcomed new experiences (hallmark of the psychological trait of openness).[55]

Hove and colleagues' fMRI study, meanwhile, looked at the effect of listening to group drumming. They recruited fifteen participants with long-term experience (average = 9.3 years) in Michael Harner's "core shamanism," which is based on cross-cultural similarities in shamanic traditions. These participants listened to rhythmic drumming during an eight-minute brain scan, while either entering a trance state or remaining in a nontrance state. Compared to the nontrance state, these shamans showed a consistent pattern of reconfigured brain activity in areas associated with internal thought and cognitive control, along with reduced sensory processing. According to the researchers, "This network configuration could enable an extended internal train of thought wherein integration and moments of insight can occur."[56] This led to the conclusion that "shamanism might capture something fundamental about our human experience and the capabilities of the mind."[57]

Together, these studies suggest that group activities common in ritual such as singing, chanting, and drumming produce meaningful changes within and between participants, whether they are a performer or observers.

TWO'S COMPANY: SACRED SEX

Whether it be tantra, sex magick, sacred sexuality, or some other term, the ritual use of sex is a ubiquitous topic in occult circles. While it can certainly be practiced alone, it is appropriate to touch on the subject in this chapter, which looks at the effects of magick involving more than just the individual magician. Shelves of books have been written on the psychology of sex, so it's impossible to fully cover this material. However, studies of sacred sex are relatively uncommon. They tend to fall into one of two categories: sexual sanctification and sexual mindfulness.

Sexual sanctification refers to treating sex as something holy or sacred. This practice need not be theistic: Indeed, the relationship between religion and sex is complex and often fraught. However, regarding sex as something sacred influences both how one thinks about, and how one engages another in, sex. Sanctification leads to greater sexual and marital satisfaction, sexual and spiritual intimacy, and more frequent intercourse. Paradoxically, while religion can provide a basis for sexual sanctification—which in turn leads to greater sexual satisfaction—the direct effect of religion on sexual satisfaction is negative. This reveals how sex and the sacred can be at odds in some faiths.[58]

Sexual mindfulness, meanwhile, refers to engaging in sex with a focus on being present in the moment, and approaching it with "curiosity, openness and acceptance."[59] A review of the research reveals a consistent connection between mindfulness and relationship satisfaction.[60] More recent research also associated sexual mindfulness with better body awareness, sexual activity, and sexual fantasy.[61] Other studies link sexual mindfulness to improved self-esteem,[62] as well as relational flourishing, sexual harmony, and consistent orgasms.[63] In a group of women with sexual dysfunction, mindfulness training provided benefits that endured twelve weeks after the training intervention, cutting their risk of dysfunction in half and improving their overall sexual satisfaction.[64] For men, yogic breathing could help avoid premature ejaculation.[65] Finally, one study compared yoga or meditation practitioners to (a) people who regularly engage in sports, and (b) a control group who did neither. All components of mindfulness—engagement, novelty seeking, novelty producing, and flexibility—were associated with better sexuality, with yoga/meditation practitioners displaying the highest levels of novelty-seeking. The authors of this study concluded that "people who develop mindfulness seem to improve their sexuality."[66]

Interestingly, Karremans and colleagues compared relationship well-being for two groups: those involved in a two-week guided mindfulness training versus those involved in two weeks of guided relaxation exercises. Both groups showed similar improvements in relationship well-being, satisfaction, connection, and acceptance, as well as reduced relationship distress.[67] As we have seen previously, many of the magical techniques we've discussed are also related to the relaxation response, so this finding may not be as surprising as it first seems.

Recent neurotheology research by Andrew Newburg and colleagues at Thomas Jefferson University, Philadelphia, has uncovered a provocative connection between meditation, sex, and mystical experiences. In chapter 4, we summarized the many ways that meditation affects the brain's functioning, even its physiological structure. Newberg's team examined a group of forty people with extensive experience in Orgasmic Meditation (OM), a partnered exercise involving meditative focus on clitoral stimulation. Neuroimaging revealed that OM practitioners' resting brain metabolism was substantially lower than that of non-meditators, particularly in regions associated cognition, attention and emotion regulation.[68] Newberg also noted that the areas of the brain activated by OM mirror in many ways the same areas associated with ecstatic religious experiences.[69] This finding potentially expands our understanding of the complex relationship between sex and religion, which are often at odds or in competition, yet in some traditions potently conjoined. While Newberg doesn't explicitly link this observation to sex magick, he comes close by arguing that all religions were originally sexual in nature.[70] This idea echoes the assertions of eighteenth- and nineteenth-century phallicists, who arrived at their conclusions through an anthropological lens.[71] Phallicism generated an enormous literature,[72] which in turn informed the development of sex magick.[73] For twenty-first century science to arrive at the same conclusion about sex and religion is a fascinating convergence.

Taken together, these studies show that approaching sex from a sacred or sex-positive spiritual perspective leads to greater intimacy and satisfaction. Engaging in this sacred act in an open and present mindset leads to enhanced well-being and satisfaction. Approaching sex in a healthy, positive, and sacred way (as opposed to the often-conflicted messaging promoted in popular media)* also reduces the likelihood of sexual dysfunction in both men and women. Ultimately, it can produce ecstatic spiritual experiences on par with those of other religious mystics and ascetics.

ALL TOGETHER, NOW

Taken together, this chapter demonstrates how impactful magical work with another person or group of people can be. While the Philip experiment resides on the fringes, solid empirical research on group ritual nevertheless paints a compelling picture. On an individual level, group rituals can lead to experiences unavailable in a solitary setting, including transcending one's sense of identity through participation in a group. In addition, group ritual also affects social bonding and cooperation.

---

*See Grace Sinclair and D. Gage Jordan, "Generation OnlyFans: Examining the Effects of 'Raunch Culture' on Depression via Social Media Use and Social Comparisons," *Sexuality and Culture* 27 (2022): 517–38, which found that endorsement of raunch culture "is associated with more intense consumption of social media, which in turn can lead to higher rates of social comparison and ultimately affect depressive symptoms." Meanwhile, endorsement of purity culture values correlates with rape culture and myths about domestic violence. See Amanda M. Ortiz, Bretlyn C. Sunu, M. Elizabeth Lewis Hall, Tamara L. Anderson, and David C. Wang, "Purity Culture: Measurement and Relationship to Domestic Violence Myth Acceptance," *Journal of Psychology and Theology* 51, no. 4 (2023), 537–56 and Bretlyn C. Owens, M. Elizabeth Lewis Hall, and Tamara L. Anderson, "The Relationship between Purity Culture and Rape Myth Acceptance," *Journal of Psychology and Theology* 49, no. 4 (2021): 405–18.

These effects are enhanced by common ritualistic elements involving synchrony, such as drumming, singing, and chanting. If participation in group rituals can form or reinforce social bonds to said group, then the next logical step is to formally join the group through initiation: the topic of our next chapter.

10
Initiation

Changing Your Mind

Naked, blindfolded, and bound, the aspiring witch stands on the northeast side of the clearing, the cool night air standing every hair on end. Without warning, the sharp point of a sword comes to rest upon their heart. The Priestess proclaims, For I say verily, it were better to rush on my blade and perish, than make the attempt with fear in thy heart. Throat dry, voice quivering, the postulant replies, "I have two passwords: Perfect love and perfect trust."

INITIATION IS A CEREMONY OF ADMISSION into a magical group: a rite of passage. For hierarchical groups, it can also be a ceremony of advancement (or recognition of advancement) to the next grade in a member's journey. For instance, there are three degrees in Gardnerian Wicca, Craft Freemasonry, Ordo Aurum Solis, and the G∴B∴G∴; eight degrees in the Rectified Scottish Rite; nine or ten grades in Rosicrucian-based systems such as the Golden Dawn, Societas Rosicruciana, A∴A∴, and their kin; twelve degrees in O.T.O.; thirty-three in the Scottish Rite; and nearly a hundred in the Rites of Memphis or Misraïm.

In the previous chapter, we saw how sociologists, anthropologists, and psychologists have found that group rituals promote social cohesion and norms. Those factors apply equally, if more so, to initiation rituals, which make one a member of a closed mystical society. Wiccan author Thorn Mooney emphasizes the social meaning of initiation when she remarks that, "in traditional Wicca, initiation marks the seeker's transformation from outsider to insider"[1] and that "for a traditional Wiccan, initiation is the acceptance of a new member into the tradition."[2]

Rather than focus on the effects of initiation on the group, this chapter—like the others in this book—will focus on how initiation impacts the individual initiate. From that perspective, I propose three functions of initiation:

1. It acts as a rite of passage accepting the initiate into, or deeper into, a formal magical group. This typically occurs through a symbolic ritual drama that affirms their bonds of membership in the group.
2. It provides instruction in the group's mysteries, practices, or norms.
3. It leads to a transformation of the initiate, which can bring about a change of behavior in light of this new perspective.

Let's take a look at each in turn.

RITE OF PASSAGE: THE TIES THAT BIND

What it is about the experience of initiation that results in an individual feeling connected to the group they have joined? Two psychological theories address why people like the groups they join . . . whether it be an exclusive country club, a college fraternity/sorority, a magical order, or something else. The *severity-attraction hypothesis* suggests that an initiate feels more attraction to the group because of the ordeal itself. The *severity-affiliation-attraction hypothesis*, meanwhile, proposes that the severity-attraction relationship happens through the influence of *affiliation*. In other words, fellow initiates bond over having something in common—the shared experience of initiation—and this common ground leads to feeling more attraction for the group as a whole.

The Severity-Attraction Hypothesis

He must teach; but he may make severe the ordeals.
THE BOOK OF THE LAW, I:38

Severity-attraction has its roots in Leon Festinger's theory of *cognitive dissonance*.[3] Simply put, when two cognitions are inconsistent, the resulting psychological tension wants to be resolved. This happens by changing either one's attitudes or behaviors. For instance, if Andy Adept believes that keeping a magical record is essential, but recalls times that they skipped a day, these two thoughts create cognitive dissonance. The memory of past lapses may prompt a behavior change, with Andy being more conscientious about keeping up with their magical record.

In the classic 1959 study of cognitive dissonance, sixty Stanford University psychology student volunteers spent an hour doing tedious tasks. First, they put spools on a tray over and over again for thirty minutes. This was followed by turning forty-eight square pegs a quarter of a turn using only the right hand; when all the pegs were turned, they went back and turned all the pegs another quarter turn, and so on for half an hour. Throughout this exercise, the experimenter stood by silently with a stopwatch, taking notes on a clipboard.

After the hour was up, the experimenter explained to the volunteer that there was a second group in the study who received a pep talk from a prior participant, saying the experience was enjoyable and rewarding. "Unfortunately, they were a no-show. We now have a study volunteer waiting to begin. Would you be willing to tell them how much fun the study was?" Almost everyone agreed to do so. Half were paid one dollar, and half were paid twenty dollars.

Here's the plot twist: The students who were paid one dollar to say how exciting the study was would go on to rate their experience as more enjoyable than those who were paid twenty dollars. A dollar was hardly enough incentive to mislead a fellow student about how mind-numbingly dull the experiment was. Since they could not reconcile their feelings about the study with what they told their fellow student, the only way to resolve the cognitive dissonance was to convince themselves that the study actually *was* fun.[4]

Princeton University psychologist Joel Cooper notes, "The theory of cognitive dissonance has been a staple of social psychology for more than half a century."[5] Cooper's research—sometimes referred to as the New Look model[6] or the Self-Standards model[7]—clarified the conditions under which cognitive dissonance does or does not occur. Dissonance will not occur, for instance, if someone is forced to do something inconsistent. The event must occur willingly.[8] Neither does it happen if the inconsistent event has no consequences; it must lead to an undesired or unintended outcome (e.g., misleading someone).[9] Finally, for cognitive dissonance to occur, the person in question needs to be aware of their inconsistent cognitions, attitudes, or behaviors. If they don't see an inconsistency, there is no dissonance to resolve.[10]

Cognitive dissonance plays a role in initiation, too. In another study from the golden age of social psychology, Aronson and Mills (1959) examined the relationship between the severity of initiation and liking for the group. Sixty-three women signed up to participate in a discussion group about the psychology of sex. These volunteers learned that the group was already meeting, but due to someone dropping out, a replacement spot had opened. The experimenter explained that he needed to screen prospective group members with an "embarrassment test" to determine if they were a good fit. The test involved reading sexually explicit material out loud in front of the experimenter, who "would make a clinical judgment of her degree of embarrassment, based upon hesitation, blushing, etc."[11] The embarrassment test was actually the experimental manipulation: severity of "initiation." Half the subjects were in the *mild* condition, reading out loud words such as "prostitute," "virgin," and "petting." The *severe* condition, meanwhile, had obscene words like "fuck," "cock," and "screw." (Yes, "screw." It was the 1950s.)

After the embarrassment test, test subjects learned that the group met via intercom to reduce inhibition and allow everyone to feel comfortable speaking freely. Since the subject hadn't yet read *Sexual Behavior in Animals*, which the group was discussing, they were asked to silently listen to the group meeting to get a feel for how it worked. In reality, every subject was played the same recording of a mind-numbingly dull

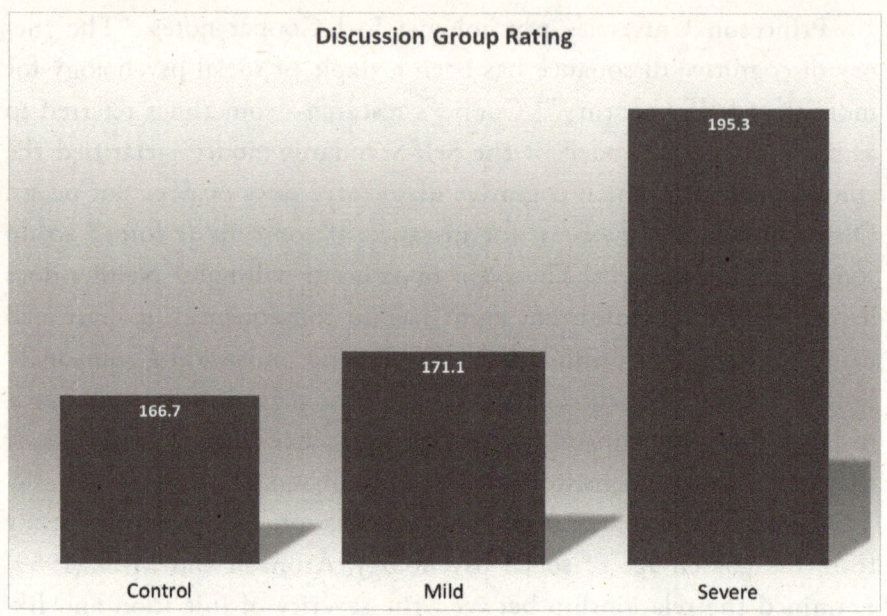

Fig. 10.1. The effect of initiation severity on overall liking of the sexual behavior discussion group (Aronson and Mills, 1959).

discussion. This ensured that every subject heard the identical group conversation. In short, the study created an ordeal required to join a group, but the group wound up being far less titillating than the embarrassment test led them to believe. The ordeal and the outcome were inconsistent, and they were intended to create cognitive dissonance.

So what did these recruits think of the discussion group? Subjects given the mild condition rated the group unfavorably, very close to how control subjects (who were subjected to no embarrassment test) rated it. By comparison, those in the severe group rated their enjoyment of the discussion, participants, and overall experience significantly higher. *Subjects liked the group more in order to justify to themselves the severity of their initiation.*

Researchers have since proposed alternative explanations for this enhanced liking of the dull discussion group. Perhaps the subjects didn't know what the obscene words meant, and hoped to find out. Or perhaps they rated the discussion group higher because the obscene words sexually aroused them. Or maybe "passing" the severe test filled them with a greater sense of relief. These possibilities and others were ruled out in follow-up studies, which generally supported the original finding that *attraction* to a group is enhanced by *initiation severity*.[12]

One modern test of the severity-attraction hypothesis is particularly relevant to initiation into a magical society. Caroline Kamau sought to replicate Aronson and Mills's original study on initiation severity and group liking, but with a twist: After completing an automated, time-limited math test in which the computer chastised incorrect answers with responses like "Wrong answer, dummy!" half of the participants received a reward:

> The experimenter ostentatiously took out the certificate titled "Certificate of Achievement: Number Task." The experimenter wrote the date and asked the participant to write his/her name in a section titled "awarded to." Many participants seemed pleased to receive the certificate and many asked if they could keep it or commented that it would be nice to keep it.[13]

Those receiving the reward reported greater identity with the fictitious focus group they had joined. Interestingly, the ostentatious presentation of a certificate of achievement mirrors the tradition in many initiations where the candidate, upon completing the ceremony, receives a certificate, piece of regalia, text for study, or other gift/token. It isn't just tradition: It also promotes identification with the group.

A more subtle source of both the ordeal and attractiveness of initiation into a secret society comes from the secret nature of the group itself. At the dawn of the twentieth century, sociologist Georg Simmel, writing on secret societies, suggested that "secrecy involves a tension which, at the moment of revelation, finds its release."[14] Over a century later, Gardnerian witch Thorn Mooney recognized the power of secrecy when she wrote of Wiccan initiation, "Secrets *feel* powerful and can make the experience that much more profound."[15] Thus, the very nature of secrets, and their communication during initiation, creates (and resolves) its own kind of ordeal. This communication furthermore boosts the group's attractiveness. As van Gulik writes of initiatory Wicca, one function of secrecy is "a means of drawing a line between the people who have internalized and lived-through the basics of Wicca" and those who have not.[16] This sentiment holds for any secret society. Indeed, secrecy has been proposed as the glue binding together secret societies from the ancient cult of Mithras[17] to modern Freemasonry.[18] Secrecy elevates the desirability, power, and significance of one's spiritual practice,[19] and of the group in which it is practiced.

The (Severity-)Affiliation-Attraction Hypothesis

An elaboration of the severity-attraction hypothesis proposes that a sense of camaraderie with fellow initiates is the secret sauce that explains the relationship between initiation severity and group attractiveness. We like a group because everyone has gone through the same experience. Describing the perception of their coven by a newly initiated witch, Mooney writes, "Knowing that they've all joined via the same rite creates a profound bond that unites members of a community."[20]

In 1959, social psychologist Stanley Schachter proposed a linkage between anxiety and affiliation[21] (which later generations would echo in the *tend and befriend* stress response, discussed later in this chapter). In his original study, Schachter told his female volunteers that, as part of his study, they would receive an electrical shock. Half were told it was painless, and the other half were told it was painful but harmless. They were next given the option of waiting their turn either alone or with other participants. Significantly more of the "painful but harmless" group, compared to the painless shock group, chose to wait their turn with others. This suggested that, in times of stress (such as in an initiation), we seek reassurance in companionship.

Recently, researchers from Duke, University of North Carolina, and Université Catholique de Louvain collaborated on three studies of how religiosity impacts affiliation behavior. When selecting where to sit in a waiting room, those who rated God as important in their lives sat closer to a chair occupied by an unknown other person. In a follow-up study, if the other person was identified as a Christian or an atheist, religious people would sit closer to the Christian. Finally, in a virtual ball-throwing game with a Christian, atheist, and neutral player, religiosity was associated with favoring the fellow Christian. In other words, all three experiments showed a tendency for religious people to want to affiliate with others, especially others with putatively similar views or values. (An alternative explanation is that those with a stronger need to affiliate are more likely to become religious.)[22]

Not only do we have an innate drive for affiliation, but sharing experiences with others also enhances those experiences. A study at Yale University examined how people rated chocolate when they tasted it in the presence of another person. This other person either (a) also tried the chocolate, or (b) did something unrelated. Although the two people did not communicate with each other, those in the first group rated the pleasant-tasting chocolate as more pleasant, and bitter chocolate as less pleasant, compared to the second group. In other words, sharing the experience in the presence of another person amplifies the experience, whether positive or negative.[23]

Instead of studying laboratory-based initiation ordeals, Lodewijkx and colleagues went with a real-life setting: initiation into a Dutch college sorority. The process that 202 novices went through involved three stages:

1. Separation. Novices spent a week at a rural campground, where they dressed in similar "bag-like" clothes, were assigned a new name for the duration, had no clocks, and spent their days doing physical labor like digging ditches and pulling trees. At night, they slept in tents, rotating tentmates daily to discourage social bonding. Random roll calls lasting up to four hours could take place any time of day or night. The experience left them exhausted from insufficient food, water, and sleep.
2. Transition. Returning to the city, they attended evening gatherings where they learned about the sorority, its customs, and its norms. Throughout this phase, the sorority members embarrassed and bullied the novices.
3. Incorporation. Finally, the novices attended a solemn induction ceremony at the eighteenth-century academy building on campus.

Church bells greeted them as they filed out after the ceremony and returned to the club for their first meal as full members of the sorority.

Contrary to the severity-attraction hypothesis, the novices' perception of initiation severity correlated with *less* liking of the sorority. Instead, the main driver of liking the sorority was the companionship they felt with their fellow initiates.[24] Lodewijkx and colleagues' follow-up paper argued, "Findings suggest the existence of a mere initiation-affiliation-attraction relationship: Irrespective of their severity, initiations seem to induce a common fate, increasing newcomers' attraction to the group through the process of short-term, affiliate exchanges."[25]

In a subsequent study, Lodewijkx and colleagues looked at *anticipation* of a severe initiation, rather than an actual initiation. The researchers told volunteers that they were going to undergo an initiation ritual lasting about twenty minutes, then evaluated the volunteers while they awaited the ritual. No initiation took place, however. In this sense, the study resembled Schachter's study, where people were told they were going to receive an electrical shock, and their behavior while waiting was observed. Unlike their previous studies, Lodewijkx and colleagues

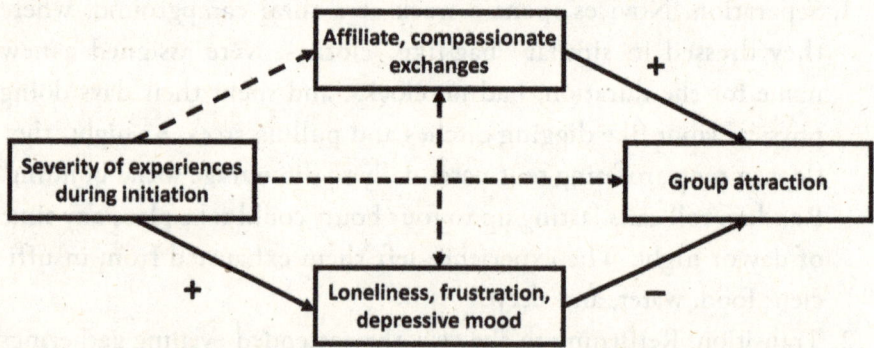

Fig. 10.2. Lodewijkx and colleagues' study of initiation into a Dutch sorority found that greater affiliation led to greater group attraction, while severity resulted in less. Solid lines indicate significant associations; dashed lines are insignificant.

Image by the author based on data from Lodewijkx and Syroit, "Severity of Initiation Revisited" and Lodewijkx, Zomeren, and Syroit, "The Anticipation of Severe Initiation"

recruited a mix of male and female subjects. Women showed the same affiliation-attraction pattern observed in the previous Dutch sorority study. The men, however, showed the more classic severity-attraction pattern. The authors summarized their findings as follows:

> When applying these findings to naturalistic initiations, they suggest that when females are confronted with (anticipated) mild to moderate real initiation situations, the building blocks for strengthening the bonds between them in terms of expressive, affiliate kinship tendencies are already there. They do not need to undergo harsh treatments to trigger and express these needs. Moreover, the reasoning further implies that the imposition of degrading and embarrassing practices of a moderate degree during real initiations might not be functional for female newcomers to increase group attraction and enhance group formation.
>
> However, when males are confronted with real initiation situations, or when they anticipate such situations, the Schachterian (1959) threat-affiliation sequence will apply, activating a need for comradeship in them that subsequently fosters their feelings of group belongingness.[26]

In other words, men tend to respond more to initiation severity, whereas women tend to seek affiliation regardless of the severity or mildness of their initiation. Conversely, Hautaluoma and Spungin report that severe initiations elicit more negative responses from men than women.[27] Either way, the presence of a sex difference suggests there may not be a one-size-fits-all approach to promoting solidarity with the group one initiates into. Particularly with a mixed-sex group, striking a balance may be necessary.

Hazing

The "severe" initiations in some studies are not representative of initiations into most magical groups. Initiation into college fraternities and sororities, in particular, often crosses the line into *hazing*. What, exactly, is the difference between an initiatory ordeal and hazing? Kent State

University anthropologist Aldo Cimino has been studying hazing—or, as he calls it, "aversive initiation practices"—since his 2013 doctoral dissertation.[28] He defines *hazing* as "non-accidental, costly aspects of group induction activities that: a) do not appear to be group-relevant assessments/preparations, or b) appear excessive in their application."[29] Lodewijkx and colleagues' study of university fraternities and sororities noted that initiations at Utrecht University involved irrelevant and excessive practices such as:

> smearing of excrements in the hair of newcomers; the forced drinking of cod-fish oil; the licking of the shoes of senior members; the pushing of a person's head onto a plate when, against orders, that person dared to speak; the embarrassing of newcomers by forcing them to say offensive and degrading words about themselves while facing a large crowd of people; the forcing of newcomers to do too many push-ups in the mud; the forcing of newcomers to perform roll-calls that took too long, causing fainting; and the forcing of newcomers to crowd into too small rooms, also causing fainting.[30]

Other commonly coerced behaviors associated with college fraternities and sororities include eating disgusting food, forced drinking games, simulated or actual sexual activity, getting tattooed/pierced/branded, and physical assault. Consequently, the list of hazing-related deaths on campuses is extensive and concerning.

Cimino and Thomas studied six sets of fraternity inductees from 2012 to 2014, 126 inductees total, as they underwent their ten-week induction. They found that severity was unrelated to liking of the group and only slightly related to solidarity. Whether the inductee thought it was "fun" was a much better predictor of liking the group. In the end, they concluded that "hazing may not be the social glue it has long been assumed to be."[31] This echoes Hautaluoma and colleagues' caution that "severe initiations can have strong negative side effects and . . . might not be the most effective in producing desired outcomes."[32] Lest there be any doubt, Mann and colleagues' three studies of severe initiations with 435 novices concluded that "severe initiations may, due to experi-

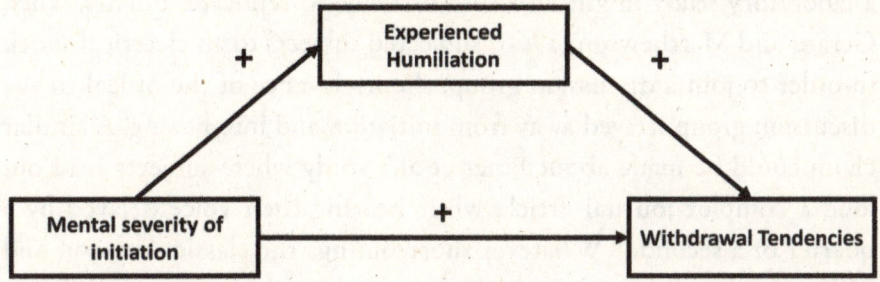

Fig. 10.3. Initiation severity and humiliation reduce group affiliation and promote a tendency to withdraw.
Image by the author based on data from Mann et al., "Withdraw or Affiliate?"

enced humiliation, result in less rather than more affiliation with fellow novices."[33] The diagram (fig. 10.3) illustrates how initiation severity and humiliation both contribute to less affiliation to a group, and may even lead to exiting the group.

The compulsion to haze newcomers is prevalent among the general population. Since putting research subjects through the extreme hazing typical of college fraternities is unethical, Cimino did a thought experiment in which a representative sample of the United States imagined themselves to be members of a longstanding and highly cooperative group. The overwhelming majority (84 percent) chose to add a stressful component to the initiation of new members. Women and older respondents indicated less of a desire to haze inductees.[34]

Initiation Ordeals Redux

Given this body of research, one might assume that a laboratory study is a poor approximation of real-life initiations. Is having to say "screw" out loud really comparable to a weeks-long process of intimidation and humiliation? As Aldo Cimino points out, it's like comparing stubbing a toe to losing a leg:[35] "It is also unclear that the experience of joining strange and ephemeral laboratory groups is a good psychological proxy for the experience of joining the kind of serious and enduring coalitions that tend to engage in non-trivial hazing in the real world."[36] One factor driving attraction to a group is how interesting it is[37] . . . something that a laboratory study might also find difficult to replicate. Finally, when Gerard and Matthewson (1966) subjected subjects to an electrical shock in order to join a discussion group, the irrelevance of the ordeal to the discussion group strayed away from initiation and into hazing. A similar claim could be made about Finer et al.'s study where subjects read out loud a complex journal article while hearing their voice delayed by a quarter of a second.[38] Whatever shortcomings the classic Aronson and Mills (1959) study may have had in hindsight, at least the ordeal (being able to say sexually explicit words without undue embarrassment) was relevant to the group (discussion of sexuality).

Several follow-up studies have affirmed the severity-attraction hypothesis. Adding a wrinkle to this trend, when Kamau (2012) failed to replicate this study, they mused that, in their version of the study, "the initiation might not have been severe enough to create dissonance."[39] But too severe an ordeal—such as hazing—leads to dislike, anger, humiliation, or resentment, pushing people away. The same could be said of an irrelevant ordeal. Taken together, there may be an optimal level of initiation severity—neither too much nor too little—which results in the initiate perceiving a group as more attractive. This optimal level, however, may differ for male versus female initiates.

"HE MUST TEACH"

The teaching function of initiation is well-suited to the physiological responses common in candidates.* When someone encounters a novel or stressful situation, the brain kicks into action to perform two tasks: evaluate whether the situation is dangerous, and decide how best to react. These two tasks follow distinct pathways in the brain. Both start with the amygdala, a pair of almond-shaped structures on either side of the brain involved in emotions, learning, and decision-making. It is part of

---

*My description in *Perdurabo* of Aleister Crowley's initiation into the Golden Dawn once received the criticism, "How do you know his throat was dry?" Dry throat being one of the common experiences of hyperarousal, I thought to myself, "You've never been initiated, have you?"

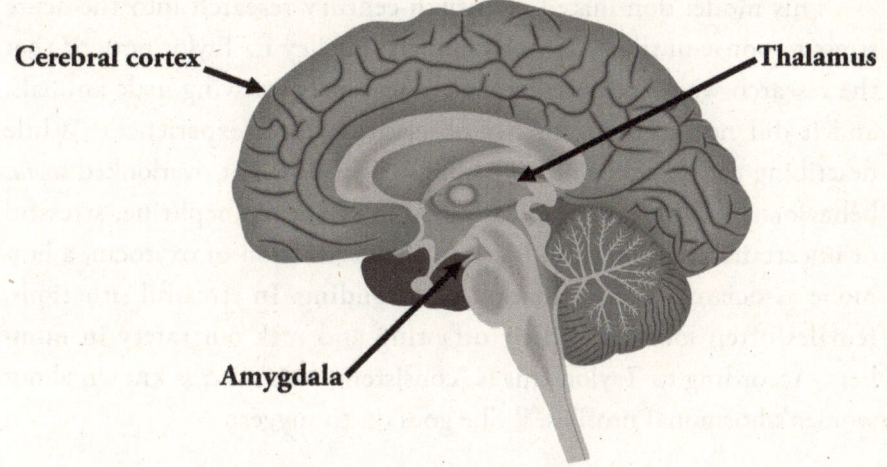

Fig. 10.4. The human brain, highlighting a few relevant areas.
DataBase Center for Life Science (DBCLS), labels added by author

the limbic system, which is the brain's danger-detector or, generally speaking, stimulus-definer. In uncertain settings, the amygdala signals the sympathetic nervous system—including the adrenal and pituitary glands—to release hormones such as ACTH and epinephrine, which speeds the heart rate and prepares the body to take action. This is the quicker-acting of the two processes. Next, the cerebral cortex kicks in. This part of the brain is involved in thinking, learning, and problem-solving. It's our thinky-bits. The cerebral cortex evaluates whether the novel situation is dangerous. If it is, the body is ready to take action. If not, the parasympathetic nervous system calms things down again.

Fight-or-Flight (or . . . ?)

Human responses to this activation of the brain and body have been the subject of study for more than a century, and our understanding has evolved over the years. In the early twentieth century, Walter Bradford Cannon first described what came to be widely known as the fight-or-flight response: In response to a threat, the adrenal or sympathetic nervous system prepares an animal to protect itself by taking one of two actions: fighting or fleeing.[40]

This model dominated twentieth-century research into the acute stress response until UCLA psychologist Shelley E. Taylor noticed that the research was developed by male researchers studying male animals, and it did not account for her observations and experiences. While describing the response of individuals, fight-or-flight overlooked *social* behaviors. In addition to releasing ACTH and epinephrine, stressful or uncertain situations also increase the production of oxytocin, a hormone associated with affiliation and bonding. In stressful situations, females often look after their offspring and seek out safety in numbers. According to Taylor, this is "consistent with what is known about women's hormonal profiles."[41] She goes on to suggest:

> The causes of death that largely account for men's early mortality are those related to the fight or flight response, namely aggressive responses to stress, withdrawal in the form of substance abuse, and coronary artery disease, the risk for which is exacerbated by frequent or recurrent stress exposure. By contrast, women more reliably turn to their social contacts in times of stress, responses that are, as just noted, protective of health and longevity. The fact that men may be somewhat more likely to cope with stress via fight or flight and women to cope with stress via tend and befriend may help to explain the worldwide gender gap in mortality.[42]

In 2000, Taylor and colleagues coined the term *tend-and-befriend* as a counter to *fight-or-flight*.[43] This idea wasn't entirely new—Schachter, as described earlier, noted the relationship between stress and social affiliation back in the 1950s, and it became one of the prevailing theories in the psychology of initiation. However, Taylor and colleagues accounted for a gender difference, and framed it as an alternative to fight-or-flight, inspiring new research on hyperarousal.

This new research has largely supported tend-and-befriend as a different response to stress, generally more common among women than men. For example, Turton and Campbell administered a questionnaire containing sixty-one items describing responses to stress to forty participants, eighteen male and twenty-two female. They analyzed the data using a statistical technique known as factor analysis, which identifies sets of questions that tend to correlate or elicit similar responses, grouping or clustering these items together into underlying "factors" or concepts that account for the data. Turton and Campbell found that their questions fell into four categories, which described the responses of fight, flight, tend, and befriend. Women responded more favorably to items depicting the tend and befriend responses to stress.[44]

Researchers at the University of Chicago examined the self-report and decision-making behavior of sixty men and sixty women. Half constituted a control group, while half experienced psychosocial stress through the Trier Social Stress Test. This standardized test is used to simulate psychosocial stress in a laboratory setting. Subjects were told to prepare a five-minute presentation on themselves for a mock job interview in front of two judges making up the selection committee. This presentation would be video recorded for later analysis. The judges—accomplices of the researcher(s)—maintained neutral expressions and provided no feedback. If the person stopped speaking before their five minutes were up, the judges would sit silently, waiting for the speaker to continue. When the five minutes were up, the subject was asked to subtract seventeen from 2023 out loud, repeating until they reached zero. If at any point the subject made a mistake, the judges would point out the mistake and ask them to start over again. This stressful ordeal completed, subjects next engaged in a standard decision-making task, such as the Prisoner's Dilemma game, in which one engages with another player to maximize their own score. It can be played either competitively or cooperatively, with competitive approaches typically leading to a breakdown of trust and both players' scores being dismal. Researchers concluded that "stress renders males more selfish and competitive, while stressed females become more other-oriented, more generous, and more cooperative. These effects are consistent with the 'flight or fight' pattern for males and the 'tend and befriend' pattern for females, respectively."[45] Observations like these have led to a blending of these two alternative responses into a more general hyperarousal model of fight, flight, or fawn (i.e., trying to appease or reduce the threat).

More recently, researchers have proposed a fourth possible behavior:

freeze. This refers to a state of attentive immobility. Those who have undergone, witnessed, or officiated initiations will be familiar with what is often referred to as "deer in the headlights" behavior from candidates: Wide-eyed, overwhelmed, and uncertain what to do, the initiate simply goes along for the ride while taking in as much as they can. What they take in may be fairly limited: Oftentimes initiates, later observing the initiation of another, will remark that they didn't recall, or had forgotten, experiencing certain of the things they saw the other person go through. This is consistent with our discussion in chapter 3 about the unreliability of autobiographical memory in the context of ritual.

Such memory lapses are not exclusive to initiation. In late 2023, social media was abuzz with reports of people who spent large sums of money, sometimes traveling great distances, to attend Taylor Swift's "Eras" tour, only to complain of "post-concert amnesia." Reading reviews of fellow attendees, these fans could not recall certain songs

Fig. 10.5. Hyperarousal led some attendees of Taylor Swift's Eras tour (2023–2024) to report "post-concert amnesia," a kind of memory lapse familiar to candidates for initiation into magical groups.
Photo by Paolo V

or other events taking place. Looking at their phones, they could not remember snapping the photos, and did not recognize the videos they shot. This experience has been attributed to a combination of hyperarousal and being distracted by one's devices (rather than being present in the moment).[46]

Some have added to fight, flight, fawn, or freeze a fifth option: flop. It refers to literal incapacitation in the face of hyperarousal, such as fainting. These observations emerge from experiences working on trauma response, particularly post-traumatic stress disorder (PTSD).

Whatever the model—fight, flight, fawn, freeze, flop, or something else—psychosocial stress produces a physiological response that plays out at both the hormonal and information-processing levels. The unknown and unexpected nature of initiation elicits this response. The enhanced information processing and environment evaluation state of the candidate renders initiation an ideal vehicle for instruction.

Cognitive Resource Depletion

According to Schjoedt and colleagues' theory of cognitive resource depletion, hyperarousal in rituals and other religious interactions creates conditions that "facilitate the transmission of cultural ideas."[47] This happens through three mechanisms:

1. Expressive suppression. High-arousal rituals limit how much perceptual information one can process, opening the way for ideas to be received from the ceremony itself.
2. Goal-demoted and causally opaque actions. Ritualized behavior lacking a concrete cause-effect relationship can suppress comprehension and meaning construction.
3. Charismatic authority. The presence of a religious leader or similar figure will "down-regulate regions in the frontal executive network that are involved with error monitoring and updating."[48]

Taken together, they argue, these three features prevent participants "from forming their own accounts of religious interactions," thereby allowing them "to experience rituals in accordance with authoritative suggestions, narratives, and interpretations."[49] This framework has been subject to serious criticism: The authors' sweeping literature review and theoretical model concludes with thirty pages of commentary from other readers providing detailed critiques. In my own experience, attendees of rituals or candidates for initiation are not constrained from drawing their own conclusions. Indeed, aside from post-initiation knowledge lectures that point out the historical or symbolic nature of certain details of the ceremony, initiates are encouraged—if not outright challenged—to ponder their experience to find further meaning independently.

Surprise!

Surprise is defined as "the sense of astonishment and wonder that one feels toward the unexpected."[50] It plays a key element in initiation, as these ceremonies often rely on the candidate not knowing what is going to happen. This keeps the candidate engaged and open to the psychological benefits of surprise.

The psychological study of surprise is a relatively new field, but one thing is clear: Brains like surprises. Dopamine neurons in monkeys fire when receiving a reward, and fire greatest when the reward is unexpected.[51] A 2001 functional MRI study in human volunteers showed that activation of the dorsolateral prefrontal cortex (which is associated with learning and executive function) is highest under conditions of unpredictability and violations of learned associations or expectations.[52] Another fMRI study done that same year at Emory University looked at the brain's reward centers (nucleus accumbens and medial orbitofrontal cortex). Participants indicated whether they preferred water or juice, and then received random tastes of water or juice. While cortical brain activity increased when participants received their favored drink, activity in the reward centers increased as a function of unpredictability.[53]

Not only is surprise pleasing to our brains, but it's also conducive to learning. "We learn more from surprising information," Mellers and colleagues write, "and we are often more persuaded by a surprising argument."[54] This phenomenon has been well-understood in psychology for decades. The Pearce Hall model of Pavlovian learning proposes that unexpected or surprising events command an animal's attention toward both the surprising event and the accompanying stimuli. This in turn leads to quicker learning.[55] Extending this to humans, infants and children learn faster from impossible events (e.g., those accomplished through sleight of hand or other trickery), which Stahl and Feigenson dub *expectancy violations*.[56] As they note, "When children's basic expectations about object behavior were violated by impossible outcomes, children learned better than when their expectations were confirmed."[57] Similarly, in an fMRI study among a group of twenty-five adults, expectancy violations in magic tricks produced increased activity in the caudate nucleus, an area of the brain associated with learning, reward, and goal-directed activity.[58]

In initiation, surprise helps the candidate enter an attentive and receptive state for the information to be communicated, whether it be instruction, passwords, secret handshakes, or anything else. As Masons tell the viewer in the documentary series *Inside the Freemasons*, "We try and keep bits of it secret because that makes it more enjoyable," and "It's like having a surprise party and knowing everybody who's coming, and what your gifts are. It's not going to be the same if it's not a surprise."[59] Exposés of initiation rituals have been widely published in books and posted online. However, "reading ahead" by candidates only spoils the surprise, and it deprives themselves of the intended transformative effect of the ritual.

Insight, or the Eureka Experience

In the course of initiation, a candidate may confront or be presented with a question, asked to contemplate a puzzle, or prompted to take an unspecified action. One classic example comes from Sophocles' play *Oedipus Rex*. As the tragic Greek character Oedipus sets out on his initiatory journey from Thebes and Delphi, he encounters the Sphinx, whose riddle he must answer in order to pass. "What walks on four feet in the morning, two in the afternoon, and three at night?" Oedipus provides the correct answer: humans. They crawl on all fours as infants, walk on two legs as adults, and in old age walk with a cane.

The answer in initiation doesn't always come as easily as it did to

Fig. 10.6. In Sophocles' play *Oedipus Rex*, Oedipus at the outset of his journey encounters the sphinx and must answer its riddle to continue (from François Xavier Fabre, *Oedipus and the Sphinx*, circa 1807).

Oedipus. But when it happens, that "Aha!" or "Eureka!" moment of realization is very powerful. It's the difference between knowing something and discovering it. This is another argument for why reading exposés of an initiation before taking it only cheats oneself of the benefits of a full, rich experience.

In the laboratory, figuring out the "trick" behind magic tricks has proven to be a good way to simulate the satisfying "Aha!" experience.[60] These experiences tend to be accompanied by feelings of pleasure, the sudden onset of the solution, and certainty in the solution's correctness.[61] The downside is that people who have insights that produce incorrect solutions (or associate the insight with incorrect facts) can be very attached to these beliefs.[62]

Within the brain, fMRI reveals that insight is associated with increased activity in areas associated with comprehension and making connections between pieces of information (in the right hemisphere anterior superior temporal gyrus); also, EEG reveals a burst of gamma band activity in the same region a third of a second before the "Aha!" moment dawns on the person.[63]

From a learning and initiation standpoint, solutions attained through insight are recalled better two weeks later than solutions arrived at through other means.[64] This suggests that any lessons conveyed by the ritual experience will be more enduring. In addition, the "Aha!" experience is an instance of what cognitive psychologists call *discovery learning*, or learning through exploration and play. This stands in contrast to *direct instruction*, in which information is taught by lecture or presentation.[65] Both styles have their advantages: Direct instruction favors achievement tests, while discovery learning favors creativity and problem-solving. An initiation with opportunities for each gives the candidate the best of both worlds.

Nor does the opportunity to learn end when the ceremony does. Attending the initiation of future candidates is an opportunity to play a supportive role in the induction of another person, while vicariously reliving one's own initiation. The inaccuracy of autobiographical memory around high-arousal rituals also means that people will notice details that they don't recall from their initiation. This provides an opportunity to refresh and reaffirm all the experiences, lessons, oaths, or other experiences of one's initiation.

Initiatory groups often require people to demonstrate the instructions of their initiation in order to attend future ceremonies. A guard may be posted outside the meeting room, and—like the sphinx in Oedipus's journey—require communication of the appropriate signs and words before they can enter. In some cases, attendees may face "questions to be answered," interrogations about their initiation for which a specifically worded answer is provided. Such testing may be required not only when attending the initiation of others but also for attending other meetings.

Aside from proving that somebody meets the requirements to enter a secure, sacred space, these modes of recognition serve other functions. Degree testing recapitulates key moments from an initiation, refreshing and reaffirming the experience in a similar way to attending the initiation of another candidate. In addition, repetition and rehearsal are fundamental elements in learning and moving knowledge into long-term memory. Degree testing therefore provides an opportunity to exercise one's knowledge, and to be mindful of the lessons of one's initiation.

Along these lines, Oman and colleagues found that memorization and meditation on biblical passages promote not only attention to and retention of the passage's principles but also increase behavioral change through spiritual modeling (an idea that will be discussed below).[66] These benefits are not necessarily exclusive to scripture: They could also apply to memorization and meditation on other meaningful texts, including one's oaths, modes of recognition, and other elements of initiation.

Lessons Learned

Taken together, we've seen theories and research in psychology describe how people undergoing the ordeal of initiation are in a state of arousal, primed to pay attention to their surroundings, taking in information to assess the situation. Provided the ordeals are in that sweet spot—enough to create a state of arousal, but not so much as to breed resentment or withdrawal from the group—the initiates are primed to take in instruction. This is further facilitated by other common features provided by initiation: surprising events and moments of insight.

CH-CH-CHANGES

If an initiate indeed receives new information and new experiences through which to understand the world and their place in it, one would hope to see this reflected in changed behavior. Indeed, an initiate may take specific oaths to do or not do certain things. Like a New Year's resolution, there's great potential for change, but also for these changes to taper off over time. Let's look at the features of initiation, and magical groups, that impact one's behavior in both the short and long term.

Cognitive Dissonance

One mechanism for behavioral change is cognitive dissonance, discussed earlier in this chapter. As a reminder, we like our attitudes and behavior to be consistent. When they are not, we experience tension and seek resolution. In initiation, a candidate may pledge, in front of their community, to do (or not do) certain things. This creates a drive to behave consistently with this publicly sworn oath. While one could trivialize the seriousness of one's oath and break it with one's behavior, that would be challenging to do in a community that takes these things seriously. The more likely route is that the initiate will attempt to adhere to their vows and acclimate to the group norms. In her 1989 ethnographic study of Wiccan and ceremonial magick groups, anthropologist Tanya Luhrmann used the term *interpretive drift* to describe the process of a member's views gradually aligning with those of the group.[67]

Role-Playing

Initiation, as a dramatic ritual, may thrust the candidate unexpectedly into playing the role of a historical figure; a biblical, mythical, or heroic character; or some person other than themselves in the mundane world. The place where the initiation occurs may symbolize a location—real or symbolic—other than the physical temple, meeting room, basement, garage, or woods: the mount of initiation, the Vault of Christian Rosenkreutz, the outdoor gathering place of generations of witches. The officiants in the ceremony may also take on unfamiliar roles . . . even if that role is High Priestess in a sacred rite, rather than the person you had coffee with at the local pagan Meetup.

Role-playing, thus, plays a big role (ha!) in initiation. While psychologists generally haven't focused on role-playing specifically in magical initiation, they *have* looked at the psychology of role-playing games, debate teams, acting, therapy, and education. According to game researcher and designer Sarah Lynne Bowman, "Roleplaying creates the potential for self-exploration in the form of identity alteration, problem-solving in the form of scenario building, and establishment of *communitas* as a modern-day ritual practice."[68] The concept of identity alteration is particularly interesting in the context of initiation, as it "allows the player to explore possibilities otherwise unavailable to him/her in the mundane world."[69]

Research on role-playing predates the emergence of popular imaginative games such as Dungeons and Dragons in the 1970s. As far back as the 1950s and 1960s, psychologists examined how role-playing influences attitudes and behavior. One early study by Janis and King (1954) demonstrated that active role-playing of a particular viewpoint produced more attitude change than silently reading a similar argument. They concluded that "overt verbalization induced by role playing tends to augment the effectiveness of a persuasive communication."[70] In their follow-up study, King and Janis (1956) reported that role-play that involves improvising a position different from one's own produces more attitude change than simply reading aloud a prepared argument provided by the experimenter. This clarified the previous study, showing that attitude change did not result from merely speaking out loud, but that "improvisation heightens the acceptance of new ideas."[71]

In the late 1960s, psychological experiments tackled the public good of smoking cessation. In his 1966 study, Alan Elm randomly assigned eighty smokers to one of two conditions: Half of them role-played a nonsmoker, while the others listened to a role-player's improvised arguments in favor of quitting smoking. As with King and Janis (1956), Elms found that the role-players' attitudes changed more than the listeners'. One powerful predictor of attitude change among the role-players was *empathic fantasy ability*: the ability to imagine situations other than the present moment, which includes imagining oneself holding different attitudes.[72]

Other studies of "emotional" role-playing asked smokers to imagine themselves as lung cancer victims who required surgery and would need to stop smoking. In one study, the scenario was powerful enough that attitudes changed for both the role-players and the controls who simply listened to a recording of a role-playing session.[73] Mann and Janis (1968) found in their eighteen-month follow-up that the lung cancer role-players smoked significantly less than those who simply listened to an audio recording.[74]

In the 1990s, McGregor conducted a meta-analysis of twenty-six published studies that reported forty-three relevant sets of results on role-playing and antiracist education. When the findings of these studies were mathematically combined, role-playing emerged as being very effective at reducing racial prejudice.[75]

Role-playing may, however, inhibit one of the other mechanisms of group ritual: synchrony. A 2024 study by Lim and colleagues found a complex interaction between culture, sex, and role-playing. Broadly speaking, however, cooperative role-play resulted in more synchrony than competitive role-playing. However, role-playing appeared to create a state of inwardly focused self-regulation (for instance, concentrating on the role being played) rather than attending to cues from others, which would otherwise facilitate synchrony.[76] In the context of initiation, however, this may facilitate the goal of having the initiate to identify with their character in the sacred drama of initiation, instead of synchronizing or empathizing with other officers in the ritual (as might be the intention with communal group rituals).

If briefly stepping into someone else's shoes for a psychological lab experiment can cause attitude change, then the roles a candidate may adopt during their initiation—which is arguably far more important to them—must be influential indeed.

Leaders, Mood, and Modeling
As stated earlier, the lessons of initiation and their implications for behavioral change don't end with the ceremony. Attending the initiation of others, rehearsing modes of recognition, and other degree testing are all ways of recapitulating those lessons. Furthermore, the initiator and significant others in the group set the mood for both the initiation and subsequent meetings. They also serve as role models for new initiates.

Research on *emotional contagion* or *mood contagion* tends to focus on the psychology of leadership, where the mood of supervisors in the workplace—whether positive or negative—affects the mood of subordinates.[77] The same principle, however, can apply to how the mood of the initiator spreads to the other officers, the attendees, and the candidates. Furthermore, the mood of the master, priest/ess, or group leader (if different from the initiator) likewise sets the tone for other gatherings.

Neumann and Strack found that listening to the same emotionally neutral speech, spoken in either a sad or happy voice, produced a corresponding affective change in the listener.[78] Similarly, team leaders influence the mood of both individuals as well as the group as a whole.[79] Fortunately, a positive mood is more contagious than a negative mood.[80] Not only does a leader's positive mood transfer to other group members, but it also decreases conflict and promotes both cooperation and perceptions of work performance.[81] Fisher and Hess propose that mirroring another's emotions serves an affiliative function[82] . . . something salient to a fraternal or initiatory group. Wróbel and Imbir, meanwhile, propose that mood contagion and emotional mimicry may depend upon *social appraisal* of the other person: Whether a smile is reciprocated may depend on whether or not the smiler is liked or disliked.[83] Putting this all together, initiators should be conscious of how a positive mood can buoy the mood of attendees and candidates alike.

If people tend to mirror or mimic the mood of others, they are equally prone to mimic their behavior. The classic study of behavior modeling was Alfred Bandura's 1963 study of how children—after witnessing adults punch, kick, and otherwise abuse a large Bo-Bo the Clown inflatable doll—imitated this behavior.[84] That this behavior was imitated whether it was observed in person, on film, or (to only a slightly lesser degree) in a cartoon set off a firestorm of concern about how early exposure to violence, from television to video games to the internet, could cause aggressiveness in children.

In the context of occult groups, Luhrmann's ethnographic research illustrates how new members go through a period of acculturation, learning the group's norms.[85] More recently, Doug Oman at the University of California, Berkeley, along with Albert Bandura himself,[86] extended the latter's social cognitive theory[87] to the topic of *spiritual modeling* to explain "the social learning of spiritual or religious beliefs, attitudes, and practices."[88] Spiritual modeling says that spiritual behaviors are often learned from people in their tradition—either everyday or prominent—who exemplify the spiritual qualities to which the respondent aspires. These exemplars can be either *community-based models* (e.g., clergy and other spiritual leaders, fellow congregants, parents, friends) as well as *prominent models* (famous people or scriptural figures associated with a given tradition, such as Mother Theresa and Mahatma Gandhi; or, for occultists, the likes of H. P. Blavatsky, Aleister Crowley, or Gerald Gardner). These spiritual models can serve as exemplars of compassion, forgiveness, meditation, charity, temperance, faith . . . or pretty much anything else that the individual values and seeks to emulate. Nearly every religious tradition affirms the importance of spiritual modeling. Self-efficacy can also be heightened by *divine proxy agency*, or calling on gods, angels, spirits, or other divine assistance in attaining goals.[89] The downside to spiritual modeling, as Silberman points out, is that people can also turn to negative figures as models, as was the case with the 9/11 terrorist attacks.[90]

Mahmud provides a succinct explanation of how spiritual modeling occurs through mentorship in Italian Freemasonry: "More advanced Maestre or Maestri teach Apprentices by example, guiding them along the path, teaching them how to recognize the signs; in the end, however, every initiation path is different. That is perhaps the most important and coveted secret of Freemasonry: that the secret cannot be revealed in words."[91] As it is often said in magick, the real secrets are incommunicable.

Within an occult initiatory tradition, the lesson is that Initiators, as well as all the other members of the group, must remain mindful that they are role models for newer members, and that their conduct is not only normative but also reflects on the group as a whole.

Demand Characteristics

The setting of an initiation may—intentionally or unwittingly—predispose a candidate to behave or experience things in a certain way. This can include behaving differently than they might under ordinary circumstances. In psychology, these behavior-shaping characteristics of the setting are called *demand characteristics*. Some of the most famous experiments in psychology demonstrate the role of demand characteristics.

Coinciding with the popularity of political thriller *The Manchurian Candidate* (1959) and its story of brainwashing,[92] research seemed to suggest that hypnotism could make people do antisocial or even self-harmful things that they would never otherwise do.[93] Martin Orne and Frederick Evans conducted their replication at the University of Pennsylvania, with the added wrinkle that some participants simply pretended to be hypnotized. In both conditions, subjects readily thrust their hand into a terrarium to pick up a venomous red-bellied black snake or threw "acid" into the face of a lab assistant. At no point was the participant—or lab assistant—in any actual danger. When the participants were debriefed, researchers asked the nonhypnotized participants why they did these seemingly dangerous things. They responded that being in a laboratory at a prestigious university, in a study conducted by respected scientists, they didn't believe these things were actually dangerous.[94] In other words, the experiment setting itself created a situation where volunteers behaved out of character.

Around this same time, Yale University psychologist Stanley Milgram did his famous experiment on obedience and authority. In what was presented as a study of the effect of punishment on learning, research subjects paired off into the roles of teacher and learner (the latter was an accomplice of the researcher). The learner was connected to a device designed to administer a mild electrical shock. The teacher was instructed to read a list of word pairs to the learner, and then repeat the first word of each pair, prompting the learner to give the second word. If the answer was incorrect, the teacher would administer a shock, turn up the shock level one notch, and continue the process. If at any point the teacher hesitated, the researcher, with his white lab coat and clipboard, would stress the scientific importance of proceeding. The real purpose of the experiment was to see how far the research subjects would go in administering punishment, as the actor in the learner role pretended to be shocked: Merely twitching at first, but subsequently expressing more pain, crying out, pleading to stop, and ultimately becoming unresponsive. The researchers, subjects, and readers of the study alike were horrified by how far one would go at the coaxing of an authority figure (the researchers) at a respected university such as Yale.*[95] While this study demon-

---

*As examples of how much this study has seeped into popular awareness, in 1976 William Shatner starred in *The Tenth Level*, a television movie inspired by Milgram's experiment; and Peter Gabriel's 1986 hit album *So* contained a track titled "We Do What We're Told (Milgram's 37)."

strated how people do inhumane things under authoritarian rule—Nazi Germany being the obvious metaphor—it also, like Orne, shows how the setting of an experiment can influence a participant's behavior.

In a study a little closer to the initiation experience, Orne and Schiebe's 1964 study examined how demand characteristics can lead to sensory deprivation experiences. All subjects were told they were in an experiment on sensory deprivation. Half the subjects (ten in all) were told they were the control group, and they were placed in a six-by-seven-foot room with a drapery-covered window and a two-by-four-foot observation window. There was a desk with two chairs. On the desk was a thermos of ice water, drinking glass, sandwich, microphone, and a stack of paper number sheets. Meanwhile, for the ten subjects making up the experimental group, the experimenter wore a white lab coat. In the room was a tray of medications and medical implements labeled "emergency tray"; although visible, the experimenter never referred to it. After taking down the subject's medical history, the experimenter recited these prepared instructions:

> While you are in the chamber, you will be under constant observation. Also, there will be a microphone through which anything you might say will be recorded. It is important that you report your experiences freely and completely. You are not expected to talk a great deal, but you should report any visual imagery, fantasies, special or unusual feelings, difficulties in concentration, hallucinations, feelings of disorientation, or the like. Such experiences are not unusual under the conditions to which you are to be subjected.
>
> If at any time you feel very discomforted, you may obtain release immediately by pressing the button which I will show you once we enter the chamber. Do not hesitate to use this button if the situation becomes difficult. However, try to stick it out if you can.
>
> Should you feel upset, or should anything untoward develop, a physician is immediately at hand.
>
> Remember, I should like you to pay special attention to any special visual or other sensations, or feelings of disorientation, and to report these experiences as they happen.[96]

They were then placed in *the exact same room* as the control group participants, with the addition of a red button labeled "Emergency Alarm." Even though the experimental group subjects were not actually in a sensory deprivation situation, they described perceptual anomalies: The walls wavered, or colorful spots appeared. The fluorescent lighting became dimmer, or yellower, or buzzed as loud as a jackhammer. Objects on the desk began moving, and the number sheets became blurry and turned into inkblot shapes. One of the ten experimental subjects even hit the panic button to end their session.

This experiment showed that explaining to subjects beforehand possible experiences they may have, as well as creating a setting with lab coats, medical implements, and a panic button, can prime them to experience sensory deprivation-like effects in decidedly ordinary settings. There is a lesson here for initiators to pay attention to what is in the space where the initiation will occur, taking care to remove any extraneous objects or symbols that might have an unknown or unexpected impact on the candidate's experience. The founder of the Society of Inner Light, Dion Fortune, who had a background in psychotherapy and counseling, echoed the thoughts of many magicians when she wrote, "Every object in a Lodge should be a symbolic representation of the different aspects of the force functioning upon the plane to which it is intended to raise the consciousness of the candidate. Nothing should be omitted, and nothing extraneous included."[97] (This is good advice for any ritual space, not just during initiations; as Crowley wrote, "The first point is the Banishing: Everything is to be removed from the room which is not absolutely necessary to the Work."[98])

Sitting alone in a room is a common experience for many candidates awaiting the start of their initiation. Perceptual distortions like those described in Orne and Schiebe (1964) could potentially occur here. There may be experimental support for individuals experiencing sensory deprivation-like effects from two common features of initiations: sequestration and blindfolding. Mason and Brady demonstrated that subjects placed in a dark, anechoic chamber can experience perceptual disturbances and hallucinations in as little as fifteen minutes.[99] It is worth noting that this experiment also used a panic button, which might have created similar demand characteristics to Orne and Schiebe.[100] Daniel and colleagues then replicated the Mason and Brady study, eliminating the panic button and adding a "secluded office" condition, in which participants sat in a vacant office for the same duration as subjects in the sensory deprivation room. Interestingly, even the "secluded office" controls reported significantly increased perceptual distortions and reduced pleasure after their seclusion.[101]

Finally, Orne and Schiebe's experiment shows that expectations or demand characteristics of a setting can prompt hallucinations and altered states of consciousness. Just as practices such as astral visions and pathworking help with thinking outside the box, initiation challenges initiates to look at the world through a different pair of glasses. Seeing the world or themselves differently ultimately prompts a genuine transformation of the Self.

CLOSING THE TEMPLE

In this chapter, we have looked at three main functions of initiation: a rite of passage, a method of instruction, and a force of change. An optimal level of initiation severity can increase liking for the group being joined. The physiological arousal of initiation—whether it's fight or flight, tend or befriend, flop or freeze—creates an attentional state conducive to learning, especially when coupled with opportunities for surprise and insight during the ceremony. In the end, the insights garnered from the experience can be transformative, especially when prompted by an oath, observed in the initiations of other candidates, and demonstrated by role models or others in the community.

11
The Method of Science and You

THE GUIDING PRINCIPLE OF THIS BOOK has been to feature scientific research whose results shed light on psychological processes at work/play while practicing magick. Likewise, in chapter 3 we talked about how keeping a journal helps to assess your work critically. Mystics and magicians—from Blavatsky to Crowley to Vivekananda—have praised science and described their approach as spiritual science. This position has been telegraphed in book titles such as Rudolf Steiner's *An Outline of Occult Science*, Dion Fortune's *Spiritualism in the Light of Occult Science*, Franz Hartmann's *Occult Science in Medicine*, Gerard Encausse's *Absolute Key to Occult Science*, among many others.[1] Israel Regardie similarly described magick as a "spiritual science . . . having for its objective the training and strengthening of Will and Imagination."[2]

Aleister Crowley, in particular, championed the notion of spiritual science. He coined the term *Scientific Illuminism* to describe his empirical, pragmatic, and skeptical approach to magick, subjecting his spiritual research to scientific rigor. "Magick," he wrote, "is the science and art of causing change to occur in accordance with the will. (Obviously then all scientific methods can be included in this term.)"[3] The motto of *The Equinox*, official organ of the A∴A∴, was "The Method of Science, the Aim of Religion," and he encouraged students to subject all spiritual claims to critical scrutiny. This was not easy, and he acknowledged the difficulty inherent in practicing Scientific Illuminism:

> Indubitably, Magick is one of the subtlest and most difficult of the sciences and arts. There is more opportunity for errors of comprehension, judgment and practice than in any other branch of physics. It is above all needful for the student to be armed with scientific knowledge, sympathetic apprehension and common sense.[4]

In his magnum opus, *Magick in Theory and Practice*, Crowley wrote, "No scientific hypothesis can adduce stronger evidence of its validity than the confirmation of its predictions by experimental evidence."[5] However, despite stressing its importance,[6] neither he nor any of the aforementioned writers clearly articulated *how* they applied science to their spirituality, let alone instruct others how to do so with the critical eye of a scientist.

Fig. 11.1. Cover design for volume I of *The Equinox* (1909–1913), proclaiming its mission to promote "The method of science, the aim of religion."

For ten years, I taught graduate-level classes in statistics and research design and methodology, plus medical school classes in evidence-based medicine. For my entire professional career, I have worked as a statistician. It's impossible to cover in one chapter a discipline about which entire books have been written, or which requires a semester-long course to explore the fundamentals, but we will take a whirlwind tour of the topic, including examples of how to apply these principles to your practices.

EPISTEMOLOGY: SOME WAYS OF KNOWING THE WORLD

At the outset, let's acknowledge that the scientific method isn't the only way of learning about the world. Here is a not-necessarily-complete list with examples.

Induction involves observation, from which one develops a hunch or theory. This is the first step in producing a hypothesis. A famous example involves smallpox, one of the deadliest diseases in human history. British physician Edward Jenner heard tales that milkmaids and other farm workers who had become ill with cowpox were immune to smallpox. This observation inspired Jenner to develop (and test) a theory of *inoculation*; that is, injecting nonimmune persons with a small dose of a virus in order to confer disease resistance. This would pave the way for the modern practice of immunization.[7] While Jenner wasn't the first person to make or test this theory, he is the one who became famous for it.

Deduction involves starting with a theory, belief, or hypothesis, and gathering data to see whether the facts support the idea. This is typically referred to as the scientific method, and this chapter will dive further into the details.

Dreams can be a way for our subconscious mind to work out solutions that evade our conscious thought processes. One notable example of such a breakthrough involves the molecular structure of benzene (C_6H_6), whose solution posed a major stumbling block to the advancement of organic chemistry until the early 1860s. Researcher

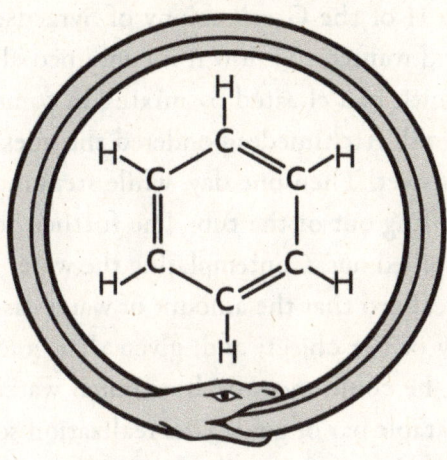

Fig. 11.2. Kekulé's daydream of the ouroboros eating its tail reputedly inspired discovery of the benzene ring.

Friedrich Kekulé's daydream of the ouroboros snake inspired the solution, which is known today as the benzene ring. Kekulé told his colleagues, "Let us learn to dream, gentlemen, then perhaps we shall find the truth . . . But let us beware of publishing our dreams till they have been tested by the waking understanding."[8]

Sometimes discoveries are made by *accident*. Rubber was originally soft and sticky, good for little more than an eraser because it melted in hot weather, and it became brittle when cold. Then one day in 1839, inventor and rubber salesman Charles Goodyear—who was experimenting on ways to "tan" or "cure" rubber the way one does with animal hides—gesticulated with a sample of sulfur-coated rubber in the shop of a prospective customer in Woburn, Massachusetts. Goodyear accidentally dropped his sample onto the general store's potbellied stove. As he apologetically scraped up the mess, Goodyear made a surprising discovery: The sample had become tough and resistant to the ravages of temperature extremes. He would spend the next five years perfecting this transformative process, which he dubbed "vulcanization" after Vulcan, the Roman god of fire.[9] Today, a line of automotive tires bears his name.

The so-called *Eureka* experience (discussed in chapter 10 as a revelatory experience that might happen in initiation) describes an unexpected flash of insight. The term comes from Archimedes' sudden solution to a puzzle. King Hieron II of the Greek colony of Syracuse had commissioned a gold crown and wanted to know if it contained all the gold provided, or if the goldsmith had cheated by mixing in some silver and keeping the rest of the gold. Archimedes pondered the question for several days without an answer. Then one day, while stepping into his bath, he noticed water spilling out of the tub. The further he sank into the tub, the more water spilled out. Contemplating the watery mess he had created, Archimedes realized that the amount of water displaced depended upon the density of the object; and, given that gold and silver have different densities, he could measure how much water the crown displaced versus a comparable bar of gold. This realization so overjoyed Archimedes that he hopped out of the tub and ran through the streets shouting "Eureka!"—Greek for "I've got it!"—on his way to tell the king.

Breakthroughs can also happen through *serendipity*: a stroke of luck or happy coincidence.[10] For example, the vasodilator known as minoxidil was originally produced as a treatment for high blood pressure. It just so happens that a significant side effect was later discovered: Minoxidil promoted hair regrowth. This led to the drug being reformulated as a topical application to treat androgenic alopecia (male or female pattern baldness).[11]

A subset of serendipity may be described as *dumb luck*. Consider Harvard political science student Stephen Young. The son of Kenneth Todd Young (U.S. ambassador to Thailand from 1961 to 1963), Stephen was canvassing Thai homes in 1966 with an opinion poll for his master's thesis. While walking through the village of Ban Chiang, he tripped on the root of a kapok tree and fell to the ground . . . finding himself face-first with the rim of a buried clay pot that had been exposed by a recent monsoon. This mishap led to the discovery of Southeast Asia's earliest Bronze Age site. The *New York Times* called it "one of the biggest accidental discoveries in archaeology."[12]

Some breakthroughs happen through *trial and error*. In the mid-1970s, mathematician Mitchell Feigenbaum with the Los Alamos National Laboratory was messing on his calculator with nonlinear equations for chaotic systems. He noticed the number 4.6692016090 popping up. The more equations he checked for the ratio of convergence, the more he found this value. Feigenbaum's constant, as it became known, demonstrated that there is a universal characteristic to nonlinear systems. This discovery revolutionized our understanding of chaos theory.[13]

Altered states of consciousness can open more than the doors of perception: They can open the doors to scientific breakthroughs. Francis Crick, co-discoverer of the double helix structure of DNA, enjoyed experimenting with cannabis and LSD, a fact that led to the controversial claim that Crick was tripping when he made the double helix breakthrough.[14] For a less controversial example, mathematician Bart Kosko arrived at some of his breakthroughs in the emerging field of fuzzy logic while experiencing a runner's high.[15]

Meditation or *introspection* can likewise be revelatory. Wilhelm Wundt, the father of experimental psychology and one of the founders of psychology as a scientific field in general, practiced *Selbstbeobachtung* or "self-observation," a form of controlled introspection that allowed methodical observations about thought processes and reactions to be replicated in a laboratory setting. While this exercise is arguably a form of induction based on self-reflection, the image of Wundt and his students systematically observing their mental processes always struck me as similar to structured meditational practices that involve observing the flow of consciousness and understanding its source.

While insights about the world can be gleaned from various experiences, they are ultimately tested and verified using the scientific method.

WHY NOT TRUST YOUR INSTINCTS?

You may be thinking, "Why make a big production of it? Can't I just go with my gut?" The short answer is no. Human beings are bad at things like judging probability, randomness, and coincidences—and at identifying cause-effect relationships. This is especially true when they are the ones doing the causing.

Consider "shuffle mode" on your favorite music device or app. As mentioned briefly back in chapter 2, shuffle mode originally played songs in truly random order. But companies began fielding complaints from customers that they were hearing songs from the same artist, or even off the same album, too close together. The problem is that, in a truly random list, the same song could repeat, and songs by the same artist might appear consecutively. When they do, however, people do not hear it as random. Instead, they perceive a pattern. "We don't like the idea of random meaning four Drake songs then three Kanye songs," Harrison Brockelhurst wrote for The Tab website. "We can't process the concept of random well, and it's in our nature to look for patterns and solutions when there aren't any."[16] Perversely, this has prompted companies to modify their algorithms to make them less random in order to make them feel *more* random.[17]

Those who believe in pseudoscience or superstition—the paranormal, anomalous or supernatural—perform even worse at gauging randomness.* Studies suggest that paranormal belief goes hand-in-hand with poorer probabilistic reasoning.[18] A fascinating twist emerged in one study comparing skeptics to believers in ESP using the classic Zener cards with five symbols: circle, square, wave, star, and cross. Different combinations of skeptics and believers paired up to act as senders and receivers in a test of telepathy (thought-transference). All participants did five trials with ten cards, or fifty guesses total. Believers estimated that they had more "hits" (correct guesses) than actually occurred, whereas skeptics' estimates were more accurate. Even more interesting, however, is that the chance rate of guessing one of the five symbols—20 percent—was achieved only in trials where both participants were believers. The other conditions, which included a skeptic in one or both roles, scored significantly *below* chance ($t_{19} = 2.23$, $p = .04$).[19] In short, while paired believers performed poorly on one metric (guessing the number of "hits" they got), groups with a skeptic in them performed poorly in another way (performing at less-than-chance levels).

---

*Many of the studies discussed cast a very wide net, lumping together belief in good luck charms or lucky numbers with things like Bigfoot, UFOs, astrology, ESP, nontraditional spiritual beliefs and the like, as if they were all the same thing, and may suffer from methodological pitfalls as explored in chapter 1. It is nevertheless wise to be aware of human foibles, so that we may better understand the need to avoid them.

Fig. 11.3. The five symbols in a deck of twenty-five Zener cards, commonly used in ESP experiments.

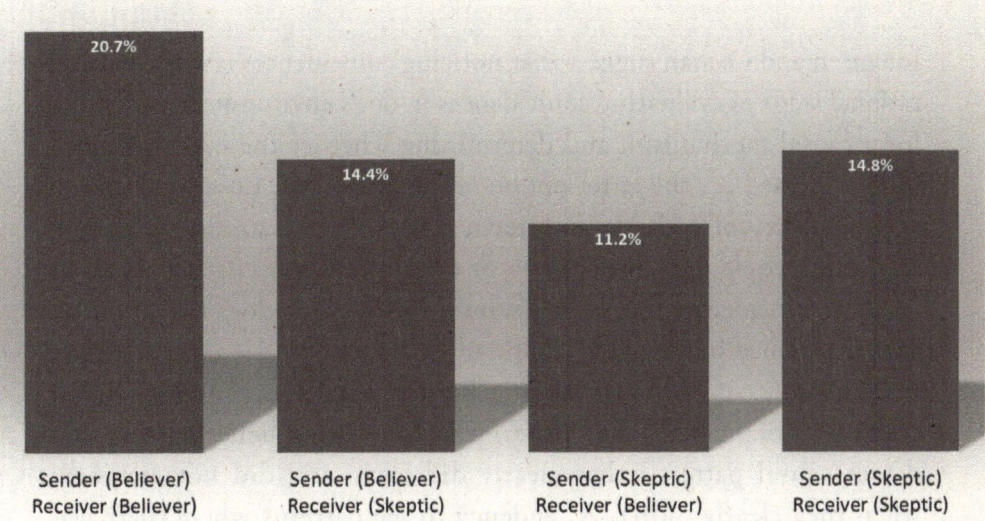

Fig. 11.4. Pairs of ESP believers performed at chance (20 percent) when guessing one of five symbols on fifty Zener cards, whereas groups with a skeptic in one or both roles performed significantly below chance.
Image by the author using data from Schienle, Vaitl, and Stark, "Covariation Bias and Paranormal Belief"

Despite the evidence that paranormal believers are simply bad at guessing probability and chance occurrence—especially when it comes to coincidences—something else may be accounting for this result. Bressan's study on coincidences, probability estimation, and paranormal beliefs concluded that believers do not underestimate the probability of chance occurrences. Instead, they have a greater tendency to see meaningful patterns and require less evidence to conclude there is a cause-effect relationship. This goes back to patternicity, discussed in chapter 2. As Bressan noted,

> Extreme scepticism appears biologically unnatural, and only possible in a culture where observed connections must carry the burden of proof before becoming established facts. The condition we are genetically equipped for is the search for bonds, patterns, meanings: paranormal belief represents its byproduct at least as much as the ability to classify, the love for music, or the gift for scientific discovery.[20]

Johansen and Osman suggest that noticing coincidences is a normal and rational stage of evaluating coincidences in one's environment, searching for a causal mechanism, and determining whether the event was random or caused . . . the latter option keeping open the door to suspicion and discovery of hitherto unknown causes.[21] As Cao and Feigenson reported, people may dismiss two or even three co-occurring events as "just" a coincidence, but as that number goes up, so does the suspicion that there must be some explanation.[22]

The idea of believers having higher patternicity tendencies is echoed by Blanco and colleagues, who found that believers correctly detect causal patterns that clearly did exist, and did not see them when they clearly didn't. A tendency to see patterns where there was none occurred only in situations where the pattern was ambiguous.[23] Similarly, Dagnall and colleagues have concluded from their studies that believers are perfectly capable of probabilistic reasoning; the difference occurs in perceptions of randomness (or seeing patterns where there are none).[24]

In short, patternicity may lead us to see patterns in randomness, whether it be in judging probability or seeing a cause-effect relationship.

While a great deal of research focuses on how believers are more likely to spot patterns, the converse is also true: Skeptics are more likely to miss (or dismiss) real patterns. In a study at Zurich University, twenty self-identified paranormal believers and twenty skeptics were asked to pick out real words or faces from images that mixed in scrambled words (making nonwords) or faces (with some features swapped around). Skeptics recognized fewer real words and real faces than did believers.[25] In short, while believers may be more likely to see a pattern where none exists, skeptics are more likely *not* to see a pattern where there really is one.

Humans also have biases about cause-effect relationships in which they are personally involved. In 1975, Ellen Langer defined *illusion of control* as "an expectancy of a personal success probability inappropriately higher than the objective probability would warrant."[26] She found that subjects doing a variety of tasks like cutting a deck of cards to see what card they get, selecting a lottery ticket, or betting on a racehorse, tended to equate these tasks with skill rather than chance. They overestimated their degree of control over the outcome. Rather than see this as a negative, Langer viewed it as "the inverse of learned helplessness,"[27] which could boost well-being among people who are debilitated by lost control over aspects of their lives, such as those in hospitals, retirement homes, or institutions. Similarly, Studer and colleagues suggest that boosting a sense of control can counteract quitting behavior when things get hard, encouraging people to persist in challenging circumstances such as rehabilitation, training, and maintaining an exercise routine.[28] Blanco and Matute point out that illusory control is also associated with optimism and positive attitudes.[29] These perspectives echo the view that ritual and magick increase in times of uncertainty as a way of creating a feeling of control over an uncontrollable situation. To the extent that magick increases feelings of control, it may be that extra dose of persistence that encourages the magician to persevere and attain their goals.

Griffiths and colleagues demonstrated the illusion of control in 2018. In their study, subjects (160 undergraduates who participated for course credit) sat at a computer with an image of an unlit light bulb. A button would appear for three seconds, which they could click or not. After the three seconds were up, the button was replaced by text indicating what the subject chose to do, either "Button pressed" or "Button not pressed." Sometimes the bulb lit up at the same time the text appeared. The screen would then clear, and a new trial would start. After forty trials, subjects were asked how much control their pushing the button had over the light. (In actuality, the light was programmed to randomly light up 60 percent of the time regardless of whether the button was pressed.) Most participants believed they had some degree of control over the light.[30]

In nonclinical samples, illusory control has received some interesting, if benign, interpretations. Some researchers suggest that illusions of control happen among individuals who are sensitive to cause-effect relationships, who respond to signal-like randomness, or who have a lower threshold for surprise at remarkable coincidences.[31] In other words, they are responding to evidence in what they see, and not uncritically seeing control everywhere they look. In comparison to others, those with a lower threshold for surprise or for seeing patterns will encounter more coincidences that are difficult to explain, and this may lead to entertaining—and ultimately accepting—supernatural explanations.[32]

As with probabilistic judgment, illusion of control seems to be higher among paranormal believers. In Griffiths and colleagues' study described above, superstitious beliefs correlated with perceived control over the light bulb. In a related study, van Elk reported that attendees of a psychic fair in the Netherlands were more likely to attribute positive outcomes to their control over the situation, while negative outcomes were written off as being due to something separate from themselves.[33] For the magical practitioner, this is a warning not to take credit only for your successes while disregarding your failures.

To sum it all up: Humans have hardwired biases toward seeing signals in noise, patterns where there are none, control over random outcomes, and agency over only positive outcomes. Believers may see evidence of success where there is none, while skeptics may dismiss important supporting evidence. The magician needs to keep these predilections in mind when trying to be a critical and objective evaluator of one's successes or failures. This is why we can't simply "trust our gut" when it comes to evaluating the efficacy of our magical work. We need to be objective and methodical. This is where the scientific method helps.

START WITH A HYPOTHESIS

Science begins with a question: a *hypothesis* about how the world works. Traditionally, hypotheses arise from observing the world and forming theories to account for one's observations. These theories are then tested for veracity through experimental manipulation. To be scientific, a hypothesis needs to satisfy several conditions:

1. It must posit some kind of cause-effect relationship between two things. The effect, in research jargon, is called the *dependent variable* because what happens to it depends on the causal (or experimentally manipulated) factor, which is called the *independent variable*.
2. A hypothesis must be measurable. If you can't measure the outcome, you have no idea whether your working *worked*. For this reason, magicians should begin evaluating their track record with intentions that are easy to measure, saving ambiguous concepts like wisdom, inspiration, or glory/thanks to one's patron deity until after you've honed your skills.
3. A hypothesis must be *falsifiable*. This means there is a possibility that your hypothesis could be disproved. Philosopher Karl Popper, who coined the term, observed among his Freudian and Marxist colleagues that whenever their theories failed to predict an outcome, they invoked some other part of the theory to explain why. No amount of contrary evidence could sway them from their beliefs.[34]

Avoid making excuses when things don't work out. A magician must be willing to say, "This didn't work."

To scientifically assess your magical work, you must state your intention clearly. It is not enough to say, "Making a talisman for money will work." Be specific and say, "Making a Jupiter talisman for money will bring in extra income." One could even add a time limit, such as "within two weeks." This hypothesis meets the three requirements described above: It posits a cause-effect relationship between the independent variable (Jupiter talisman) and the dependent variable (extra money). Money can be measured (with more on that below in "Operationalize your study variables"). Finally, the hypothesis could be disproven if no extra income arrives within a reasonable time.

Once you have a solid hypothesis, you're halfway there. Just like Hobbits have second breakfast, scientists have a second hypothesis. That's because hypothesis testing requires *two* hypotheses: A *null hypothesis* (H_0) that says nothing is going on—there is no cause-effect relationship; and an *alternative hypothesis* (H_A) that says there is a relationship.

An experiment evaluates the null hypothesis. This is typically *not* what we are interested in, otherwise we wouldn't be bothering with the experiment. So why take this seemingly backward approach? It's because there is no universally accepted burden of proof to demonstrate that a statement is true. For instance, someone might claim that "All magicians wear black." How many black-clad occultists would it take to prove this statement? One? Ten? A hotel-full? The answer is that you'd have to see *all* of them to prove this claim to be true... an impossibility in most cases. However, producing only *one* occultist in tie-dye (or some other color) would disprove the statement. And if H_0 is false, then its opposite, the alternative hypothesis (H_A), must be true. In short, the only way to prove something is to *dis*prove its opposite. For the Jupiter talisman example, the null hypothesis (H_0) might be "Consecrating a Jupiter talisman for money will not affect my income," while the alternative (H_A) would be "Consecrating a Jupiter talisman for money will produce an increase in my income."

Fig. 11.5. Proving a statement like "All magicians wear black" to be true requires observing the entire universe of magicians. Disproving it takes only one exception.

WHAT: MEASUREMENT

Having established your null and alternative hypotheses about your independent and dependent variables, the next step is to *operationalize* the study variables. This involves defining how the concepts represented by your independent and dependent variables will be measured in practice. For example, it's the difference between intelligence (a concept), and an IQ score (a way of measuring intelligence). Since science relies upon replication to verify research findings and build up a body of evidence, it is critical that the experimenter (or someone else) can *exactly* reproduce the experiment and its findings.

Two concepts related to measurement are *reliability* and *accuracy*. *Reliability* says whether a measure is consistent; in other words, do repeated measurements of the same thing produce more or less the same number? One's magical robe size, for instance, is very consistent. Heart rate, on the other hand, can vary quite a lot from moment to moment depending on activity level. Neither one, however, is an *accurate* measure of financial status. While the error in this example is pretty obvious on the surface (what scientists call *face validity*), choosing the best way to measure a variable is not always so clear. This is nevertheless a critical element in research. Doing good science requires measures that are both appropriate and consistent.

For our Jupiter talisman example, the following are questions to consider regarding the *independent variable*: What Jupiter talisman will be consecrated? Does its design come from a particular grimoire, book of shadows, or similar source? What will it be made of? What color will it be? What specific ritual will you do to consecrate it? When will it be consecrated? For the *dependent variable* or *outcome*: How will you assess your financial status? Will you go by your bank balance? How much money is in your wallet? Your crypto account? Something else? To get a clear picture of income, a series of different measures may be necessary. It could be a combination of one's checking account balance, savings account, wallet, PayPal balance, and so on. Thus, we could identify a particular Jupiter talisman for money, a specific ceremony for its consecration, and define "money" as "any income above and beyond my regular paycheck."

WHO: THE TARGET POPULATION

The goal of research is to make a statement about some *population*. "Population" need not mean everyone in the world, but it *does* mean everyone in the world who meets particular inclusion criteria. For example, a study population may be defined as "likely voters," "women using hormone replacement therapy," or "U.S. Gulf War veterans." Even so, it is impractical to measure every person in a population.

Since an entire population cannot be measured, members of that population are *sampled* for inclusion in the study. If a sample from the population is selected both *randomly* (meaning that everyone has an equal chance of being selected) and *independently* (meaning that who gets selected isn't influenced by whether or not anyone else is selected), then there's a good chance that the sample will be a pretty faithful representation of the entire population. Failure to follow these rules can produce a *biased* or distorted picture of the population. Conclusions drawn from a biased sample will be misleading or incorrect.

There's no guarantee that a random and independent sample will resemble the population. The luck of the draw may produce a weird sample no matter how careful the researcher is. It's the nature of random selection. This possibility can be minimized by using a large sample: The bigger the sample, the better the odds that it will be representative of the population. This is easy to imagine if taken to extremes: In a sample of three people, each individual accounts for one-third of the data; one outlier will have an oversized influence on your results. Taken to the other extreme, if a particular population contains one hundred people, a sample of ninety-nine of them will resemble the entire population more than a sample of three.

In practice, a magician will have a very different definition of a sample or population. The only person observed, for instance, may well be oneself—or, at best, a small group of friends or students. As magician Rodney Orpheus notes about fellow magicians using the scientific method, "Unlike a conventional scientist, you are performing experiments on yourself, not on some inert substance."[35] Even if the population consists of only you, a single observation doesn't provide a complete picture of what you're like from day to day. A study with one observation also has very low statistical power for rejecting the null hypothesis.

If you are the only magician participating in the "study"—as will be the case with most people—one solution is to repeat the "experiment" on multiple occasions. For instance, you could consecrate a Jupiter talisman and measure its effect on your financial status once a month for a year. This is where keeping a magical record is valuable.

What if you are fortunate enough to have a group of people willing to participate in the experiment with you? Ensure that everyone follows the exact same procedure. Be aware that the participants constitute a *convenience sample*: It consists of participants who are convenient to the researcher; their selection is neither random nor independent. Thus, the results may not be representative of the target population. You and your circle of co-experimenters may differ in experience, study, or some other quality from the general population of "magicians," "ceremonial magicians," "Wiccans," and so on. This doesn't mean that evaluating your work is impossible: It simply means that you must be cautious in extending your findings to those who did not participate in your study. (This will be discussed further in "Conclusions.")

HOW: RESEARCH DESIGN

Having decided on who and what to measure, the "how" is crucial for evaluating whether the null or alternative hypothesis better accounts for your results. There are a lot of different ways to do a study, and these designs all have inherent strengths and weaknesses. No one approach is bulletproof, and science relies on replication using different methodologies to thoroughly vet research findings.

The most basic research design—consisting of the intervention followed by observation of the outcome—can be illustrated as in figure 11.6. The pentagram indicates the intervention (the magick), the horizontal line represents time, and the Eye of Horus represents observing and assessing the outcome. In our example, this would mean consecrating a Jupiter talisman, followed by checking your bank balance.

Fig. 11.6. Intervention and observation only.

Fig. 11.7. Pretest and post-test.

This is a pretty poor design because you don't know what was in your bank account before you made the talisman.

A better design might look something like figure 11.7. Here, you have a *pretest* and a *post-test*; in other words, measurements made both before and after the experiment. This allows you to detect a change in your bank balance.

Variations in research design include adding a *control group*, in which a comparable observation is made but there is no experimental manipulation. For a solitary magician, this would mean observing a comparable time period without the talisman, either before doing your working or after you've destroyed the talisman. This could be represented like figure 11.8 or figure 11.9 on page 242, depending on whether the control condition has a pre-test.

You may recall from chapter 10 that Martin Orne's criticism of prior studies on hypnosis and antisocial behavior was the lack of a comparison or control group; when he added one, he found that subjects who were not hypnotized behaved in a similar way to the experimental group.[36] The example shown in figure 11.9 is the most common

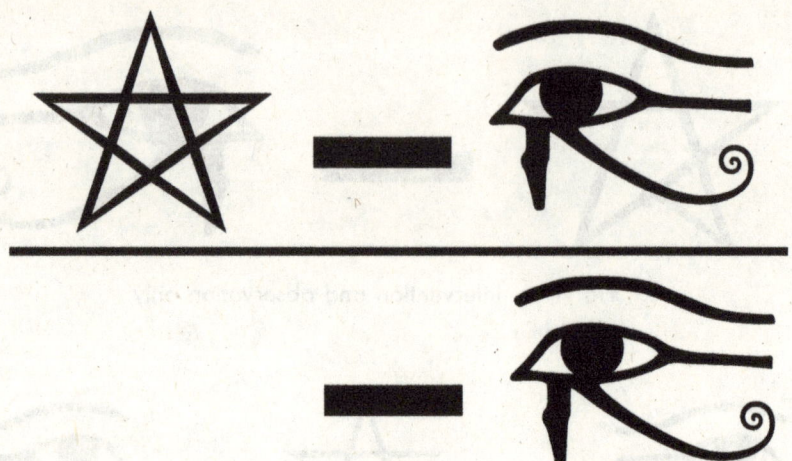

Fig. 11.8. Control condition (*below* the line) with no pre-test.

Fig. 11.9. Control condition (*below* the line) with a pre-test.

experimental design. It can detect change over time, plus determine if change in the experimental condition is greater than any change in the control condition. Many of the studies we've looked at use this design.

Finally, one could do a *time series* design, where multiple observations are made over time, as shown in figure 11.10. The advantage of this approach is that a single post-test observation could miss the moment when there is a change. One might measure too soon or too late. Multiple observations also allow one to see how enduring the effects of the experimental manipulation are.

Fig. 11.10. Time series, multiple observations made over time.

Research design will determine how you conduct your experiment and how you evaluate your results. For our purposes, let's keep things simple and go with the basic pre-post design: The magician will check their financial status, consecrate their talisman, wait two weeks to allow for the magick to happen, and then check their financial status again.

The next steps are easy: Conduct the experiment and collect your data!

WHAT HAPPENED?

Once you're on the other side of data collection, your study results are compared to the null hypothesis (H_0). Recall that this is the hypothesis that says nothing is going on: no cause-effect relationship. Researchers will ask "Do my results look like what I expected?" (according to H_0). Bear in mind that every outcome is possible due to chance even if H_0 is true; some outcomes are more likely than others, and some are extremely unlikely. If your results are too unlikely to be due to chance, you would reject H_0 (and accept H_A). If the results seem fairly likely—"nothing to see here"—then you would *not* reject H_0.

Regardless of which decision is made, there is always a chance you've made the wrong decision. You could reject the null hypothesis when it is actually true. And you might fail to reject the null hypothesis when it is wrong. These situations are ingeniously named the Type I and Type II errors. Not being the most obvious names, it might be helpful instead to think of these scenarios as "false positive" and "false negative," respectively.

Someone might arrive at the wrong conclusion for a variety of reasons. The researcher may simply have gotten "lucky" and obtained a very unusual finding. This is like being dealt a full house, or winning the lottery: Both are possible, but not likely. Alternately, a real cause-effect relationship could be obscured by too much "noise" in the data—random variation or other relevant effects that were not taken into account.

Fortunately, the field of statistics has solutions to these issues. It provides clear methods for calculating probabilities for any scenario. Statistics asks a technical version of the basic question "How unusual are my results?" Its question is "How far are my results from what I expected, relative to the amount of variation in my data?" For example, if you have only one source of income (your paycheck) and you receive the same amount every two weeks like clockwork, then a difference of one hundred dollars, fifty dollars, or even ten dollars would be unusual. By contrast, for someone whose work is seasonal, irregular, part of the gig economy, or otherwise unpredictable, an extra hundred dollars may not be that unusual. Statistics provides formulas and rules for making these decisions. The mathematics are too involved to explore here, but they are worth investigating for those interested in learning about empirical ways of calculating probability.

Let's look at a simple example for a basic idea of how this might work. Suppose you are debating whether to create a Jupiter talisman from your favorite grimoire versus consecrating a prosperity candle to Jupiter. You try a coin toss: heads for grimoire, tails for candle. To be sure, you toss the coin three times and take the best two out of three. If you got tails for all three tosses, you might wonder if something fishy is going on. Is the coin weighted strangely? Does it have tails on both sides? If we assume that you have a normal coin (H_0), then the chance of heads versus tails is 50/50, or .5. Half the time you expect heads, and half the time you expect tails. Thus, the probability of getting tails once is .5, and the probability of getting tails three times in a row is $.5 \times .5 \times .5 = .125$, or 12.5 percent. In other words, if you flipped a coin three times, you would expect three tails once out of eight attempts. That isn't very unusual—in statistics, 5 percent or one time in twenty is often the line to cross to reject the null hypothesis.

COMPETING EXPLANATIONS

After deciding whether to reject the null hypothesis, another consideration is whether you've correctly identified the cause-effect relationship. This is referred to as *internal validity*. Classic texts on the subject identify various *threats to internal validity*, or possible alternative explanations that could account for your findings.[37] (There are also threats or competing explanations focused on statistical validity, construct validity, and external validity—thirty-seven in all—but for simplicity, we will focus on internal, cause-effect alternatives here.) As would any scientist, your job as a critical and rational evaluator of your magical work is to consider whether you can rule these out. If one or more of these seem plausible, then acknowledge that your conclusion isn't ironclad. Here's a quick rundown of some major competing explanations:

The outcome might be due to *history*. Some event completely unrelated to your experiment may have happened in the world at large that caused the outcome you observed. For the Jupiter talisman example, this could include situations where your employer is doing well and gives *all* employees, not just you, a profit-sharing check; or where everyone at your company receives a holiday bonus.

The change may be associated with *maturation*, a natural growth process over time. Maturational factors influencing one's income, for instance, could include the following: your annual review period at work has come up and you're overdue for a raise; it's your birthday, and you receive a gift; or you retire and receive new benefits.

Another explanation is *selection*: Something about the sample is different from the population at large. For instance, you'd like to use your magical experiment as an example for all magicians, but you may be more entrepreneurial than your peers, even if you match them in magical study and experience. Consider the research finding from chapter 10 that religious people are more likely to sit near another person in a waiting room. While one might claim that religiosity predicts affiliative tendencies, the converse could be true: People may seek out religion because they are gregarious, making them inherently different from others.[38] A similar question could be raised about studies comparing long-term meditators to nonmeditators (as reviewed in chapter 4): Might long-term meditators be healthier in other lifestyle factors that contribute to their positive outcomes?

Mortality happens when certain participants drop out of a study (either through death, or simply withdrawing), leaving behind a sample that—although initially random and independent—is now biased. An analogy for the practical magician would be the situation where you get discouraged if your ritual doesn't seem to be working. Enthusiasm flags and magical recordkeeping suffers; but when things are going well, successes are enthusiastically recorded. Such "selective editing" of a journal gives a false impression that your magick is more effective than it truly is.

Or perhaps the change is due to *testing*. This acknowledges that the act of measuring something—such as taking a pretest measurement—can affect what you're studying, including what you see at the post-test. This is true at the level of quantum physics, and it could be true in the macroverse as well. If you go to your human resources person at work and start asking about your 401k balance or other benefits, it might unintentionally trigger a conversation between HR and your boss that results in a bonus or unexpected pay raise: an increase that wouldn't have happened had you not taken that pre-experiment measurement of your financial status.

Additional threats to internal validity include *ambiguous temporal precedence*, which reflects chicken-or-egg uncertainty about which variable causes which; *regression to the mean*, which is the tendency for people who perform extremely badly or well to subsequently have less extreme scores, a predictable phenomenon that can be mistaken for an experimental effect; *instrumentation*, in which the way something is measured changes, potentially accounting for pre-post differences. In addition, two or more of these phenomena can combine to create complex interactions. As an example, *selection x maturation* would describe a situation where members of a sample start out looking the same, but diverge over time due not to your intervention, but due to differences in how they grow or mature.

This list is long, and we've only scratched the surface. The idea, however, is to consider whether anything other than your talisman could have produced the results you obtained. This is arguably the hardest part of evaluating your work. After all the effort that goes into doing a magick ritual, we *want* to find out that all the effort was worth it. Yet we wouldn't be looking at the scientific method unless we wanted to get at the truth and consider things objectively. Hopefully, what you want and what seems to be true will agree.

DRAWING CONCLUSIONS

Weighing all the factors discussed above, the scientist *finally* concludes: Did the experiment work? The conclusion may support the alternative hypothesis (H_A), or it may favor the null hypothesis (H_0). It may come with some caveats. And it may come with lessons learned from doing the study. Likewise, a magician applying these principles needs to be able to evaluate their work, acknowledge any limitations, include any appropriate caveats, and consider how the "experiment" could be improved the next time around.

A critical part of one's conclusion is *generalizing* the findings to the larger population from which the sample was drawn. If the sample is indeed representative of the population, then the findings should be true for the entire population (however "population" is defined). This does *not* mean that the finding applies to any other group. For this reason, how you define your population is important not only because it ensures that you are observing the appropriate group; it also confines the people or objects to which your findings generalize. Thus, if your population consists of one magician, then your findings apply to that one person alone. You cannot generalize your findings to anyone else. This will be sufficient for most magicians. Crowley adhered to this principle, writing that a spiritual teacher:

> can do good only in one way, that is by publishing the methods by which he attained illumination: in other words, by adding his experience to the sum of scientific knowledge. I have myself striven

strenuously to do this, always endeavouring to make it clear that my results are of value only to myself, and that even my methods may need modification in every case.[39]

Another important part of science, as mentioned earlier, is *replication*. An experiment should be replicated to verify that the cause-effect mechanism works as described. If the findings cannot be replicated, then the original conclusion may be incorrect. As an example: Scientists have confirmed Mendel's findings on inheritance in pea plants—from which the fundamental laws of genetics are based—but comparing these replications to the original study suggests that Mendel's data are too good to be true. This has led some to argue that he may have tampered with or unconsciously edited his data to make them look better.[40] Replication can also be valuable given the expense and difficulty of large-scale studies: A series of similar studies with smaller samples can be combined in a process called *meta-analysis* to re-evaluate a body of research with the cumulative sample size of all the papers combined. While this is common in medical research where sample sizes are limited due to cost, this methodology can be applied to other research questions. This book has referenced many studies that have used meta-analysis. Building a body of evidence by replicating your results is extraordinarily valuable.

METHOD OF SCIENCE REDUX

The scientific method can be adapted to the rigorous study of one's magical work. No experiment will be perfect, but the keys are to (a) do the best you possibly can, (b) acknowledge the limitations of your particular approach, (c) critically evaluate possible competing explanations, and (d) avoid the temptation to rationalize why your study "really" worked even though your data don't support that claim. Proceed without "lust of result," and you just may surprise yourself.

In brief, here are the main steps to take in evaluating your magical work:

- Choose an intention that has a concrete outcome that you can easily measure.
- Rephrase your intention as a precise cause-effect statement. Also, have a competing statement that says there is no cause-effect relationship.
- Pick a magical working to enact your intention. Be explicit about what you will do in your ritual so that you can repeat it if it works.
- Decide on a study design. (Do you want a pretest? A control group?)
- Do your ritual.
- Look at the results: Is there evidence of a cause-effect relationship? If so, have you ruled out other possible explanations for what you saw?
- Ask yourself, Is there anything you could have done better or could do differently for next time?
- Repeat your experiment (with any lessons learned) and amass a body of evidence.

12
Last Writes

LIFE AS A MAGICIAN IS DEMANDING. Like any skill or lifestyle, it requires discipline, study, and continual practice. But the rewards are many: All that discipline—from keeping a journal to doing regular practices—teaches us to structure our activities and manage our time. Our practices challenge us to remain ever-vigilant of the beauty, joy, and spiritual quality of all that we do. Such mindfulness, along with other meditation exercises, leads to better health, well-being, and longevity. Ritual empowers us to pursue and realize our goals—to persevere in the face of adversity—and that feeling of control over one's fate can likewise translate into less stress and better health.* Through the practice of magick, we seek and experience the divine in the world, as well as our own inner divinity. That search opens us to new knowledge and new experiences. By gaining a better awareness of ourselves and the journey of transformation ahead, we strive to become the best we can be. This is the alchemical work of transmuting the inner self. As Lon Milo DuQuette says, the goal of magick isn't to make us super-human, but extra-human.[1] Engaging in group rituals and even initiation builds ties with a community of like-minded and supportive individuals—social

---

*When research identifies a significant correlation or trend with certain outcomes, bear in mind this indicates a *tendency* for certain things to happen, or to happen more often. Due to individual differences and other factors, there's no guarantee of a specific outcome. However, the chances of it happening are more likely.

support being another important predictor of wellness—but we also open ourselves to the transformative power of sacred drama. Finally, learning what psychological research has to tell us about the practice of magick also helps us to apply similar empirical methods to evaluating our work, identifying those practices that are best suited to our individual natures.

In traditions where one chooses a magical motto (as in the Golden Dawn or A∴A∴, for example), that motto is an aspirational goal for one's self-transformation. In other traditions, one's chosen name may represent a deity or other figure with which the magician identifies, or seeks to emulate: It is an ongoing act of invocation. In Thelema, for example, one seeks to discover one's True Will, and then marshal one's resources to achieve that ideal. In other mystical paths, the student strives for self-realization. Ultimately, all these practices lead to a sense of purpose in life. And this is a powerful way of being.

PURPOSE IN LIFE: EUDAIMONIA AND IKIGAI

The notion of "purpose in life" dates back some two thousand years to Aristotle, who called it *eudaimonia*. Psychologists have embraced both the concept and the term in recent years. Instead of being pleasure-centered (i.e., *hedonic*, or doing that which feels good or satisfies our appetites), eudaimonia suggests that a flourishing and satisfying existence is potential-centric: striving to become the best version of ourselves. As echoed by Veronika Huta of the University of Ottawa, "A hedonic orientation involves seeking happiness, positive affect, life satisfaction, and reduced negative affect; a eudaimonic orientation includes seeking authenticity, meaning, excellence, and personal growth."[2] Carol D. Ryff of the University of Wisconsin-Madison elaborates, "Eudaimonia thus captured the essence of the two great Greek imperatives: first, to know yourself, and second, to become what you are."[3] I often use a similar two-step explanation of Crowley's approach—namely, using the tools of magick to discover one's True Will, and then using those same tools to accomplish it.

Eudaimonia entered the psychology of happiness and well-being lexicon around 1990 through the work of Alan S. Waterman at the College of New Jersey[4] and Carol D. Ryff at the University of Wisconsin-Madison.[5] In 1989, Ryff referenced eudaimonia in her six-factor model of psychological well-being, which integrated theoretical perspectives from a range of psychologists including Abraham Maslow (hierarchy of needs including self-actualization), Carl Jung (individuation), Carl Rogers (fully functioning person), Viktor Frankl (will to meaning) and others. More than just the usual measure of subjective happiness, its six components included purpose in life, environmental mastery, positive relationships, personal growth, autonomy, and self-acceptance.

Eudaimonia is difficult to define in English. Ryff's conceptualization includes purposeful engagement in life, the realization of personal talents/capacities, and enlightened self-knowledge. Waterman, Schwartz, and Conti define *eudaimonia* as "the feelings present when one is moving toward self-realization in terms of the developing one's potentials and furthering one's purposes in living."[6] Kinderen and Khapova wrote that eudaimonia reflects "agentic and spiritual elements of well-being such as personal growth, positive relationships, autonomy, and meaning . . . through behaviors and cognitions that are within our control and influence and that inspire striving and goal attainment."[7] Heintzelman identifies self-determination, meaning in life, and flow among its various components.[8] Finally, Huta and Waterman list four core elements of eudaimonia: *authenticity* (identifying your true self and acting accordingly); *meaning* (the self-transcendent experience of seeing the bigger picture of the world in which you are part); *excellence* (striving for higher standards in accord with your true nature); and *growth* (pursuing your goals and fulfilling your potential).[9]

Japanese approaches to well-being employ a related concept. Although there is no equivalent term in English, *ikigai* is often translated as "what makes life worth living." It includes characteristics of both eudaimonia and hedonia. "For example," a recent study of Japanese older adults explained, "some people may derive their *Ikigai* through activities that promote purpose in life such as volunteering, others may cultivate *Ikigai* by fulfilling one's own need (e.g., reading books to satisfy curiosity) or simply indulging in pleasure (e.g., enjoying drinks with peers)."[10]

Kotera and colleagues define *ikigai* as "a feeling that arises in your body when you are living your mission."[11] Meta-analyses and longitudinal studies find that having ikigai is related to better physical health, and protects against disability, mortality, and cardiovascular disease.[12]

WILLPOWER

Both concepts of meaningful existence—eudaimonia and ikigai—echo the goals and results of magick discussed throughout this book, from empowerment to flow to awe. They express the heart of magick as a tool to achieve self-knowledge and liberation, recognize one's potential, and discover one's purpose in life. This goal-oriented focus recalls the question "To what end?" repeated in the Thelemic ritual of Saying Will with a meal (discussed in chapter 3):

> "What is thy will?"
> "It is my will to eat and to drink."
> "To what end?"
> "That my body may be fortified thereby."
> "To what end?"
> "That I may accomplish the Great Work."

Huta restates the Thelemic principle of "Do what thou wilt shall be the whole of the Law" in psychological terms when explaining that eudaimonia involves "acting in line with objectively valid and enduring psychological needs rather than momentary impulses."[13] Similarly, the notion that ikigai varies from person to person, depending on their "mission," sits comfortably alongside the individualistic idea of finding and doing one's True Will.

Dolores Ashcroft-Nowicki—a member of Dion Fortune's Society of the Inner Light, and Director of Studies of the Servants of Light from 1976 to 2018—tells us in no uncertain terms that "real magic is the realization of what you are and what you can become. It is being able to see your potential and knowing you can achieve it."[14] French occultist Éliphas Lévi likewise described magick in terms that reflect self-determination, another key concept in eudaimonia: "The Great Work is, above all else, the creation of man by himself, that is to say the full and entire conquest of his faculties and his future; it is above all the perfect emancipation of his will."[15] Lest there be any doubt about the nature of will in magick, ceremonial magician William Gray, founder of the Sangreal Sodality, left us with these words: "This is the True Will in us which is referred to in the summation of Law: 'DO WHAT *Thou* WILT,' which has nothing to do with the little petty wishes, whims and ill feelings of our personalized projections, but is the Real Reason in us that makes us WHAT WE ARE."[16] As magician J. R. Marscaro recently wrote, "Magic is meant to bring you to a transcendent state, a clarity of will, and a singularity of purpose."[17] This then is the essence of magick: To discover your purpose, your potential, and to transform yourself in pursuit of that ideal.

THE MONOMYTH AND YOU

This transformative quest of self-discovery often involves identification with a significant or heroic figure from history, myth, scripture, or literature. As we've seen previously, this can happen by reenacting their ordeals as part of the sacred drama of initiation; spiritually modeling idealized others; assuming the patronage of a deity or spirit; devoting oneself through bhakti yoga; invocation to become more like them; or adopting an aspirational magical motto or name. Such identification conjures a trope (or archetype, if you prefer) popularized by Joseph Campbell: the Hero's Journey. Sometimes referred to as the monomyth, Campbell proposed that all great myths follow, to a greater or lesser degree, a universal model of separation, initiation, and return: "A hero ventures forth from the world of common day into a region of supernatural wonder: fabulous forces are there encountered and a decisive victory is won: the hero comes back from this mysterious adventure with the power to bestow boons on his fellow man."[18] Folklorists have criticized Campbell for ignoring important details that make each myth culturally unique, and homogenizing the world's folkloric traditions into a single generic, male-centric model that (in its full form) involves seventeen vague and overly broad steps.[19]

Whether or not the monomyth stands up to scrutiny, it has exerted tremendous influence on modern thought, becoming archetypal in its own right. From the Cthulhu mythos to Harry Potter to the Marvel Cinematic Universe, the mythic arc has become a staple of popular culture.[20] Stanley Kubrick and Arthur C. Clarke both read *Hero with a Thousand Faces* while working on *2001: A Space Odyssey*.[21] George Lucas acknowledged his debt to Joseph Campbell's ideas in the Star Wars franchise:[22] The original trilogy told the tale of a naive youth (Luke Skywalker) who is taken in by a "crazy old wizard" (Obi-Wan Kenobi), instructed how to tap into the mystical power that interpenetrates the universe (the Force), initiated through his ordeals into a secretive order (the Jedi Knights . . . just like his father),* and ultimately saves the galaxy. This reminds me of an undergraduate anthropology text I had that argued that the Hero's Journey in *Star Wars* echoes elements of *The Wizard of Oz*; this includes parallels between farm-raised Dorothy and Luke Skywalker, whose quest leads to them to unlikely companions in the Tin Woodsman/C3P0, the Cowardly Lion/Chewbacca, and the Scarecrow/Han Solo. But that's a conversation best saved for too many drinks or bong hits.

The monomyth has also influenced modern occultism. Many magicians find that the concept of a universal transformative ordeal affirms Carl Jung's magick-friendly ideas of archetypes and the collective unconscious.† These also fit together with the notion of the perennial tradition, which posits that there is a single universal Truth that prophets, mystics, and other messengers repeat down through the ages.

Mythmaking one's spiritual journey goes hand-in-hand with magick and meaning in life. Recently, a group of researchers from the Universities of North Carolina at Chapel Hill, California Irvine,

---

*The son ascending to the throne of the father, through the agency of the daughter, is an interpretation of the magical formula of Y-H-V-H, which is the Hebrew tetragrammaton or four-lettered name of God. In ceremonial magick, Y represents the Father, the first H the Mother, V the Son, and the final H the daughter. For details, see "Chapter III: The Formula of Tetragrammaton" in Crowley, *Magick in Theory and Practice*.

†Joseph Campbell even edited and introduced Carl Gustav Jung, *The Portable Jung* (New York: Viking Press, 1971), cementing the connection between himself and Jung.

Koblenz-Landau, and Pennsylvania reported results from eight studies involving the Hero's Journey. Those who viewed their lives relative to the Hero's Journey narrative expressed better well-being and more meaning in life. This finding led to the development of a *restorying* intervention designed to help people see their lives in terms of Campbell's model, "prompting people to reflect on important elements of their lives and connecting them into a coherent and compelling narrative."[23] This intervention resulted in increased meaning in life and improved psychological resilience. (As discussed earlier, these are also benefits of eudaimonia and ikigai.) As the study authors wrote, "Meaning in life is tied to the stories people tell about their lives."[24] And that story can beneficially include the Hero's Quest, or similar spiritual models such as the Path of Return up the Tree of Life.

This finding extends beyond just the Hero's Journey. In a series of three studies involving approximately one thousand subjects, Ryan Goffredi and Kennon M. Sheldon at the University of Missouri, Columbia, demonstrated that seeing oneself as a major character in one's life story (as compared to those seeing themselves as subject to the tides of fate) comes with several psychological benefits. These include higher well-being, need satisfaction, autonomous goal pursuit, and personal agency.[25] In short, you need not see yourself as a mythic hero to reap these benefits (though it may help!).

THE BELIEVER AND THE SKEPTIC

One of the "big five" personality traits associated with eudaimonic well-being is openness to experience.[26] In my doctoral research, questing (i.e., a spirituality that is actively open to new information and experiences) was the main predictor of having had a transformative spiritual experience.[27] Here we find belief/openness and empiricism/doubt existing in a state of tension. Humans are hardwired to seek patterns and cause-effect relationships in ambiguous situations, and to overestimate our own control over random events. The tendency to see patterns in ambiguous situations is greater among believers, or those with a lower threshold for surprising coincidence. But these patterns could be misperceptions.

Conversely, doubt can make one closed to experiences, rejecting real patterns or true information. In chapter 11 we saw how skeptics were less able to distinguish real words from scrambled words, and real faces from scrambled faces.[28] Likewise, ESP skeptics performed significantly below chance on telepathy trials with a Zener deck.[29] Phenomena like these—where believers perform slightly better than chance, and nonbelievers perform worse—was first noticed by parapsychology researcher Gertrude Schmeidler, who dubbed it the *sheep-goat effect*.[30] The analogy of separating sheep from goats comes from Matthew 25, which states that when the Lord returns He will separate the sheep on his right hand and the goats on his left (welcoming the sheep into the kingdom of God and condemning the goats to eternal fire). Meta-analyses of the psi literature have concluded that a slight but significant sheep-goat effect has been demonstrated over the past seventy years of studies.[31]

Jeffrey Kripal drives this point home in *How to Think Impossibly* when he says that:

> beliefs limit what is possible. Beliefs shut down. Beliefs decide. If specific beliefs can be thought of as fishhooks that sometimes catch real fish, it can also be said that beliefs generally only catch fish, and particular kinds of fish that the hook is designed to catch, no less. But, if we extend the metaphor, we can also say that the waters are filled with other sorts of beings, most of which couldn't care less about these particular belief-hooks. Which is another way of saying beliefs can miss a great deal, really almost everything.[32]

Your beliefs can either leave you open to new experiences, or close you off to these possibilities. This echoes an observation by Gerald Gardner, the founder of Wicca: "As in the case of dowsing, if a man believes that when insulated from the ground by rubber insoles he cannot find water, this belief inhibits him."[33] If the studies mentioned above show us anything, it's that neither belief nor skepticism is a "pure" or unbiased way to see the world. I submit that finding a balance between the two is the way to go. Be both a scientist *and* an illuminist.

☆

Having reached the end of this book, we've seen that research tells us a lot about how psychology plays a role in the powerful and transformative practice of magick. Not because magick is all psychology, but because psychology is a vital part of these experiences. From simple daily exercises to elaborate group rituals, magick tweaks the magician's consciousness to facilitate encountering the numinous. Our practices resonate profoundly in the mind, giving us hope, empowerment, and a sense of purpose. The benefits of magick—physical, mental, social . . . or, if you prefer, eudaimonia or ikigai—are as valid and real as those of mainstream spiritualities. Ultimately, what we get out of magick depends on what we put in. Understanding the psychological processes that drive or enhance a ritualist's experience will help maximize the payoff of your magical practice.

If you're a seasoned practitioner, I hope this book has helped you to see your work in a new light, and that it encourages you to engage fully and mindfully with your practices. If you're relatively new at this, I hope this book makes sense of the sometimes-bewildering new things you are reading, trying, or experiencing. And if you are curious or just sticking your toe into the water for the first time, may these words be an encouragement. You may find that there's *something* to it.

Notes

CHAPTER 1. SOMETHING

1. *The Mysterious Monsters*, dir. Robert Guenette, Sunn Classic Pictures, November 5, 1975; *In Search Of*, hosted by Leonard Nimoy, NBC, 1977–1982; *Kolchak: The Night Stalker*, starring Darren McGavin, ABC, 1974–1975.
2. Israel Regardie, *The Golden Dawn: An Account of the Teachings, Rites and Ceremonies of the Hermetic Order of the Golden Dawn*, 3rd printing (St. Paul, MN: Llewellyn, 1978).
3. For information on Gundella, see John E. L. Tenney, "Gundella: Michigan's Good Witch," Weird Lectures website, December 11, 2018, and Bart Bealmear, "'Gundella, the Green Witch' of Detroit Explains How to Cast Spells," Dangerous Minds (.net) website, September 29, 2017.
4. Antonio Pagliarulo, "Why Paganism and Witchcraft Are Making a Comeback," *NBC News* website, October 30, 2022.
5. Harry Enten, "What Statistics Can Tell Us about Americans' Skyrocketing Belief in Ghosts," CNN Politics website, September 21, 2021.
6. Live Science Staff, "Americans' Belief in Paranormal Phenomena" (infographic), Live Science website, October 28, 2011.
7. Becka A. Alper, Michael Rotolo, Patricia Tevington, Justin Nortey, and Asta Kallo, "Spirituality among Americans," Pew Research Center (.org) website, December 7, 2023.
8. Taylor Orth, "One in Four Americans Say They Believe in Astrology," YouGov website, April 26, 2022.
9. Whitley Strieber, *Communion: A True Story* (New York: Avon Books, 1987).

10. Whitley Strieber and Jeffrey J. Kripal, *The Super Natural: A New Vision of the Unexplained* (New York: TarcherPerigee, 2016), 32.
11. Jeffrey J. Kripal, *How to Think Impossibly about Souls, UFOs, Time, Belief, and Everything Else* (Chicago: University of Chicago Press, 2024), 96.
12. Kripal, *How to Think Impossibly*, 56.
13. Christopher D. Bader, Joseph O. Baker, and F. Carson Mencken, *Paranormal America: Ghost Encounters, UFO Sightings, Bigfoot Hunts, and Other Curiosities in Religion and Culture*, 2nd ed. (New York: New York University Press, 2017), 231–33.
14. See Daniele Fanelli, "How Many Scientists Fabricate and Falsify Research? A Systematic Review and Meta-analysis of Survey Data," *PLOS ONE* 4, no. 5 (2009): e5738; Yu Xie, Kai Wang, and Yan Kong, "Prevalence of Research Misconduct and Questionable Research Practices: A Systematic Review and Meta-analysis," *Science and Engineering Ethics* 27 (2021): 41.
15. See Carl Gustav Jung, *The Red Book = Liber Novus*, ed. and trans. Sonu Shamdasani, Mark Kyburz, John Peck, and Ulrich Hoerni (New York: W.W. Norton & Company, 2009) and Carl Gustav Jung, *The Black Books: 1913–1932: Notebooks of Transformation*, ed. and trans. Sonu Shamdasani (New York: W.W. Norton & Company, 2020).
16. Christopher Hauke, "Keeping Secrets (and Deciding What Can Be Told): Individuation, Power and the *Red Book*," *International Journal of Jungian Studies* 3, no. 2 (2011): 159–68 (p. 159).
17. See Anthony Storr, *Feet of Clay: Saints, Sinners and Madmen, A Study of Gurus* (New York: Free Press, 1996), 89; Paul J. Stern, *C. G. Jung: The Haunted Prophet* (New York: G. Braziller, 1976).
18. One notable exception is Michael White, *Isaac Newton: The Last Sorcerer* (Reading, MA: Addison-Wesley, 1997).
19. For more on Fuller, see Richard Kaczynski, *Friendship in Doubt: Aleister Crowley, J. F. C. Fuller, Victor B. Neuburg, and British Agnosticism* (New York: Oxford University Press, 2024).
20. C. R. Snyder, "Why Horoscopes Are True: The Effects of Specificity on Acceptance of Astrological Interpretations," *Journal of Clinical Psychology* 30, no. 4 (1974): 577–80.
21. See, e.g., Chr. Scharfetter, "Okkultismus, parapsychologie und esoterik in der sicht der psychopathologie," *Fortschritte der Neurologie-Psychiatrie* 66, no. 10 (1998): 474–82.
22. See Gertrude R. Schmeidler, "Predicting Good and Bad Scores in a

Clairvoyance Experiment: A Preliminary Report," *Journal of the American Society for Psychical Research* 37 (1943): 103–10; Michael A. Thalbourne and Peter S. Delin, "A New Instrument for Measuring the Sheep-Goat Variable: Its Psychometric Properties and Factor Structure," *Journal of the Society for Psychical Research* 59, no. 832 (1993): 172–86.

23. For some examples and critiques of the marginality hypothesis, see Robert Wuthnow, "Astrology and Marginality," *Journal for the Scientific Study of Religion* 15, no. 2 (1976): 157–68; Charles F. Emmons and Jeff Sobal, "Paranormal Beliefs: Testing the Marginality Hypothesis," *Sociological Focus* 14, no. 1 (1981): 49–56; James J. McGarry and Benjamin H. Newberry, "Belief in Paranormal Phenomena and Locus of Control: A Field Study," *Journal of Personality and Social Psychology* 41, no. 4 (198): 725–36; Harvey J. Irwin, "Belief in the Paranormal: A Review of the Empirical Literature," *Journal of the American Society for Psychical Research* 87, no. 1 (1993): 1–39.
24. For the history of modern paganism and witchcraft, see, for instance, Margot Adler, *Drawing Down the Moon: Witches, Druids, Goddess-Worshippers, and Other Pagans in America Today* (New York: Viking Press, 1979); Ronald Hutton, *The Triumph of the Moon: A History of Modern Pagan Witchcraft* (Oxford: Oxford University Press, 1999); or Shai Feraro and Ethan Doyle White, eds., *Magic and Witchery in the Modern West: Celebrating the Twentieth Anniversary of* The Triumph of the Moon (Cham, Switzerland: Palgrave Macmillan, 2019).
25. Frank D. Drake, "Project Ozma," *Physics Today* 14, no. 4 (1961): 40–46.
26. McGarry and Newberry, "Belief in Paranormal Phenomena."
27. Anna Stone, "Rational Thinking and Belief in Psychic Abilities: It Depends on Level of Involvement," *Psychological Reports* 118, no. 1 (2016): 74–89.
28. Richard Kaczynski, "The Structure and Correlates of Metaphysical Beliefs in a Behaviorally Committed Sample" (doctoral dissertation, Wayne State University, November 1993).
29. Richard Kaczynski, *Perdurabo: The Life of Aleister Crowley*, rev. exp. ed. (Berkley: North Atlantic Books, 2010); Kaczynski, *Friendship in Doubt*.

CHAPTER 2. HEAD LIKE A WHOLE

1. Josh Levin, "Jesus on a Tortilla," Slate website, November 17, 2012.
2. "'Virgin Mary Grilled Cheese' Sells for $28,000," *NBC News* website, November 17, 2004.

3. Li-Jun Ji, Zhiyong Zhang, and Richard E. Nisbett, "Is It Culture or Is It Language? Examination of Language Effects in Cross-cultural Research on Categorization," *Journal of Personality and Social Psychology* 87, no. 1 (2004): 57–65.

4. Michael Cohanpour, Mariam Aly, and Jacqueline Gottlieb, "Neural Representations of Sensory Uncertainty and Confidence Are Associated with Perceptual Curiosity," *Journal of Neuroscience* 44, no. 33 (2024): e0974232024.

5. "California Probes Rock Music 'Devil,'" *Chicago Tribune*, April 29, 1982, A2; "'Devil Messages' in Music," *Vancouver Sun*, April 28, 1982, 31; "Bedeviled: A Fear That Satan Speaks When Disc Is Put in Reverse," *Philadelphia Inquirer*, April 30, 1982, 3.

6. Michael A. Nees and Charlotte Phillips, "Auditory Pareidolia: Effects of Contextual Priming on Perceptions of Purportedly Paranormal and Ambiguous Auditory Stimuli," *Applied Cognitive Psychology* 29 (2014): 129–34; Stephen C. Benoit and Roger L. Thomas, "The Influence of Expectancy in Subliminal Perception Experiments," *Journal of General Psychology* 119, no. 4 (1992): 335–41; Stephen B. Thorne and Philip Himelstein (1984), "The Role of Suggestion in the Perception of Satanic Messages in Rock-and-Roll Recordings," *Journal of Psychology* 116 (1984): 245–48; D. J. Bruce (1958), "The Effect of Listeners' Anticipations on the Intelligibility of Heart Speech," *Language and Speech* 1, no. 2 (1958): 79–97.

7. Leonard Zusne and Warren H. Jones (1989), *Anomalistic Psychology: A Study of Magical Thinking*, 2nd ed. (Hillsdale, NJ: Lawrence Earlbaum Associates), 79; Jerome S. Bruner and Mary C. Potter, "Interference in Visual Recognition," *Science* 144, no. 3617 (1964): 424–25.

8. Michael Shermer, *The Believing Brain: From Ghosts and Gods to Politics and Conspiracies—How We Construct Beliefs and Reinforce Them As Truths* (New York: Time Books, 2011), 99.

9. Lyle C. Swart and Cynthia L. Morgan, "Effects of Subliminal Backward-Recorded Messages on Attitudes," *Perceptual and Motor Skills* 75 (1992): 1107–13; John R. Vokey and J. Don Read, "Subliminal Messages: Between the Devil and the Media," *American Psychologist* 40, no. 11 (1985): 1231–39; Erica Yalch, "Backmasking: Annihilating the Effects of Good and Evil," paper presented at the April 2009 37th Annual Western Pennsylvania Undergraduate Psychology Conference, Moon Township, PA.

10. Klaus Conrad, *Die beginnende Schizophrenie. Versuch einer Gestaltanalyse des Wahns* (Stuttgart, Germany: Georg Thieme, 1958).
11. Jan-Willem van Prooijen, Karen M. Douglas, and Clara De Inocencio, "Connecting the Dots: Illusory Pattern Perception Predicts Belief in Conspiracies and the Supernatural," *European Journal of Social Psychology* 48 (2018): 320–35.
12. Ubuka Tagami and Shu Imaizumi, "No Correlation Between Perception of Meaning and Positive Schizotypy in a Female College Sample," *Frontiers in Psychology* 11 (2020): 1323.
13. Christian Rominger, Günter Schulter, Andreas Fink, Elisabeth M. Weiss, and Ilona Papousek, "Meaning in Meaninglessness: The Propensity to Perceive Meaningful Patterns in Coincident Events and Randomly Arranged Stimuli Is Linked to Enhanced Attention in Early Sensory Processing," *Psychiatry Research* 263 (2016): 225–32; Paola Bressan, Peter Kramer, and Mara Germani, "Visual Attentional Capture Predicts Belief in a Meaningful World," *Cortex* 44 (2008): 1299–1306.
14. Johannes H. Salge, Stefan Pollmann, and Reshanne R. Reeder, "Anomalous Visual Experience Is Linked to Perceptual Uncertainty and Visual Imagery Vividness," *Psychological Research* 85, no. 5 (2021): 1848–65.
15. David Smailes, Emma Burdis, Constantina Gregorius, Bryony Fenton, and Rob Dudley, "Pareidolia-Proneness, Reality Discrimination Errors, and Visual Hallucination-like Experiences in a Non-clinical Sample," *Cognitive Neuropsychiatry* 25, no. 2 (2020): 113–25.
16. van Prooijen et al., "Connecting the Dots"; M. Lindeman and K. Aarnio, "Superstitious, Magical, and Paranormal Beliefs: An Integrative Model," *Journal of Research in Personality* 41 (2007): 731–44; R. Wiseman and C. Watt, "Belief in Psychic Ability and the Misattribution Hypothesis: A Qualitative Review," *British Journal of Psychology* 97 (2006): 323–38.
17. van Prooijen et al., "Connecting the Dots," 321.
18. Mai-Britt Herslund and Niels O. Jørgensen (2003), "Looked-but-failed-to-see-errors in Traffic," *Accident Analysis and Prevention* 35, no. 6 (2003): 885–91; A Special Correspondent, "What Causes Road Accidents?" *The British Medical Journal* 2, no. 6147 (1978): 1272–74.
19. Daniel J. Simons and Daniel T. Levin, "Failure to Detect Changes to People During a Real-World Interaction," *Psychosomatic Bulletin and Review* 5, no. 4 (1998): 644–49.
20. Daniel J. Simons and Christopher F. Chabris, "Gorillas in Our Midst:

Sustained Inattentional Blindness for Dynamic Events," *Perception* 28, no. 9 (1999): 1059–74. For video demonstrations of these perceptual blindness experiments, see the Invisible Gorilla website.

21. Leonid Zhmud, "Pythagoras' Northern Connections: Zalmoxis, Abaris, Aristeas," *Classical Quarterly* 66, no. 2 (2016): 446–62; Nora Dimitrova, "Inscriptions and Iconography in the Monuments of the Thracian Rider," *Hesperia* 71, no. 2 (2002): 209–229; Mircea Eliade and Willard R. Trask (1972), "Zalmoxis," *History of Religions* 11, no. 3 (1972): 257–302; Mircea Eliade, *Zalmoxis: The Vanishing God*, trans. Willard R. Trask (Chicago: University of Chicago Press, 1972); Eric R. Dodds, *The Greeks and the Irrational* (Berkeley: University of California Press, 1951).

22. Yulia Ustinova, *Caves and the Ancient Greek Mind: Descending Underground in the Search for Ultimate Truth* (New York: Oxford University Press, 2009).

23. David Whitmer, *An Address to All Believers in Christ by a Witness to the Divine Authenticity of the Book of Mormon* (Richmond, MO: David Whitmer, 1887), 12.

24. Shahar Arzy, Moshe Idel, Theodor Landis, and Olaf Blanke (2005), "Why Revelations Have Occurred on Mountains? Linking Mystical Experiences and Cognitive Neuroscience," *Medical Hypotheses* 65, no. 5 (2005): 841–45; Peter Brugger, Marianne Regard, Theodor Landis, and Oswald Oelz, "Hallucinatory Experiences in Extreme-Altitude Climbers," *Neuropsychiatry, Neuropsychology and Behavioral Neurology* 12, no. 1 (1999): 67–71.

25. Erica Reiner, "Fortune-telling in Mesopotamia," *Journal of Near Eastern Studies* 19, no. 1 (1960): 24.

26. S. Davis (1955), "Divining Bowls: Their Uses and Origin: Some African Examples, and Parallels from the Ancient World," *Man* 55, no. 143 (1955): 132–35.

27. Lucya Starza, *Pagan Portals—Scrying: Divination using Crystals, Mirrors, Water and Fire* (Winchester, UK: Moon Books, 2022).

28. Stuart Campbell, Elizabeth Healey, Yaroslav Kuzmin, and Michael D. Glascock, "The Mirror, the Magus and More: Reflections on John Dee's Obsidian Mirror," *Antiquity* 95, no. 384 (2021): 1547–64.

29. See Stephen Skinner, *Dr. John Dee's Spiritual Diary (1583–1608)*, 2nd ed. (St. Paul, MN: Llewellyn, 2020).

30. Joscelyn Godwin, *The Theosophical Enlightenment* (Albany: State University of New York Press, 1994), 169. Godwin's chapter 9, "Visions

in the Crystal" (169–86) provides an overview of crystallomancy in the eighteenth century.

31. Frederick Hockley, *Invocating by Magic Crystals and Mirrors*, intro. R. A. Gilbert (York Beach, ME: Teitan Press, 2010); John Hamill and R. A. Gilbert, *The Rosicrucian Seer: Magical Writings of Frederick Hockley* (York Beach, ME: Teitan Press, 2009).
32. Godwin, *Theosophical Enlightenment*, 170.
33. Kenneth R. H. Mackenzie, "Visions in Mirrors and Crystals," *The Spiritualist, and Journal of Psychological Science* 12, no. 13 (March 29, 1878): 151–54. This was a transcript of a March 25, 1878, talk given to the British National Association of Spiritualists on "The Spirit-World as seen through Crystals, Mirrors, and Vessels of Water."
34. Godwin, *Theosophical Enlightenment*, 211–12; Sirius [Emma Hardinge Britten], "Occultism Defined," *The Two Worlds* 1, no. 1 (1887): 3–4.
35. Emma Hardinge Britten, *Ghost Land; or Researches into the Mysteries of Occultism Illustrated in a Series of Autobiographical Sketches in Two Parts* (Boston: for the editor, 1876), 100–106.
36. Robert H. Fryar, *The History and Mystery of the Magic Crystal* (London: J. Burns, 1870); One of the Six Hundred [Robert H. Fryar], "'Visions and Mirrors in Crystals,'" A Response to Mackenzie, 'Visions,'" *The Spiritualist, and Journal of Psychological Science* 13, no. 6 (1878): 71; Robert H. Fryar, "Crystal Gazing," *Notes and Queries and Historic Magazine* 25 (1907): 241–43. For more on Fryar, see Sydney T. Chapman, "A Victorian Occultist and Publisher: Robert H. Fryar of Bath," *The Road: A Journal of History, Myth and Legend* 4 (2011): 3–11.
37. J. Lawrence, *Hypnotism, or Health and Wealth within the Reach of Everybody: A Practical, Concise, and Up-To-Date Method* (London: Electric and Magnetic Institute), 32.
38. Fryar, "Visions and Mirrors in Crystals."
39. Paschal Beverly Randolph, *"Clairvoyance: How to Produce It, and Perfect It,"* with an Essay on *"Hashish, Its Benefits and Its Dangers."* Also *"How to Make the Magic Glass, or Mirror of the Dead, by means of which the Oriental Magi are Said to Have Held Intelligent Commerce with Spirits"* (Boston: Albert Renne & Co., 1860). For a detailed treatment of Randolph, his magic mirrors, and his special (and likely sexual) method of charging them, see John Patrick Deveney, *Paschal Beverly Randolph: A Nineteenth-Century Black American Spiritualist, Rosicrucian, and Sex*

Magician (Albany: State University of New York Press, 1997), 77–88.
40. Paschal Beverly Randolph, *The Wonderful Story of Ravalette: Also, Tom Clark and His Wife and the Curious Things That Befell Them; Being the Rosicrucian's Story* (Toledo, OH: K. Corson Randolph, 1876), 113–14 (originally published in 1863); Anonymous, *The Guide to Clairvoyance and Clairvoyant's Guide: A Practical Manual for Those Who Aim at Perfect Clear Seeing and Psychometry; also a Special Paper Concerning Hashish, Its Uses, Abuses, and Dangers, Its Extasia, Fantasia, and Illuminati. Printed for People of Common Sense Only* (Boston: Rockwell & Rollins, 1867); Paschal Beverly Randolph, *Seership! The Magnetic Mirror. A Practical Guide to Those Who Aspire to Clairvoyance-Absolute. Original and Selected from Various European and Asiatic Adepts* (Boston: Randolph Publishing Co., 1870).
41. Opening to "The Cry of the 28th Æthyr BAG" in Aleister Crowley, Victor B. Neuburg, and Mary Desti, *The Vision and the Voice with Commentary and Other Papers, The Equinox Volume IV Number II* (York Beach, ME: Samuel Weiser, 1998).
42. William Walker Atkinson, *Practical Psychomancy and Crystal Gazing: A Course of Lessons on the Psychic Phenomena of Distant Sensing, Clairvoyance, Psychometry, Crystal Gazing, Etc.* (Chicago: Advanced Thought Publishing, 1908).
43. Frater Achad [Charles Stansfeld Jones], *Crystal Vision through Crystal Gazing, or the Crystal as a Stepping-Stone to Clear Vision: A Practical Treatise on the Real Value of Crystal-Gazing* (Chicago: Yogi Publication Society, 1923).
44. Jeane Dixon and Rene Noorbergen, *Jeane Dixon: My Life and Prophecies* (New York: William Morrow & Company, 1969).
45. Morton Prince, "An Experimental Study of Visions," *Journal of the Boston Society of Medical Sciences* 3, no. 3 (1898): 47–50.
46. Page 165 in Morton Prince, "An Experimental Study of the Mechanism of Hallucinations," *British Journal of Medical Psychology* 2, no. 3 (1922): 165–208.
47. Wolfgang Metzger, "Optische Untersuchungen am Ganzfeld. II: Zur Phänomenologie des homogenen Ganzfelds," *Psychologische Forschung* 13 (1930): 6–29.
48. Julian E. Hochberg, William Triebel, and Gideon Seaman (1951), "Color Adaptation under Conditions of Homogeneous Visual Stimulation

(Ganzfeld)," *Journal of Experimental Psychology* 41, no. 2 (1951): 153–59.
49. Timo T. Schmidt and Julia C. Prein, "The Ganzfeld Experience—A Stably Inducible Altered State of Consciousness: Effects of Different Auditory Homogenizations," *PsyCh Journal* 8 (2019): 66–81.
50. Jiří Wackermann, Peter Pütz, and Carsten Allefeld (2008), "Ganzfeld-Induced Hallucinatory Experience, Its Phenomenology and Cerebral Electrophysiology," *Cortex* 44 (2008): 1364–78 (p. 1368).
51. Paul Foster Case, *The True and Invisible Rosicrucian Order: An Interpretation of the Rosicrucian Allegory and an Explanation of the Ten Rosicrucian Grades* (York Beach, ME: Samuel Weiser, 1985), 178.
52. van Prooijen et al., "Connecting the Dots."
53. Roderick Main, "The Cultural Significance of Synchronicity for Jung and Pauli," *Journal of Analytical Psychology* 59 (2014): 174–80 (p. 176).
54. Dan Hocoy (2012), "Sixty Years Later: The Enduring Allure of Synchronicity," *Journal of Humanistic Psychology* 52, no. 4 (2012): 467–78 (p. 468).
55. Harald Atmanspacher and Wolfgang Fach, "Synchronistic Mind-Matter Correlations in Therapeutic Practice: A Commentary on Connolly (2015)," *Journal of Analytical Psychology* 61 (2016): 79–85 (p. 79).
56. Pninit Russo-Netzer and Tamar Ickeson, "Engaging with Life: Synchronicity Experiences as a Pathway to Meaning and Personal Growth," *Current Psychology* 41 (2022): 597–610; W. Fach, H. Atmanspacher, K. Landolt, T. Wyss, and W. Rössler (2013), "A Comparative Study of Exceptional Experiences of Clients Seeking Advice and of Subjects in an Ordinary Population," *Frontiers in Psychology* 4 (2013): 65; S. L. Coleman, B. D. Beitman, and E. Celebi, "Weird Coincidences Commonly Occur," *Psychiatric Annals* 39, no. 5 (2009): 265–70.
57. Eric Dietrich and Chris Fields (2015), "Science Generates Limit Paradoxes," *Axiomathes* 25 (2015): 409–32.
58. Hocoy, "Sixty Years Later," 468.
59. Carl Gustav Jung, *Memories, Dreams, Reflections*, ed. Aniela Jaffé, trans. Richard and Clara Winston (New York: Vintage Books, 1965), 374.
60. Angela Connolly, "Bridging the Reductive and the Synthetic: Some Reflections on the Clinical Implications of Synchronicity," *Journal of Analytical Psychology* 60, no. 2 (2015): 159–78 (p. 160).
61. [Aleister Crowley], "John St. John: The Record of the Magical Retirement of G. H. Frater, O∴ M∴," *The Equinox* I, no. 1 (March 1909): supplement (p. 11).

62. Russo-Netzer and Ickeson, "Engaging with Life."
63. Kaczynski, "The Structure and Correlates of Metaphysical Beliefs."
64. The Master Therion [Aleister Crowley], *Magick in Theory and Practice* (Paris: Lecram Press, 1929–1930), xvi.
65. Christopher Penczak, *The Inner Temple of Witchcraft: Magick, Meditation and Psychic Development* (St. Paul, MN: Llewellyn, 2002), 77.
66. Thorn Mooney, *The Witch's Path: Advancing Your Craft at Every Level* (Woodbury, MN: Llewellyn, 2021), 95.
67. See, e.g., Stanislav Grof, *Psychology of the Future: Lessons from Modern Consciousness Research* (Albany: State University of New York Press, 2000), 136.

CHAPTER 3. RIGAMAROLE MODELS

1. Deborah Blake, *Everyday Witchcraft: Making Time for Spirit in a Too-Busy World* (St. Paul, MN: Llewellyn, 2015).
2. Jenn Stevens, *The Mindful Witch: Daily Practice and Reflection for a Truly Magickal Life* (New York: Castle Point Books, 2019).
3. Originally published in Israel Regardie, *The Middle Pillar* (Chicago: Aries Press, 1938), the ritual has been widely used, adapted, and modified ever since.
4. Ann M. Graybiel (2008), "Habits, Rituals, and the Evaluative Brain," *Annual Review of Neuroscience* 31 (2008): 359–87 (p. 361).
5. Evan Imber-Black and Janine Roberts, *Rituals for Our Times: Celebrating, Healing, and Changing Our Lives and Our Relationships* (New York: HarperPerennial, 1992).
6. Dimitris Xygalatas, *Ritual: How Seemingly Senseless Acts Make Life Worth Living* (New York: Little, Brown Spark, 2022).
7. Pierre Liénard and Pascal Boyer, "Whence Collective Rituals? A Cultural Selection Model of Ritualized Behavior," *American Anthropologist* 108, no. 4 (2006): 814–27 (p. 814).
8. Radha J. Parker and H. Shelton Horton, Jr., "A Typology of Ritual: Paradigms for Healing and Empowerment," *Counseling and Values* 40 (1996): 82–97 (p. 87).
9. Harvey Whitehouse, *Modes of Religiosity: A Cognitive Theory of Religious Transmission* (Walnut Creek, CA: Alta Mira, 2004); Worwach Tungjitcharoen and Dorthe Berntsen, "Belief-Related Memories:

Autobiographical Memories of the Religious Self," *Memory* 29, no. 5 (2021): 573–86.

10. Cristine H. Legare and André L. Souza, "Evaluating Ritual Efficacy: Evidence from the Supernatural," *Cognition* 124, no. 1 (2012): 1–15.

11. See, e.g., Stanley Jeyaraja Tambiah, "A Performative Approach to Ritual," *Proceedings of the British Academy* 45 (1979): 113–69; Alison Wood Brooks, Juliana Schroeder, Jane L. Risen, Francesca Gino, Adam D. Galinsky, Michael I. Norton, and Maurice E. Schweitzer, "Don't Stop Believing: Rituals Improve Performance by Decreasing Anxiety," *Organizational Behavior and Human Decision Process* 137 (2016): 71–85; Allen Ding Tian, Juliana Schroeder, Gerald Häubl, Jane L. Risen, Michael I. Norton, and Grancesca Gino, "Enacting Rituals to Improve Self-Control," *Journal of Personality and Social Psychology* 114, no. 6 (2018): 851–76; Nicholas M. Hobson, Juliana Schroeder, Jane L. Risen, Dimitris Xygalatas, and Michael Inzlicht, "The Psychology of Rituals: An Integrative Review and Process-based Framework," *Personality and Social Psychology Review* 22, no. 3 (2018): 260–84.

12. Wai Kai Hou, Francisco TT Lai, Menachem Ben-Ezra, and Robin Goodwin, "Regularizing Daily Routines for Mental Health during and after the COVID-19 Pandemic," *Journal of Global Health* 10, no. 2 (2020): 020315; Greg Murray, John Gottlieb, and Holly A Swartz, "Maintaining Daily Routines to Stabilize Mood: Theory, Data, and Potential Intervention for Circadian Consequences of COVID-19," *Canadian Journal of Psychiatry* 66, no. 1 (2021): 9–13; Julian Zubek, Karolina Ziembowicz, Marek Pokropski, Paweł Gwiaździński, Michał Denkiewicz, and Anna Boros, "Rhythms of the Day: How Electronic Media and Daily Routines Influence Mood during COVID-19 Pandemic," *Applied Psychology: Health and Well-Being* 14, no. 2 (2021): 519–36.

13. Xygalatas, *Ritual*, 61–66, cites studies that show ritual being more prevalent in stressful times or places, providing a sense of control over external events over which the individual has little or no actual control.

14. Daniel Mochon, Michael I. Norton, and Dan Ariely, "Getting Off the Hedonic Treadmill, One Step at a Time: The Impact of Regular Religious Practice and Exercise on Well-being," *Journal of Economic Psychology* 29 (2008): 632–42.

15. Francis King and Stephen Skinner, *Techniques of High Magic* (New York: Destiny Books, 1976), 26.

16. David Conway, *Magic: An Occult Primer* (New York: Bantam, 1973), 60.
17. Janet Farrar and Stewart Farrar, *Eight Sabbats for Witches* (London: Robert Hale, 1985), 47.
18. Maevius Lynn, "Guide to Saying Will," video posted December 12, 2023 on YouTube.
19. Rodney Orpheus, *Abrahadabra: Understanding Aleister Crowley's Thelemic Magick*, 2nd ed. (York Beach, ME: Weiser, 2005), 61.
20. David Shoemaker, *Living Thelema: A Practical Guide to Attainment in Aleister Crowley's System of Magick* (Sacramento: Anima Solis, 2013; rpt. Newburyport, MA: Red Wheel/Weiser, 2022), 34–35.
21. Orpheus, *Abrahadabra*, 14.
22. Éliphas Lévi, *The Doctrine and Ritual of High Magic: A New Translation*, trans. John Michael Greer and Mark Anthony Mikituk (New York: TarcherPerigee, 2017), 213.
23. Lon Milo DuQuette, *The Magick of Thelema: A Handbook of the Rituals of Aleister Crowley* (York Beach, ME: Weiser, 1993), 1.
24. Lévi, *Doctrine and Ritual*, 209.
25. Phillippa Lally, Cornelia H. M. van Jaarsveld, Henry W. W. Potts, and Jane Wardle, "How Habits Are Formed: Modelling Habit Formation in the Real World," *European Journal of Social Psychology* 40 (2010): 998–1009; Katherine R. Arlinghaus and Craig A. Johnston, "The Importance of Creating Habits and Routine," *American Journal of Lifestyle Medicine* 13, no. 2 (2019): 142–44.
26. Chic Cicero and Sandra Cicero, *Golden Dawn Magic: A Complete Guide to the High Magical Arts* (St. Paul, MN: Llewellyn, 2019), 43.
27. Arin Murphy-Hiscock, *The Witch's Book of Self-Care* (Avon, MA: Adams Media, 2018), 28.
28. Sarah Lyons, *How to Study Magic: A Guide to History, Lore, and Building Your Own Practice* (New York: Running Press, 2022), 28–29.
29. James Wasserman, ed. and intro., *Aleister Crowley and the Practice of the Magical Diary* (Tempe, AZ: New Falcon, 1993; rev. exp. ed., San Francisco, Weiser, 2006).
30. Valerie van Mulukom, "Remembering Religious Rituals: Autobiographical Memories of High-Arousal Religious Rituals Considered from a Narrative Processing Perspective," *Religion, Brain and Behavior* 7, no. 3 (2017): 191–205 (p. 10). See also Daniel L. Schacter, *Searching for Memory: The Brain, the Mind, and the Past* (New York: Basic Books, 2006) and Frederic

C. Bartlett, *Remembering: A Study in Experimental and Social Psychology* (Cambridge: Cambridge University Press, 1932).

31. See, e.g., Harvey Whitehouse and James Laidlaw, eds., *Ritual and Memory: Toward a Comparative Anthropology of Religion* (Walnut Creek, CA: AltaMira, 2004).

32. Dimitris Xygalatas, Uffe Schjoedt, Joseph Bulbulia, Ivana Konvalinka, Else-Marie Jegindo, Paul Reddish, Armin W. Geertz, and Andreas Roepstoff, "Autobiographical Memory in a Fire-walking Ritual," *Journal of Cognition and Culture* 13, no. 1 (2013): 1–16.

33. Mulukom, "Remembering Religious Rituals," 5.

34. Xygalatas et al., "Autobiographical Memory," 12.

35. Philip M. Ullrich and Susan K. Lutgendorf, "Journaling about Stressful Events: Effects of Cognitive Processing and Emotional Expression," *Annals of Behavioral Medicine* 24, no. 2 (2002): 244–50. While this article deals with processing traumatic events, the idea arguably extends to processing the experiences of magical rituals.

36. Frances A. Yates, *The Art of Memory* (London: Routledge & Kegan Paul, 1966).

37. David L. Bimler, "Some Renaissance, Baroque, and Contemporary Cultural Elaborations of the Art of Memory," *Behavioral and Brain Sciences* 36, no. 6 (2013): 608–9.

38. J. H. Chajes, *The Kabbalistic Tree: האילן הקבלי* (University Park: Pennsylvania State University Press, 2022).

39. Sue Llewellyn, "Such Stuff as Dreams Are Made On? Elaborative Encoding, the Ancient Art of Memory, and the Hippocampus," *Behavioral and Brain Sciences* 36 (2013): 589–659.

40. Mukaila Alade Rahman, Benjamin Segun Aribisala, Irfan Ullah, and Hammad Omer, "Association between Scripture Memorization and Brain Atrophy Using Magnetic Resonance Imaging," *Acta Neurobiologiæ Experimentalis* 80 (2020): 90–97.

41. Janet L. Jacobs, "The Effects of Ritual Healing on Female Victims of Abuse: A Study of Empowerment and Transformation," *Sociological Analysis* 50, no. 3 (1989): 265–79.

42. Tian et al., "Enacting Rituals to Improve Self-control"; Hobson et al., "Psychology of Rituals," 267.

43. Ann O'Leary, "Self-efficacy and Health," *Behaviour Research and Therapy* 23, no. 4 (1985): 437–51.

44. Albert Bandura, "Self-efficacy: Toward a Unifying Theory of Behavior Change," *Psychological Research* 84 (1977): 191–215. See also Albert Bandura, *Social Learning Theory* (Englewood Cliffs, NJ: Prentice-Hall, 1977).
45. Alexander D. Stajkovic, Albert Bandura, Edwin A. Locke, Dongseop Lee, and Kayla Sergent, "Test of Three Conceptual Models of Influence of the Big Five Personality Traits and Self-efficacy on Academic Performance: A Meta-analytic Path-analysis," *Personality and Individual Differences* 120 (2018): 238–45; Michelle Richardson, Charles Abraham, and Rod Bond, "Psychological Correlates of University Students' Academic Performance: A Systematic Review and Meta-analysis," *Psychological Bulletin* 138 (2012): 353–87.
46. O'Leary, "Self-efficacy and Health."
47. Tian et al., "Enacting Rituals to Improve Self-control"; Lysann Damisch, Barbara Stoberock, and Thomas Mussweiler, "Keep Your Fingers Crossed! How Superstition Improves Performance," *Psychological Science* 21 (2010): 1014–20; Daniel R. Czech, A. J. Ploszay, and Kevin L. Burke, "An Examination of the Maintenance of Preshot Routines in Basketball Free Throw Shooting," *Journal of Sport Behavior* 27, no. 4 (2004): 323–29; Hobson et al., "Psychology of Rituals."
48. Brooks et al., "Don't Stop Believing," 83.
49. Michaéla C. Schippers and Paul A. M. Van Lange, "The Psychological Benefits of Superstitious Rituals in Top Sport: A Study among Top Sportspersons," *Journal of Applied Social Psychology* 36, no. 10 (2006): 2532–53.
50. Michael I. Norton and Francesca Gino, "Rituals Alleviate Grieving for Loved Ones, Lovers, and Lotteries," *Journal of Experimental Psychology: General* 143, no. 1 (2014): 266–72.
51. Donald Tyson, *Kinesic Magic: Channeling Energy with Postures and Gestures* (Woodbury, MN: Llewellyn, 2020).
52. James D. Laird, "Self-attribution of Emotion: The Effects of Expressive Behavior on the Quality of Emotional Experience," *Journal of Personality and Social Psychology* 29 (1974): 475–86.
53. Nicholas A. Coles, David S. March, Fernando Marmolejo-Ramos, Jeff T. Larsen, Nwadiogo C. Arinze, Izuchukwu L. G. Ndukaihe, Megan L. Willis, "A Multi-lab Test of the Facial Feedback Hypothesis by the Many Smiles Collaboration," *Nature Human Behavior* 6 (2022): 1731–42.

54. John H. Riskind and Carolyn C. Gotay, "Physical Posture: Could It Have Regulatory or Feedback Effects on Motivation and Emotion?" *Motivation and Emotion* 6, no. 3 (1982): 273–98 (p. 292).
55. Tom F. Price, Lauritz W. Dieckman, and Eddie Harmon-Jones, "Embodying Approach Motivation: Body Posture Influences Startle Eyeblink and Event-related Potential Responses to Appetitive Stimuli," *Biological Psychology* 90 (2012): 211–217.
56. Felicitas Wieneck, Matthias Messner, Gernot Hauke, and Olga Pollatos, "Improving Interoceptive Ability through the Practice of Power Posing: A Pilot Study," *PLoS ONE* 14, no. 2 (2019): e0211453 (p. 14).
57. Patty Van Cappellen and Megan Edwards, "Emotion Expression in Context: Full Body Postures of Christian Prayer Orientations Compared to Specific Emotions," *Journal of Nonverbal Behavior* 45, no. 4 (2021): 633; Patty Van Cappellen, Stephanie Cassidy, and Ruixi Zhang, "Religion as an Embodied Practice: Organizing the Various Forms and Documenting the Meanings of Christian Prayer Postures, *Psychology of Religion and Spirituality* 15, no. 2 (2023): 251–61.
58. Felicitas D. Goodman, *Where the Spirits Ride the Wind: Trance Journeys and Other Ecstatic Experiences* (Bloomington: Indiana University Press, 1990), 216–18.
59. Raquel Romberg, "'Gestures That Do'": Spiritist Manifestations and the Technologies of Religious Subjectivation and Affect," *Journal of Material Culture* 22, no. 4 (2017): 385–405.
60. Romberg, "Gestures That Do," 386.
61. Linda Larkey, Roger Jahnke, Jennifer Etnier, and Julie Gonzales, "Meditative Movement as a Category of Exercise: Implications for Research," *Journal of Physical Activity and Health* 6, no. 2 (2009): 230–38; Peter Payne and Mardi A. Crane-Godreau, "Meditative Movement for Depression and Anxiety," *Frontiers in Psychiatry* 4 (2013): 71; Pasi Pölönen, Otto Lappi, and Mari Tervaniemi, "Effect of Meditative Movement on Affect and Flow in Qigong Practitioners," *Frontiers in Psychology* 10 (2019): 2375; Ryan Abbott and Helen Lavretsky, "Tai Chi and Qigong for the Treatment and Prevention of Mental Disorders," *Psychiatric Clinics of North America* 36, no. 1 (2013): 109–119.
62. Starhawk, *The Spiral Dance: A Rebirth of the Ancient Religion of the Great Goddess* (San Francisco: Harper & Row, 1979), 58.
63. Chenchen Wang, Raveendhara Bannuru, Judith Ramel, Bruce Kupelnick,

Tammy Scott, and Christopher H. Schmid, "Tai Chi on Psychological Well-being: Systematic Review and Meta-analysis," *BioMed Central Complementary and Alternative Medicine* 10 (2010): 23; Abbott and Lavretsky, "Tai Chi and Qigong"; Payne and Crane-Godreau, "Meditative Movement."

64. Payne and Crane-Godreau, "Meditative Movement."
65. Herbert Benson, John F. Beary, and Mark P. Carol, "The Relaxation Response," *Psychiatry: Journal for the Study of Interpersonal Processes* 37, no. 1 (1974), 37–46; Herbert Benson and Miriam Z. Klipper, *The Relaxation Response* (New York: William Morrow & Co., 1975); Herbert Benson, Martha M. Greenwood, and Helen Klemchuk, "The Relaxation Response: Psychophysiologic Aspects and Clinical Applications," *International Journal of Psychiatry in Medicine* 6, nos. 1–2 (1975): 87–98.
66. Sara Martin, "The Power of the Relaxation Response: A Behavioral Medicine Pioneer Reports on a Time-tested Technique That Reverses Aging and Improves Health," *Psychological Monitor* 39, no. 9 (2008): 32.
67. Gregg D. Jacobs, "Clinical Applications of the Relaxation Response and Mind-Body Interventions," *Journal of Alternative and Complementary Medicine* 7, no. 1 (2001): S93–S101; Manoj K. Bhasin, Jeffery A. Dusek, Bei-Hung Chang, Marie G. Joseph, John W. Denninger, Gregory L. Fricchione, Herbert Benson, and Towia A. Libermann, "Relaxation Response Induces Temporal Transcriptome Changes in Energy Metabolism, Insulin Secretion and Inflammatory Pathways," *PLoS ONE* 8, no. 5 (2013): e62817.
68. James E. Stahl, Michelle L. Dossett, A. Scott LaJoi, John W. Denninger, Darshan H. Mehta, Roberta Goldman, Gregory L. Fricchione, and Herbert Benson, "Relaxation Response and Resiliency Training and Its Effect on Healthcare Resource Utilization," *PLoS ONE* 10, no. 10 (2015): e0140212.
69. Bhasin et al., "Relaxation Response."
70. Fred B. Bryant and Joseph Veroff, *Savoring: A New Model of Positive Experience* (Mahwah, NJ: Lawrence Erlbaum Associates, 2007), 3.
71. Laura G. Kiken, Kristjen B. Lundberg, and Barbara L. Frederickson, "Being Present and Enjoying It: Dispositional Mindfulness and Savoring the Moment are Distinct, Interactive Predictors of Positive Emotions and Psychological Health," *Mindfulness* 8 (2017): 1280–90.
72. Kiken et al., "Being Present and Enjoying It"; Jordi Quoidbach, Elizabeth V. Berry, Michel Hansenne, and Moïra Mikolajczak," Positive Emotion Regulation and Well-being: Comparing the Impact of Eight Savoring and

Dampening Strategies," *Personality and Individual Differences* 49, no. 5 (2010): 368–73; Jennifer L. Smith and Fred B. Bryant, "Savoring and Wellbeing: Mapping the Cognitive-Emotional Terrain of the Happy Mind," in Michael D. Robinson and Michael Eid, eds., *The Happy Mind: Cognitive Contributions to Well-Being* (Cham, Switzerland: Springer, 2017), 139–56.

73. Eric L. Garland, Adam W. Hanley, Michael R. Riquino, Sarah E. Reese, Anne K. Baker, Karen Salas, Brook P. Yack, Carter E. Bedford, Myranda A. Bryan, Rachel Atchley, Yoshio Nakamura, Brett Froeliger, and Matthew O. Howard, "Mindfulness-Oriented Recovery Enhancement Reduces Opioid Misuse Risk via Analgesic and Positive Psychological Mechanisms: A Randomized Controlled Trial," *Journal of Consulting and Clinical Psychology* 87, no. 10 (2019): 927–40.

74. Jenifer L. Smith and Fred B. Bryant, "The Benefits of Savoring Life: Savoring as a Moderator of the Relationship between Health and Life Satisfaction in Older Adults," *International Journal of Aging and Human Development* 84, no. 1 (2016): 3–23.

75. Eric L. Garland and Barbara L. Fredrickson, "Positive Psychological States in the Arc from Mindfulness to Self-transcendence: Extensions of the Mindfulness-to-Meaning Theory and Applications to Addiction and Chronic Pain Treatment," *Current Opinion in Psychology* 28 (2019): 184–91.

76. Daniel B. Hurley and Paul Kwon, "Results of a Study to Increase Savoring the Moment: Differential Impact on Positive and Negative Outcomes," *Journal of Happiness Studies* 13 (2012): 579–88.

77. Bryant and Veroff, *Savoring*, 204–9.

78. Bryant and Veroff, *Savoring*, 209.

79. Kathleen D. Vohs, Yajin Wang, Francesca Gino, and Michael I. Norton, "Rituals Enhance Consumption," *Psychological Science* 24, no. 9 (2013): 1714–21. See also the literature review in Eleanor Ratcliffe, Weston Lyle Baxter, and Nathalie Martin, "Consumption Rituals relating to Food and Drink: A Review and Research Agenda," *Appetite* 134 (2019): 86–93.

80. Rohan Kapitány and Mark Nielsen, "Adopting the Ritual Stance: The Role of Opacity and Context in Ritual and Everyday Actions," *Cognition* 145 (2015): 13–29.

81. Vohs et al., "Rituals Enhance Consumption," 86.

82. Israel Regardie, *Foundations of Practical Magic: An Introduction to Qabalistic, Magical and Meditative Techniques* (Wellingborough, Northamptonshire: Aquarian Press, 1979), 30.

83. Marc Andersen, Kristoffer L. Nielbo, Uffe Schjoedt, Thies Pfeiffer, Andreas Roepstorff, and Jesper Sørensen, "Predictive Minds in Ouija Board Sessions," *Phenomenology and the Cognitive Sciences* 18 (2019): 577–88.

84. Justin L. Barrett, "Exploring the Natural Foundations of Religion," *Trends in Cognitive Sciences* 4, no. 1 (2000): 29–34 (p. 31).

85. Michiel van Elk, "Paranormal Believers Are More Prone to Illusory Agency Detection Than Skeptics," *Consciousness and Cognition* 22 (2012): 1041–46 (p. 1041).

86. Stephen D. Krau, "The Multiple Uses of Guided Imagery," *Nursing Clinics of North America* 55 (2020): 467–74; Joe Utay and Megan Miller, "Guided Imagery as an Effective Therapeutic Technique: A Brief Review of Its History and Efficacy Research," *Journal of Instructional Psychology* 33, no. 1 (2006): 40–43; Dani Veena and Sana Alvi, "Guided Imagery Intervention for Anxiety Reduction," *Indian Journal of Health and Wellbeing* 7, no. 2 (2016): 198–203.

87. Clair Mellenthin, "Guided Imagery," in Heidi Gerard Kaduson and Charles E. Schafer, eds., *Play Therapy with Children: Modalities for Change* (Washington, DC: American Psychological Association, 2021), 125–139 (p. 186).

88. Kristine Kwekkeboom, Karen Huseby-Moore, and Sandra Ward, "Imaging Ability and Effective Use of Guided Imagery," *Research in Nursing and Health* 21 (1998): 189–98; Krau, "Multiple Uses of Guided Imagery," 468.

89. Mellenthin, "Guided Imagery," 125–126.

90. Recommendations for this kind of exercise can be found in Lindsay Squire, *Earth Magick: Ground Yourself with Magick. Connect with the Seasons in Your Life and in Nature* (London: Leaping Hare Press, 2022); Lisa McSherry, *A Witch's Guide to Crafting Your Practice: Create a Magical Path That Works for You* (St. Paul, MN: Llewellyn, 2022); Deborah Blake, *A Year and a Day of Everyday Witchcraft: 366 Ways to Witchify Your Life* (St. Paul, MN: Llewellyn, 2017).

91. Conway, *Magic*, 62.

92. Conway, *Magic*, 63.

93. Morwyn, *Secrets of a Witch's Coven* (West Chester, PA: Whitford Press, 1988), 50.

94. See the chapter "Meditation and Visualization Practices" in Shoemaker, *Living Thelema*.

95. Daniel Gould, Dana K. Voelker, Nicole Damarjian, and Christy Greenleaf, "Imagery Training for Peak Performance," in J. Van Raalte and B. Brewer, eds., *Exploring Sport and Exercise Psychology*, 3rd ed. (Washington, DC: American Psychological Association, 2014), 55–82 (p. 67).
96. Gould et al., "Imagery Training," 71.
97. Gould et al., "Imagery Training," 75.
98. Gould et al., "Imagery Training," 76.
99. Elizabeth Bigham, Lauren McDannel, Isabel Luciano, and Guadalupe Salgado-Lopez, "Effect of a Brief Guided Imagery on Stress," *Biofeedback* 42, no. 1 (2014): 28–35.
100. Ephraim C. Trakhtenberg, "The Effects of Guided Imagery on the Immune System: A Critical Review," *International Journal of Neuroscience* 118 (2008): 839–55.
101. Samira Foji, Moosa Alreza Tadayonfar, Mohaddesh Mohsenpour, and Mhammad Hasan Rakhshani, "The Study of the Effect of Guided Imagery on Pain, Anxiety and Some Other Hemodynamic Factors in Patients Undergoing Coronary Angiography," *Complementary Therapies in Clinical Practice* 21 (2015): 119–23; Kelly King, "The Review of the Effects of Guided Imagery on Cancer Patients with Pain," *Complementary Health Practice Review* 15, no. 2 (2010): 98–107.
102. María Dolores Onieva-Zafra, María Laura Parra-Fernández, and E. Fernandez-Martinez, "Benefits of a Home Treatment Program Using Guided Imagery Relaxation Based on Audio Recordings for People with Fibromyalgia," *Holistic Nursing Practice* 33, no. 2 (2019): 111–20.
103. Bigham et al., "Effects of a Brief Guided Imagery."
104. Kwekkeboom et al., "Imaging Ability and Effective Use."
105. Sidney J. Blatt, "Projective Techniques," in Alan E. Kazdin, ed., *Encyclopedia of Psychology*, vol. 6 (Washington, DC: American Psychological Association, 2000), 317–321 (p. 317).
106. See, e.g., Scott O. Lilienfeld, James M. Wood, and Howard N. Garb, "The Scientific Status of Projective Techniques," *Psychological Science in the Public Interest* 1, no. 2 (2000): 27–66; Stephen Hibbard, "A Critique of Lilienfeld et al.'s (2000) 'The Scientific Status of Projective Techniques,'" *Journal of Personality Assessment* 80, no. 3 (2003): 260–71; James P. Choca and Edward D. Rossini, *Assessment Using the Rorschach Inkblot Test* (Washington, DC: American Psychological Association, 2018).
107. Choca and Rossini, *Assessment Using the Rorschach Inkblot Test*, 103.

108. Blatt, "Projective Techniques," 319.
109. Blatt, "Projective Techniques," 320.
110. Choca and Rossini, *Assessment Using the Rorschach Inkblot Test*, 87.
111. Blatt, "Projective Techniques," 317.
112. Julia A. Mossbridge and Dean Radin, "Precognition as a Form of Prospection: A Review of the Evidence," *Psychology of Consciousness: Theory, Research, and Practice* 5 (2018): 78–93; Dean Radin, *The Conscious Universe* (San Francisco: HarperEdge, 1997).
113. Daryl J. Bem and Charles Honorton, "Does Psi Exist? Replicable Evidence for an Anomalous Process of Information Transfer," *Psychological Bulletin* 115 (1994): 4–18; Daryl J. Bem, John Palmer, and Richard S. Broughton, "Updating the Ganzfeld Database: A Victim of Its Own Success?" *Journal of Parapsychology* 65, no. 3 (2001): 207–218.
114. Charles Honorton and Diane C. Ferrari, "Future Telling": A Meta-analysis of Forced-choice Precognition Experiments, 1935–1987," *Journal of Parapsychology* 53 (1989): 281–308.
115. Radin, *Conscious Universe*; Patrizio E. Tressoldi and Lance Storm, "Stage 2 Registered Report: Anomalous Perception in a Ganzfeld Condition: A Meta-analysis of More than 40 Years Investigation," *F1000 Research* 10 (2024): 234.
116. Daryl J. Bem, "Feeling the Future: Experimental Evidence for Anomalous Retroactive Influences on Cognition and Affect," *Journal of Personality and Social Psychology* 100, no. 3 (2011): 407–25.
117. Bem (2011), "Feeling the Future," 419.
118. Daryl Bem, Patrizio Tressoldi, Thomas Rabeyron, and Michael Duggan, "Feeling the Future: A Meta-analysis of 90 Experiments on the Anomalous Anticipation of Random Future Events [version 2; referees: 2 approved], *F1000 Research* 4 (2016): 1188.
119. Zoltan Kekecs, Bence Palfi, Barnabas Szaszi, Peter Szecsi, Mark Zrubka, Marton Kovacs, Bence E. Bakos et al., "Raising the Value of Research Studies in Psychological Science by Increasing the Credibility of Research Reports: The Rransparent Psi Project," *Royal Society of Open Science* 10 (2023): 191375.
120. Mahlon W. Wagner and Mary Monnet, "Attitudes of College Professors toward Extra-sensory Perception," *Zetetic Scholar* 5 (1979): 7–17.
121. Bethany Butzer, "Bias in the Evaluation of Psychology Studies: A Comparison of Parapsychology versus Neuroscience," *Explore* 16 (2020): 382–91.

122. Bem et al. (2016), "Feeling the Future," 13.
123. Thomas Rabeyron, "Why Most Research Findings about Psi Are False: The Replicability Crisis, the Psi Paradox and the Myth of Sisyphus," *Frontiers in Psychology* 11 (2020): 562992, (p. 4).
124. Rabeyron, "Why Most Research Findings about Psi Are False," 6.
125. Mat Auryn, *Psychic Witch: A Metaphysical Guide to Meditation, Magick and Manifestation* (Woodbury, MN: Llewellyn, 2020); Mat Auryn, *Mastering Magick: A Course in Spellcasting for the Psychic Witch* (Woodbury, MN: Llewellyn, 2022); Mat Auryn, *The Psychic Art of Tarot: Opening Your Inner Eye for More Insightful Readings* (Woodbury, MN: Llewellyn, 2024).

CHAPTER 4. THINK BETTER

1. Debra Diamond and Molly E. Aitken, *Yoga: The Art of Transformation* (Washington, DC: Arthur M. Sackler Gallery, Smithsonian Institution, 2013); Elizabeth De Michelis, *A History of Modern Yoga: Patañjali and Western Esotericism* (London: Continuum, 2004); Swami Vivekananda, *Rāja Yoga: Conquering the Internal Nature* (London: Longmans, Green, and Co., 1896).
2. "Bargains in Hatha Yoga for a Short Time Only: Professor Will Throw in Yoga Breathing and Vibration of Colors Gratis: All Can Be Done in Two Weeks: But It Is Expressly Stipulated That Customers Are Not to Yoga in the Professor's Preserves," *Brooklyn Daily Eagle*, November 11, 1900, 33.
3. "Fearing Jail, She Kills Self: Miss Ida Craddock, High Priestess of Yoga, Inhales Gas: She Was an Admirer of the Danse du ventre," *Atlanta Constitution*, October 18, 1902, 1; "Author Ends Her Life: 'High Priestess of Yoga' Commits Suicide: Miss Ida C. Craddock, writer and leader in peculiar religions, convicted of sending improper literature through mails and fearing imprisonment in insane asylum, kills herself in New York," *Chicago Daily Tribune*, October 18, 1902; "Ida Craddock Ends Her Earthly Troubles: Suicide of High Priestess of 'Church of the Yoga,'" *Los Angeles Times*, October 18, 1902. For more on Ida Craddock and the Church of Yoga, see Leigh Eric Schmidt, *Heaven's Bride: The Unprintable Life of Ida C. Craddock, American Mystic, Scholar, Sexologist, Martyr and Madwoman* (New York: Basic Books, 2010), 120–35.
4. "The Newest Way to Beauty: Oriental health hints as gathered from the yoga book and here set down for the benefit of the fair and those who would

be fair," *St. Louis Post Dispatch* Sunday magazine, August 19, 1906, 8.
5. "Mrs. Stone Becomes a Yoga: Wife of Purdue University President Withdraws from the World and Family," *New York Times*, May 3, 1908, 1; "Dr. Stone Would Take Back Wife Now a Mystic: Yoga philosophy of individualism wrecks home of Purdue's president: He wants to resign," *St. Louis Post Dispatch*, May 3, 1908, A2; "Wife Leaves College Head: Mrs. Stone Will Become a Yoga Priestess: Purdue University declines husband's resignation: Fad course in philosophy led to desertion," *Boston Daily Globe*, May 3, 1908, 17.
6. "Wreckage: Quits Husband for Yoga Cult: Purdue's President Wifeless: He gets divorce when she forsakes home for weird philosophy: Victim of fad would live on cocoanuts and wear garb of nature: Educator tenders resignation but college trustees stand by him," *Los Angeles Times*, June 20, 1911; "Joins Yoga Colony: Educator's Wife Goes to Follow Strange God: Purdue University head divorced after Indian philosophy is said to have taken wife to South Sea islands," *Chicago Defender*, July 29, 1911, 3.
7. "Paul Morton Headed Strange Yoga Cult: Filing of a Suit in New York Brings Lights to an Interesting Story," *Nashville Tennessean*, June 19, 1908, 8.
8. "Taught Mystic Love: Barber Tells of Mrs. Bull's Bhakti Yoga Lessons: Sought stage of divinity: At trial of action to set aside will of violinist's widow, pupil relates weird instructions—followers breathed through left nostrils and imagined lotus blossoms in hearts," *Washington Post*, May 24, 1911, 1; "Danger in Raja Yoga: It May Have Unhinged Mrs. Bull's Mind, Vedante Leader Says: Too difficult for women," *New York Tribune*, June 10, 1911, 5.
9. "Seattle Yoga Scandal Grows," *Tacoma Times*, August 3, 1915, 1; "'Burbanking Souls'" May Land Head of Yoga Cult in Prison: Dr. Gerber won't stand for 'mental alchemy' between his wife and 'Dr.' DeBit: Arrests yoga prophet on statutory charge: Fights for the custody of his daughter," *Salt Lake Telegram*, August 15, 1915; "Both Parents Denied Custody of Child," *San Francisco Examiner*, September 10, 1915, 8.
10. "Poet and Magus Explains Magic on a Basis of Scientific Facts: Defends Yoga and Mystic Rites," *Washington Post*, December 26, 1915, R2.
11. Frater Perdurabo [Aleister Crowley] and Soror Virakam [Mary d'Este Sturges], *Book 4*, part 1 (London: Wieland, 1912); J. F. C. Fuller, *Yoga: A Study of the Mystical Philosophy of the Brahmins and Buddhists* (London: William Rider, 1925); Mahatma Guru Sri Paramahansa Shivaji [Aleister

Crowley], *Eight Lectures on Yoga* (London: O.T.O., 1939); Nancy Wasserman, *The Weiser Concise Guide to Yoga for Magick*, ed. and intro. James Wasserman (Newburyport, MA: Red Wheel/Weiser, 2007).

12. David Shoemaker, *Living Thelema: A Practical Guide to Attainment in Aleister Crowley's System of Magick* (Sacramento: Anima Solis, 2013; rpt. Newburyport, MA: Red Wheel/Weiser, 2022), 28.

13. Morwyn, *Secrets of a Witch's Coven* (West Chester, PA: Whitford Press, 1988), 43.

14. "Probe Queer Cult of Rich N.Y. Women: Two Vanderbilt sisters in club of "Oom," once jailed for orgies," *Quad City Times*, October 24, 1919. For more on Bernard, see Robert Love, *The Great Oom: The Improbable Birth of Yoga in America* (New York: Viking, 2010).

15. Theos Casimir Bernard, *Penthouse of Gods: A Pilgrimage into the Heart of Tibet and the Sacred City of Lhasa* (New York: Scribner's Sons, 1939), *Heaven Lies Within Us* (New York: Scribner's Sons, 1939), *Hatha Yoga: The Report of a Personal Experience* (New York: Columbia University Press, 1944), and *Philosophical Functions of India* (London: Rider and Company, 1945). For more on Theos Bernard, see Douglas Veenhof, *White Lama: The Life of Tantric Yogi Theos Bernard Tibet's Lost Emissary to the New World* (New York: Doubleday Religion, 2011).

16. Suzanne Newcombe, *Yoga in Britain: Stretching Spirituality and Educating Yogis* (Bristol, CT: Equinox, 2019), 28–38.

17. Mark Singleton, *Yoga Body: The Origins of Modern Posture Practice* (Oxford, UK: University Press, 2010).

18. Anya P. Foxen, *Inhaling Spirit: Harmonialism, Orientalism, and the Western Roots of Modern Yoga* (Oxford, UK: University Press, 2020), 2.

19. See, e.g., David Gordon White's preface to *Kiss of the Yogini: "Tantric Sex" in Its South Asian Contexts* (Chicago: University of Chicago Press, 2003); Karl Baier, Philipp A. Maas, and Karin Preisendanz, eds., *Yoga in Transformation: Historical and Contemporary Perspectives* (Göttingen: Vienna University Press, 2018).

20. Kurt Leland, *Rainbow Body: A History of the Western Chakra System from Blavatsky to Brennan* (Lake Worth, FL: Ibis Press, 2016); Phil Hine, *Wheels within Wheels: Chakras and Western Esotericism* (London: Twisted Trunk, 2024).

21. Deane H. Shapiro and Roger N. Walsh, *Meditation Classic and Contemporary Perspectives* (New York: Aldine, 1984); Robin Monro,

A. K Ghosh, and Daniel Kalish, *Yoga Research Bibliography: Scientific Studies on Yoga and Meditation* (Cambridge, England: Yoga Biomedical Trust, 1989); Maria Ospina, *Meditation Practices for Health: State of the Research* (Rockville, MD: Agency for Healthcare Research and Quality, 2007); K. Ramakrishna Rao, *Foundations of Yoga Psychology* (Singapore: Springer, 2017); Narayanan Srinivasan, ed., *Meditation*, vol. 244 in *Progress in Brain Research* (Cambridge, MA: Academic Press, 2019).

22. Rao, *Foundations of Yoga Psychology*, 137.
23. R. G. Torrens, *The Golden Dawn: The Inner Teachings* (New York: Samuel Weiser, 1969; rpt. 1977), 39. For a description of relaxation aimed at witches, see Morwyn, *Secrets of a Witch's Coven*, 48–49.
24. S. Kobayashi and K. Koitabashi, "Effects of Progressive Muscle Relaxation on Cerebral Activity: An fMRI Investigation," *Complementary Therapies in Medicine* 26 (2016): 33–39.
25. Kobayashi and Koitabashi, "Effects of Progressive Muscle Relaxation," 33.
26. Masoomeh Noruzi Zamenjani, Behnam Masmouei, Behdi Harorani, Rezvan Ghafarzadegan, Fahimeh Davodabady, Sima Zahedi, and Zakie Davodabady, "The Effect of Progressive Muscle Relaxation on Cancer Patients' Self-efficacy," *Complementary Therapies in Clinical Practice* 34 (2019): 70–75.
27. Kyriakoula Merakou, Konstantinos Tsoukas, Georgios Stavrinos, Eirini Amanaki, Antonia Daleziou, Ntina Kourmousi, Georgia Stamatelopoulou, Evi Spourdalaki, and Anastasia Barbouni, "The Effect of Progressive Muscle Relaxation on Emotional Competence: Depression-anxiety-stress, Sense of Coherence, Health-related Quality of Life, and Well-being of Unemployed People in Greece: An Intervention study," *Explore* 15, no. 1 (2019): 38–46.
28. Merakou et al., "The Effect of Progressive Muscle Relaxation," 39.
29. Friedhelm Stetter and Sirko Kupper, "Autogenic Training: A Meta-analysis of Clinical Outcome Studies," *Applies Psychophysiology and Biofeedback* 27, no. 1 (2002): 45–98.
30. Chris C. Streeter, J. Eric Jensen, Ruth M. Perlmutter, Howard J. Cabral, Hua Tian, Devin B. Terhune, Domenic A. Ciraulo, and Perry F. Renshaw, "Yoga Asana Sessions Increase Brain GABA Levels: A Pilot Study," *Journal of Alternative and Complementary Medicine* 13, no. 4 (2007): 419–26.
31. Chantal Villemure, Marta Čeko, Valerie A. Cotton, and M. Catherine Bushnell, "Neuroprotective Effects of Yoga Practice: Age-, Experience-,

and Frequency-dependent Plasticity," *Frontiers in Human Neuroscience* 9 (2015): 281.

32. Christina Grof and Stanislav Grof, *Holotropic Breathwork: A New Approach to Self-Exploration and Therapy* (Albany: State University of New York Press, 2010).

33. Guy W. Fincham, Amy Kartar, Malin V. Uthaug, Brittany Anderson, Lottie Hall, Yoko Nagai, Hugo Critchley, and Alessandro Colasanti, "High Ventilation Breathwork Practices: An Overview of Their Effects, Mechanisms, and Considerations for Clinical Applications," *Neuroscience and Biobehavioral Reviews* 155 (2023): 105453.

34. Originally appearing as a series of articles in *The Theosophist*, the collected volume Ráma Prasád, *The Science of Breath and the Philosophy of the Tatwas (Translated from the Sanskrit): With Fifteen Introductory and Explanatory Essays on Nature's Finer Forces* (London: Theosophical Society, 1890) had an expanded edition in 1894, with many subsequent reprintings.

35. Thomas Lake Harris, *The Breath of God with Man: An Essay on the Grounds and Evidences of Universal Religion* (New York: Brotherhood of the New Life, 1867). This book, too, has been reprinted many times.

36. Torrens, *The Golden Dawn*, 40; Israel Regardie, *The Golden Dawn: An Account of the Teachings, Rites and Ceremonies of the Order of the Golden Dawn* (St. Paul, MN: Llewellyn, 1971; rpt. 1978), 105.

37. J. F. C. Fuller, "The Temple of Solomon the King," *The Equinox* I, no. 4 (September 1910): 101.

38. [Aleister Crowley], "Liber RV vel Spiritus sub figura CCVI," *The Equinox* I, no. 7 (March 1912): 62.

39. Guy W. Fincham, Clara Strauss, and Kate Cavanagh, "Effect of Coherent Breathing on Mental Health and Wellbeing: A Randomised Placebo-controlled Trial," *Scientific Reports* 13 (2023): 22141.

40. Guy William Fincham, Clara Strauss, Jesus Montero-Marin, and Kate Cavanagh, "Effect of Breathwork on Stress and Mental Health: A Meta-analysis of Randomised-controlled Trials," *Scientific Reports* 13 (2023): 432; Stephany Campanelli, Adriano Bretanha Lopes Tort, and Bruno Lobão-Soares, "Pranayamas and Their Neurophysiological Effects," *International Journal of Yoga* 13, no. 3 (2020): 183–92; Apar Avinash Saoji, B. R. Raghavendra, and N. K. Manjunath, "Effects of Yogic Breath Regulation: A Narrative Review of Scientific Evidence," *Journal of Ayurveda and Integrative Medicine* 10 (2019): 50–58.

41. Jeniffer Z. Brandani, Julio Mizuno, Emmanuel G. Ciolac, and Henrique L. Monteiro, "The Hypotensive Effects of Yoga's Breathing Exercises: A Systematic Review," *Complementary Therapies in Clinical Practice* 28 (2017): 38–46.
42. Karamjit Singh, Hemant Bhargav, and T. M. Srinivasan, "Effect of Uninostril Yoga Breathing on Brain Hemodynamics: A Functional Near-infrared Spectroscopy Study," *International Journal of Yoga* 9, no. 1 (2016)): 12–19.
43. C.-K. Peng, Isaac C. Henry, Joseph E. Mietus, Jeffrey M. Hausdorff, Gurucharan Khalsa, Herbert Benson, and Ary L. Goldberger, "Heart Rate Dynamics during Three Forms of Meditation," *International Journal of Cardiology* 95 (2004): 19–27 (p. 19); see also C.-K. Peng, Joseph E. Mietus, Yanhui Liu, Gurucharan Khalsa, Pamela S. Douglas, Herbert Benson, and Ary L. Goldberger, "Exaggerated Heart Rate Oscillations during Two Meditation Techniques," *International Journal of Cardiology* 70 (1999): 101–7.
44. Andrew Newberg, *Sex, God and the Brain* (Nashville: Turner, 2024), 30–31.
45. Alexander T. Duda, Adam R. Clarke, and Robert J. Barry, "Mindfulness Meditation Alters Neural Oscillations Independently of Arousal," *International Journal of Psychophysiology* 205 (2024): 112439.
46. Josh Brahinsky, Jonas Mago, Mark Miller, Shaila Catherine and Michael Lifshitz (2024), "The Spiral of Attention, Arousal, and Release: A Comparative Phenomenology of Jhāna Meditation and Speaking in Tongues," *American Journal of Human Biology*, 36 (2024): e24189.
47. James C. Corby, Walton T. Roth, Vincent P. Zarcone Jr., and Bert S. Kopell, "Psychophysiological Correlates of the Practice of Tantric Yoga Meditation," *Archives of General Psychiatry* 35 (1978): 571–77.
48. Alberto Chiesa, Alessandro Serretti, and Janus Christian Jakobsen, "Mindfulness: Top-down or Bottom-up Emotion Regulation Strategy?" *Clinical Psychology Review* 33 (2013): 82–96.
49. Xin Qi, Jiajin Tong, Senlin Chen, Zhonghui He, and Xiangyi Zhu, "Comparing the Psychological Effects of Meditation- and Breathing-focused Yoga Practice in Undergraduate Students," *Frontiers in Psychology* 11 (2020): 560152.
50. Christine Tara Peterson, Sarah M. Bauer, Deepak Chopra, Paul J. Mills, and Raj K. Maturi, "Effects of *Shambhavi Mahamudra Kriya*, a

Multicomponent Breath-based Yogic Practice (*Pranayama*), on Perceived Stress and General Well-being," *Journal of Evidence-Based Complementary and Alternative Medicine* 22, no. 4 (2017): 788–97.

51. Maria von Salisch and Katharina Voltmer, "A Daily Breathing Practice Bolsters Girls' Prosocial Behavior and Third and Fourth Graders' Supportive Peer Relationships: A Randomized Controlled Trial," *Mindfulness* 14 (2023): 1622–35.

52. Willem Kuyken, Susan Ball, Catherine Crane, Poushali Ganguli, Benjamin Jones, Jesus Montero-Marin, Elizabeth Nuthall et al., "Effectiveness and Cost-effectiveness of Universal School-based Mindfulness Training Compared with Normal School Provision in Reducing Risk of Mental Health Problems and Promoting Well-being in Adolescence: The MYRIAD Cluster Randomised Controlled Trial," *Evidence Based Mental Health* 25 (2022): 99–109; Lauren Meyer and Katie Eklund, "The Impact of a Mindfulness Intervention on Elementary Classroom Climate and Student and Teacher Mindfulness: A Pilot Study," *Mindfulness* 11 (2020): 991–1005; Xiaolu Dai, Nan Du, Songyun Shi, and Shuang Lu, "Effects of Mindfulness-based Interventions on Peer Relationships of Children and Adolescents: A Systematic Review and Meta-analysis," *Mindfulness* 13 (2022): 2653–75.

53. Salisch and Voltmer, "A Daily Breathing Practice."

54. Barbara L. Fredrickson, Aaron J. Boulton, Ann M. Firestine, Patty Van Cappellen, Sara B. Algoe, Mary M. Brantley, Sumi Loundon Kim, Jeffrey Brantley, and Sharon Salzberg, "Positive Emotion Correlates of Meditation Practice: A Comparison of Mindfulness Meditation and Lovingkindness Meditation," *Mindfulness* 8 (2017): 1623–33; Philip D. Zelazo and Kristen E. Lyons, "The Potential Benefits of Mindfulness Training in Early Childhood: A Developmental Social Cognitive Neuroscience Perspective," *Child Development Perspectives* 6 (2012): 154–60.

55. Richard P. Brown and Patricia L. Gerbarg, "Yoga Breathing, Meditation, and Longevity," *Annals of the New York Academy of Science* 1172 (2009): 54–62 (p. 58).

56. Patton E. Burchett, "The 'Magical' Language of Mantra," *Journal of the American Academy of Religion* 76, no. 4 (2008): 807–43 (p. 815).

57. M. M. Delmonte, "Mantras and Meditation: A Literature Review," *Perceptual and Motor Skills* 57 (1983): 64–66; Shirley Telles, R. Nagarathna, and H. R. Nagendra, "Autonomic Changes while Mentally Repeating Two

Syllables—One Meaningful and the Other Neutral," *Indian Journal of Physiology and Pharmacology* 42, no. 1 (1998): 57–63.
58. Delmonte, "Mantras and Meditation," 65.
59. Gemma Perry, Vince Polito, and William Forde Thompson, "Rhythmic Chanting and Mystical States across Traditions," *Brain Sciences*, 11 (2021): 101.
60. Barbara Stöckigt, F. Jeserich, H. Walach, M. Elies, B. Brinkhaus, and M. Teut, "Experiences and Perceived Effects of Rosary Praying: A Qualitative Study," *Journal of Religion and Health* 60, no. 6 (2021): 3886–3906.
61. Junling Gao, Hang Kin Leung, Bonnie Wai Yan Wu, Stavros Skouras, and Hin Hung Sik, "The Neurophysiological Correlates of Religious Chanting," *Scientific Reports* 9 (2019): 4262 (p. 4).
62. Gao et al., "Neurophysiological Correlates," 5.
63. Dharma Singh Khalsa, Daniel Amen, Chris Hanks, Nisha Money, and Andrew Newberg, "Cerebral Blood Flow Changes during Chanting Meditation," *Nuclear Medicine Communications* 39 (2009): 956–61 (p. 961).
64. Holger Cramer, Romy Lauche, Jost Langhosrt, and Gustav Dobos, "Is One Yoga Style Better Than Another? A Systematic Review of Associations of Yoga Style and Conclusions in Randomized Yoga Trials," *Complementary Therapies in Medicine* 25 (2016): 178–87 (p. 178). The authors acknowledge, however, that only five styles of yoga had more than ten trials, so their conclusions may not be definitive.
65. Kieran C. R. Fox, Matthew L. Dixon, Savannah Nijeboer, Manesh Girn, James L. Floman, Michael Lifshitz, Melissa Ellamil, Peter Sedlmeier, and Kalina Christoff, "Functional Neuroanatomy of Meditation: A Review and Meta-analysis of 78 Functional Neuroimaging Investigations," *Neuroscience and Biobehavioral Reviews* 65 (2016): 208–28 (p. 225).
66. Bruno Neri, Alejandro Luis Callara, Nicola Vanello, Danilo Menicucci, Andrea Zaccaro, Andrea Piarulli, Marco Laurino et al., "Report from a Tibetan Monastery: EEG Neural Correlates of Concentrative and Analytical Meditation," *Frontiers in Psychology* 15 (2024): 1348317.
67. Frederick Travis, "On the Neurobiology of Meditation: Comparison of Three Organizing Strategies to Investigate Brain Patterns during Meditation Practice," *Medicina* 56 (2020): 712. For another take on the complexity of classifying types of meditation practice, see Tracy

Brandmeyer, Arnaud Delorme, and Helané Wahbeh, "The Neuroscience of Meditation: Classification, Phenomenology, Correlates, and Mechanisms," *Progress in Brain Research* 244 (2019): 1–29.

68. Juliana Yordanova, Vasil Kolev, Valentina Nicolardi, Luca Simione, Federica Mauro, Patrizia Garberi, Antonio Raffone, and Peter Malinowski, "Attentional and Cognitive Monitoring Brain Networks in Long-term Meditators Depend on Meditation States and Expertise," *Scientific Reports* 11 (2021): 4909; David Laneri, Verena Schuster, Bruno Dietsche, Andreas Jansen, Ulrich Ott, and Jens Sommer, "Effects of Long-term Mindfulness Meditation on Brain's White Matter Microstructure and Its Aging," *Frontiers in Aging Neuroscience* 7 (2016): 254; Tim Gard, Maxime Taquet, Rohan Dixit, Britta K. Hölzel, Bradford C. Dickerson, and Sara W. Lazar, "Greater Widespread Functional Connectivity of the Caudate in Older Adults Who Practice Kripalu Yoga and Vipassana Meditation Than in Controls," *Frontiers in Human Neuroscience* 9 (2015): 137; Eileen Luders, Kristi Clark, Katherine L. Narr, and Arthur W. Toga, "Enhanced Brain Connectivity in Long-term Meditation Practitioners," *NeuroImage* 57 (2011): 1308–16.

69. Cyril R. Pernet, Nikolai Belov, Arnaud Delorme, and Alison Zammit, "Mindfulness Related Changes in Grey Matter: A Systematic Review and Meta-analysis," *Brain Imaging and Behavior* 15, no. 5 (2021): 2720–30; Radhika Desai, Anisha Tailor, and Tanvi Bhatt, "Effects of Yoga on Brain Waves and Structural Activation: A Review," *Complementary Therapies in Clinical Practice* 21 (2015): 112–18.

70. M. G. Ramesh Babu, Rajagopal Kadavigere, Prakashini Koteshwara, Brijesh Sathian, and Kiranmai S. Rai, "Rajayoga Meditation Induces Grey Matter Volume Changes in Regions That Process Reward and Happiness," *Scientific Reports* 10 (2020): 16177.

71. Sergio Elías Hernández, José Suero, Alfonso Barros, José Luis González-Mora, and Katya Rubia, "Increased Grey Matter Associated with Long-term Sahaja Yoga Meditation: A Voxel-Based Morphometry Study," *PLoS One* 11, no. 3 (2016): e0150757.

72. Kieran C. R. Fox, Savannah Nijeboer, Matthew L. Dixon, James L. Floman, Melissa Ellamil, Samuel P. Rumak, Peter Sedlmeier, and Kalina Christoff (2014), "Is Meditation Associated with Altered Brain Structure? A Systematic Review and Meta-analysis of Morphometric Neuroimaging in Meditation Practitioners," *Neuroscience and Biobehavioral Reviews* 43: 48–73 (p. 48).

73. Fox et al., "Is Meditation Associated with Altered Brain Structure?" 48.

74. Eileen Luders, Owen R. Phillips, Kristi Clark, Florian Kurth, Arthur W. Toga, and Katherine L. Narr, "Bridging the Hemispheres in Meditation: Thicker Callosal Regions and Enhances Fractional Anisotrophy (FA) in Long-term Practitioners," *NeuroImage* 61 (2012): 181–87.

75. Joshua A. Grant, Emma G. Duerden, Jérôme Courtemanche, Mariya Cherkasova, Gary H. Duncan, and Pierre Rainville, "Cortical Thickness, Mental Absorption and Meditative Practice: Possible Implications for Disorders of Attention," *Biological Psychology* 92 (2013): 275–81. See also David Chan and Marjorie Woollacott, "Effects of Level of Meditation Experience on Attentional Focus: Is the Efficiency of Executive or Orientation Networks Improved?" *Journal of Alternative and Complementary Medicine* 13, no. 6 (2007): 651–57.

76. Sara W. Lazar, Catherine E. Kerr, Rachel H. Wasserman, Jeremy R. Gray, Douglas N. Greve, Michael T. Treadway, Metta McGarvey et al., "Meditation Experience Is Associated with Increased Cortical Thickness," *NeuroReport* 16, no. 17 (2005): 1893–97.

77. Shirley Telles, Nilkamal Singh, Ram Kumar Gupta, and Acharya Balkrishna, "A Selective Review of *Dharana* and *Dhyana* in Healthy Participants," *Journal of Ayurveda and Integrative Medicine* 7 (2016): 255–60; B. R. Raghavendra and Shirley Telles, "Performance in Attentional Tasks Following Meditative Focusing and Focusing without Meditation," *Ancient Science of Life* 32, no. 1 (2013) 49–53; Sanjay Kumar and Shirley Telles, "Meditative States Based on Yoga Texts and Their Effects on Performance of a Letter-cancellation Task," *Perceptual and Motor Skills* 109, no. 3 (2009): 679–89.

78. Grant et al., "Cortical Thickness, Mental Absorption and Meditative Practice"; Lazar et al., "Meditation Experience Is Associated with Increased Cortical Thickness"; Laneri et al., "Effects of Long-term Mindfulness Meditation."

79. Eileen Luders, Nicolas Cherbuin, and Christian Gaser, "Estimating Brain Age Using High-resolution Pattern Recognition: Younger Brains in Long-term Meditation Practitioners," *NeuroImage* 134 (2016): 508–13 (p. 508).

80. Florian Kurth, Nicolas Cherbuin, and Eileen Luders, "Reduced Age-related Degeneration of the Hippocampal Subiculum in Long-term Meditators," *Psychiatry Research: Neuroimaging* 232 (2015): 214–18 (p. 216).

81. Rinske A. Gotink, Rozanna Meijboom, Mieke W. Vernooij, Marion Smits, and M. G. Myriam Hunink, "8-week Mindfulness Based Stress Reduction

Induces Brain Changes Similar to Traditional Long-term Meditation Practice—A systematic Review," *Brain and Cognition* 108 (2016): 32–41.

82. Alessandra Dodich, Maurizio Zollo, Chiara Crespi, Stefano F. Cappa, Daniella Laureiro Martinez, Andrea Falini, and Nicola Canessa, "Short-term Sahaja Yoga Meditation Training Modulates Brain Structure and Spontaneous Activity in the Executive Control Network," *Brain and Behavior* 9, no. 1 (2018): e01159.

83. Elke Gizewski, Ruth Steiger, Michaela Waibel, Sergiy Pereverzyev, Patrick J. D. Sommer, Christian Siedentopf, Astrid E. Grams, Lukas Lenhart, and Nicolas Singewald, "Short-term Meditation Training Influences Brain Energy Metabolism: A Pilot Study on 31PMR Spectroscopy," *Brain and Behavior* 11 (2020): e01914.

84. Shao-Wei Xue, Yi-Yuan Tang, Rongxiang Tang, and Michael I. Posner, "Short-term Meditation Induces Changes in Brain Resting EEG Theta Networks," *Brain and Cognition* 87 (2014): 1–6.

85. Rita Sleimen-Malkoun, Louise Devillers-Réolon, and Jean-Jacques Temprado, "A Single Session of Mindfulness Meditation May Acutely Enhance Cognitive Performance Regardless of Meditation Experience," *PLoS One* 18, no. 3 (2023): e0282188; Lorenza S. Colzato, Roberta Sellaro, Iliana Samara, and Bernhard Hommel, "Meditation-induced Cognitive-control States Regulate Response-conflict Adaptation: Evidence from Trial-to-trial Adjustments in the Simon Task," *Consciousness and Cognition* 35 (2015): 110–114.

86. Susan A. Gaylord, Olafur S. Palsson, Eric L. Garland, John Douglas Mann, Karen Bluth, William Whitehead and Keturah R. Faurot, "Mindfulness Training Has Long-Term Therapeutic Benefits in Women with Irritable Bowel Syndrome," *Mindfulness*, 15 (2024): 2233–2244.

87. Marco Schlosser, Olga M. Klimecki, Fabienne Collette, Julie Gonneaud, Matthias Kliegel, Natalie L. Marchant, Gaël Chételat, and Antoine Lutz, "An 18-month Meditation Training Selectively Improves Psychological Well-being in Older Adults: A Secondary Analysis of a Randomised Controlled Trial," *PLoS ONE* 18, no. 12 (2023): e0294753. This study consisted of nine months of mindfulness meditation followed by nine months of loving-kindness meditation; significant changes relative to controls were observed after the loving-kindness training, but not after nine months of mindfulness training.

88. María Elena Gutiérrez-Hernández, Luisa Fernanda Fanjul Rodríguez,

Alicia Díaz Megolla, Cristián Oyanadel, and Wenceslao Peñate Castro, "The Effect of Daily Meditative Practices Based on Mindfulness and Self-compassion on Emotional Distress under Stressful Conditions: A Randomized Controlled Trial," *European Journal of Investigation in Health, Psychology and Education* 13, no. 4 (2023): 762–75.

89. Julieta Galante, Claire Friedrich, Collaboration of Mindfulness Trials (CoMinT), Tim Dalgleish, Peter B. Jones, and Ian R. White, "Systematic Review and Individual Participant Data Meta-analysis of Randomized Controlled Trials Assessing Mindfulness-based Programs for Mental Health Promotion," *Nature Mental Health* 1 (2023): 462–76.

90. Julieta Galante, Jesús Montero-Marín, Maris Vainre, Géraldine Dufour, Javier García-Campayo, and Peter B. Jones, "Altered States of Consciousness Caused by a Mindfulness-based Programme Up to a Year Later: Results from a Randomised Controlled Trial," *PloS ONE* 19, no. 7 (2024): e0305928.

91. Catherine Hobbs, Sarah Jelbert, Laurie R. Santos, and Bruce Hood, "Long-term Analysis of a Psychoeducational Course on University Students' Mental Well-being," *Higher Education* 10 (2024): 1007.

92. Joseph Pilates, Judd Robbins, and Lin Van Heuit-Robbins, *Pilates' Return to Life through Contrology* (n.p.: Presentation Dynamics, 2012), 11–17.

93. Roos Vonk and Anouk Visser, "An Exploration of Spiritual Superiority: The Paradox of Self-enhancement," *European Journal of Social Psychology* 51, no. 1 (2019): 152–65; Jochen E. Gebauer, Andreas D. Nehrlich, Dagmar Stahlberg, Constantine Sedikides, Anke Hackenschmidt, Doreen Schick, Clara A. Stegmaier, Cara C. Windfelder, Anna Bruk, and Johannes Mander, "Mind-body Practices and the Self: Yoga and Meditation Do Not Quiet the Ego but Instead Boost Self-enhancement," *Psychological Science* 29, no. 8 (2018): 1299–1308; Anthony D. Hermann and Robert C. Fuller, "Grandiose Narcissism and Religiosity," in Anthony D. Hermann, Amy B. Brunell, and Joshua D. Foster, eds., *Handbook of Trait Narcissism: Key Advances, Research Methods, and Controversies* (Singapore: Springer, 2018).

CHAPTER 5. GREATER (AND LESSER) MAGICAL RETIREMENTS

1. For the first English translation, see Samuel Liddell MacGregor Mathers, *The Book of the Sacred Magic of Abra-Melin the Mage, as Delivered*

by *Abraham the Jew unto His Son Lamech, A.D. 1458* (London: John M. Watkins, 1898). A modern translation from earlier and more complete manuscripts is Abraham von Worms, *The Book of Abramelin: A New Translation*, ed. Georg Dehn and trans. Steven Guth (Lake Worth, FL: Ibis Press, 2006).
2. Lon Milo DuQuette, foreword in von Worms, *The Book of Abramelin*, xv.
3. Aleister Crowley, "Liber Samekh" in *Magick in Theory and Practice* (Paris: Lecram Press, 1929–1930), 265–301.
4. [Aleister Crowley], "John St. John: The Record of the Magical Retirement of G. H. Frater O∴ M∴," *The Equinox* I, no. 1 (March 1909): supplement.
5. Juan Siliezar, "Life on the Ice," *Harvard Gazette*, September 11, 2019. See also Kat Long, "Wind, Cold, and Altitude Sickness: Winter at the South Pole," *National Geographic*, June 20, 2016; Amy Lowitz, "Captain's web log(10)—11 June 2016—What's the inside of the station like?" blog post available at amylowitz.com/SouthPole; Svati Kirsten Narula, "On Getting Naked in Antarctica," *The Atlantic*, January 7, 2014.
6. Arreed F. Barabasz, "Effects of Isolation on States of Consciousness," in Albert A. Harrison, Yvonne A. Clearwater, and Christopher P. McKay, eds., *From Antarctica to Outer Space: Life in Isolation and Confinement* (New York: Springer New York, 1991), 201–208 (p. 205).
7. Andrew Neher, *Paranormal and Transcendental Experience: A Psychological Examination* (New York: Dover Publications, 2011), 22.
8. Kristoffer Jonsson, Katarina Grim, and Anette Kjellgren, "Do Highly Sensitive Persons Experience More Nonordinary States of Consciousness during Sensory Isolation?" *Social Behavior and Personality* 42, no. 9 (2014): 1495–1506.
9. Christopher R. Long and James R. Averill, "Solitude: An Exploration of Benefits of Being Alone," *Journal for the Theory of Social Behavior* 33, no. 1 (2003): 21–44 (definitions found on pages 23 and 37).
10. William E. Hammitt, "Cognitive Dimensions of Wilderness Solitude," *Environment and Behavior* 14 (1982): 478–93.
11. Long and Averill, "Solitude, "26; paraphrasing Anthony Storr, *Solitude: A Return to the Self* (New York: Ballantine, 1982).
12. David T. Bradford, "Brain and Psyche in Early Christian Asceticism," *Psychological Reports* 109, no. 2 (2011): 461–520 (p. 470).
13. Éliphas Lévi, *Transcendental Magic: Its Doctrine and Ritual*, trans. A. E. Waite (New York: Samuel Weiser, 1974), 210.

14. Aleister Crowley, *The Confessions of Aleister Crowley*, ed. John Symonds and Kenneth Grant (London: Jonathan Cape, 1969), 113.
15. Aleister Crowley, *Little Essays Toward Truth* (London: Ordo Templi Orientis, 1938; rpt. Scottsdale, AZ: New Falcon Publications, 1991), 71.
16. Karynna Okabe-Miyamoto and Julia K. Boehm, "Hedonic Adaptation," in Bernardo J. Carducci, Christopher S. Nave, Jeffrey S. Mio, and Ronald E. Riggio, eds., *The Wiley Encyclopedia of Personality and Individual Differences: Volume I, Models and Theories* (Hoboken, NJ: John Wiley & Sons, 2020).
17. Jordi Quoidbach and Elizabeth W. Dunn, "Give It Up: A Strategy for Combating Hedonic Adaptation," *Social Psychological and Personality Science* 4, no. 5 (2012) 563–68.
18. Stephen D. Anton, Keelin Moehl, William T. Donahoo, Krisztina Marosi, Stephanie A. Lee, Arch G. Mainous III, Christiaan Leeuwenburgh, and Mark P. Mattson, "Flipping the Metabolic Switch: Understanding and Applying the Health Benefits of Fasting," *Obesity* 26, no. 2 (2018): 254–68; Dimitrios Kapogiannis, Apostolos Manolopoulos, Roger Mullins, Konstantinos Avgerinos, Francheska Delgado-Peraza, Maja Mustapic, Carlos Nogueras-Ortiz et al., "Brain Responses to Intermittent Fasting and the Healthy Living Diet in Older Adults," *Cell Metabolism* 36, no. 8 (2024): 1668–78.
19. Mark P. Mattson, Valter D. Longo, and Michelle Harvie, "Impact of Intermittent Fasting on Health and Disease Processes," *Ageing Research Reviews* 39 (2017): 46–58.
20. Mark P. Mattson, Keelin Moehl, Nathaniel Ghena, Maggie Schmaedick, and Aiwu Cheng, "Intermittent Metabolic Switching, Neuroplasticity and Brain Health," *Nature Reviews Neuroscience* 19, no. 2 (2018): 63–80.
21. Xuefeng Yang, Xiu Miao, Franziska Schweiggart, Sophia Großmann, Karsten Rauss, Manfred Hallschmid, Jan Born et al., "The Effect of Fasting on Human Memory Consolidation," *Neurobiology of Learning and Memory*, 218 (2025): 108034.

CHAPTER 6. HOLD THAT THOUGHT

1. Russell W. Belk, "Possessions and the Extended Self," *Journal of Consumer Research* 15 (1988): 139–68 (p. 140).
2. Belk, "Possessions and the Extended Self," 160.

3. Aleister Crowley, Mary Desti, and Leila Waddell, *Magick: Liber ABA, Book 4, Parts I–IV*, ed. Hymenaeus Beta, 2nd rev. ed. (San Francisco: Red Wheel/Weiser, 2008), 73, 86, 95.
4. Christian Derbaix and Alain Decrop, "Colours and Scarves: An Ethnographic Account of Football Fans and their Paraphernalia," *Leisure Studies* 30, no. 3 (2011): 271–91 (p. 283).
5. Michael Shermer, *The Believing Brain: From Ghosts and Gods to Politics and Conspiracies—How We Construct Beliefs and Reinforce Them as Truths* (New York: Time Books, 2011), 89–90.
6. Laura Shapiro, *Something from the Oven: Reinventing Dinner in 1950s America* (New York: Viking, 2004); Veronique Greenwood, "Why Cake Mix Lacks One Essential Ingredient," *BBC Future* website, November 9, 2017; Michael Y. Park, "A History of the Cake Mix, the Invention That Redefined 'Baking,'" *Bon Appétit* website, September 26, 2013; David Mikkelson, "Requiring an Egg Made Instant Cake Mixes Sell?" *Snopes* website, January 30, 2008.
7. Michael I. Norton, Daniel Mochon, and Dan Ariely, "The IKEA Effect: When Labor Leads to Love," *Journal of Consumer Psychology* 22 (2012): 453–60.
8. Simone Dohle, Sina Rall, and Michael Siegrist, "I Cooked It Myself: Preparing Food Increases Liking and Consumption," *Food Quality and Preference* 33 (2014): 14–16.
9. Norton et al., "The IKEA Effect"; Lukasz Walasek, Tim Rakow, and William J. Matthews, "When Does Construction Enhance Product Value? Investigating the Combined Effects of Object Assembly and Ownership on Valuation," *Journal of Behavioral Decision Making* 30 (2015): 144–56.
10. Daniel Mochon, Michael I. Norton, and Dan Ariely, "Bolstering and Restoring Feelings of Competence via the IKEA Effect," *International Journal of Research on Marketing* 29 (2012): 363–69.
11. Lauren E. March, Patricia Kanngiesser, and Bruce Hood, "When and How does Labour Lead to Love? The Ontogeny and Mechanisms of the IKEA Effect," *Cognition* 170 (2018): 245–53 (p. 252).
12. See, e.g., Skye Alexander, *The Modern Witchcraft Grimoire: Your Complete Guide to Creating Your Own Book of Shadows* (New York: Simon and Schuster, 2016) or Alferian Gwydion MacLir, *The Witch's Wand: The Craft, Lore, and Magick of Wands and Staffs* (St. Paul, MN: Llewellyn, 2015).

13. Kathleen D. Vohs, Yajin Wang, Francesca Gino, and Michael I. Norton, "Rituals Enhance Consumption," *Psychological Science* 24, no. 9 (2013): 1714–21.
14. Rohan Kapitány and Mark Nielsen, "Adopting the Ritual Stance: The Role of Opacity and Context in Ritual and Everyday Actions," *Cognition* 145 (2015): 13–29.
15. Kapitány and Nielsen, "Adopting the Ritual Stance," 27.
16. Hilke Plassmann, John O'Doherty, Baba Shiv, and Antonio Rangel, "Marketing Actions Can Modulate Neural Representations of Experienced Pleasantness," *PNAS* 105, no. 3 (2008): 1050–54.
17. Aleister Crowley, "Letter B," *Magick Without Tears*, ed. Israel Regardie (St. Paul, MN: Llewellyn, 1973), 6.
18. For details of the various Golden Dawn implements, along with practical instructions on how to make them, see Robert Wang, *The Secret Temple* (New York: Weiser, 1980) and Chic Cicero and Sandra Tabatha Cicero, *Secrets of a Golden Dawn Temple* (St. Paul, MN: Llewellyn, 1992). Compare to practical instructions from the Servants of the Light in Dolores Ashcroft-Nowicki, *The Ritual Magic Workbook: A Practical Course of Self-Initiation* (London: Aquarian/Thorsons, 1986).
19. [Aleister Crowley], "Liber A vel Armorum sub figura CDXII," *The Equinox* I, no. 4 (September 1910): 15–19; rpt. Aleister Crowley, *Magick in Theory and Practice* (Paris: Lecram Press, 1929–1930), 435–36.
20. Dion Fortune, *The Esoteric Orders and Their Work* (St. Paul, MN: Llewellyn, 1978), 92.
21. Wolfgang von Goethe, *Theory of Colours*, trans. Charles Lock Eastlake (London: John Murray, 1840).
22. J. Jastrow, "The Popular Aesthetics of Color," *Popular Science Monthly* 50 (1897): 361–68.
23. Hans J. Eysenck, "A Critical and Experimental Study of Color Preferences," *American Journal of Psychology* 54, no. 3 (1941): 385–94.
24. Andrew J. Elliot, "Color and Psychological Functioning: A Review of Theoretical and Empirical Work," Frontiers in Psychology 6 (2015): 368; J. S. Nakashian, "The Effects of Red and Green Surroundings on Behavior," Journal of General Psychology 70 (1964): 143–61; Ayn E. Crowley, "The Two-dimensional Impact of Color on Shopping," Marketing Letters 4 (1993): 59–69.
25. Christian Cajochen, Mirjam Münch, Szymon Kobialka, Kurt Kräuchi,

Roland Steiner, Peter Oelhafen, Selim Orgül, and Anna Wirz-Justice, "High Sensitivity of Human Melatonin, Alertness, Thermoregulation, and Heart Rate to Short Wavelength Light," *Journal of Clinical Endocrinology and Metabolism* 90, no. 3 (2005): 1311–16; Steven W Lockley, Erin E. Evans, Frank A. J. L. Scheer, George C. Brainard, Charles A. Czeisler, and Daniel Aeschbach, "Short-wavelength Sensitivity for the Direct Effects of Light on Alertness, Vigilance, and the Waking Electroencephalogram in Humans," *Sleep* 29, no. 2 (2006): 161–68.

26. Anya C. Hurlbert and Yazhu Ling, "Biological Components of Sex Differences in Color Preference," *Current Biology* 17, no. 16 (2007): R623–R625.

27. Mark A Changizi, Qiong Zhang, and Shinsuke Shimojo, "Bare Skin, Blood and the Evolution of Primate Colour Vision," *Biology Letters* 2, no. 2 (2006): 217–21; Mark Changizi, *The Vision Revolution* (Dallas: Benbella, 2009).

28. Stephen E. Palmer and Karen B. Schloss, "An Ecological Valence Theory of Human Color Preference," *PNAS*, 107 no. 19 (2010): 8877–882.

29. Andrew J. Elliot and Markus A. Maier, "Color-in-context Theory," in Patricia Devine and Ashby Plant, eds., *Advances in Experimental Social Psychology* 45 (San Diego: Academic Press, 2012), 61–125; Andrew J. Elliot and Markus A. Maier, "Color Psychology: Effects of Perceiving Color on Psychological Functioning in Humans," Annual Review of Psychology 65 (2014): 95–120.]

30. Chloe Taylor, Alexandra Clifford, and Anna Franklin, "Color Preferences Are Not Universal," Journal of Experimental Psychology: General 142, no. 4 (2013): 1015–27.

31. Mubeen M. Aslam, "Are You Selling the Right Colour? A Cross-cultural Review of Colour as a Marketing Cue," Journal of Marketing Communications 12, no. 1 (2006): 15–30. For a wide-ranging survey of color in literature, history, art, and science, see David Scott Kastan and Stephen Farthing, On Color (New Haven, CT: Yale University Press, 2018).

32. Taylor et al., "Color Preferences Are Not Universal."

33. W. R. Crozier, "The Psychology of Colour Preferences," *Coloration Technology* 26, no. 1 (1996): 63–72.

34. Elliot and Maier, "Color Psychology," 99.

35. Mark G. Frank and Thomas Gilovich, "The Dark Side of Self- and Social Perception: Black Uniforms and Aggression in Professional Sports,"

Journal of Personality and Social Psychology 54 (1988): 74–85. See also Duje Kodžoman, "The Psychology of Clothing: Meaning of Colors, Body Image and Gender Expression in Fashion," Textile and Leather Review 2, no. 2 (2019): 90–103.

36. Russell Hill, "Psychology: Red Enhances Human Performance in Contests," Nature 435 (2005): 293.
37. Adam K. Fetterman, Tianwei Liu, and Michael D. Robinson, "Extending Color Psychology to the Personality Realm: Interpersonal Hostility Varies by Red Preferences and Perceptual Biases," Journal of Personality 83, no. 1 (2015): 106–116.
38. Diana Su Yun Tham, Paul T. Sowden, Alexandra Grandison, Anna Franklin, Anna Kai Win Lee, Michelle Ng, Juhyun Park, Weiguo Pang, and Jingwen Zhao , "A Systematic Investigation of Conceptual Color Associations," Journal of Experimental Psychology: General 149, no. 7 (2019): 1311–32.
39. Rezvan Rafatjou, Bahar Ahmadi, Maryam Farhadian, and Niloofar Entezari Moghadam, "Evaluation Effect of Color in Dental Office and Dentist's Uniform while Using Two Different Distraction Techniques on Injection Anxiety of 6–9 years' Old Children Referring to Hamedan Dental School: Randomized Clinical Trial," Dental Research Journal 18 (2021): 71.
40. Kattakayam Annamary, Gajula Shivashankarappa Prathima, Renganathan Sajeev, Gurusamy Kayalvizhi, Venkatesan Ramesh, and Govindasamy Ezhumalai, "Colour Preference to Emotions in Relation to the Anxiety Level among School Children in Puducherry: A Cross-sectional Study," Journal of Clinical and Diagnostic Research 10, no. 7 (2016): ZC26–ZC30.
41. Guobin Xia, Muzi Li, Philip Henry, Stephen Westland, Francisco Queiroz, Qiwei Peng, and Luwen Yu, "Aroused and Impulsive Effects of Colour Stimuli on Lateral and Logical Abilities," Behavioral Sciences 11 (2021): 24.
42. David Allen Hulse, *The Key of It All: An Encyclopedic Guide to the Sacred Languages and Magickal Systems of the World*, vol 1 (St. Paul, MN: Llewellyn, 1993), 53.
43. Bill Heidrick, "An Introduction to the Qabalah: Part X—The Rose and Scales," *Thelema Lodge Calendar*, December 1995.
44. Pat Zalewski and Chris Zalewski, *The Magical Tarot of the Golden Dawn* (London: Aeon, 2008), 25–26. This is slightly expanded from the author's assessment originally appearing in Pat Zalewski, *Kabbalah of the Golden Dawn* (St. Paul, MN: Llewellyn, 1993), 75–76.
45. Aleister Crowley, *777 vel Prolegomena Symbolica ad Systemam Sceptico-*

Mysticae Viae Explicandae Fundamentum Hieroglyphicum Sanctissimorum Scientiae Summae (London: W. Scott, 1909); Israel Regardie, *The Golden Dawn: An Account of the Teachings Rites and Ceremonies of the Order of the Golden Dawn* (Chicago: Aries Press, 1937).

46. Thanks to Emily Auger, Tony Iannotti, Amy Hale, and Jesse Bransford for pointing me to literature on the Golden Dawn colors.

47. Sandra Tabatha Cicero, *The Book of the Concourse of the Watchtowers: An Exploration of Westcott's Enochian Tablets* (Elfers, FL: H.O.G.D. Books, 2012), 63.

48. Ira Robinson, *Moses Cordovero's Introduction to Kabbalah: An Annotated Translation of His Or Ne'erav* (New York: Michael Scharf Publication Trust of the Yeshiva University Press, 1994), 133; Bill Heidrick, "An Introduction to Qabalah: Part IX—Color and Qabalah," *Thelema Lodge Calendar*, November 1995.

49. Meyer Waxman, *A History of Jewish Literature* (South Brunswick, NY: Thomas Yoseloff, 1960), 370.

50. William James, *The Principles of Psychology*, vol. 1 (New York: Henry Holt & Co., 1890), 292.

51. Introduced by Daryl J. Bem, "Self-perception: An Alternative Interpretation of Cognitive Dissonance Phenomena," *Psychological Review* 74 (1967): 183–200 and Daryl J. Bem, "Self-perception Theory," in L. Berkowitz, ed., *Advances in Experimental Social Psychology*, vol. 6 (New York: Academic Press, 1972), 1–62.

52. Joan M. Kellerman and James D. Laird, "The Effect of Appearance on Self-perceptions," Journal of Personality 50, no. 3 (1982): 296–315.

53. Joy V. Peluchette and Katherine Karl, "The Impact of Workplace Attire on Employee Self-perceptions," Human Resource Development Quarterly 18 (2007): 345–60.

54. Philip G. Zimbardo, "The Human Choice: Individuation, Reason and Order versus Deindividuation, Impulse, and Chaos," in W. J. Arnold and D. Levine, eds., Nebraska Symposium on Motivation, vol. 18 (Lincoln: University of Nebraska Press, 1970).

55. Robert D. Johnson and Leslie L. Downing, "Deindividuation and Valence of Cues: Effects on Prosocial and Antisocial Behavior," Journal of Personality and Social Psychology 37, no. 9 (1979): 1531–38.

56. Hajo Adam and Adam D. Galinsky, "Enclothed Cognition," Journal of Experimental Social Psychology 48 (2012): 918–25.

57. Sandra Blakeslee, "Mind Games: Sometimes a White Coat Isn't Just a White Coat," New York Times, April 2, 2012.
58. Charles A. Van Stockum Jr. and Marci S. DeCaro, "Enclothed Cognition and Controlled Attention during Insight Problem-solving," Journal of Problem Solving 7 (2014): 73–83.
59. Michael W. Kraus and Wendy Berry Mendes, "Sartorial Symbols of Social Class Elicit Class-Consistent Behavioral and Physiological Responses: A Dyadic Approach," Journal of Personality and Social Psychology 143, no. 6 (2014): 2330–40.
60. Michael L. Slepian, Simon N. Ferber, Joshua M. Gold, and Abraham M. Rutchick, "The Cognitive Consequences of Formal Clothing," Social Psychological and Personality Science 6, no. 6 (2015): 661–68. See also Joseph K. Kim, Brian C. Holtz, and Ryan M. Vogel, "Wearing Your Worth at Work: The Consequences of Employees' Daily Clothing Choices," Academy of Management Journal, September 20, 2022.
61. Melissa Dahl, "How 'Casual Fridays' Suppress Creativity," CNN Health website, May 29, 2015.
62. J. N. Belding, R. E. Petty and P. Briñol, "Embodied Objects: Wearing Unfamiliar Objects Can Influence Information Processing and Evaluation" (presented at the annual meeting of the Midwestern Psychological Association, Chicago, IL, 2013); Pablo Briñol, Richard E. Petty, and Jennifer Belding, "Objectification of People and Thoughts: An Attitude Change Perspective," British Journal of Social Psychology 56 (2017): 233–49.
63. Belén López-Pérez, Tamara Ambrona, Ellie Wilson, and Marina Khalil, "The Effect of Enclothed Cognition on Empathic Responses and Helping Behaviour," Social Psychology 47 (2016): 223–31.
64. Ciro Civile and Sukhvinder S. Obhi, "Students Wearing Police Uniforms Exhibit Biased Attention toward Individuals Wearing Hoodies," Frontiers in Psychology 8 (2017): 62.
65. Saaid A. Mendoza and Elizabeth J. Parks-Stamm, "Embodying the Police: The Effects of Enclothed Cognition on Shooting Decisions," Psychological Reports 123, no. 6 (2020): 2363–71.
66. Adam Galinsky, "Why Outfitting Police in Military Uniforms Encourages Brutality," Fast Company website, June 17, 2020.
67. Hajo Adam and Adam D. Galinsky, "Reflections on Enclothed Cognition: Commentary on Burns et al.," Journal of Experimental Social Psychology 83 (2019): 157–59 (p. 159).

68. Rebecca Womack, "Enclothed Cognition: The Effect of Attire on Attention Task Performance," *Samford Undergraduate Research Journal* (spring 2016): 94–99; Devi M. Burns, Elizabeth L. Fox, Michael Greenstein, Gayla Olbright, and DeMaris Montgomery, "An Old Task in New Clothes: A Preregistered Direct Replication Attempt of Enclothed Cognition Effects on Stroop Performance," *Journal of Experimental Social Psychology* 83 (2019): 150–56.
69. Burns et al., "An Old Task in New Clothes," 155.
70. Womack, "Enclothed Cognition," 98.
71. King and Skinner, *Techniques of High Magic*, 24–25.

CHAPTER 7. SACRED HEAD SPACE

1. William Gray, *Inner Traditions of Magic* (New York: Weiser, 1978), 124.
2. Ying Yang, Constantine Sedikides, Yuqi Wang, and Huajian Cai, "Nature Nurtures Authenticity: Mechanisms and Consequences," *Journal of Personality and Social Psychology: Interpersonal Relations and Group Processes* 126, no. 1 (2024): 79–104.
3. Howard Frumkin, Gregory N. Bratman, Sara Jo Breslow, Bobby Cochran, Peter H. Kahn Jr., Joshua J. Lawler, Philip S. Levin et al., "Nature Contact and Human Health: A Research Agenda," *Environmental Health Perspectives* 125, no. 7 (2017): 075001.
4. Dongmei Mei, Ding Yang, Tong Li, Xin Zhang, Kang Rao, and Liman Man Wai Li, "Nature Contact Promotes Prosociality: The Mediating Roles of Self-transcendence, Nature Connectedness, and Materialism," *Journal of Environmental Psychology* 96 (2024): 102324.
5. Matthew P. White, Sabine Pahl, Katherine Ashbullby, Stephen Herbert, and Michael H. Depledge, "Feelings of Restoration from Recent Nature Visits," *Journal of Environmental Psychology* 35 (2013): 40–51.
6. Chorong Song, Harumi Ikei, Bum-Jin Park, Juyoung Lee, Takahide Kagawa, and Yoshifumi Miyazaki, Psychological benefits of walking through forest areas, *International Journal of Environmental Research and Public Health* 15 (2018): 2804.
7. Matthew P. White, Ian Alcock, James Grellier, Benedict W. Wheeler, Terry Hartig, Sara L. Warber, Angie Bone, Michael H. Depledge, and Lora E. Fleming, "Spending at Least 120 Minutes a Week in Natures is Associated with Good Health and Wellbeing," *Scientific Reports* 9 (2019): 7730.

8. This is a primary thesis throughout Dimitris Xygalatas, *Ritual: How Seemingly Senseless Acts Make Life Worth Living* (New York: Little, Brown Spark, 2022).
9. Quote in Brian Resnick, "The Weird Science of the Placebo Effect Keeps Getting More Interesting," *Vox* website, May 5, 2021.
10. Resnick, "The Weird Science of the Placebo Effect."
11. Gary Greenberg, "What if the Placebo Effect Isn't a Trick?" *New York Times Magazine*, November 7, 2018.
12. Melina von Wernsdorff, Martin Loef, Brunna Tuschen-Caffier, and Stefan Schmidt, "Effect of Open-label Placebos in Clinical Trials: A Systematic Review and Meta-analysis," *Scientific Reports* 11 (2021): 3855. A more recent study found open-label placebos effective for treating COVID-19-related stress. See Darwin A. Guevarra, Christopher T. Webster, Jade N. Moros, Ethan Kross, and Jason S. Moser, "Remotely Administered Non-Deceptive Placebos Reduce COVID-Related Stress, Anxiety, and Depression," Applied Psychology: Health and Well-Being, 16 (2024): 2204–2224.
13. See, e.g., Johannes Alfons Karl and Ronald Fischer, "Rituals, Repetitiveness and Cognitive Load: A Competitive Test of Ritual Benefits for Stress," *Human Nature* 29 (2018): 418–41; Xygalatas, *Ritual*.
14. Andrew Newberg, *Neurotheology: How Science Can Enlighten Us about Spirituality* (New York: Columbia University Press, 2018), 185 et seq.
15. Nicholas M. Hobson, Juliana Schroeder, Jane L. Risen, Dimitris Xygalatas, and Michael Inzlicht, "The Psychology of Rituals: An Integrative Review and Process-based Framework," *Personality and Social Psychology Review* 22, no. 3 (2018): 260–84.
16. Éliphas Lévi, *Doctrine and Ritual of High Magic*, trans. Mark Anthony Mikituk (New York: TarcherPerigee, 2017), 128. For the original French, see *Dogme et Rituel de la Haute Magie* (Paris: Germer Baillière, 1861), 268–69.
17. Guangyu Zhou, Jonas K. Olofsson, Mohamad Z. Koubeissi, Georgios Menelaou, Joshua Rosenow, Stephan U. Schuele, Pengfei Xu, Joel L. Voss, Gregory Lane, and Christina Zelano, "Human Hippocampal Connectivity Is Stronger in Olfaction Than Other Sensory Systems," *Progress in Neurobiology* 201 (2021): 102027.
18. Charles Spence, "Using Ambient Scent to Enhance Well-being in the Multisensory Built Environment," Frontiers in Psychology 11 (2020): 598859.

19. M. A. M. Smeets and G. B. Dijksterhuis, "Smelly Primes: When Olfactory Primes Do or Do Not Work," Frontiers in Psychology 5 (2014): 96.
20. Spence, "Using Ambient Scent."
21. Kandhasamy Sowndhararajan and Songmun Kim, "Influence of Fragrances on Human Psychophysiological Activity: With Special Reference to Human Electroencephalographic Response," Scientia Pharmaceutica 84 (2016): 724–51.
22. Mitsumi Ijima, Mikio Osawa, Nobuyuki Nishitani, and Makoto Iwata, "Effects of Incense on Brain Function: Evaluation Using Electroencephalograms and Event-related Potentials," Neuropsychobiology 59 (2009): 80–86.
23. Sowndhararajan and Kim, "Influence of Fragrances."
24. Craig Warren and Stephen Warrenburg, "Mood Benefits of Fragrance," *Perfumer Flavor* 18 (1993): 9–16.
25. Meihui Ba and Jian Kang, "A Laboratory Study of the Sound-odour Interaction in Urban Environments," *Building and Environment* 147 (2019): 314–26.
26. [Lisa Chamberlain], "Tools of Wiccan Ritual: The Bell," Wicca Living website, under the Wiccan Ritual tab, choose the Tools of Magic menu.
27. See, e.g., Darinda J. Congdo, "'Tibet Chic': Myth, Marketing, Spirituality and Politics in Musical Representations of Tibet in the United States" (doctoral dissertation, University of Pittsburgh, 2007); Ben Joffe, "Tripping on Good Vibrations: Cultural Commodification and Tibetan Singing Bowls," Savage Minds (.org) website, October 31, 2015; and Tenzin Dheden, "'Tibetan Singing Bowls' Are Not Tibetan. Sincerely, a Tibetan Person," *Toronto Star* website, February 18, 2020; Deoin, "Singing Bowl or Standing Bell: Appropriation or Misattribution?" The Pagan Minister website, February 20, 2020.
28. Jayan Marie Landry, "Physiological and Psychological Effects of a Himalayan Singing Bowl in Meditation Practice: A Quantitative Analysis," American Journal of Health Promotion 28, no. 5 (2014): 306–9.
29. L. Pigaiai, M. Casini, L. Bidin, P. Seghini, and L. Cavanna, "Psychological and Physical Benefits in Metastatic Cancer Patients Using Tibetan Singing Bowls: A Pilot Study in an Italian Oncology Unit," Annals of Oncology 27, supplement 4 (2016): 55–58.
30. Melanie Bergmann, Stefan Riedinger, Ambra Stefani, Thomas Mitterling, Evi Holzknecht, Peter Grassmayr, and Birgit Högl, "Effects of Singing

Bowl Exposure on Karolinska Sleepiness Scale and Pupillographic Sleepiness Test: A Randomised Crossover Study," PLOS One 15, no. 6 (2020): e0233982.
31. Tamara L. Goldsby, Michael E. Goldsby, Mary McWalters, and Paul J. Mills, "Effects of Singing Bowl Sound Meditation on Mood, Tension, and Well-being: An Observational Study," Journal of Evidence-Based Complementary and Alternative Medicine 22, no. 3 (2017): 401–6.
32. Jessica Stanhope and Philip Weinstein, "The Human Health Effects of Singing Bowls: A Systematic Review," Complementary Therapies in Medicine 51 (2020): 102412.
33. Islay Campbell, Roya Sharifpour, and Gilles Vandewalle, "Light as a Modulator of Non-image-forming Brain Functions: Positive and Negative Impacts of Increasing Light Availability," Clocks and Sleep 5 (2023): 116–40.
34. Takatsugu Deguchi and Masahiko Sato, "The Effect of Color Temperature of Lighting Sources on Mental Activity Level," Annals of Physiological Anthropology 11, no. 1 (1992): 37–43.
35. Islay Campbell, Roya Sharifpour, Jose Fermin Balda Aizpurua, Elise Beckers, Ilenia Paparella, Alexandre Berger, Ekaterina Koshmanova et al., "Regional Response to Light Illuminance across the Human Hypothalamus," Elife 13 (2024): RP96576.
36. Yi-Man Mu, Xiao-Dan Huang, Sui Zhu, Zheng-Fang Hu, Kwok-Fai So, Chao-Ran Ren, and Qian Tao, "Alerting Effects of Light in Healthy Individuals: A Systematic Review and Meta-analysis," Neural Regeneration Research 17, no. 9 (2022): 1929–37.
37. Christian Cajochen, Sylvia Frey, Doreen Anders, Jakub Späti, Matthias Bues, Achim Pross, Ralph Mager, Anna Wirz-Justice, and Oliver Stefani, "Evening Exposure to a Light-emitting Diodes (LED)-backlit Computer Screen Affects Circadian Physiology and Cognitive Performance," Journal of Applied Physiology 110 (2011): 1432–38.
38. Igor Knez, "Effects of Indoor Lighting on Mood and Cognition," Journal of Environmental Psychology 15 (1995): 39–51.
39. C. L. B. McCloughan, P. A. Aspinall, and R. S. Webb, "The Impact of Lighting on Mood," Lighting Research and Technology 31, no. 3 (1999): 81–88.
40. L. Werth, A. Steidle, and E. Hanke, "Getting Close in the Dark: Darkness Increases Cooperation," paper presented at Experiencing Light 2012,

International Conference on the Effects of Light on Wellbeing, November 12–13, 2012, the Netherlands.

41. Anna Steidle and Lioba Werth, "Freedom from Constraints: Darkness and Dim Illumination Promote Creativity," *Journal of Environmental Psychology* 35 (2013): 67–80.
42. Yadan Li, Wenjuan Ma, Qin Kang, Lei Qiao, Dandan Tang, Jiang Qiu, Qinglin Zhang, and Hong Li, "Night or Darkness, Which Intensifies the Feeling of Fear?" *International Journal of Psychophysiology* 97 (2015): 46–57.
43. See, for example, Stephen Skinner, *Techniques of Graeco-Egyptian Magic* (Singapore: Golden Hoard, 2014); Brian Alt, *Interlinear Magic: An Anthology of the Greek Magical Papyri* (Kickstarter currently in production). For more traditional academic examples, see Christopher A. Faraone and Sofía Torallas Tovar, *Greek and Egyptian Magical Formularies: Text and Translation*, vol. 1 (Berkeley: California Classical Studies, 2022) and Christopher A. Faraone and Sofía Torallas Tovar, *The Greco-Egyptian Magical Formularies: Libraries, Books, and Individual Recipes* (Ann Arbor, MI: University of Michigan Press, 2022).
44. Hans Dieter Betz, *The Greek Magical Papyri in Translation, Including the Demotic Spells, Volume One: Texts*, 2nd ed. (Chicago: University of Chicago Press, 1992), 187.
45. Scire [Gerald B. Gardner], *High Magic's Aid* (London: Michael Houghton, 1949).
46. J. F. C. Fuller, "The Black Arts," *Form* 2, no. 1 (November/December 1921): 57–66; rpt. *Occult Review* 43, no. 1 (January 1926): 227–36. See also Ronald Hutton, *The Triumph of the Moon: A History of Modern Pagan Witchcraft* (Oxford: Oxford University Press, 1999), 231–32 and Richard Kaczynski, *Friendship in Doubt: Aleister Crowley, J. F. C. Fuller, Victor B. Neuburg, and British Agnosticism* (Oxford: Oxford University Press, 2024), 166–70.
47. Hereward Carrington, *The Invisible World* (London: Rider & Co., 1949), 120.
48. Kenneth Grant, *The Magical Revival* (New York: Samuel Weiser, 1973), 110.
49. Aleister Crowley, *Magick in Theory and Practice* (Paris: Lecram Press, 1929–1930), 69.
50. Israel Regardie, *The Tree of Life: A Study in Magic* (London: Rider & Co., 1932), 144.

51. Grant, *Magical Revival*, 183.
52. Wolfgang Köhler, *Gestalt Psychology* (New York: Liveright, 1929).
53. Vilayanur S. Ramachandran and Edward Michael Hubbard, "Synaesthesia—A Window into Perception, Thought and Language," *Journal of Consciousness Studies* 8, no. 12 (2001): 3–34.
54. Yang-Chen Shen, Yi-Chuan Chen, and Pi-Chun Huang, "Seeing Sounds: The Role of Vowels and Consonants in Crossmodal Correspondences," *i-Perception* 13, no. 2 (2022): 1–11; Charles Spence, "Crossmodal Correspondences: A Tutorial Review," *Attention, Perception, and Psychophysics* 73 (2011): 971–95.
55. Gwilym Lockwood and Mark Dingemanse, "Iconicity in the Lab: A Review of Behavioral, Developmental, and Neuroimaging Research into Sound-symbolism," *Frontiers in Psychology* 6 (2015): 1246; Annette D'Onofrio, "Phonetic Detail and Dimensionality in Sound-shape Correspondences: Refining the *Bouba-kiki* Paradigm," *Language and Speech* 57 (2014): 367–93; Alan K. S. Nielsen and Drew Rendall, "Parsing the Role of Consonants versus Vowels in the Classic Takete-Maluma Phenomenon," *Canadian Journal of Experimental Psychology* 67 (2013): 153–63.
56. Mutsumi Imai and Sotaro Kita, "The Sound Symbolism Bootstrapping Hypothesis for Language Acquisition and Language Evolution," *Philosophical Transactions of the Royal Society B: Biological Sciences* 369 (2014): 20130298.
57. Shao-Min Hung, Suzy J. Styles, and Po-Jang Hsieh, "Can a Word Sound Like a Shape Before You Have Seen It? Sound-shape Mapping Prior to Conscious Awareness," *Psychological Science* 28 no. 3 (2017): 263–75.
58. Imai and Kita, "Sound Symbolism Bootstrapping Hypothesis"; Spence, "Crossmodal Correspondences."
59. Andrew Newberg, *Neurotheology: How Science Can Enlighten Us About Spirituality* (New York: Columbia University Press, 2018), 58.
60. Jeff Galak and Joseph P. Redden, "The Properties and Antecedents of Hedonic Decline," *Annual Review of Psychology* 69 (2018): 1–25.
61. Cammy Crolic and Chris Janiszewski, "Hedonic Escalation: When Food Just Tastes Better and Better," *Journal of Consumer Research* 43, no. 3 (2016): 388–406.
62. See, e.g., Mohammed Elgendi, Parmoud Kumar, Skye Barbic, Newton Howard, Derek Abbott, and Andrzej Cichocki, "Subliminal Priming—State of the Art and Future Perspectives," *Behavioral Sciences* 8 (2018):

54; Dario Krpan, "Behavioral Priming 2.0: Enter a Dynamical Systems Perspective," *Frontiers in Psychology* 8 (2017): 1204.
63. Gustav Kuhn, *Experiencing the Impossible: The Science of Magic* (Cambridge, MA: MIT Press, 2019), 148.
64. This example is inspired by Philip G. Zimbardo, Robert L. Johnson, and Vivian McCann, *Psychology: Core Concepts*, 7th ed. (Boston: Pearson Education, 2014), 127.
65. Kuhn, *Experiencing the Impossible*, 158–59.
66. Joshua Gold and Joseph Ciorciari, "A Review on the Role of Neuroscience of Flow States in the Modern World," *Behavioral Sciences* 10 (2020): 137.
67. Susie Cranston and Scott Keller, "Increasing the "Meaning Quotient" of Work," *McKinsey Quarterly* 1 (2013):48–59.
68. Dennis Coon and John O. Mitterer, *Introduction to Psychology: Gateways to Mind and Behavior*, 13th ed. (Mason, OH: Cenage Learning, 2013), 624–25.
69. Mihaly Robert Csikszentmihályi, *Flow: The Psychology of Optimal Experience* (New York: Harper and Row, 1990).
70. Robert M. Yerkes and John D. Dodson, "The Relation of Strength of Stimulus to Rapidity of Habit-formation," *Journal of Comparative Neurology and Psychology* 18, no. 5 (1908): 459–82.
71. Corinna Peifer, Hartmut Schächinger, Stefan Engeser, and Conny H. Antoni, "Cortisol Effects on Flow-experience," *Psychopharmacology* 232 (2015): 1165–73.
72. Marcelo Felipe de Sampaio Barros, Fernando M. Araújo-Moriera, Luis Carlos Trevelin, and Rémi Radel, "Flow Experience and the Mobilization of Attentional Resources," *Cognitive, Affective, and Behavioral Neuroscience* 18 (2018): 810–23.
73. Kazuki Yoshida, Daisuke Sawamura, Yuji Inagaki, Keita Ogawa, Katsunori Ikoma, and Shinya Sakai, "Brain Activity during the Flow Experience: A Functional Near-infrared Spectroscopy Study," *Neuroscience Letters* 573 (2014): 30–34.
74. Coon and Mitterer, *Introduction to Psychology*, 624–25.
75. Keith A. Kaufman, Carol R. Glass, and Timothy R. Pineau, *Mindful Sport Performance Enhancement: Mental Training for Athletes and Coaches* (Washington, DC: American Psychological Association, 2018).
76. Shih-Han Hung, Ching-Yung Hwang, Chun-Yen Chang, "Is the Qi Experience Related to the Flow Experience? Practicing Qigong in Urban Green Spaces," *PLoS ONE* 16, no. 1 (2021): e0240180.

77. Gold and Ciorciari, "Review on the Role of Neuroscience."
78. Lynda Flower, "Spiritual Experiences of Post-performance Career Ballet Dancers: A Qualitative Study of How Peak Performance Spiritual Lived Experiences Continued into and Influences Later Teaching Lives," *Research in Dance Education* 20, no. 2 (2019): 184–96.
79. Crowley, *Magick in Theory and Practice*, 72.
80. Kylie Loveday, David L. Neumann, and Linda Hassall, "The Peak Performance Experience in Professional Screen Acting," *Current Psychology* 42 (2023): 1456–66.
81. W. E. Butler, *The Magician: His Training and Work* (London: Aquarian Press, 1959).
82. Arne Dietrich, "Neurocognitive Mechanisms Underlying the Experience of Flow," *Consciousness and Cognition* 13 (2004): 746–61.
83. Dietrich, "Neurocognitive Mechanisms," 757.
84. Dietrich, "Neurocognitive Mechanisms," 758.
85. Andrew Neher, *Paranormal and Transcendental Experience: A Psychological Examination* (New York: Dover Publications, 2011), 21–22.
86. Crowley, *Magick in Theory and Practice*, 129.
87. Regardie, *Tree of Life*, 106.

CHAPTER 8. SIGNIFICANT OTHERS

1. Ernest Shackleton, *South: The Story of Shackleton's Last Expedition 1914–1917* (New York: Macmillan, 1920), 211.
2. See Lawrence Rainey, ed., *The Annotated Waste Land with Eliot's Contemporary Prose* (New Haven: Yale University Press, 2006).
3. Nathan I. Comer, Leo Madow, and James J. Dixon, "Observations of Sensory Deprivation in a Life-threatening Situation," *American Journal of Psychiatry* 124, no. 2 (1967): 164–69.
4. Hugh Rutledge, *Everest 1933* (London: Hodder & Stoughton, 1934), 164.
5. Charles A. Lindbergh, *The Spirit of St. Louis* (New York: Scribner, 1953, 1981), 389.
6. Eric Shipton, *Upon That Mountain* (London: Hodder & Stoughton, 1943), 89.
7. Macdonald Critchley, "Idea of a Presence," *Acta Psychiatrica Neurologica* 30, nos. 1–2 (1955)): 155–68 (p. 157).
8. Captain Joshua Slocum, *Sailing Alone Around the World* (New York: Blue Ribbon Books, 1900), 39.

9. "Girl, 6, Disappears on Hike in Buffalo River Area," *Daily American Republic*, May 1, 2001, 3.
10. Bob Clausen and Bill Smith, "Haley Zega Recounts Her Three Days Alone in the Arkansas Wilderness as a 6-year-old," KARK website, May 10, 2023.
11. Benjamin Hale, "Who Walks Always Beside You? A Disappearance in Arkansas," *Harper's Magazine*, August 2023. For more information, see Haley Zega, "19 Years Later: Missing Child Haley Zega Tells Her Story," video posted on YouTube May 1, 2020.
12. See John Geiger, *The Third Man Factor: Surviving the Impossible* (New York: Weinstein Books, 2009) and Ben Alderson-Day, *Presence: The Strange Science and True Stories of the Unseen Other* (New York: St. Martin's Press, 2023).
13. Peter Suedfeld and Jane S. P. Mocellin, "The 'Sensed Presence' in Unusual Environments," *Environment and Behavior* 19, no. 1 (1987): 33–52.
14. Christopher D. Bader, Joseph O. Baker, and F. Carson Mencken, *Paranormal America: Ghost Encounters, UFO Sightings, Bigfoot Hunts, and Other Curiosities in Religion and Culture*, 2nd ed. (New York: New York University Press, 2017), 220.
15. John Geiger, *The Angel Effect: We Are Never Alone* (Philadelphia: Weinstein, 2013); Patricia Tevington and Manolo Corichi, "Many Americans Report Interacting with Dead Relatives in Dreams or Other Ways," Pew Research Center (.org) website, August 23, 2023.
16. Geiger, *Angel Effect*, 203.
17. Critchley, "Idea of a Presence," 158.
18. Critchley, "Idea of a Presence," 161.
19. William James, *The Varieties of Religious Experience: A Study in Human Nature* (New York: Modern Library, 1902), 58.
20. Elizaveta Solomonova, Elena Frantova, and Tore Nielsen, "Felt Presence: The Uncanny Encounters with the Numinous Other," *AI and Society* 26, no. 2 (2011): 179–86.
21. Alderson-Day, *Presence*, 90–92.
22. C. M. Cook and M. A. Persinger, "Experimental Induction of the 'Sensed Presence' in Normal Subjects and an Exceptional Subject," *Perceptual and Motor Skills* 85 (1997): 683–93.
23. See Alderson-Day, *Presence*, 186, 191; Geiger, *Angel Effect*, 99.
24. Cook and Persinger, "Experimental Induction," 683.
25. Geiger, *Angel Effect*, 39.

26. T. M. Luhrmann, "Hallucinations and Sensory Overrides," *Annual Review of Anthropology* 40 (2011): 71–85.
27. Solomonova et al., "Felt Presence," 179.
28. Geiger, *Angel Effect*, 79.
29. Andrew Neher, *Paranormal and Transcendental Experience: A Psychological Examination* (New York: Dover Publications, 2011), 7.
30. George Estabrooks, *Hypnotism* (New York: Dutton, 1957), 93–94.
31. Quoted in Alderson-Day, *Presence*, 197–200.
32. Luhrmann, "Hallucinations," 79.
33. Alderson-Day, *Presence*, 188.
34. Aleister Crowley, *The Equinox of the Gods* (London: Ordo Templi Orientis, 1936), 117–18.
35. Jung, *Memories, Dreams, Reflections* (New York: Vintage Books, 1963) 190–91.
36. William Butler Yeats, *A Vision: An Explanation of Life Founded upon the Writings of Giraldus and upon Doctrines Attributed to Kusta ben Luka* (London: privately printed, 1925); William Butler Yeats, *A Vision* (London: Macmillan, 1937). For critical editions of these two redactions, see George Mills Harper and Walter Kelly Hood, eds., *A Critical Edition of Yeats's* A Vision *(1925)* (London: Macmillan, 1978) and Margaret Mills Harper and Catherine E. Paul, eds., *A Vision: The Revised 1937 Edition* (New York: Scribner, 2015).
37. Geiger, *Angel Effect*, 23.
38. Geiger, *Angel Effect*, 210.
39. Ella Embry, "The Art of the Dress: How Getting into Costume Affects an Actor's Self-Perception" (bachelor's thesis, University of Southern Mississippi, May 2018), 18.
40. Embry, "Art of the Dress," 23.
41. Isabella Rossellini, *Some of Me* (New York: Random House, 1997), 62. See also "Celebrating Movie Icons: Isabella Rossellini," interview with Terry Gross, *Fresh Air*, National Public Radio, August 29, 2024.
42. Stephen Reysen, Courtney N. Plante, Sharon E. Roberts, and Kathleen C. Gerbasi, "'Who I Want To Be': Self-perception and Cosplayers' Identification with Their Favorite Characters," The Phoenix Papers 3, no. 2 (2018): 1–7.
43. Osmud Rahman, Liu Wing-Sun, and Brittany Hei-man Cheun, "'Cosplay': Imaginative Self and Performing Identity," Fashion Theory 16, no. 3 (2012): 317–41 (p. 333–34).

44. Aleister Crowley, *Hymn to Pan* (Chicago: Argus Bookshop, 1919), rpt. *The Equinox* III, no. 1 (September 1919): 5.
45. Crowley, "Hymn to Pan," 7.
46. See, for example, Maya Deren, *Divine Horsemen: The Living Gods of Haiti* (London: Thames and Hudson, 1953).
47. Erika Bourguignon, "World Distribution and Patterns of Possession States," in R. Prince, ed., *Trance and Possession States* (Montreal: R. M. Bucke Memorial Society, 1968).
48. Colleen Ward, "Spirit Possession and Mental Health: A Psychoanthropological Perspective," *Human Relations* 33, no. 3 (1980): 149–63.
49. *The Book of the Law* I:54. *The Book of the Law* was first published in [Aleister Crowley], ΘΕΛΗΜΑ, vol. 3 (London: privately printed, 1909), and has since been reprinted widely, both as stand-alone volumes and as part of other books by or about Crowley.
50. *The Book of the Law* III:47.
51. *The Book of the Law* II:11.
52. See, for example, Alice W. Flaherty, *The Midnight Disease: The Drive to Write, Writer's Block, and the Creative Brain* (Boston: Houghton Mifflin, 2004).
53. William James, *The Principles of Psychology*, vol. I (New York: Henry Holt and Company, 1890), 399.
54. E. Walsh, M.A. Mehta, D.A. Oakley, D.N. Guilmette, A. Gabay, P.W. Halligan, and Q. Deeley, "Using Suggestion to Model Different Types of Automatic Writing," *Consciousness and Cognition* 26 (2014): 24–36 (p. 33).
55. Walsh et al., "Using Suggestion," 34.
56. Szabolcs Kéri, Imre Kállai, and Katalin Csigó, "Attribution of Mental States in Glossolalia: A Direct Comparison with Schizophrenia," *Frontiers in Psychology* 11 (2020): 638.
57. Szabolcs Kéri, Imre Kállai, and Katalin Csigó, "Enhanced Verbal Statistical Learning in Glossolalia," *Cognitive Science* 44 (2020): e12865.
58. [Aleister Crowley and Victor B. Neuburg], "Liber XXX Aerum vel Saeculi sub figura CCCCXVIII: Being of the Angels of the 30 Aethyrs: The Vision and the Voice," *The Equinox* I, no. 5 (March 1911): 164.
59. Dacher Keltner and Jonathan Hadit, "Approaching Awe, a Moral, Spiritual, and Aesthetic Emotion," *Cognition and Emotion* 17 (2003): 297–314.
60. Dacher Keltner, *Awe: The New Science of Everyday Wonder and How It Can Transform Your Life* (New York: Penguin, 2023), 7.

61. Steve Paulson, Lisa Sideris, Jennifer Stellar, and Piercarlo Valdesolo, "Beyond Oneself: The Ethics and Psychology of Awe," *Annals of the New York Academy of Sciences* 1501 (2021): 30–47; Paul Pearsall, *Awe: The Delights and Dangers of our Eleventh Emotion* (Deerfield Beach, FL: Health Communications, Inc., 2007).
62. Paulson et al., "Beyond Oneself," 31.
63. Paulson et al., "Beyond Oneself," 32.
64. Huanhuan Zhao, Heyun Zhang, Yan Xu, Wen He, and Jiamei Lu, "Why Are People High in Dispositional Awe Happier? The Roles of Meaning in Life and Materialism," *Frontiers in Psychology* 10 (2019): 1208.
65. David B. Yaden, Scott Barry Kaufman, Elizabeth Hyde, Alice Chirico, Andrea Gaggioli, Jia Wei Zhang, and Dacher Keltner, "The Development of the Awe Experience Scale (AWE-S): A Multifactorial Measure for a Complex Emotion," *Journal of Positive Psychology* 14, no. 4 (2019): 474–88.
66. Jeffrey L. Saver and John Rabin, "The Neural Substrates of Religious Experience," *Journal of Neuropsychiatry* 9, no. 3 (1997): 498–510 (p. 507).
67. Alexander A. Fingelkurts and Andrew A. Fingelkurts, "Is Our Brain Hardwired to Produce God, or Is Our brain Hardwired to Perceive God? A Systematic Review of the Role of the Brain in Mediating Religious Experience," *Cognitive Processing* 10 (2009): 293–326 (p. 294–95).
68. See David B. Yaden, Jonathan Iwry, Kelley J. Slack, Johannes C. Eichstaedt, Yukun Zhao, George E. Vaillant, and Andrew B. Newberg, "The Overview Effect: Awe and Self-transcendent Experience in Space Flight," *Psychology of Consciousness: Theory, Research, and Practice* 3, no. 1 (2016): 1–11.
69. William Shatner, *Boldly Go: Reflections on a Life of Awe and Wonder* (New York: Atria, 2022), 89–90.
70. Thomas J. L. van Rompay, Sandra Oran, Mirjam Galetzka, and Agnes E. van den Berg, "Lose Yourself: Spacious Nature and the Connected Self," *Journal of Environmental Psychology* 91 (2023): 102108.
71. Daniel 8:17.
72. Ezekiel 1:7, 10: 14–21.
73. Zhao et al., "Why Are People High in Dispositional Awe Happier?"
74. Piercarlo Valdesolo and Jesse Graham, "Awe, Uncertainty, and Agency Detection," *Psychological Science* 25, no. 1 (2014): 170–78.
75. Elliott D. Ihm, Raymond F. Paloutzian, Michiel van Elk, and Jonathan W. Schooler, "Awe as a Meaning-making Emotion: On the Evolution of

Awe and the Origin of Religions," in Jay R. Feierman and Lluis Oviedo, eds., *The Evolution of Religion, Religiosity and Theology: A Multi-Level and Multi-Disciplinary Approach* (London: Routledge, 2019).

CHAPTER 9. FULL CIRCLE

1. Iris M. Owen and Margaret H. Sparrow, "Generation of a Paranormal Physical Phenomena in Connection with an Imaginary Communicator," *New Horizons* 1, no. 3 (1974): 6–13 (p. 7).
2. K. J. Batcheldor, "Report on a Case of Table Levitation and Associated Phenomena," *Journal of the Society for Psychical Research* 43, no. 729 (1966): 339–56; C. Brookes-Smith and D. W. Hunt, "Some Experiments in Psychokinesis," *Journal of the Society for Psychical Research* 45, no. 744 (1970): 265–81.
3. Owen and Sparrow, "Generation," 9.
4. Iris M. Owen, "'Philip's' Story Continued," *New Horizons* 2, no. 1 (1975): 14–20 (p. 16).
5. Owen, "'Philip's' Story Continued," 17.
6. Iris M. Owen and Margaret Sparrow, *Conjuring up Philip: An Adventure in Psychokinesis* (Toronto, ON: Fitzhenry & Whiteside, 1976).
7. Iris M. Owen, "Philip's Fourth Year," *New Horizons* 2, no. 3 (1977): 11–15.
8. Owen and Sparrow, "Generation," 12–13.
9. Owen and Sparrow, *Conjuring up Philip*, 124.
10. Zolar, *Zolar's Encyclopedia of Ancient and Forbidden Knowledge* (Los Angeles: Nash Publishing, 1970; rpt. London: Peerage Books, 1990), 152.
11. Richard Reichbart, "Group Psi: Comments on the Recent Toronto PK Experiment as Recounted in *Conjuring Up Philip*," *Journal of the American Society for Psychical Research* 71, no. 2 (1977): 201–212 (p. 210).
12. See, e.g., Donna Zuckerbrot, dir., *Conjuring Philip* (Toronto: Reel Time Images, 2008).
13. Hélène L. Gauchou, Ronald A. Resink, and Sidney Fels, "Expression of Nonconscious Knowledge via Ideomotor Actions," *Consciousness and Cognition* 21 (2012): 976–82 (p. 979).
14. Owen and Sparrow, "Generation," 10.
15. Owen, "'Philip's' Story Continued," 17.
16. Iris M. Owen, "Continuation of the Philip Experiment," *New Horizons* 2, no. 2 (1976): 3–6.

17. Peter Lamont, "Spiritualism and a Mid-Victorian Crisis of Evidence," *Historical Journal* 47, no. 4 (2004): 897–920.
18. Carlos M. N. Eire, *The Flew: A History of the Impossible* (New Haven, CT: Yale University Press, 2023).
19. Francis Young, "History Takes Flight," First Things website, November 13, 2023.
20. See, for example, Matt J. Rossano, "The Essential Role of Ritual in the Transmission and Reinforcement of Social Norms," *Psychological Bulletin* 138, no. 3 (2012): 529–49.
21. Khushbeen Kaur Sohi, Purnima Singh, and Krutika Bopanna, "Ritual Participation, Sense of Community, and Social Well-being: A Study of *Seva* in the Sikh Community," *Journal of Religion and Health* 57 (2018): 2066–78.
22. Sarah J. Charles, Valerie van Mulukom, Jennifer E. Brown, Fraser Watts, Robin I. M. Dunbar, and Miguel Farias, "United on Sunday: The Effects of Secular Rituals on Social Bonding and Affect," *PLoS ONE* 16, no. 1 (2021): e0242546.
23. Charles et al., "United on Sunday."
24. Charles et al., "United on Sunday."
25. Kaitlin Woolley and Aylet Fishbach, "Shared Plates, Shared Minds: Consuming from a Shared Plate Promotes Cooperation," *Psychological Science* 30, no. 4 (2019): 541–52 (p. 541).
26. Jiyin Cao, Dejun Tony Kong, and Adam D. Galinsky, "Breaking Bread Produces Bigger Pies: An Empirical Extension of Shared Eating to Negotiations and a Commentary on Woolley and Fishbach (2019)," *Psychological Science* 31, no. 10 (2020): 1340–45 (p. 1344).
27. Daniel H. Stein, Juliana Schroeder, Nicholas M, Hobson, Francesca Gino, and Michael I. Norton, "When Alterations Are Violations: Moral Outrage and Punishment in Response to (Even Minor) Alterations to Rituals," *Journal of Personality and Social Psychology* 123, no. 1 (2022): 123–53 (p. 123).
28. Kiersten Riedford, "New NCAA Women's Volleyball Rule Change Draws Big Controversy Online," *NBC Chicago* website, February 23, 2024; Jon Hoefling, "This New Rule Change for College Volleyball Has Sent Players into a Frenzy," *USA Today*, February 22, 2024.
29. Stein et al., "When Alterations Are Violations," 123.
30. Dimitris Xygalatas, *Ritual: How Seemingly Senseless Acts Make Life Worth Living* (New York: Little, Brown Spark, 2022).

31. Ellen M. Lee, Kathryn R. Klement, James K. Ambler, Tonio Loewald, Evelyn M. Comber, Sarah A. Hanson, Bria Pruitt, and Brad J. Sagarin, "Altered States of Consciousness during an Extreme Ritual," *PLoS ONE* 11, no. 5 (2016): e0153126 (p. 1). See also Kathryn R. Klement, Ellen M. Lee, James K. Ambler, Sarah A. Hanson, Evelyn Comber, David Wietting, Michael F. Wagner et al., "Extreme Rituals in a BDSM Context: The Physiological and Psychological Effects of the 'Dance of Souls,'" *Culture, Health and Sexuality* 19, no. 4 (2017): 453–469.

32. Ronald Fischer, Dimitris Xygalatas, Panagiotis Mitkidis, Paul Reddish, Penny Tok, Ivana Konvalinka, and Joseph Bulbulia, "The Fire-walker's High: Affect and Physiological Responses in an Extreme Collective Ritual," *PLoS ONE* 9, no. 2 (2014): e883555.

33. Ivana Kovalinka, Dimitris Xygalatas, Joseph Bulbulia, Uffe Schjødt, Else-Marie Jegindø, Sebastian Wallot, Guy Van Orden, and Andreas Roepstorff, "Synchronized Arousal between Performers and Related Spectators in a Fire-walking Ritual," *PNAS* 108, no. 20 (2011): 8514–19.

34. G. Baranowski-Pinto, V. L. S. Profeta, M. Newson, H. Whitehouse, and D. Xygalatas, "Being in a Crowd Bonds People via Physiological Synchrony," *Scientific Reports* 12 (2022): 613.

35. Nan Zhao, Xian Zhang, J. Adam Noah, Mark Tiede, and Joy Hirsch, "Separable Processes for Live "In-person" and Live "Zoom-like" Faces," *Imaging Neuroscience* 1 (2023): 1–17.

36. Heather Freeman, "Ancient Technopagans: Magicians, Witches, and Neopagans of the Early Internet," season 1, episode 2 of the podcast *Magic in the United States*, PRX, October 31, 2023.

37. Kyle M. Jasmin, Carolyn McGettigan, Zarinah K. Agnew, Nadine Lavan, Oliver Josephs, Fred Cummins, and Sophie K. Scott, "Cohesion and Joint Speech: Right Hemisphere Contributions to Synchronized Vocal Production," *Journal of Neuroscience* 36, no. 17 (2016): 4669–80 (p. 4669).

38. Michael J. Hove and Jane L. Risen, "It's All in the Timing: Interpersonal Synchrony Increases Affiliation," *Social Cognition* 27, no. 6 (2009): 949–61.

39. Birgit Rauchbauer, Jasminka Majdandžić, Allan Hummer, Christian Windischberger, and Claus Lamm, "Distinct Neural Processes Are Engaged in the Modulation of Mimicry by Social Group-membership and Emotional Expressions," *Cortex* 70 (2015): 49–67 (p. 49).

40. S. Cacioppo, H. Zhou, G. Monteleone, E. A. Majka, K. A. Quinn,

A. B. Ball, G. J. Norman, G. R. Semin and J. T. Cacioppo, "You Are in Sync with Me: Neural Correlates of Interpersonal Synchrony with a Partner," *Neuroscience* 277 (2014): 842–58.

41. Scott S. Wiltermuth and Chip Heath, "Synchrony and Cooperation," *Psychological Science* 20, no. 1 (2009): 1–5 (p. 5).

42. Paul Reddish, Ronald Fischer, and Joseph Bulbulia, "Let's Dance Together: Synchrony, Shared Intentionality and Cooperation," *PLoS ONE* 8, no. 8 (2013): e71182.

43. Ronald Fischer, Rohan Callander, Paul Reddish, and Joseph Bulbulia, "How Do Rituals Affect Cooperation? An Experimental Field Study Comparing Nine Ritual Types," *Human Nature* 24 (2013): 115–25.

44. Angela Frances Yap, Yu Heng Kwan, and Seng Bin Ang, "A Systematic Review on the Effects of Active Participation in Rhythm-centered Music Making on Different Aspects of Health," *European Journal of Integrative Medicine* 9 (2017): 44–49; Carine Smith, Jeandre T. Viljoen, and Lauren McGeachie, "African Drumming: A Holistic Approach to Reducing Stress and Improving Health?" *Federazione Italiana di Cardiologia (Italian Federation of Cardiology)* 15, no. 6 (2014): 441–46; Daisy Fancourt, Rosie Perkins, Sara Ascenso, Louise Atkins, Stephen Kilfeather, Livia Carvalho, Andrew Steptoe, and Aaron Williamon, "Group Drumming Modulates Cytokine Response in Mental Health Service Users: A Preliminary Study," *Psychotherapy and Psychosomatics* 85 (2016): 53–55.

45. Daisy Fancourt, Rosie Perins, Sara Ascenso, Livia A. Carvalho, Andrew Steptoe, and Aaron Williamon, "Effects of Group Drumming Interventions on Anxiety, Depression, Social Resilience and Inflammatory Immune Response among Mental Health Service Users," *PLoS ONE* 11, no. 3 (2016): e0151136.

46. Idil Kokal, Annerose Engel, Sebastian Kirschner, and Christian Keysers, "Synchronized Drumming Enhances Activity in the Caudate and Facilitates Prosocial Commitment—If the Rhythm Comes Easily," *PLoS One* 6, no. 11 (2011): e27272.

47. Melanie Wald-Fuhrmann, Sven Boenneke, Thijs Vroegh, and Klaus Peter Dannecker, "'He Who Sings, Prays Twice'? Singing in Roman Catholic Mass Leads to Spiritual and Social Experiences That Are Predicted by Religious and Musical Attitudes," *Frontiers in Psychology* 11 (2020): 570189.

48. Arthur Saniotis, "Understanding Mind/Body Medicine from Muslim

Practices of *Salat* and *Dhikr*," *Journal of Religion and Health* 57 (2018): 849–57.

49. Carly Reagon, Nichola Gale, Stephanie Enright, Mala Mann, and Robert van Deursen, "A Mixed-method Systematic Review to Investigate the Effect of Group Singing on Health Related Quality of Life," *Complementary Therapies in Medicine* 27 (2016): 1–11.

50. Moshe Bensimon and Ehud Bodner, "Playing with Fire: The Impact of Football Game Chanting on Level of Aggression," *Journal of Applied Social Psychology* 41, no. 10 (2011): 2421–33.

51. Melissa Holm and Jon Sewell, *Aleister Crowley's The Rite of Mars* (Seattle: Eleusive Productions, 2014), DVD of musical production.

52. Nella Moisseinen, Lotta Ahveninen, Noelia Martínez-Molina, Viljami Sairanen, Susanna Melkas, Boris Kleber, Aleksi J. Sihvonen, and Teppo Särkämö, "Choir Singing Is Associated with Enhanced Structural Connectivity across the Adult Lifespan," *Human Brain Mapping* 45 (2024): e26705.

53. Junling Gao, Hang Kin Leung, Bonnie Wai Yan Wu, Stavros Skouras, and Hin Hung Sik, "The Neurophysiological Correlates of Religious Chanting," *Scientific Reports* 9 (2019): 4262.

54. Jasmin et al., "Cohesion and Joint Speech," 4669.

55. Wolfgang Tschacher, Steven Greenwood, Christian Weining, Melanie Wald-Fuhrmann, Chandrasekhar Ramakrishnan, Christoph Seibert, and Martin Tröndle, "Physiological Audience Synchrony in Classical Concerts Linked with Listeners' Experiences and Attitudes," *Nature: Scientific Reports* 14 (2024): 16412.

56. P. 3122 in Michael J. Hove, Johannes Stelzer, Till Nierhaus, Sabrina D. Thiel, Christopher Gundlach, Daniel S. Margulies, Koene R. A. Van Dijk, Robert Turner, Peter E. Keller, and Björn Merker, "Brain Network Reconfiguration and Perceptual Decoupling during an Absorptive State of Consciousness," *Cerebral Cortex* 26 (2016): 3116–24.

57. Hove et al., "Brain Network Reconfiguration," 3122.

58. Nathan D. Leonhardt, Dean M. Busby, Veronica R. Hanna-Walker, and Chelom E. Leavitt, "Sanctification or Inhibition? Religious Dualities and Sexual Satisfaction," *Journal of Family Psychology* 35, no. 4 (2021): 433–44.

59. Lori A. Brotto, "Editorial: Orienting to the Present Moment," *Sexual and Relationship Therapy* 28, nos. 1–2 (2013): 1–2.

60. Anna Kozlowski, "Mindful Mating: Exploring the Connection between

Mindfulness and Relationship Satisfaction," *Sexual and Relationship Therapy* 28, nos. 1–2 (2013): 92–104. See also, more recently, Christopher A. Pepping, Timothy J. Cronin, Anthony Lyons, and Jon G. Caldwell, "The Effects of Mindfulness on Sexual Outcomes: The Role of Emotion Regulation," *Archives of Sexual Behavior* 47 (2018): 1601–12.

61. Laura C. Sánchez-Sánchez, María Fernanda Valderrama Rodríguez, José Manuel García-Montes, Cristina Petisco-Rodríguez, and Rubén Fernández-Garcia, "Mindfulness in Sexual Activity, Sexual Satisfaction and Erotic Fantasies in a Non-clinical Sample," *International Journal of Environmental Research and Public Health* 18 (2021): 1161.

62. Chelom E. Leavitt, Eva S. Lefkowitz, and Emily A. Waterman, "The Role of Sexual Mindfulness in Sexual Wellbeing, Relational Wellbeing, and Self-esteem," *Journal of Sex and Marital Therapy* 45, no. 6 (2019): 497–509.

63. Chelom E. Leavitt, Tawniele F. Maurer, Tiffany L. Clyde, Rebecca W. Clarke, Dean M. Busby, Jeremy B. Yorgason, Erin K. Holmes, and Spencer James, "Linking Sexual Mindfulness to Mixed-sex Couples' Relational Flourishing, Sexual Harmony, and Orgasm," *Archives of Sexual Behavior* 50 (2021): 2589–2602.

64. Izabela Jąderek, Katarzyna Obarska, and Michał Lew-Starowicz, "Assessment of the Effect of Mindfulness Monotherapy on Sexual Dysfunction Symptoms and Sex-related Quality of Life in Women," *Sexual Medicine* 11, no. 3 (2023): 1–17.

65. Lori A. Brotto, Lisa Mehak, and Cassandra Kit, "Yoga and Sexual Functioning: A Review," *Journal of Sex and Marital Therapy* 55 (2009): 378–90; Vikas Dhikav, Girish Karmarkar, Mallika Gupta, and Kuljeet Singh Anand, "Yoga in Premature Ejaculation: A Comparative Trial with Fluoxetine," *Journal of Sexual Medicine* 4 (2007): 1726–32; Anjali Mangesh Joshi, Raveendran Arkiath Veettil, and Sanjay Deshpande, "Role of Yoga in Management of Premature Ejaculation," *World Journal of Men's Health* 38, no. 4 (2020): 495–505.

66. Asimina Lazaridou and Christina Kalogianni, "Mindfulness and Sexuality," *Sexual and Relationship Therapy* 28, nos. 1–2 (2013): 29–38 (p. 33).

67. Johan C. Karremans, Gesa Kappen, Melanie Schellekens, and Dominik Schoebi, "Comparing the Effects of a Mindfulness versus Relaxation Intervention on Romantic Relationship Wellbeing," *Scientific Reports* 10 (2020): 21696.

68. Andrew B. Newberg, Nancy A. Wintering, Chloe Hriso, Faezeh Vedaei, Sara Gottfried, and Reneita Ross, "Neuroimaging Evaluation of the Long Term Impact of a Novel Paired Meditation Practice on Brain Function," *Frontiers in Neuroimaging*, 3 (2024): 1368537.
69. Andrew Newberg, *Sex, God and the Brain* (Nashville: Turner, 2024).
70. Newberg, *Sex, God and the Brain*.
71. For the original thesis that ancient faiths involved worship of the generative principle, as expressed through imagery of the sexual organs, see Richard Payne Knight, *An Account of the Remains of the Worship of Priapus, Lately Existing at Isernia, in the Kingdom of Naples* (London: T. Spilsbury, 1786). Released in a small edition subsequently recalled by the author, its 1865 republication in London ushered in a tidal wave of writers on phallicism.
72. Roger Goodland, *A Bibliography of Sex Rites and Customs: An Annotated Record of Books, Articles and Illustrations in All Languages* (London: George Routledge & Sons, 1931).
73. The popularity and influence of these ideas within Western esotericism are described in Joscelyn Godwin, *The Theosophical Enlightenment* (Albany, NY: State University of New York Press, 1994), 1–25 and Richard Kaczynski, "Continuing Knowledge from Generation unto Generation: The Social and Literary Background of Aleister Crowley's Magick," in Henrik Bogdan and Martin P. Starr (eds.), *Aleister Crowley and Western Esotericism* (New York: Oxford University Press, 2012), 141–179.

CHAPTER 10. INITIATION

1. Thorn Mooney, *Traditional Wicca: A Seeker's Guide* (Woodbury, MN: Llewellyn, 2018), 45.
2. Mooney, *Traditional Wicca*, 49.
3. Leon Festinger, *A Theory of Cognitive Dissonance* (Evanston, IL: Row Peterson, 1957).
4. Leon Festinger and James M. Carlsmith, "Cognitive Consequences of Forced Compliance," *Journal of Anormal and Social Psychology* 58 (1959): 203–10. See also J. Merrill Carlsmith, Barry E. Collins, and Robert L. Helmreich, "Studies in Forced Compliance: 1. The Effect of Pressure for Compliance on Attitude Change Produced by Face-to-face Role Playing and Anonymous Essay Writing," *Journal of Personality and Social Psychology* 4, no. 1 (1966): 1–13, which replicated these results in

face-to-face interactions (the results differed, however, for those asked to write an anonymous essay).

5. Joel Cooper, "Cognitive Dissonance Theory," in Paul A. M. Van Lange et al., *Handbook of Theories of Social Psychology* (Los Angeles: SAGE Publications, 2011), 377–97 (p. 377).
6. Joel Cooper and Russell H. Fazio, "A New Look at Dissonance Theory," in L. Berkowitz, ed., *Advances in Experimental Social Psychology* 17 (1984): 229–62.
7. J. Stone and Joel Cooper, "A Self-standards Model of Cognitive Dissonance," *Journal of Experimental Social Psychology* 37 (2001): 228–43.
8. Darwin E. Linder, Joel Cooper, and Edward E. Jones, "Decision Freedom as a Determinant of the Role of Incentive Magnitude in Attitude Change," *Journal of Personality and Social Psychology* 6 (1967): 245–54.
9. Joel Cooper and Stephen Worchel, "Role of Undesired Consequences in Arousing Cognitive Dissonance," *Journal of Personality and Social Psychology* 16, no. 2 (1970): 312–20.
10. Cooper, "Cognitive Dissonance Theory."
11. Elliot Aronson and Judson Mills, "The Effect of Severity of Initiation on Liking for a Group," *Journal of Abnormal and Social Psychology* 59, no. 2 (1959): 177–81 (p. 178).
12. See, for example, John Schopler and Nicholas Bateson, "A Dependence Interpretation of the Effects of a Severe Initiation," *Journal of Personality* 30 (1962): 633–49 and Harold B. Gerard and Grover C. Mathewson, "The Effects of Severity of Initiation on Liking for a Group: A Replication," *Journal of Experimental Social Psychology* 2 (1966): 278–87.
13. Caroline Kamau, "What Does Being Initiated Severely into a Group Do? The Role of Rewards," *International Journal of Psychology* 48, no. 3 (2012): 399–406 (p. 402).
14. Georg Simmel, "The Sociology of Secrecy and of Secret Societies," *American Journal of Sociology* 11, no. 4 (1906): 441–98.
15. Mooney, *Traditional Wicca*, 45.
16. Léon A. van Gulik, "Cleanliness Is Next to Godliness, but Oaths are for Horses: Antecedents and Consequences of the Institutionalization of Secrecy in Initiatory Wicca," *Pomegranate* 14, no. 2 (2012): 233–55 (p. 250).
17. Olympia Panagiotidou, "Secrecy in the Mithras cult: Concealment, Cognition and Social Cohesion," *Acta Antiqua Academiae Scientiarum Hungaricae* 58, no. 1 (2018): 667–79.

18. Lilith Mahmud, "'The World Is a Forest of Symbols': Italian Freemasonry and the Practice of Discretion," *American Ethnologist* 38, no. 2 (2012): 425–38. For a comparative examination of the function secrecy in various occult societies, see Hugh B. Urban, *Secrecy: Silence, Power, and Religion* (Chicago: University of Chicago, 2021).
19. Tanya M. Luhrman (1989), "The Magic of Secrecy," *Ethos* 17, no. 2 (1989): 131–65.
20. Mooney, *Traditional Wicca*, 46.
21. Stanley Schachter, *The Psychology of Affiliation; Experimental Studies of the Sources of Gregariousness* (Stanford: University Press, 1959).
22. Patty Van Cappellen, Barbara L. Fredrickson, Vassilis Saroglou, and Olivier Cornielle, "Religiosity and the Motivation for Social Affiliation," *Personality and Individual Differences* 113 (2017): 24–31.
23. Erica J. Boothby, Margaret S. Clark, and John A. Bargh, "Shared Experiences Are Amplified," *Psychological Science* 25, no. 12 (2014): 2209–16.
24. Hein F. M. Lodewijkx and Joseph E. M. M. Syroit, "Severity of Initiation Revisited: Does Severity of Initiation Increase Attractiveness in Real Groups?" *European Journal of Social Psychology* 27 (1997): 275–300.
25. Hein F. M. Lodewijkx and J. E. M. M. Syroit, "Affiliation during Naturalistic Severe and Mild Initiations: Some Further Evidence against the Severity-attraction Hypothesis," *Current Research in Social Psychology* 6, no. 7 (2001): 90–107 (p. 90).
26. Hein F. M. Lodewijkx, Martijn Van Zomeren, Jef E. M. M. Syroit, "The Anticipation of Severe Initiation: Gender Differences in Effects on Affiliation Tendency and Group Attraction," *Small Group Research* 36, no. 2 (2005): 237–62 (p. 257–58).
27. Jacob E. Hautaluoma and Helene Spungin, "Effects of Initiation Severity and Interest on Group Attitudes," *Journal of Social Psychology* 93 (1974): 245–59.
28. Aldo Nicholas Cimino, "Hazing as a Manifestation of Evolved Psychology" (doctoral dissertation, University of California Santa Barbara, June 2013).
29. Aldo Cimino, "Defining Hazing: Why Popular Definitions Are Misleading and Counterproductive," *Journal of Higher Education Management* 32, no. 1 (2017): 135–48 (p. 144).
30. Lodewijkx et al., "The Anticipation of Severe Initiation," 237–38.
31. Aldo Cimino and Benjamin Thomas, "Does Hazing Actually Increase

Group Solidarity? Re-examining a Classic Theory with a Modern Fraternity," *Evolution and Human Behavior* 43 (2022): 408–417 (p. 408).

32. Jacob B. Hautaluoma, Ray S. Enge, Thomas M. Mitchell, and Frank J. Rittwager, "Early Socialization into a Work Group: Severity of Initiations Revisited," *Journal of Social Behavior and Personality* 6, no. 4 (1991): 725–48 (p. 725).

33. Liesbeth Mann, Allard R. Feddes, Bertjan Doosje, and Agneta H. Fischer, "Withdraw or Affiliate? The Role of Humiliation during Initiation Rituals," *Cognition and Emotion* 30, no. 1 (2016): 80–100 (p. 80).

34. Aldo Cimino, "Predictors of Hazing Motivation in a Representative Sample of the United States," *Evolution and Human Behavior* 34 (2013): 446–52.

35. Cimino, "Hazing as a Manifestation," 137.

36. Cimino and Thomas, "Does Hazing Actually Increase Group Solidarity?" 410.

37. Ward D. Finer, Jacob B. Hautaluoma, and Larry J. Bloom, "The Effects of Severity and Pleasantness of Initiation on Attraction to a Group," *Journal of Social Psychology* 111 (1980): 301–2.

38. Finer et al., "The Effects of Severity."

39. Kamau, "What Does Being Initiated Severely into a Group Do?" 405.

40. See, e.g., Walter Bradford Cannon, *Bodily Changes in Pain, Hunger, Fear, and Rage* (New York: Appleton-Century-Crofts, 1915), 211, and Walter B. Cannon, *The Wisdom of the Body* (New York: Norton, 1932).

41. Shelley E. Taylor, "Tend and Befriend Theory," in Paul A. M. Van Lange et al., *Handbook of Theories of Social Psychology* (Los Angeles: SAGE Publications, 2011), 32–49 (p. 42).

42. Taylor, "Tend and Befriend Theory," 42.

43. Shelley E. Taylor, Laura Cousino Klein, Brian P. Lewis, Tara L. Gruenewald, Regan A. R. Gurung, and John A. Updegraff, "Biobehavioral Responses to Stress in Females: Tend-and-befriend, not Fight-or-flight," *Psychological Review* 107, no. 3 (2000): 411–29; Shelly E. Taylor, *The Tending Instinct: How Nurturing is Essential to Who We Are an How We Live* (New York: Holt, 2002); Shelley E. Taylor, "Tend and Befriend: Biobehavioral Bases of Affiliation under Stress," *Current Directions in Psychological Science* 15, no. 6 (2006): 273–77.

44. Stuart Turton and Carol Campbell, "Tend and Befriend versus Fight or Flight: Gender Differences in Behavioral Response to Stress among

University Students," *Journal of Applied Biobehavioral Research* 10, no. 4 (2005): 209–32.
45. Nora Nickels, Konrad Kubicki, and Dario Maestripieri, "Sex Differences in the Effects of Psychosocial Stress on Cooperative and Prosocial Behavior: Evidence for 'Flight or Fight' in Males and 'Tend and Befriend' in Females," *Adaptive Human Behavior and Physiology* 3 (2017): 171–83 (p. 171).
46. Angela Haupt, "Why You Can't Remember That Taylor Swift Concert All Too Well," *Time* website, May 26, 2023; Robert N. Kraft, "Why Fans Are Forgetting Their Experience of the Taylor Swift Concert," *Psychology Today* website, May 30, 2023; "Some Taylor Swift Fans Are Reporting 'Amnesia' after Going to Her Concert," *Morning Edition*, NPR website, June 14, 2023.
47. Uffe Schjoedt, Jesper Sørensen, Kristoffer Laigaard Nielbo, Dimitris Xygalatas, Panagiotis Mitkidis, and Joseph Bulbulia, "Cognitive Resource Depletion in Religious Interactions," *Religion, Brain and Behavior* 3, no. 1 (2013): 39–86 (p. 39).
48. Schjoedt et al., "Cognitive Resource Depletion," 49.
49. Schjoedt et al., Cognitive Resource Depletion," 49.
50. Barbara Mellers, Katrina Fincher, Caitlin Drummond, and Michelle Bigony, "Surprise: A Belief or an Emotion?" *Progress in Brain Research* 202 (2013): 3–19 (p. 3).
51. Wolfram Schultz, Paul Apicella, Eugenio Scarnati, and Tomas Ljungberg, "Neuronal Activity in Monkey Ventral Striatum Related to the Expectation of Reward," *Journal of Neuroscience* 12 (1992): 4594–4610; Wolfram Schultz, Paul Apicella, and Tomas Ljungberg, "Responses of Monkey Dopamine Neurons to Reward and Conditioned Stimuli during Successive Steps of Learning a Delayed Response Task," *Journal of Neuroscience* 13 (1993): 900–913.
52. P. C. Fletcher, J. M. Anderson, D. R. Shanks, R. Honey, T. A. Carpenter, T. Donovan, N. Papadakis, and E. T. Bullmore, "Responses of Human Frontal Cortex to Surprising Events Are Predicted by Formal Associative Learning Theory," *Nature Neuroscience* 4, no. 10 (2001): 1043–48.
53. Gergory S. Berns, Samuel M. McClure, Giuseppe Pagnoni, and P. Read Montague, "Predictability Modulates Human Brain Response to Reward," *Journal of Neuroscience* 21, no. 8 (2001): 2793–98.
54. Mellers et al., "Surprise," 3.
55. John M. Pearce and Geoffrey Hall, "A Model for Pavlovian Learning:

Variations in the Effectiveness of Conditioned but Not of Unconditioned Stimuli," *Psychological Review* 87 (1980): 532–52.
56. Aimee E. Stahl and Lisa Feigenson, "Observing the Unexpected Enhances Infants' Learning and Exploration," *Science* 348 (2015): 91–94; Aimee E. Stahl and Lisa Feigenson, "Expectancy Violations Promote Learning in Young Children," *Cognition* 163 (2017): 1–14.
57. Stahl and Feigenson, "Expectancy Violations," 13.
58. Amory H. Danek, Michael Öllinger, Thomas Fraps, Benedikt Grothe, and Virginia L. Flanagin, "An fMRI Investigation of Expectation Violation in Magic Tricks," *Frontiers in Psychology* 6 (2015): 84.
59. Emporium Productions, *Inside the Freemasons* (2017), episode 1, 31:09–31:20.
60. See Amory H. Danek, Thomas Fraps, Albrecht von Müller, Benedikt Grothe, and Michael Öllinger, "It's a Kind of Magic: What Self-reports Can Reveal about the Phenomenology of Insight Problem Solving," *Frontiers on Psychology* 5 (2014): 1408; Amory H. Danek, Thomas Fraps, Albrecht von Müller, Benedikt Grothe, and Michael Öllinger, "Working Wonders? Investigating Insight with Magic Tricks," *Cognition* 130 (2014): 174–85.
61. Amory H. Danek and Jennifer Wiley, "What about False Insights? Deconstructing the Aha! Experience along Its Multiple Dimensions for Correct and Incorrect Solutions Separately," *Frontiers in Psychology* 7 (2017): 2077.
62. Ruben E. Laukkonen, Benjamin T. Kaveladze, Jason M. Tangen, and Jonathan W. Schooler, "The Dark Side of Eureka: Artificially Induced Aha Moments Make Facts Feel True," *Cognition* 196 (2020): 104122.
63. Mark Jung-Beeman, Edward M. Bowden, Jason Haberman, Jennifer L. Frymiare, Stella Arambel-Liu, Richard Greenblatt, Paul J. Reber, and John Kounios, "Neural Activity When People Solve Verbal Problems with Insight," *PLoS Biology* 2, no. 4 (2003); 500–510.
64. Amory H. Danek, Thomas Fraps, Albrecht von Müller, Benedikt Grothe, and Michael Öllinger, "Aha! Experiences Leave a Mark: Facilitated Recall of Insight Solutions," *Psychological Research* 77 (2013): 659–69.
65. David Dean Jr. and Deanna Kuhn, "Direct Instructions vs. Discovery: The Long View," *Science Education* 91, no. 3 (2007): 384–97.
66. Doug Oman, Shauna L. Shapiro, Carl E. Thoresen, Tim Flinders, Joseph D. Driskill, and Thomas G. Plante, "Learning from Spiritual Models and

Meditation: A Randomized Evaluation of a College Course," *Pastoral Psychology* 54 (2007): 473–93.
67. Tanya M. Luhrmann, *Persuasions of the Witch's Craft: Ritual Magic in Contemporary England* (Cambridge, MA: Harvard University Press, 1989).
68. Sarah Lynne Bowman, "The Psychological Power of the Roleplaying Experience," *Journal of Interactive Drama* 2, no. 1 (2007): 1–14 (p. 1).
69. Bowman, "Psychological Power," 7. For more on the transformational power of role-playing games, see Sarah Lynne Bowman, *The Functions of Role-Playing Games: How Participants Create Community, Solve Problems, and Explore Identity* (Jefferson, NC: McFarland & Company, Inc., 2010); Sarah Lynne Bowman and Kjell Hedgard Hugaas, "Magic Is Real: How Role-playing Can Transform Our Identities, Our Communities, and Our Lives," in Kari Kvittingen Djukastein, Marcus Irgens, Nadja Lipsyc, and Lars Kristian Løveng Sunde, eds., *Book of Magic: Vibrant Fragments of Larp Practices* (Oslo, Norway: Knutepunkt, 2021); and Josephine Baird and Sarah Lynne Bowman, "The Transformative Potential of Immersive Experiences within Role-playing Communities," *Revista de Estudos Universitário* 48 (2022): 1–48.
70. Irving L. Janis and Bert T. King, "The Influence of Role Playing on Opinion Change," *Journal of Abnormal Social Psychology* 49, no. 2 (1954): 211–18 (p. 218).
71. Bert T. King and Irving L. Janis, "Comparison of the Effectiveness of Improvised versus Non-improvised Role-playing in Producing Opinion Changes," *Human Relations* 9, no. 2 (1956): 177–86 (p. 182).
72. Alan C. Elms, "Influence of Fantasy Ability on Attitude Change through Role Playing," *Journal of Personality and Social Psychology* 4, no. 1 (1966): 36–43.
73. Edward Lichtenstein, Carolin S. Keutzer, and Kenneth H. Himes, "'Emotional' Role-playing and Changes in Smoking Attitudes and Behavior," *Psychological Reports* 23 (1969): 379–87.
74. Leon Mann and Irving L. Janis, "A Follow-up Study on the Long-term Effects of Emotional Role Playing," *Journal of Personality and Social Psychology* 8, no. 4 (1968): 339–42. For their original study, see Irving L. Janis and Leon Mann, "Effectiveness of Emotional Role Playing in Modifying Smoking Habits and Attitudes," *Journal of Experimental Research in Personality* 1 (1965): 84–90.
75. Josette McGregor, "Effectiveness of Role Playing and Antiracist Teaching

in Reducing Student Prejudice," *Journal of Educational Research* 86, no. 4 (1993): 215–26.

76. Mengyu Lim, Alessandro Carollo, Andrea Bizzego, Annabel SH Chen, and Gianluca Esposito, "Culture, Sex and Social Context Influence Brain-to-brain Synchrony: An fNIRS Hyperscanning Study," *BMC Psychology* 12 (2024): 350.

77. For a review of the literature, see Gerben A. van Kleef and Agneta H. Fischer, "Emotional Collectives: How Groups Shape Emotions and Emotions Shape Groups," *Cognition and Emotion* 30, no. 1 (2016): 3–19.

78. Roland Neumann and Fritz Strack, "'Mood Contagion': The Automatic Transfer of Mood between Persons," *Journal of Personality and Social Psychology* 79, no. 2 (2000): 211–23.

79. Judith Volmer, "Catching Leaders' Mood: Contagion Effects in Teams," *Administrative Sciences* 2 (2012): 203–20.

80. Naureen Bhullar, "Relationship between Mood and Susceptibility to Emotional Contagion: Is Positive Mood More Contagious?" *North American Journal of Psychology* 14, no. 3 (2012): 517–30.

81. Thomas Sy, Stéphane Côté, and Richard Saavedra, "The Contagious Leader: Impact of the Leader's Mood on the Mood of Group Members, Group Affective Tone, and Group Processes," *Journal of Applied Psychology* 90, no. 2 (2005): 295–305; Sigal G. Barsade, "The Ripple Effect: Emotional Contagion and Its Influence on Group Behavior," *Administrative Science Quarterly* 47 (2002): 644–75; Joyce E. Bono and Remus Ilies, "Charisma, Positive Emotions and Mood Contagion," *Leadership Quarterly* 17 (2006): 317–54; Stefanie K. Johnson, "Do You Feel What I Feel? Mood Contagion and Leadership Outcomes," *Leadership Quarterly* 20 (2009): 814–27.

82. Agneta Fisher and Ursula Hess, "Mimicking Emotions," *Current Opinion in Psychology* 17 (2017): 151–55.

83. Monika Wróbel and Kamil K. Imbir, "Broadening the Perspective on Emotional Contagion and Emotional Mimicry: The Correction Hypothesis," *Perspectives on Psychological Science* 14, no. 3 (2019): 437–51.

84. Albert Bandura, Dorothea Ross, and Sheila A. Ross, "Imitation of Film-mediated Aggressive Models," *Journal of Abnormal and Social Psychology* 67 (1963): 3–11.

85. Luhrmann, *Persuasions of the Witch's Craft*.

86. Albert Bandura, "On the Psychosocial Impact and Mechanisms of Spiritual

Modeling," *International Journal for the Psychology of Religion* 13, no. 3 (2003): 167–73.

87. Albert Bandura, *Social Foundations of Thought and Action: A Social Cognitive Theory* (Englewood Cliffs, NJ: Prentice Hall, 1986).

88. Doug Oman, "Spiritual Modeling and the Social Learning of Spirituality and Religion," in Kenneth I. Pargament, Julie J. Exline, and James W. Jones, eds., *APA Handbook of Psychology, Religion, and Spirituality (Vol. 1): Context, Theory, and Research* (Washington, D.C.: American Psychological Association, 2013), 187–204 (p. 188). For Oman and colleagues' publications contemporary with Bandura (2003), see Doug Oman and Carl E. Thoresen, "Spiritual Modeling: A Key to Spiritual and Religious Growth?" *International Journal for the Psychology of Religion* 13, no. 3 (2003): 149–65; Doug Oman and Carl E. Thoresen, "The Many Frontiers of Spiritual Modeling," *International Journal for the Psychology of Religion* 13, no. 3 (2003): 197–213.

89. Doug Oman, Carl E. Thoresen, Crystal L. Park, Philip R. Shaver, Ralph W. Hood, and Thomas G. Plante, "Spiritual Modeling Self-Efficacy," *Psychology of Religion and Spirituality* 4, no. 4 (2012): 278–97; Doug Oman, Thomas G. Plante, Eric P. Boorman, and Kevin A. Harris, "Spiritual Modeling Self-Efficacy (SMSE): A Stand-alone Measure," in Amy L. Ai, Paul Wink, Raymond F. Paloutzian, and Kevin A. Harris, eds., *Assessing Spirituality in a Diverse World* (Cham, Switzerland: Springer, 2021), 521–52.

90. Israela Silberman, "Spiritual Role Modeling: The Teaching of Meaning Systems," *International Journal for the Psychology of Religion* 13, no. 3 (2003): 175–95.

91. Mahmud, "The World Is a Forest of Symbols," 435.

92. Richard Condon, *The Manchurian Candidate* (New York: McGraw Hill, 1959) has been twice adapted as a movie, in 1962 and 2004.

93. See, e.g., Loyd W. Rowland, "Will Hypnotized Persons Try to Harm Themselves or Others?" *Journal of Abnormal and Social Psychology* 34 (1939): 114–17 and Paul C. Young, "Antisocial Uses of Hypnosis," in Leslie M. LeCron, ed., *Experimental Hypnosis* (New York: Macmillan, 1952), 376–409.

94. Martin T. Orne and Frederick J. Evans, F. J., "Social Control in the Psychological Experiment: Antisocial Behavior and Hypnosis," *Journal of Personality and Social Psychology* 1 (1965): 189–200.

95. Stanley Milgram, "Behavioral Study of Obedience," *Journal of Abnormal and Social Psychology* 67, no. 4 (1963): 371–78. See also Stanley Milgram, *Obedience to Authority; An Experimental View* (New York: Harper & Row, 1974). For a modern evaluation of the study, see Gina Perry, Augustine Brannigan, Richard A. Wanner, and Henderikus Stam, "Credibility and Incredulity in Milgram's Obedience Experiments: A Reanalysis of an Unpublished Test," *Social Psychology Quarterly* 83, no. 1 (2020): 88–106.
96. Martin T. Orne and Karl E. Schiebe, "The Contribution of Nondeprivation Factors in the Production of Sensory Deprivation Effects: The Psychology of the "Panic Button," *Journal of Abnormal and Social Psychology*, 68, no. 1 (1964): 3–12 (p. 5).
97. Dion Fortune, *The Esoteric Orders and Their Work* (St. Paul, MN: Llewellyn, 1978), 100.
98. See Aleister Crowley, *Magick Without Tears*, ed. Israel Regardie (St. Paul, MN: Llewellyn, 1973), 168.
99. Oliver J. Mason and Francesca Brady, "The Psychotomimetic Effects of Short-term Sensory Deprivation," *Journal of Nervous and Mental Disease* 197, no. 10 (2009): 783–85.
100. Vaughan Bell, "An Alternative Interpretation of 'The Psychotomimetic Effects of Short-term Sensory Deprivation," *Journal of Nervous and Mental Disease* 198, no. 2 (2010): 166.
101. Christina Daniel, Anna Lovatt and Oliver John Mason, "Psychotic-like Experiences and Their Cognitive Appraisal under Short-term Sensory Deprivation," *Frontiers in Psychiatry* 5 (2014): 106.

CHAPTER 11. THE METHOD OF SCIENCE AND YOU

1. Rudolf Steiner, *An Outline of Occult Science* (Chicago: Rand McNally, 1914); Dion Fortune, *Spiritualism in the Light of Occult Science* (London: Rider, 1931); Franz Hartmann, *Occult Science in Medicine* (London: Theosophical Publishing Co., 1893); and Papus [Gerard Encausse], *Absolute Key to Occult Science: The Tarot of the Bohemians. The Most Ancient Book in the World: For the Exclusive Use of Initiates*, trans. A. P. Morton (London: George Redway, 1896).
2. Israel Regardie, *The Tree of Life: A Study in Magic* (London: Rider & Co., 1932), 105–6.

3. Aleister Crowley, *Magick Without Tears*, ed. Israel Regardie (St. Paul, MN: Llewellyn, 1973), 499–500.
4. Aleister Crowley, *The Confessions of Aleister Crowley*, ed. John Symonds and Kenneth Grant (London: Jonathan Cape, 1969), 177.
5. Aleister Crowley, *Magick in Theory and Practice* (Paris: Lecram Press, 1929–1930), 58.
6. Egil Asprem, "Magic Naturalized? Negotiating Science and Occult Experience in Aleister Crowley's Scientific Illuminism," *Aries* 8, no. 2 (2008): 139–65.
7. Stefan Riedel, "Edward Jenner and the History of Smallpox and Vaccination," *Baylor University Medical Center Proceedings* 18, no. 1 (2005): 21–25.
8. Byron Vanderbilt, "Kekulé's Whirling Snake: Fact or Fiction," *Journal of Chemical Education* 52, no. 11 (1975): 709.
9. "Charles Goodyear: Vulcanized Rubber: Consumer Devices," Inventor Archive: Invention Education Resources, Lemelson MIT (.edu) website..
10. For an overview, see Telmo Pievani, *Serendipity: The Unexpected in Science*, trans. Michael Gerard Kenyon (Cambridge, MA: MIT Press, 2024).
11. Alfredo Rossi, Carmen Cantisani, Luca Melis, Alessandra Iorio, Elisabetta Scali, and Stefano Calvieri, "Minoxidil Use in Dermatology, Side Effects and Recent Patents," *Recent Patents on Inflammation and Allergy Drug Discovery* 6, no. 2 (2012): 130–36.
12. Jori Finkel, "Thai Antiquities, Resting Uneasily," *New York Times*, February 17, 2008, 29. See also Anastasia Toufexis, "Science: Hidden Treasures at a Dead End," *Time*, November 19, 1984. Some of Stephen Young's research was published as Stephen B. Young, "The Northeastern Thai Village: A Non-participatory Democracy," *Asian Survey* 8, no. 11 (1968): 873–86.
13. James Gleick, *Chaos: Making a New Science* (New York: Penguin Books, 1988), 173–81.
14. Matt Ridley, *Francis Crick: Discoverer of the Genetic Code* (New York: HarperCollins, 2006).
15. Bart Kosko, *Fuzzy Thinking: The New Science of Fuzzy Logic* (New York: Hyperion, 1993).
16. Harrison Brockelhurst, "Ever Feel like the Spotify Shuffle Isn't Actually Random? Here's the Algorithm Explained," The Tab website, November 17, 2021.

17. Andrew Griffin, "Why 'Random' Shuffle Feels Far from Random," *Independent*, February 24, 2015.
18. Toby Prike, Michelle M. Arnold, and Paul Williamson, "The Relationship between Anomalistic Belief, Misperception of Chance and the Base Rate Fallacy," *Thinking and Reasoning* 26, no. 3 (2020): 447–77; Neil Dagnall, Andrew Parker, and Gary Munley, "Paranormal Belief and Reasoning," *Personality and Individual Differences* 43, no. 6 (2007): 1406–15; Peter Brugger, Theodor Landis, and Marianne Regard, "A Sheep-goat Effect in Repetition Avoidance: Extrasensory Perception as an Effect of Subjective Probability?" *British Journal of Psychology* 81, no. 4 (1990): 455–68; Susan Blackmore and Tom Troscianko, "Belief in the Paranormal: Probability Judgements, Illusory Control, and the Chance Baseline Shift," *British Journal of Psychology* 76, no. 4 (1985): 459–68.
19. Anne Schienle, Dieter Vaitl, and Rudolf Stark, "Covariation Bias and Paranormal Belief," *Psychological Reports* 78 (1996): 291–305.
20. Paola Bressan, "The Connection between Random Sequences, Everyday Coincidences, and Belief in the Paranormal," *Applied Cognitive Psychology* 16 (2002): 17–34 (p. 30).
21. Mark K. Johansen and Magda Osman, "Coincidences: A Fundamental Consequence of Rational Cognition," *New Ideas in Psychology* 39 (2015): 34–44; Mark K. Johansen and Magda Osman, "Coincidence Judgment in Causal Reasoning: How Coincidental Is This?" *Cognitive Psychology* 120 (2020): 101290.
22. Qiong Cao and Lisa Feigenson, "Children's Representation of Coincidence," *Cognition* 250 (2024): 105854.
23. Fernando Blanco, Itxaso Barberia, and Helena Matute, "Individuals Who Believe in the Paranormal Expose Themselves to Biased Information and Develop More Causal Illusions Than Nonbelievers in the Laboratory," *PLoS ONE*, 10, no. 7 (2015): e0131378.
24. Neil Dagnall, Kenneth Drinkwater, Andrew Parker, and Kevin Rowley, "Misperception of Chance, Conjunction, Belief in the Paranormal and Reality Testing: A Reappraisal," *Applied Cognitive Psychology* 28 (2014): 711–19; Neil Dagnall, Andrew Parker, and Gary Munley, "Paranormal Belief and Reasoning," *Personality and Individual Differences* 43 (2007): 1406–15.
25. Peter Krummenacher, Christine Mohr, Helene Haker, and Peter Brugger, "Dopamine, Paranormal Belief, and the Detection of Meaningful Stimuli,"

Journal of Cognitive Neuroscience 22, no. 8 (2010): 1670–81; Sharon Begley, "The Ghosts We Think We See," *Newsweek*, October 27, 2007; Peter Brugger, "Tracking a Finer Madness," *Scientific American*, October/November 2007, 76–79.

26. Ellen J. Langer, "The Illusion of Control," *Journal of Personality and Social Psychology* 32, no. 2 (1975): 311–28 (p. 313).
27. Langer, "Illusion of Control," 325.
28. Bettina Studer, Shawn N. Geniole, Maike L. Becker, Christoph Eisenegger, and Stefan Knecht, "Inducing Illusory Control Ensures Persistence When Rewards Fade and When Others Outperform Us," *Psychonomic Bulletin and Review* 27 (2020): 809–18.
29. Fernando Blanco and Helena Matute, "Base-rate Expectations Modulate the Causal Illusion," *PLoS ONE* 14, no. 3 (2019): e0212615.
30. Oren Griffiths, Noor Shehabi, Robin A. Murphy, and Mike E. Le Pelley, "Superstition Predicts Perception of Illusory Control," *British Journal of Psychology* 110, no. 3 (2018): 499–518.
31. Daniel Yon, Carl Bunce, and Clare Press, "Illusions of Control without Delusions of Grandeur," *Cognition* 205 (2020): 104429; Gergö Hadlaczky and Joakim Westerlund, "Sensitivity to Coincidences and Paranormal Belief," *Perceptual and Motor Skills* 113, no. 3 (2011): 894–908.
32. Hadlaczky and Westerlund, "Sensitivity to Coincidences," 906.
33. Michiel van Elk, "The Self-attribution Bias and Paranormal Beliefs," *Consciousness and Cognition* 49 (2017): 313–21.
34. Katherine A. Johnson, Jan R. Wiersema, and Jonna Kuntsi, "What Would Karl Popper Say? Are Current Psychological Theories of ADHD Falsifiable?" *Behavioral and Brain Functions* 5 (2009): 15; Niall McLaren, "Popper versus Freud," *Australian and New Zealand Journal of Psychiatry* 40, no. 1 (2006): 97–98; Don C. Grant and Edwin Harari, "Psychoanalysis, Science and the Seductive Theory of Karl Popper," *Australian and New Zealand Journal of Psychiatry* 39, no. 6 (2005): 446–52.
35. Rodney Orpheus, *Abrahadabra: Understanding Aleister Crowley's Thelemic Magick*, 2nd ed. (York Beach, ME: Weiser, 2005), 7.
36. Orne and Evans, "Social Control in the Psychological Experiment."
37. Donald T. Campbell and Julian C. Stanley, *Experimental and Quasi-Experimental Designs for Research* (Chicago: Rand McNally, 1963); Thomas D. Cook and Donald T. Campbell, Quasi-Experimentation: Design and Analysis Issues for Field Settings (Boston: Houghton Mifflin,

1979). For a brief and recent survey, see Ellicott C. Matthay and M. Maria Glymour, "A Graphical Catalog of Threats to Validity," *Epidemiology* 31, no. 3 (2020): 376–84.
38. Patty Van Cappellen, Barbara L. Fredrickson, Vassilis Saroglou, and Olivier Cornielle, "Religiosity and the Motivation for Social Affiliation," *Personality and Individual Differences* 113 (2017): 24–31.
39. Crowley, *Confessions*, 241.
40. Allan Franklin, A. W. F. Edwards, Daniel J. Fairbanks, Daniel L. Hartl, and Teddy Seidenfeld, *Ending the Mendel-Fisher Controversy* (Pittsburgh, PA: University of Pittsburgh Press, 2008); Daniel J. Fairbanks and Bryce Rytting, "Mendelian Controversies: A Botanical and Historical Review," *American Journal of Botany* 88 (2001): 737–52; Walter W. Piegorsch, "The Gregor Mendel Controversy: Early Issues of Goodness-of-fit and Recent Issues of Genetic Linkage." *History of Science* 24 (1983): 173–82; R. A. Fisher, "Has Mendel's Work Been Rediscovered?" *Annals of Science* 1 (1936):115–37.

CHAPTER 12. LAST WRITES

1. See Donna Zuckerbrot, *Aleister Crowley: The Beast 666* (Toronto: Reel Time Images, 2007), DVD.
2. Veronika Huta, "The Complementary Roles of Eudaimonia and Hedonia and How They Can Be Pursued in Practice," in Stephen Joseph, ed., *Positive Psychology in Practice*, 2nd ed. (Hoboken, NJ: John Wiley & Sons, 2014), 216–46 (p. 216).
3. Carol D. Ryff, "Psychological Well-being Revisited: Advances in the Science and Practice of Eudaimonia," *Psychotherapy and Psychosomatics* 83 (2014): 10–28 (p. 14).
4. Alan S. Waterman, "The Relevance of Aristotle's Conception of Eudaimonia for the Psychological Study of Happiness," *Theoretical and Philosophical Psychology* 10, no. 1 (1990): 39–44; Alan S. Waterman, "Two Conceptions of Happiness: Contrasts of Personal Expressiveness (Eudaemonia) and Hedonic Enjoyment," *Journal of Personality and Social Psychology* 64 (1993): 678–91.
5. Carol D. Ryff, "Happiness Is Everything, or Is It? Explorations on the Meaning of Psychological Well-being," *Journal of Personality and Social Psychology* 57 (1989): 1069–81.

6. Alan S. Waterman, Seth J. Schwartz, and Regina Conti, "The Implications of Two Conceptions of Happiness (Hedonic Enjoyment and Eudaimonia) for the Understanding of Intrinsic Motivation," *Journal of Happiness Studies: An Interdisciplinary Forum on Subjective Well-Being* 9, no. 1 (2008): 41–79 (p. 42).
7. Susan der Kinderen and Svetlana N. Khapova, "Positive Psychological Well-being at Work: The Role of Eudaimonia," in Satinder Dhiman, ed., *The Palgrave Handbook of Workplace Well-Being* (Cham, Switzerland: Palgrave Macmillan, 2020). The connection of goal-oriented spiritual striving to psychological well-being was earlier explored (without referencing eudaimonia) in Sarah A. Schnitker and Robert A. Emmons, "Spiritual Striving and Seeking the Sacred: Religion as Meaningful Goal-directed Behavior," *International Journal for the Psychology of Religion* 23, no. 4 (2013): 315–24.
8. Samantha J. Heintzelman, "Eudaimonia in the Contemporary Science of Subjective Well-being: Psychological Well-being, Self-determination, and Meaning in Life," in E. Diener, S. Oishi, and L. Tay, eds., *Handbook of Well-Being* (Salt Lake City: DEF Publishers, 2018).
9. Veronika Huta and Alan S. Waterman, "Eudaimonia and Its Distinction from Hedonia: Developing a Classification and Terminology for Understanding Conceptual and Operational Definitions," *Journal of Happiness Studies* 15 (2013): 1425–56.
10. Sakurako S. Okuzono, Koichiro Shiba, Eric S. Kim, Kokoro Shirai, Naoki Kondo, Takeo Fujiwara, Katunori Kondo et al., "Ikigai and Subsequent Health and Wellbeing among Japanese Older Adults: Longitudinal Outcome-wide Analysis," *The Lancet Regional Health: Western Pacific* 21 (2022): 100391.
11. Yasuhiro Kotera, Greta Kaluzeviciute, Gulcan Garip, Kirsten McEwan, and Katy. J. Chamberlain, "Health Benefits of Ikigai: A Review of Literature," in Yasuhiro Kotera and Dean Fido, eds., *Ikigai: Towards a Psychological Understanding of a Life Worth Living* (Toronto: Concurrent Disorders Society Press, 2021).
12. Sakurako et al., "Ikigai"; Kotera et al., "Health Benefits of Ikigai."
13. Veronika Huta, "Eudaimonia," in S. David, I. Boniwell, and A. C. Ayers, eds., *Oxford Handbook of Happiness* (Oxford: University Press, 2013), 201–13.
14. Dolores Ashcroft-Nowicki, *The Ritual Magic Workbook: A Practical Course of Self-Initiation* (Wellingborough, UK: Aquarian Press, 1986), 34.

15. Éliphas Lévi, *The Doctrine and Ritual of High Magic: A New Translation*, trans. John Michael Greer and Mark Anthony Mikituk (New York: TarcherPerigee, 2017), 119.
16. William Gray, *Inner Traditions of Magic* (New York: Weiser, 1978), 221.
17. J. R. Marscaro, *Seal, Sigil and Call* (Woodbury, MN: Llewellyn, 2022), 130.
18. Joseph Campbell, *The Hero with a Thousand Faces* (New York: Pantheon Books, 1949), 30.
19. See, e.g., Kent Huffman, "In the Kingdom of the Blind: The Deconstruction of *The Hero with A Thousand Faces*," *Articulāte* 1 (1996): 70–81; Sarah E. Bond and Joel Christensen, "The Man behind the Myth: Should We Question the Hero's Journey?" *Los Angeles Review of Books* website, August 12, 2021.
20. A. J. Black, *Myth-Building in Modern Media: The Role of the Mytharc in Imagined Worlds* (Jefferson, NC: McFarland, 2020).
21. Bond and Christensen, "Man behind the Myth."
22. Mary Henderson, *Star Wars: The Magic of Myth* (New York: Bantam Spectra, 1997).
23. Benjamin A. Rogers, Herrison Chicas, John Michael Kelly, Emily Kubin, Michael S. Christian, Frank J. Kachanoff, Jonah Berger, Curtis Puryear, Dan P. McAdams, and Kurt Gray, "Seeing Your Life Story as a Hero's Journey Increases Meaning in Life," *Journal of Personality and Social Psychology* 125, no. 4 (2023): 752–78 (p. 752).
24. Rogers et al., "Seeing Your Life," 752.
25. Ryan Goffredi and Kennon M. Sheldon, "The Autobiographical Critic Within: Perceiving Oneself as a Major Character in One's Life Story Predicts Well-being," *Journal of Research in Personality* 111 (2024): 104510.
26. Ryff, "Eudaimonia," 14.
27. Kaczynski, "Structure and correlates of metaphysical beliefs."
28. Peter Krummenacher, Christine Mohr, Helene Haker, and Peter Brugger, "Dopamine, Paranormal Belief, and the Detection of Meaningful Stimuli," *Journal of Cognitive Neuroscience* 22, no. 8 (2010): 1670–81.
29. Anne Schienle, Dieter Vaitl, and Rudolf Stark, "Covariation Bias and Paranormal Belief," *Psychological Reports* 78 (1996): 291–305.
30. Gertrude R. Schmeidler, "Predicting Good and Bad Scores in a Clairvoyance Experiment: A Preliminary Report," *Journal of the American Society for Psychical Research* 37 (1943): 103–10.

31. Tony R. Lawrence, "Gathering In the Sheep and Goats: A Meta-analysis of Forced-choice Sheep-goat ESP Studies, 1947–1993," *Proceedings of Presented Papers: The Parapsychological Association 36th Annual Convention* (Durham, NC: Parapsychological Association, 1993), 75–86; Lance Storm and Patrizio E. Tressoldi, "Gathering In More Sheep and Goats: A Meta-analysis of Forced-choice Sheep-goat ESP Studies, 1994–2015," *Journal of the Society for Psychical Research* 81, no. 2 (2017): 79–107.
32. Jeffrey J. Kripal, *How to Think Impossibly about Souls, UFOs, Time, Belief, and Everything Else* (Chicago: University of Chicago Press, 2024), 157.
33. Gerald Gardner, *Witchcraft Today* (New York: Citadel Press, 1955), 20.

Index

A∴A∴, 40, 80, 114
accuracy, 238
active practices. *See also* practices
   about, 45–46, 53–54
   athletes and, 55–56
   empowerment and self-efficacy, 53–54
   meditative movement, 58–60
   posture and poses, 56–58
   relaxation response, 60–61
   savoring, 61–63
Adam, Hajo, 122–23
affiliation, 193, 198, 199. *See also* severity-affiliation-attraction hypothesis
afterlife, belief in, 13
agency detection, 171
agenticity, 64–65
Aha experience, 213
alien control of movement, 165
altars, 108–9, 112, 114, 129, 132
alternative hypothesis, 236
ambiguous temporal precedence, 246
angel switch, 157–58, 161
Angel Effect, The (Geiger), 156

Antarctic research station, 102–4
apophenia, 27–28, 37
apparitions, in the house, 2–4
Art of Drawing Spirits into Crystals, The (Trithemius), 31–32
Art of Memory, 48–49
asanas, 77, 86
Ashcroft-Nowicki, Dolores, 253–54
astrology, 10, 12, 13, 115
attentive immobility, 208
autobiographical memory, 48
autogenic training, 85–86
awe
   about, 167–68
   dispositional, 170–71
   elements of, 168
   influence on well-being, 171
   in inspiring spiritual sentiments, 171
   psychometric scale, 168
   transcendent experience of, 169

Bandura, Alfred, 218
banishing rituals, 56
barbarous names, 135–37, 140
Barrett, Francis, 31–32

believers and patternicity, 230–33
Bem, Daryl, 72–74
Benson, Herbert, 60
Bernard, Pierre Arnold ("Loving Guru"), 80
Bernard, Theos, 83
Bigfoot, 4–7
"Black Arts, The" (Fuller), 136
Book of Mormon, 30, 36
Book of the Law, The (Crowley), 164–65, 194
bottom-up responses, 56
bouba-kiki effect, 140–41
brain, the
  areas of, 205
  chanting and, 92–93
  fasting and, 106
  meditation and, 93–96
  memorization and, 53
  pareidolia and, 26–27
  progressive muscle relaxation and, 85
  structuring of perceptions, 30, 36, 39
breakthroughs, 227–29
Breathing Break Intervention, 89–90
breathing exercises, 77, 88–90
Britten, Emma Hardinge, 32–33, 34
Bryant, Fred, 61–62
Bull, Sarah Chapman, 79–80
Burt, Calvin C., 181
Butler, W. E., 147

Campbell, Joseph, 254
Cannon, Walter Bradford, 205
Case, Paul Foster, 36–37
centering and grounding, 53–54, 66–67
challenge-skill balance, 144, 145

chandra bhedana (moon breath), 87
change blindness, 28
changed behavior
  about, 193, 214
  cognitive dissonance and, 214–15
  demand characteristics and, 219–23
  leaders, mood, modeling and, 217–19
  role-playing and, 215–17
chanting, 91–93, 186
chaos magick, 138
charismatic authority, 209
chastity, 105
closure principle, 24
clothing, 121–24
cognitive dissonance, 194–95, 214–15
cognitive resource depletion, 209–10
coherent breathing, 87–88
color preferences, 116–20, 131
common region principle, 19, 22
communal meals, 180
communitas, 215
community tradition, 180–81
completeness principle, 19, 24
Conjuring Up Philip (Owen and Sparrow), 176
consciousness
  altered states of, 36, 72, 104, 122, 136, 148, 166, 229
  collective, 176
  enclothed cognition and, 122–24
  fasting and asceticism and, 105
  opening of, 64
  spiritual state of, 149, 159, 165
continuity principle, 19, 23
control, illusion of, 233–34
control condition, 165, 241–42
control group, 241
convenience sample, 240
Conway, David, 43, 67

Cooper, Joel, 195
core shamanism, 187
correspondences
　about, 114
　color, 117–18, 120, 133
　as common vocabulary of associations, 114–16
　crossmodal, 140
　table of, 119
cortisol, 145
Crowley, Aleister. *See also specific books*
　expounding magick, yoga, and science, 81
　flow and, 146, 148
　on generalizing findings, 247–48
　Holy Guardian Angel encounter and, 159–60
　"Hymn to Pan," 162–63
　"Liber RV," 87
　magical routine and, 42–44
　magick and, 38–39
　Neuburg and, 34–35
　Scientific Illuminism, 224–25
　on sexual abstinence, 105
　on strings of formidable words, 136
　table of correspondences, 119
crystallomancy, 35
Csikszentmihalyi, Mihaly, 144
cup (chalice), 108

dagger (athame), 108, 109
daily practices. *See also* practices
　about, 40
　active, 53–63
　benefits of, 42–46
　importance of maintaining, 42
　intellectual, 46–53
　receptive, 53–63
　ritual and, 40–42

"Dance of Souls," 182
deduction, 226
Dee, John, 30, 160
degree testing, 213–14
deindividuation, 121
demand characteristics, 219–23
dependent variable, 235, 238
design, research, 240–43
Dietrich, Arne, 37, 147–48
direct instruction, 213
discovery learning, 213
dispositional awe, 170–71
divine encounters, 167, 170–71. *See also* awe
divine proxy agency, 219
doctrinal ritual, 42
Doctrine and Ritual of High Magic (Lévi), 129
dramatic ritual, 146–47
dreams, 49, 226–27
drumming, 141, 185–88, 191
dumb luck, 228
DuQuette, Lon Milo, 45

Ecological Valence Theory (EVT), 117
Eight Lectures on Yoga (Crowley), 80
Eire, Carlos, 179
electronic voice phenomenon (EVP), 27
Elms, Alan, 216
embarrassment test, 195–96
Embry, Ella, 161, 163
emotional contagion, 217
empathic fantasy ability, 216
empowerment, 54–56, 57, 253
enclothed cognition, 122–24, 162
epistemology, 226–29
Equinox, The, 87, 102, 115, 126, 224, 225

Estabrooks, George, 158
eudaimonia, 251–52, 253
Eureka experience, 213, 227–28
Everyday Witchcraft (Blake), 40
evocation, 41, 136, 156, 157–61
expectancy violations, 211
expressive suppression, 209

face validity, 238
false dichotomy, 9
fasting, 106–7
fight-or-flight, 205–9
Five M's, 141–42
"flashcards for the insane," 49
flotation-REST, 104
flow experiences
  about, 144
  challenge-skill balance and, 144, 145
  characteristics of, 144–45
  cortisol and, 145
  mindfulness and, 146
  from neurocognitive perspective, 147
  state, entering, 147–48
fragrance, 130–31
Friendship in Doubt, 15
Fryar, Robert, 33
Fuller, J. F. C., 79–80, 87, 136

Galinsky, Adam, 122–23
Ganzfeld, 36, 72, 73
Geiger, John, 156, 157–58, 161
generalizing findings, 247
Gerber, Rudolph and Dorothy, 80
Gestalt principles of grouping
  closure principle, 24
  common region, 19, 22
  completeness, 19, 24
  continuity, 19, 23
  proximity, 19, 21
  similarity, 19, 20
  types of, 19
Ghost Land (Britten), 32–33
ghosts, 3, 8, 64, 129, 152, 173–77
glyphs, 138–40
goal-demoted actions, 209
Golden Dawn
  color scales, 119
  Fourfold Breath and, 87
  motto, 251
  ritual implements, 113, 115
  sigils, 137, 138
  temple, 126
Golden Dawn, The (Regardie), 7
Goodman, Felicitas, 57–58
Goodyear, Charles, 227
Gould, Daniel, 68
Gray, William, 254
Greater Magical Retirement (GMR), 100–101
Great Work, the, 42–44
Greek Magical Papyri, 135
Greenberg, Gary, 127
group ritual. *See also* ritual(s)
  in bonding a community, 180–81, 250–51
  changes in, 181
  communal meals, 180
  conclusions, 190–91
  Philip experiment and, 173–77
  sacred sex, 188–90
  as social glue, 179–83
  synchronous ritual actions, 185–88
  synchrony, 183–85
guardian angels, 155–56
guided imagery, 66, 68–69

Harner, Michael, 187
Harris, Thomas Lake, 90
Hauke, Christopher, 10
hazing, 201–3
hedonic adaptation, 106
hedonic decline, 43, 142
hedonic escalation, 142
Hero's Journey, 255–56
Hockley, Frederick, 32
Holy Guardian Angel (HGA), 101, 159, 172
How to Study Magic (Lyons), 46
"Hymn to Pan," 162–63
hyperactive agency-detection device (HADD), 64–65
hypothesis, 235–37, 243

I Ching, 38
iconography, 49–53
ideomotor action, 177–78
IKEA effect, 111, 124
ikigai, 252–53
illusion of control, 233–34
imagery, mental, 65–69
imagistic ritual, 42
implements, magical
  about, 108–10
  correspondences and colors, 113–20
  creation of, 111
  design and crafting of, 109
  Golden Dawn, 113, 115
  sacralization, 110
  specialness, 113
inattentional blindness, 29
independent variable, 235, 238
induction, 226, 229
inhibiting, 147–48
initiation
  about, 192
  anticipation of, 200
  aversive practices, 202
  changed behavior from, 193, 214–23
  cognitive dissonance and, 194–95, 214–15
  cognitive resource depletion and, 209–10
  community and, 250–51
  degree testing, 213–14
  demand characteristics and, 219–23
  Dutch sorority study, 199–200
  embarrassment test and, 195–96
  fight-or-flight and tend-and-befriend and, 205–9
  functions, 193
  hazing and, 201–3
  in hierarchical groups, 192
  incorporation and, 199–200
  insight and, 211–14
  leaders, mood, modeling and, 217–19
  ordeal and attractiveness of, 197–98
  ordeals, 199, 203–4
  as rite of passage, 193–204
  rituals, exposés of, 211
  role-playing and, 215–17
  separation and, 199
  severity and humiliation, 203
  severity-attraction hypothesis, 196, 197
  sexual behavior discussion group and, 195–97
  sitting alone before, 222–23
  surprise and, 210–11
  as teaching function, 193, 204–14
  transition and, 199
insight, 97, 187, 211–14
instincts, trusting, 229–35

instrumentation, 246
intellectual practices. *See also* practices
  about, 45
  iconography, 49–53
  journals, 46–49
  memorization, 53
intention
  ascetic choices and, 105
  driving rituals, 186
  magick and, 39, 109, 125
  reality relationship, 75
  shared, 185
intermittent fasting, 106
internal validity, 245
intervention and observation, 240–41
invocation
  about, 161
  actors and, 162
  barbarous names of, 136
  as ceremonial experience, 164
  experience of, 163
  possession versus, 163–64
  psychology and, 161
  shift in perspective and, 162–63
Iyengar, B. K. S., 83

James, William, 120–21, 124, 156, 165
Jesus on a tortilla, 17, 26
Jung, Carl, 9, 37–38, 159, 255

Kamau, Caroline, 197
kapalabhati (breath of fire), 87, 89
Kekulé's daydream of the ouroboros, 227
Kellner, Carl, 78, 79
Kelly, Edward, 30–31, 160
kinesic magic, 56
King, Francis, 43

kirtan kriya, 93
Kripal, Jeffrey, 9, 257

Lamont, Peter, 179
Langer, Ellen, 233
LED lighting, 133–34
Lesser Banishing Ritual, 57–58
Lévi, Éliphas, 44, 105, 120, 129, 253–54
lighting, 133–34
Light on Yoga (Iyengar), 83
Lindbergh, Charles, 152
Living Thelema (Shoemaker), 68
locus of control, 14
Luhrmann, Tanya, 158, 215, 218

MacGregor Mathers, S. L., 101
magical journals, 46–47
magical preparation, 143
magical retirements, 100–102, 104–6
Magic: An Occult Primer (Conway), 67
magick
  Crowley definition of, 38–39
  patterns and perception and, 36–39
  psychology and, 2, 16
  in times of uncertainty, 233
  transformative practices of, 16
Magick in Theory and Practice (Crowley), 146
Magus, The (Barrett), 31–32
mantras, 90–91
marginality hypothesis, 12
Marscaro, J. R., 254
maturation, 245
meaningful coincidence, 37, 38
measurement, 238, 246

meditation
  about, 93–94
  brain studies, 93–96
  chanting and, 91
  group, 94
  guided, 67
  long-term, 94, 96
  neural activity and, 93–94
  raja yoga and, 94
  as revelatory, 229
  sahaja yoga and, 94, 96
  short-term, 96–97
  Spain experiment, 97
meditation paradox, 88–89
meditative movement, 58–60
memory, 47–48, 53, 75, 94, 106–7, 122, 146, 208
mental imagery, 65–69
meta-analysis, 248
Method of Loci, 48–49
Milgram, Stanley, 220
mindfulness, 44–45, 97, 146, 186, 188
Mindful Witch, The (Stevens), 40
monomyth, the, 254–56
Mooney, Thorn, 197
mortality, 206, 246
mythmaking, 255–56

nadi shodhana (alternate nostril breathing), 87
names, barbarous, 135–37, 140
Neuburg, Victor, 34–35
Newburg, Andrew, 189
null hypothesis, 236, 243

olfactory stimulation, 130–31
openness to experience, 256–57
Open Society (Orphic Circle), 32

Orgasmic Meditation (OM), 189
Orpheus, Rodney, 44
Ouija boards, 64, 178
overview effect, 169

Papyri Graecae Magicae (PGM), 135
Paranormal America (Bader and Mencken), 9
paranormal experience, statistics, 10
parapsychology, 71–76
pareidolia, 26–27
patternicity, 26–28, 230–33
patterns, viewing, 17–18
peak performance, 144
Pearce Hall model, 210–11
perceptual blindness, 28–29
perceptual expectancy, 25–26
perceptual grouping principles
  closure principle, 24
  common region, 19, 22
  completeness, 19, 24
  continuity, 19, 23
  proximity, 19, 21
  similarity, 19, 20
  types of, 19
periodic fasting, 106
peripheral possession, 164
Philip experiment, 173–77, 190
phi phenomenon, 18
Pilates, Joseph, 97
placebos, 127–28
planets, representation of, 13
population, 239–40
possession, 163–64
"post-concert amnesia," 208–9
posture and poses, 56–58
practices
  active, 45–46, 53–63
  agenticity and HADD, 64–65

iconography, 49–53
intellectual, 45, 46–53
journaling, 46–49
meditative movement, 58–60
memorization, 53
mental imagery, 65–69
mindfulness and, 44–45
parapsychology, 71–76
posture and poses, 56–58
projective techniques, 69–71
receptive, 46, 63–76
relaxation response, 60–61
rituals and, 40–42
savoring, 61–63
pranayama, 77, 88–90
prayer, 40, 57, 61, 91, 100, 186–87
"Precognitive Detection of Erotic Stimuli," 73–74
pretest and post-test, 241
priming, 37, 130, 143
Prince, Morton, 35
prisoner's cinema, 30
Prisoner's Dilemma game, 207
progressive muscle relaxation (PMR), 84–86
projective techniques, 69–71
proximity principle, 19, 21
psi, 71–76
psychology
　about, 1
　anomalous beliefs and experiences and, 11–12
　apophenia and, 27–28
　of fasting and asceticism, 105–7
　Gestalt, 18–24
　invocation and, 161
　magick and, 2, 16
　pareidolia and, 26–27
　perceptual blindness and, 28–29

perceptual expectancy and, 25–26
perceptual grouping and, 19–24
priming in, 143
projective techniques in, 69–71
recruitment method in, 14
of sensed presence, 156–57
undifferentiated visual conditions and, 29–36
yoga in, 83–84
purpose of life, 251–53

Radin, Dean, 72
Randolph, Paschal Beverly, 33–34
receptive practices. *See also* practices
　about, 46, 63–64
　agenticity and HADD, 64–65
　mental imagery, 65–69
　parapsychology, 71–76
　projective techniques, 69–71
Regardie, Israel, 7, 63–64, 136–37, 148–49
regression to the mean, 246
relaxation response, 60–61
reliability, 71, 238
religious chanting, 91–93
renunciation, 105–7
repetition priming, 130
repetitive prayer, 61, 91
replication, 123, 140, 238, 240, 248
research design, 240–43
restorying, 256
retirement, magical, 100–102, 104–6
"Retroactive Facilitation of Recall," 74
Rite of Mars (Crowley), 186
rites of passage. *See also* initiation
　about, 193
　hazing, 201–3
　initiation ordeals and, 203–4

severity-affiliation-attraction hypothesis, 193, 198–201
severity-attraction hypothesis, 193, 194–98
Ritual: How Seemingly Senseless Acts Make Life Worth Living (Xygalatas), 41
ritual implements
  about, 108–10
  correspondences and colors, 113–20
  design and crafting of, 109
  sacralization, 110
  specialness, 113
ritual possession, 164
ritual(s)
  about, 40–42
  anxiety and, 55
  athlete, 55–56
  banishing, 56
  centering and grounding, 53–54
  changes in, 181
  characteristics of, 42
  classification of, 41–42
  commitment, 55–56
  defined, 40–41
  doctrinal, 42
  dramatic, 146–47
  empowerment and behavior changes from, 54–55
  enjoyment enhancement and, 63
  healing, 55
  imagistic, 42
  impact of, 128–29
  meaning of, 47–48
  medical, 127–28
  olfactory stimulation and, 130–31
  research, 16
  sacred group values and, 181
  scheduling of, 134
  as social glue, 179–83
  in society, 127
  sound and, 131–33
  synchronous actions, 185–88
role-playing, 215–17
Rossellini, Isabella, 162

sacralization, 110
sacred sex, 188–90
sacred space
  about, 158
  entering, 146, 213
  magicians in, 10, 125, 126–27, 128
  temples, 124, 125–26, 146
salat (prayer) and dhiker (chanting), 186
samatha (concentration), 186
savoring, 61–63
Science of Magic, The (Kuhn), 143
Scientific Illuminism, 224–25
scientific method, 224–49
secrecy, power of, 197–98
Secrets of a Witch's Coven (Morwyn), 67–68
Selbstbeobachtung (self-observation), 229
selection, 245–46
self-efficacy, 54–55, 63, 85, 146, 219
self-enlightenment, caution, 98–99
self-perception theory, 121
self-regulation, 217
sensed presence
  about, 155–56
  fundamental properties, 157
  Holy Guardian Angel encounter and, 159
  psychology of, 156–57
  qualities of, 157
  self-hypnotic state and, 166
serendipity, 228

seva, 180
severity-affiliation-attraction hypothesis, 193, 198–201
severity-attraction hypothesis, 193, 194–98
sexual sanctification, 188–90
Shackleton, Ernest, 150–51
shapes, sounds and, 135–41
shared intention, 185
Shatner, William, 169–70
sheep-goat effect, 257
Shepperton Mine Disaster, 151
Shipton, Eric, 152
shitali (cooling breath), 87
sigils, 137–39
similarity principle, 19, 20
Simons, Daniel, 28–29
singing, group, 186
singing bowls, 132–33
Six Million Dollar Man, The 5–6
Skinner, Stephen, 43
Slocum, Joshua, 152–54
smiling, 56, 61
Smythe, Frank, 151–52
social appraisal, 218
sound(s)
 bouba-kiki effect and, 140–41
 chanting and, 91–93
 in rituals, 131–33
 shapes and, 135–41
 unfamiliar, 137
Spare, Austin Osman, 137–38, 139
Spiral Dance, The (Starhawk), 60
spiritual modeling, 218
square breathing, 87
Sri Agaymya Guru Paramahamsa (Tiger Mahatma), 79
"Stairway to Heaven" (Led Zeppelin), 26–27

statistics, 8, 74, 226, 244
Stone, Winthrop E., 78–79
Strieber, Whitley, 8, 9
Super Natural, The (Strieber and Kripal), 9
surprise, 210–11
susceptibility, 57
synchronicity, 37, 38–39
synchronous ritual actions
 about, 185
 changes produced by, 188
 drumming, 141, 185–88, 191
 singing and chanting, 186
synchrony
 about, 183–84
 cooperation and, 184
 listening and, 187
 ritual, 185
 shared intention and, 185
 social benefit and, 184
systems theory, 18

taboos, breaking, 142
target population, 239–40
Taylor, Shelley E., 206
teaching function. *See also* initiation
 about, 193, 204–5
 cognitive resource depletion and, 209–10
 fight-or-flight and, 205–9
 insight and, 211–14
 lessons learned, 214
 surprise and, 210–11
 tend and befriend and, 206, 207
Techniques of High Magic (King and Skinner), 43
temples, 119, 125–26, 146
tend and befriend, 198, 206, 207
testing, 141, 213–14, 236, 246

Theory of Color (Goethe), 116
Theosophical Society, 77, 87
They Flew: A History of the Impossible (Eire), 179
Third Man, 151, 155
thought insertion, 165
threats to internal validity, 245–47
time series design, 242–43
top-down approach, 56
Toronto Eight, 173–77
tracing boards, 49, 51
transformation. *See* changed behavior
transgressions, 141–42
trauma response, 208–9
trial and error, 228–29
Trier Social Stress Test, 207
True Will, 46
Two Worlds (Britten), 34

ujjayi (ocean breath), 87
undifferentiated visual conditions, 29–36

Veroff, Joseph, 61–62
vesica piscis, 23
Viking face on Mars, 17, 18
vipassana (mindfulness), 186
visions in darkness, 29–36
Vision and the Voice, The (Crowley), 34–36, 166–67
visualization, 66–67, 68–69, 146
Vivekananda, 78, 79

wand, 25, 108, 109, 110, 111, 114
Wasserman, James, 46
Weiser Concise Guide to Yoga for Magick (Wasserman), 80
well-being
  eudaimonia and, 251–52
  Hero's Journey and, 256
  ikigai and, 252–53
  relationship, 189
  well-being, 43
Whitehouse, Harvey, 47
Whitmer, David, 30
Wiccan initiation, 197–98
willpower, 54, 105, 253–54
witchcraft, 7–8, 14, 47, 65, 66
words, 164–67

Xygalatas, Dimitris, 41, 47–48, 181–82

Yeats, William Butler, 159, 161
Yerkes-Dodson law, 145
yoga
  about, 78–79
  asanas, 77, 86
  books on, 81, 83–84
  early years in U.S.A., 78–82
  as global phenomenon, 83
  magicians and, 98
  meditation and, 93–97
  postural, 83
  pranayama and breathing exercises, 77, 86–90
  progressive muscle relaxation (PMR) and, 84–86
  in psychology, 83–84
Yoga (Fuller), 80

Zalmoxis, 29
Zega, Haley, 154–55
Zener cards, 230, 231, 257
Zimbardo, Philip, 121
Zolar's Encyclopedia of Ancient and Forbidden Knowledge (Zolar), 176–77